*The Consumer Reports
Law Book*

THE CONSUMER REPORTS
LAW BOOK

*Your Guide to Resolving
Everyday Legal Problems*

CAROL HAAS
AND THE EDITORS OF
CONSUMER REPORTS BOOKS

CONSUMER REPORTS BOOKS
A Division of Consumers Union
Yonkers, New York

Library of Congress Cataloging-in-Publication Data

The Consumer Reports Law Book : your guide to resolving everyday legal problems / Carol Haas and the editors of Consumer Reports Books.

    p.   cm.

    Includes index.

    ISBN 0-89043-537-5 (hc : acid-free paper)

    1. Law—United States—Popular works.   2. Consumer protection—Law and legislation—United States—Popular works.   I. Haas, Carol.

II. Consumer Reports Books.

KF387.C547   1994

349.73—dc20

[347.3]

94-3971

CIP

Design by Jackie Schuman

First printing, May 1994

This book is printed on recycled paper.

Manufactured in the United States of America

The Consumer Reports Law Book is a Consumer Reports Book published by Consumers Union, the nonprofit organization that publishes *Consumer Reports*, the monthly magazine of test reports, product Ratings, and buying guidance. Established in 1936, Consumers Union is chartered under the Not-for-Profit Corporation Law of the State of New York.

The purposes of Consumers Union, as stated in its charter, are to provide consumers with information and counsel on consumer goods and services, to give information on all matters relating to the expenditure of the family income, and to initiate and to cooperate with individual and group efforts seeking to create and maintain decent living standards.

Consumers Union derives its income solely from the sale of *Consumer Reports* and other publications. In addition, expenses of occasional public service efforts may be met, in part, by noncommercial contributions, grants, and fees. Consumers Union accepts no advertising or product samples and is not beholden in any way to any commercial interest. Its Ratings and reports are solely for the use of the readers of its publications. Neither the Ratings, nor the reports, nor any Consumers Union publications, including this book, may be used in advertising or for any commercial purpose. Consumers Union will take all steps open to it to prevent such uses of its material, its name, or the name of *Consumer Reports*.

To Ken, Jake, and Adam

ACKNOWLEDGMENTS

I would like to thank my editors, Mark Hoffman and Roz Siegel, for their hard work, skills, and commitment, which were essential and greatly appreciated.

Special thanks to Atlanta attorney and writer Jim Simmons for sharing his legal knowledge and for providing moral support, Jim Rakestraw, Sue Ann Wilson, and Tom Ousley.

I would also like to acknowledge the Federal Trade Commission, the U.S. Department of Commerce, the Better Business Bureau, Mothers Against Drunk Drivers (MADD), and the American Bar Association for their cooperation.

Lastly, thank you to my family—husband Ken and sons Jake and Adam—to whom this book is dedicated.

Contents

ix

The Consumer Reports Law Book

Introduction

What do you do if your new car spends more time in the shop than on the road? What can you do if your boss consistently expects you to work through your lunch hour? What are your rights if your son's ex-wife refuses to allow you to visit your grandson? What are your options if the computer store will not honor its warranty? What do you do when you get a speeding ticket or break your leg on your neighbor's front step, or when your dry cleaner loses your jacket?

Like death and taxes, legal issues in our society cannot be avoided. Laws regulate everything in our lives—including death and taxes—from how we drive our cars to where we can build our houses. And often it is only when a problem arises that we suddenly realize how little we know about specific laws, and how much less we know about how to obtain satisfaction under them.

Sometimes our legal problems occur because other people break the law—we are denied a job because of age, an apartment because of race. But often our own acts can cause the legal problem—we default on a loan, change our minds about a contract, go through a red light. And sometimes before legal issues become problems, information is required to prevent them from becoming so—borrowing money, adopting a child, or buying a house.

The Consumer Reports Law Book will give you the knowledge you need to understand your rights as a citizen and consumer, to understand particular laws and what they cover and exclude and how best to cope with common legal issues. While the book is not intended to offer or be a substitute for professional advice, it will provide basic, practical guidance on how to solve everyday legal problems and guard against problems in the future. And it will help you recognize when your legal rights have been violated and explain what your options may be for getting satisfaction.

1

According to research based on information from the American Bar Association and various state government agencies, the largest number of civil lawsuits (criminal law is beyond the scope of this book) filed in the United States involve family law. The other issues that most frequently lead to court cases concern credit and debt, disputed bills, traffic violations, professional negligence and malpractice, problems in the workplace, real estate transactions, and automobile purchases. This book offers advice and guidance on all of these issues.

Although *The Consumer Reports Law Book* may provide all the information needed to solve certain legal problems, it is not meant to replace the services of an attorney. You must consider the complexity of the situation as well as the personal and financial stakes before deciding whether or not to hire a lawyer. Laws differ from state to state, sometimes from county to county, and complications can easily arise that might cost you far more than a lawyer's fee if you choose to handle legal issues on your own.

The strategies in this book generally favor informal, mutually agreeable solutions. To that end, we offer step-by-step advice that focuses on the most practical approach first, reserving the lawsuit as a course of last resort. This book will clarify legal issues and help you gather the information necessary to obtain satisfaction. It will aid you in presenting your case adequately—whether you consult a lawyer, utilize an alternative dispute-resolving agency, or deal with matters on your own. We hope that the information we offer helps you to act wisely in your own best interests.

In as many cases as possible, we have included hypothetical situations involving legal problems in the area of the law covered and have provided a step-by-step course of action to resolve the problem or legal issue. The sample cases and suggested solutions have been contributed by attorneys, who have used their expertise and experience to provide detailed, real-life situations and suggested remedies.

1

THE FAMILY

MARRIAGE

To most people, marriage means that two people are making a commitment with the hopes of creating a nurturing and secure emotional, social, and financial life. The law has another view. In the eyes of the law, marriage resembles a contract. As in most contracts, both parties are required to give up something in return for a benefit. In return for the joint rights and positive experiences marriage may provide, each party has certain obligations and responsibilities under the law.

Most contracts are usually agreements made among the parties, with little outside interference. If the parties mutually agree to end their contractual relationship, the contract is no longer valid. But because the state perceives that marriage and the family are an important part of a stable society, the state actually becomes a party to the contract and its termination (divorce), setting up certain terms and requirements for both.

Prenuptial Agreements

The practice of a couple entering into a written agreement before they marry is growing. This is partly because couples tend to marry later than was true in the past. Today, it is more likely that one or both parties have accumulated wealth and possessions. With the high rate of divorce, others remarry after having had children during a previous marriage. As a result of such patterns, many people approach marriage with concern about the terms of a possible divorce or how their assets will be distributed after death.

A valid prenuptial agreement should include the following elements:

- It should be in writing. An oral agreement is not usually sufficient, but this may vary from state to state.
- Both parties must enter into the agreement without being coerced or defrauded.
- There must be a full financial disclosure by both parties.
- The terms of the agreement must be reasonably fair to both parties when made and not unconscionable when and if it is ever enforced.

Each party should have an attorney review the final agreement to be sure it is fair and that all requirements have been met. In some states, there is a presumption of coercion if each party does not have a separate attorney. If the elements noted earlier are present, the court will often honor a prenuptial agreement.

The following hypothetical situation involves a prenuptial agreement.

THE PROBLEM

George and Susan are engaged to be married. Each has children from a prior marriage, and each wishes the bulk of his or her estate to pass to his or her particular children. In the state in which they reside, however, the estate laws require spouses to provide each other with a greater percentage of the estate than either George or Susan wish to provide.

WHAT TO DO

1. George and Susan should contact separate attorneys and learn the laws concerning estate rights of spouses in their state. They should each discuss with their attorneys what they hope to achieve and how best to achieve this.

2. George and Susan should each prepare a complete financial disclosure statement. This should include a schedule of

assets and liabilities, with approximate values, as well as a schedule of income and expenses.

3. A prenuptial agreement should be drafted by one of the attorneys. It should contain the necessary estate waiver and any other terms agreed to by George and Susan.

4. Each party should carefully review a draft of the agreement with his or her attorney and revise it if necessary.

5. The final agreement should be executed in the manner required under the law of their state. Four copies of the agreement should be executed—one for each of the parties to retain and one for each attorney's file for later reference.

6. Each party should prepare a will. The attorney or attorneys preparing these wills should review a copy of the parties' prenuptial agreement to ensure that the wills conform to its terms.

Getting Married

There are two kinds of marriage: ceremonial and common-law. Ceremonial marriages are recognized in all 50 states and the District of Columbia; only 11 states and the District of Columbia acknowledge common-law marriages. Ceremonial marriages entail satisfying certain requirements imposed respectively by the states. If you are intending to marry, contact your county clerk's office for the laws and rules that govern marriage in your state.

The Legal Requirements for Marriage

AGE Age requirements vary from state to state, but most allow a couple to marry at the age of 18 without parental consent. Mississippi has the most stringent requirement; the minimum age for marriage there is 21. In many states the legal age for marriage is lower if parental consent is given. For example, Arizona allows people as young as 16 to marry, provided that each partner has parental

---

Remember: *Laws governing marriage differ from state to state. Check the relevant laws in your area and/or consult an attorney.*

approval. Without this consent, the couple will have to wait until they reach 18.

PHYSICAL HEALTH   A few states require their residents to undergo physical examinations, and many require blood tests to check for the presence of venereal disease. States even vary in regard to what happens if such a test is positive; some prohibit the marriage, and others leave the decision to the couple. Some states require evidence of having received immunizations for certain diseases, such as rubella.

MENTAL HEALTH   Some states prohibit marriage by drug addicts, alcoholics, or those with severe mental disabilities.

MARITAL STATUS   There is no limit to the number of times you can be married and divorced, but you are restricted to one spouse at a time. Bigamists (those who have two spouses at one time) and polygamists (those who have more than two) may be criminally prosecuted. Second and subsequent marriages may be void if an earlier marriage was not first dissolved legally through the courts.

RELATIONSHIP   None of the states provides for marriages between members of the same sex (homosexual marriages). Eighteen states permit marriage between first cousins, but marriage between blood relatives (incest) is not provided for in the other 32 states. Some states are much more restrictive and even prohibit the legal union of those who are related only through marriage, such as a woman and her brother-in-law. Marriages that involve a transsexual (an individual who has undergone a sex-change operation) are usually valid under the law.

WAITING PERIODS   Some states require a "cooling-off period" between the time the couple gets a marriage license and the date of the wedding, a period that varies from one to seven days. More often, states require a waiting period between the time the application for a marriage license is made and the date of its issuance. The concept of a waiting period stems from the belief that friends and acquaintances should have the right to protest the union.

LICENSES   Most states require application for a license prior to a marriage ceremony. Some states will declare a marriage void if a license is not obtained.

CEREMONIES   To sanction a ceremonial marriage as valid, most states require that the marriage undergo "solemnization," either a religious ceremony performed by a clergyperson, or a civil formality performed by a public official such as a justice of the peace. State laws specify who may perform a marriage ceremony and the kind of ceremony legally required. Some states require witnesses to the ceremony, and most require filing the certificate of marriage with the county clerk.

REGISTRATION   All marriages should be registered with the state, but failing to register does not necessarily make the marriage void.

What If the Wedding Is Canceled?

Suppose things don't go as planned and your partner changes her or his mind before the marriage, canceling the wedding.

Can you sue your fiancé? Perhaps, depending on your state's laws. Being "left at the altar" or something similar can be embarrassing and emotionally devastating. You may be able to recover damages resulting from your loss of reputation, the mental anguish you suffer, and injury to your health. Some states don't permit a rejected fiancé to recover any damages.

What if you and your prospective spouse exchanged prenuptial gifts? Who owns the watch given as a birthday gift or as a "token of friendship"? What about the 2-carat diamond engagement ring? Basically, any gifts given throughout the courtship period are considered just that: gifts, and therefore nonreturnable. But engagement rings are an exception, considered to be given in contemplation of marriage. If the wedding is called off, one partner has the right to expect the other to return the ring, or at least to compensate that person for its monetary value.

If family and friends have already sent wedding gifts before the decision was made to cancel the wedding, the couple is obligated to return the gifts, preferably unopened, with an explanation. What about the deposit for the caterer, the entertainment, the cost of the bridesmaids' gowns? Technically, if the prospective groom has canceled the marriage and the bride's family was planning on paying for the wedding (as is tradition), the bride's family may be able to sue the groom under breach-of-contract law. If you are a party to a canceled wedding, you may want to consult an attorney about what rights you have in reclaiming an engagement ring or wedding expenses.

The following is a hypothetical situation involving a canceled wedding.

THE PROBLEM

Suzanne and Jeff are engaged to be married. Suzanne's parents pay the caterer a $500 deposit for the wedding reception. Two weeks before the wedding, Jeff breaks the engagement. Suzanne's parents notify the caterer to cancel the wedding reception. They attempt to reclaim the deposit, but their contract with the caterer clearly states that it is nonrefundable.

WHAT TO DO

1. If possible, Suzanne or her parents should contact Jeff to see if he is willing to reimburse Suzanne's parents.

2. If Jeff is unwilling, Suzanne's parents may be able to commence a lawsuit against Jeff for the return of the money. They can do this through an attorney. They may also be able to do this without an attorney by going to the court in their area with jurisdiction over small claims, often called a small-claims court.

It should be noted, however, that many states have enacted "heart-balm" statutes. These prohibit lawsuits concerning breach of the promise to marry. Although it may seem unfair, some of these statutes have been held to preclude lawsuits to recover wedding expenses.

Common-Law Marriage

Some people prefer not to make legal commitments. Instead, they choose to live as couples without the official approval of church or state and all the ceremonial formalities. The institution of the common-law marriage has its roots in eleventh-century feudal England, when peasants were not permitted to leave the manor. When they wanted to marry, they had two choices: to wait for several months until a cleric visited to perform a ceremony, or to declare themselves married and make it official later. The latter course was often chosen.

Today, common-law marriages are frowned upon by the courts because, in the absence of formal vows, it is sometimes difficult for courts to determine the actual intent of the parties, opening the door for fraudulent claims if the couple separates or after the death of one of the partners. Nevertheless, 11 states as well as the District of Columbia recognize common-law marriages. No formal ceremony is required. Three elements are usually required for a relationship to be recognized as a common-law marriage:

1. The couple must mutually agree that they are married at the present time, not some time in the future.
2. They must represent themselves to others as being married— for example, referring to themselves as Mr. and Mrs.
3. They must live together.

Suppose a couple lives together as husband and wife in a state that recognizes common-law marriages. They decide to move to a neighboring state that does not. They are still considered married because the "Full Faith and Credit" clause of the U.S. Constitution requires that the second state honor the laws of the first. Therefore, the common-law marriage entered into in a state that recognizes it will be recognized in all other states.

In one case, an elderly woman with health problems was abandoned after raising many children in a relationship that had lasted for many decades but had not been formally solemnized. In order to award her spousal support, the court found that the parties had entered into a common-law marriage while flying briefly in air space over Pennsylvania (a state that recognizes common-law marriage). Since the court found that they had entered into a valid common-law marriage in Pennsylvania, it was recognized in the state where the parties resided, and the woman was awarded spousal support.

Couples who have entered into a common-law marriage must go through formal divorce proceedings before they can remarry. However, suppose Bob and Jean live together, are old enough to marry, tell neighbors that they are Mr. and Mrs., hold joint checking accounts, and have taken their own personal wedding vows. In their minds they're married, but they live in a state that does not acknowledge common-law marriages. When they decide to separate, no formal divorce is required because, in the eyes of the law, they were never married.

The following is a hypothetical situation involving common-law marriage.

THE PROBLEM

Susan and Bill Singer, both 50 years old, have lived together for 22 years and have three children. Bill has supported the family, and since the birth of their first child, Susan has stayed home with the children. They have a joint checking account in the names of Susan Singer and Bill Singer, consider themselves husband and wife, and even file joint income-tax returns; however, they were never formally married, and the state in which they reside does not recognize common-law marriage. Bill moves out and tells Susan that because their marriage was never formally solemnized, he has no obligations to Susan or the children.

WHAT TO DO

1. Susan should confer with an attorney experienced in family law to learn her legal rights. She will learn that Bill has the same obligation to contribute to the support of the children that he would have had if the parties had been formally married. Susan, who has not worked for over 20 years, is not entitled to spousal support, which requires marriage.

2. Susan may have rights under other laws. For example, assume the parties had an agreement that Bill would support Susan for life, in exchange for Susan's giving up her career, raising the children, and caring for the home. Even if the agreement were only oral, the courts in most states would enforce it if Susan could prove its existence. In most states, the agreement must have been expressed and may not have been simply implied from the conduct of the parties.

Live-in Lovers

Common-law marriage should not be confused with a "live-in" relationship. Couples sometimes live together without the intent of marital commitment. Live-in partners may encounter problems if they separate and want to determine who has made tangible and intangible contributions to the relationship and who is entitled to share in which of these.

The term *palimony* was coined in 1976 when actor Lee Marvin was sued by his former live-in partner, Michelle Triola Marvin. She demanded support payments as well as half the assets they had accumulated over the seven years they had lived together. She argued that she and Marvin had an oral agreement in which she agreed to give up her career as an entertainer to become a homemaker in return for Marvin's financial support for the remainder of her life. The Marvin case opened the door for similar lawsuits across the country, but not all states acknowledge the concept of palimony. In those states in which it is recognized, proof of an agreement between the parties may be required.

What follows is a hypothetical situation involving live-in lovers.

THE PROBLEM

Joe and Nicole, who are not married, have recently begun to live together. Joe is very wealthy; Nicole is not. Joe currently provides financial support for Nicole, but he does not wish to be vulnerable to a palimony claim if he and Nicole terminate their relationship.

WHAT TO DO

1. Joe should make his intentions clear to Nicole orally and in writing so that their cohabitation can in no way be construed as an implied contract to continue to support her should their relationship end.

2. Joe should ask Nicole to sign a cohabitation agreement. Such an agreement can provide that neither party shall acquire property rights from the other party solely as a result of their cohabitation, that neither party has a legal obligation to support the other, and that each party shall retain control over his and her separate property.

3. Each party should be represented by separate counsel and should provide the other with full financial disclosure to avoid arguments of duress, fraud, or undue influence by a party seeking to overturn the agreement.

Rights of Homosexual Couples

Homosexual couples who live together often confront the same issues as live-in heterosexual lovers. However, unlike heterosexuals, homosexuals cannot marry and consequently are not protected by laws concerning property rights upon divorce or death of a spouse. Therefore, it is often useful for them to set forth their rights and obligations in cohabitation contracts, wills, and powers of attorney.

In some states, homosexuality itself is against the law; many states still treat homosexual sodomy as a crime. But some municipalities have taken steps to protect the rights of homosexuals. In 1986 the City of New York's City Council enacted legislation that outlawed discrimination against homosexuals in housing and employment. In 1989 San Francisco enacted an ordinance prohibiting discrimination against unmarried couples, regardless of sexual orientation, who register as domestic partners. In 1993 New York City established a domestic partner registration program whereby heterosexual or homosexual cohabitants receive benefits formerly afforded only to married persons. These include leave of absence from work when a partner becomes a parent or experiences the death of a child or parent; succession rights of tenancy or occupancy rights in certain buildings; and specific visitation rights in correctional and hospital facilities.

What follows is a hypothetical situation involving a homosexual couple.

THE PROBLEM

Chuck and Lou live together in a rented apartment. The real estate market is favorable, interest rates are low, and they wish to purchase a home. They wish to purchase the home in joint names and to contribute equally to the monthly mortgage payments and expenses. However, only Chuck can afford to provide the $25,000 down payment. He is willing to do so, but he is concerned about being able to recoup his investment in the event that his relationship with Lou ends or the home is sold for any other reason.

WHAT TO DO

Chuck and Lou can execute an agreement that sets forth their intentions regarding the home. This agreement should state that upon the sale or other disposition of the house, Chuck will be credited for the full amount he provided as the down payment. A sample clause to this effect might read as follows:

The parties plan to purchase a home at 123 Main Street, Anywhere, U.S.A. (the "Home") in the near future. Chuck shall pay the down payment of $25,000. Title to the home shall be in joint names, and each party shall be entitled to equal ownership rights, except that in the event of a sale or other disposition of the Home, after payment of the mortgage and other usual closing costs, Chuck shall receive the first $25,000 of the sale proceeds. The remaining balance shall be divided equally. Chuck shall be entitled to recoup his investment of $25,000 regardless of any contributions by Lou toward the mortgage or maintenance of the Home.

Alternatively, such an agreement may provide that Chuck will receive the first 10 percent of sale proceeds after payment of mortgage and other usual closing costs—giving Chuck a proportionate share of appreciation.

The relationship may change and one party may move out, leaving the remaining party little incentive to sell. For this reason, Chuck and Lou should agree in advance to exactly when the home shall be sold. Perhaps the house should be placed on the market for sale 90 days after either party makes such a written request. Contracts can provide mechanisms for determining asking and sales prices to avoid future disputes.

Chuck should have a lawyer draft the contract. Lou should show the contract to an attorney of his choosing. In other words, if parties wish to enter into a contract, they should do it properly so they know it will be enforceable in the future, if necessary.

The Rights and Duties of Spouses

Marriage vows often involve the promise to love, honor, and obey until death. But each partner also has legal obligations that are inherent in both ceremonial and common-law marriages. These include:

Financial support. The law requires each partner to provide support for the other in accordance with his or her means.

Owning property. Each spouse holds title to the property she or he owned before marriage, although the "active" appreciation of this separate property may become a marital asset. For property acquired after the marriage, the states vary in determining who owns what. In community property states—those states that consider a couple's property to be owned equally by the two spouses, except that which is acquired through inheritance or as a gift—the property merges into marital assets. (The community property states are Arizona, California, Idaho, Louisiana, Nevada, New Mexico, Texas, and Washington. Puerto Rico is also listed in this category.) In the other 42 "noncommunity" states, spouses retain private ownership of property during the marriage.

Sexual relations. Partners are legally required to participate in sexual relations with their spouses unless an illness or disability exists. Despite this right, a spouse is prohibited from compelling a partner by force to have sex; that is considered rape in many states. The only legal remedy a refused spouse has is to file for either an annulment, separation, or divorce. In many states, a spouse has the right to sue someone who has interfered with a partner's ability to engage in sexual relations. Suppose a husband is badly injured in an automobile accident, rendering him paralyzed from the neck down. In addition to the many damages he can claim against the party at fault, his wife can sue for loss of *consortium*, the term used to refer to loss of marital services.

The right to bear children and to have an abortion. A woman is not required to receive permission from her spouse to become pregnant, bear a child, or have an abortion. Although there have been challenges, the courts have held that a woman has dominion over her own body.

Lawsuits Against a Spouse
Historically, the majority of American jurisdictions did not allow spouses to sue each other. Their objections were usually based upon the rationale that such suits would disturb the marital relationship. Today, the majority of states have either abolished or limited the doctrine of interspousal immunity.

Typical situations in which spouses might sue each other include the conversion of property by the other, negligence, assault, battery, defamation, or fraud. By far the most common scenario occurs when one spouse sues the other for injuries caused by the negligent operation of an automobile. These cases generally do not disrupt family harmony, because the spouse being sued is usually covered by liability insurance. Indeed, these types of lawsuits between spouses are so common that some states have statutes requiring insurance policies to state specifically that they cover claims between spouses.

If one's spouse is injured or killed through the negligence of another person, the noninjured spouse may sue the negligent party for the loss of support, companionship, affection, and sexual relationship of the other spouse. In cases of serious injury, a once-happy marriage or family can be turned into a source of pain and suffering for even the noninjured spouse; thus, damages are awarded.

Most courts require a legal marriage and a serious, permanent injury before awarding damages. In general, the noninjured spouse demonstrates to the court the mental distress caused by a spouse's injury, deprivation of social and family activities, impairment of the sexual relationship of the spouses, and the inability to have children, if applicable. The noninjured spouse usually may not recover for lost wages and medical expenses, because these are covered in the injured spouse's lawsuit against the negligent party.

Similarly, parents can recover for the loss of a child's society, companionship, and affection, but if the parents' own negligence contributed to the child's injury, some states will bar recovery by the parents.

Attempts by children to recover for the loss of parental *consortium* caused by injury to their parents have generally failed; however, in the past decade several courts have recognized this cause of action and awarded damages.

ANNULMENT

Two legal actions can end a marriage: annulment and divorce. In divorce, a court declares that, for one of any number of reasons—often irreconcilable differences between the spouses—a valid marriage is legally ended. An annulment not only ends a marriage, it declares that the marriage never existed, through a legal finding that something took place or that a condition existed that makes the marriage void or voidable.

The grounds for annulment include:

Fraud. If one of the partners made a fraudulent representation about his or her past, character, or intentions, the other partner can file for an annulment. These misrepresentations can include claiming pregnancy, concealing a drug or alcohol addiction, failing to disclose a health problem such as a venereal disease or epilepsy, or professing to want children when the individual had no intention or desire to become a parent.

Duress. If a person forces another into marriage by threatening or using bodily harm, the marriage may be voided by the victim.

Mental retardation or mental illness. If a person is so mentally infirm at the time of the marital commitment as not to understand what she or he is doing, the marriage may be declared void.

Impotency. The marriage may be declared invalid if the husband was incurably impotent at the time it occurred.

Bigamy and incest. Because the law considers both bigamous and incestuous marriages to be illegal, they are void and are grounds for annulment.

Under age. If one partner is under age (according to state law) and married without parental consent, the union may be annulled.

If the court determines that sufficient grounds exist and grants an annulment, the marriage is declared never to have existed.

Annulments are relatively uncommon because it's often difficult to prove fraud (e.g., that one's spouse never really wanted children). But if grounds for annulment do exist, it might be more advantageous than filing for divorce, because in certain states each person's property rights would be preserved. However, in many states the same property distribution laws apply to annulments and to divorces.

Although a court will most likely declare children born out of annulled marriages to be legitimate if they were born before the annulment, in some states an annulment may eliminate some of the privileges that would have accompanied a valid marriage—inheritance rights, the right to file a lawsuit or workers' compensation claim when a spouse is killed or injured, or, in some states, the right of not testifying against a husband or wife in a criminal action.

Some states do not provide for spousal support after an annulment; other states make spousal support available only to the innocent party. Because the grounds for annulment may also be grounds for divorce, and because spousal support is sometimes difficult to obtain in an annulment, a divorce action may be preferable to an annulment in some circumstances.

If you wish to have your marriage annulled, be aware that the courts pay close attention to whether or not you cohabited after you learned of the fraudulent situation. If you continue to live with and/or have sexual relations with your spouse, the court may view that as "ratification," or approving of the fraud or the otherwise annulment-qualifying situation, and refuse to grant an annulment. In many cases divorce may be the only route to take in ending an unhappy or fraudulent relationship.

The following is a hypothetical situation involving annulment.

THE PROBLEM

Before Julie and Gary were married, they discussed marriage and their mutual plans and hopes to have a family. After two years of marriage, Julie decides that the time is right to start a family. She mentions this to Gary, who says that he is not settled in his career and that he does not want to start a family until he feels financially secure. Julie waits another year and, shortly after Gary receives a promotion and large salary increase, tells him of her strong desire to start a family. Gary tells Julie that he still does not feel ready. Julie points out that they have substantial savings and she cannot understand Gary's reluctance. Gary says that he has never wanted children, that he only told Julie he did because he loved her and knew that she would not marry him if he told her the truth. Julie is devastated.

WHAT TO DO

If Julie wishes to terminate the marriage, she may seek an annulment. She must demonstrate that Gary deceived her and that she would not have married Gary if she had known of his unwillingness to have children. Proof may be difficult. Julie must prove that Gary did not intend to have children before they were married and that he intentionally deceived her. Gary may argue that he merely had a change of heart after they married.

SEPARATION

Often, the first step in a divorce is a separation, the act of living apart from your spouse. Because formal separation is a way to test the status of a couple's relationship to determine whether the marriage should be ended, some states require a couple to go through the legal separation process before granting a divorce. This usually requires the drafting of a written separation agreement, which may contain the following information:

- a statement that the parties are separated
- a full financial disclosure of assets
- how the property, both personal and real, is to be divided
- who pays how much in spousal and child support
- who has custody and visitation rights
- who pays the cost of education for the children
- who pays children's medical and dental expenses
- who pays the couple's debts
- who claims children as dependents for tax purposes
- who pays for insurance
- who pays legal fees
- who has inheritance rights
- a clause stating whether this agreement is to be incorporated into a divorce decree

Certain matters can invalidate a separation; therefore, the following must be avoided:

- lying about or concealing your assets
- including a clause that agrees to enter into a divorce in the future
- providing for an illegal activity (such as suggesting that both parties simultaneously claim a child as a tax deduction)

Obviously, the more amicable the separation is, the quicker, less expensive, and less emotionally wrenching it will be. Except in the briefest of childless and assetless marriages, you should confer with a lawyer who specializes in domestic law to learn about the issues and your rights and obligations stemming from the marriage. Then sit down with your spouse and decide upon which issues you can both agree and which will require some negotiation and work. However, if one spouse, such as a battered spouse, may be intimidated, it is advisable that the lawyers be involved in all the negotiations.

After you have a basic picture of where you each stand on the issues, talk again to your lawyers. Perhaps you can, with the guidance of the lawyers, come up with a satisfactory agreement.

Remember that an attorney can represent the best interests of only one of you. Both spouses will have to have their own attorneys. This applies except in the briefest of childless and assetless marriages where one party or both parties may decide not to retain an attorney.

Mediation

Mediation is another alternative in separations and divorces. A couple mutually selects a professional mediator who assists the parties in negotiating their own settlement. The mediator will discuss the issues with the couple together and separately in an effort to remove stumbling blocks, present options to the couple, elicit relevant information, and encourage more flexible behavior. If the couple is successful in coming up with a mediated separation agreement, each party should have his or her attorney review it before executing it.

SEXUAL RELATIONS DURING SEPARATION Remember that separation agreements are valid only when a couple lives apart or is about to live apart. If you reconcile and move back in together, the agreement may become void. Resuming sexual relations with your spouse can hinder your chances of a divorce in some states.

FINANCIAL ARRANGEMENTS In addition to deciding about spousal and child support, separating couples must consider the assets that they've shared as a couple. Suppose that you and your spouse have separated, and you are concerned that your spouse may withdraw all the proceeds of your joint checking and savings accounts and leave the area. If there has been no prior order by the court regarding the money, you may be permitted to withdraw it and place it in a safe place, such as another account, from which it can be drawn for your necessities and those of the children. Squandering the funds or lying to the court about the location of the money can cause you severe problems. If you do take possession of the money, be sure you can account for where you spent it or where you have placed it for safekeeping.

If you and your spouse have a safe-deposit box and you're concerned that your spouse may take its contents, do an inventory of the contents in the presence of a neutral third party, such as a bank teller, and then place the box in another safe-deposit box. If the safe-deposit box is in your spouse's name, you should consider a court order preventing your spouse from having access to the contents.

If you have joint charge card accounts, you might want to close them if you believe your spouse may try to use them irresponsibly.

Credit card bills can become a problem during property settlements. Some states make credit card payments the responsibility of both parties regardless of who made the purchases; other states provide that if you are separated, the charges belong to the person who incurred them. Find out about the law in your state. Once the divorce is final, you should be sure to open a charge account in your name and be certain that the joint accounts are paid off according to the provisions of the final decree.

DIVORCE

The "trial divorce"—the separation—may convince both partners that the marriage should be legally ended. The next step is to consult with your lawyer about the grounds for a divorce. If you and your partner can agree to an uncontested divorce, consider whether you wish to proceed *pro se*, or on your own behalf, without a lawyer. Be aware that sometimes divorces that start out as uncontested run into snags as issues and assets are discussed.

No-fault Divorce

A no-fault divorce is a relatively new phenomenon. Until the recent past, a marriage could be dissolved legally only if one party could prove that the other was at fault for causing the breakup by a particular act, such as adultery, desertion, cruelty, or physical abuse. Even if both parties agreed that they wanted to end the marriage, they were often forced to invent false and humiliating charges—and "prove" them before a witness—in order to be granted the divorce.

During the 1960s the courts began to acknowledge that the law encouraged perjury and hardship and failed at its purpose of keeping marriages intact. As a result, the concept of no-fault divorce started to take hold.

No-fault divorce is just that. Its provisions are based on the assumption that no one is to blame, that the couple, or one spouse, wants to terminate the marriage. Every state has some form of no-fault divorce, although the grounds may differ, and some states require the consent of both parties. Individual states may require that divorcing couples show evidence (in sworn statements in the petition for divorce) of:

- mutual consent to divorce
- irreconcilable differences
- the marriage being irretrievably broken
- incompatibility
- the couple living separate and apart for a specified period of time (in some states, pursuant to a valid separation agreement or judicial separation)

Uncontested Divorce

Uncontested divorces don't require a trial. If you and your spouse agree to end your marriage and have no disputes concerning child or spousal support, child custody, or property settlement, call the appropriate court in your county to determine what procedure is necessary to obtain an uncontested divorce in your state. As we have noted, each state has its own requirements and grounds for divorce. You may discover that you can handle the paperwork for a simple uncontested divorce yourself, almost from start to finish. This is seldom the case, however, because the issues of support, custody, and property settlement are rarely so simple. You'll probably find that your divorce will require a great deal of negotiation and hard work before you see a final judgment.

If it becomes apparent that you're going to require an attorney, either evaluate the one you may have consulted initially or see chapter 10 for some guidance on selecting an attorney who suits you. If you decide not to consult with an attorney, the clerk's office of the court in the county in which you reside can tell you where to get the required forms and where to file them. After they're filed, the court may set a date for a hearing, which merely requires that both parties answer a few questions. The court usually grants an uncontested divorce with no further requirements as long as there is total agreement on all issues.

Fault Divorce

Some states combine the grounds for no-fault divorces with those required for fault divorces, including:

- adultery
- drug and alcohol addiction
- nonsupport
- abandonment
- physical or mental cruelty
- sexual perversions
- impotency
- insanity
- bigamy
- fraud
- coercion
- felony or imprisonment
- incestuous marriage

Divorce becomes more complex when one of the parties opposes the divorce or when a major issue, such as child custody, is unresolved. Some courts will grant a divorce even if only one spouse wants it. These states view marriage as a contract with an escape clause; if one of the parties no longer wants to fulfill her or his obligations, the contract contradicts the purpose of the marriage. Other no-fault states require both parties' consent.

The following is a hypothetical situation involving divorce.

THE PROBLEM

Lisa and Larry have been married for five years. During the past two years, Larry has become verbally abusive and caused Lisa much unhappiness. She wants to end the marriage, but Larry will not agree to an uncontested divorce.

WHAT TO DO

Lisa should contact an attorney who specializes in matrimonial law. She should then, with the help of that attorney, commence a lawsuit for divorce based on Larry's cruelty.

Lisa should use a notepad or diary to recall facts, dates, times, and places concerning each instance of cruelty. These will prove helpful in litigating the cruelty issue, especially since she knows Larry will be contesting it.

Divorce cases are always heard in state courts, not federal. The state has jurisdiction to hear a divorce case where both or either of the parties reside. This includes "quickie" Mexican divorces. But if neither party has established residency in Mexico—an appearance is not enough—the divorce will most likely be invalid in the United States, as will any order regarding the property of the party.

The Divorce Procedure

The procedure in a divorce action is the same as in any other civil action. Suppose you've been married for 12 years, and you and your spouse have two preteen children, a home, two cars, joint bank accounts, and various investments, both liquid and nonliquid. You've both been unhappy with your marriage for some time and have participated in marriage counseling in the hope of ironing out your differences. Your spouse believes that the marriage still has a chance, but you wish to end it. Assuming negotiations are fruitless, your lawyer will file and serve a Summons and Complaint for Divorce (sometimes called a Petition for Dissolution of Marriage) with the court, stating the grounds for the action. You are the plaintiff; your spouse is the defendant. Your spouse is given a specified time in which to respond, either denying the grounds or admitting them.

Suppose your spouse believes that the divorce can be avoided by going into hiding so the Summons and Complaint for Divorce cannot be served. Avoiding service may make divorce a little more complicated, but it doesn't prevent it. Your lawyer can ask the court to permit service by "publication." You'll be required to demonstrate that you were unable to effect service by another method with due diligence. Then you must publish notice of the filing of your divorce petition in a local newspaper and allow your elusive spouse a certain number of days in which to come forward. If your spouse does not respond and you have complied with your state's requirements for service by publication, you may be granted a divorce by default.

If your spouse does answer (contest) the Complaint, both parties will begin preparing for trial through "discovery," gathering evidence and seeking out reliable witnesses. (See chapter 11.)

Your divorce decree may not become a reality for many months; in the meantime you'll probably have some financial and custodial issues that require immediate resolution. Suppose that your spouse has been the primary breadwinner because you have stayed at home to care for your child. If you and your spouse cannot agree to what support you should temporarily receive, you have the right to petition the court for temporary spousal or child support. You'll be required to provide the court with detailed financial information, including your sources of income and liquid assets as well as monthly expenses.

The issue of child custody must also be resolved before a final divorce decree is issued. As a general rule, the parent who remains in the marital home will have custody of the child to avoid disrupting the child's normal routine and friendships.

If you take a job in another state and move with your child to the site of your new job without obtaining permission from the court or your spouse, your spouse's attorney will probably promptly file a petition requesting that your child be returned and accusing you of kidnapping the child.

SHOULD YOU LEAVE HOME?   Suppose you've filed for divorce, but your spouse refuses to leave. Judges prefer not to become involved in ordering spouses out of their own homes unless they have become violent or abusive. Some spouses may decide to take it upon themselves to force their spouse off the property, but this can create serious legal problems and should not be undertaken without the advice of an experienced divorce attorney.

Others find the marital situation so unbearable that they leave the home instead of demanding that their spouse do so. If you are absent from home for a certain length of time, the final divorce decree may grant the home to the one who is in possession. Be sure to seek legal advice before leaving the marital home.

MEDIATION   Divorce mediation can greatly reduce the stress and expense of divorce. In a mediation procedure, a skilled mediator assists the parties in arriving at their own settlement. The mediator does not issue a decision or recommendation; instead, he or she supports the couple in working out their own solutions, providing a structured setting and impartial guidance. Mediation can take place before a divorce action is filed or any time before the court issues a final decree.

Some judges believe in the concept of mediation so strongly that they require all divorce actions to submit to mediation before engaging in a court action. If the couple reaches a settlement agreement through either mediation or negotiation, it will be reviewed by the court and incorporated into the final divorce judgment. If negotiation and mediation fail, the process of preparing for trial continues.

You can get recommendations for a mediator from your state bar association.

ARBITRATION   Another alternative to court is having someone other than a judge resolve the issues of your case. An arbitrator usually is a lawyer but may be anyone the parties agree on, including a clergyperson, a relative, a mental-health professional, or a trusted friend. Both parties must agree to take their dispute out of the courts and to be bound by the arbitrator's decision.

Both parties, with or without lawyers, argue their case before the arbitrator. Arbitration may take place in the arbitrator's office or any place agreed on by the arbitrator and parties. The arbitration setting is less formal than court, although usually the rules of evidence apply. In general, the arbitrator's decision will be absolutely final and binding and will be incorporated into a court order that may not be appealed.

The advantages of arbitration are speed and informality. Long court delays and the adversarial and formal process of court litigation can be avoided. Although costs are usually connected with it, arbitration is often far less costly than court litigation because of its speed.

The disadvantage of arbitration is that the parties have given up their rights to judicial review. If a judge makes a mistake, the case may be appealed. Except for custody issues, an arbitrator's decision generally may not be reviewed. Since many divorcing parties cannot afford the expensive process of an appeal, giving up the right to appeal may often not be important.

PRETRIAL CONFERENCES TO RESOLVE DISPUTES   After the discovery process has been completed—interrogatories answered, depositions taken, witnesses interviewed, documentation developed—the court will schedule a pretrial conference to resolve remaining differences. This type of pretrial conference can take place anytime the judge believes that an informal discussion may resolve an issue. For example, suppose you go before a judge on a temporary motion to grant visitation rights. The judge may sense that the parties could reach an agreement if they retired to chambers and discussed their differences, perhaps avoiding a trial. In certain instances a spouse and that spouse's lawyer may meet privately with the judge without the other spouse and lawyer present or being involved with the conference.

If a resolution does not take place during the pretrial conference, the trial proceeds.

THE TRIAL   As in any civil trial, the attorneys and judge usually meet in a pretrial conference to decide what issues will be resolved during the trial. Such a conference can be used as the last formal attempt to reach a settlement.

A divorce trial follows the procedures of a general trial: opening arguments; plaintiff's case presented through evidence and witnesses, followed by the defendant's case; rebuttal by the plaintiff; rebuttal by the defendant; and finally, closing arguments. (See chapter 11.) Sometimes, when testimony in an open court is considered awkward, particularly in the case of children, the judge will hold an *in camera* hearing, that is, one held in chambers.

The judge will either rule at the conclusion of the trial or decide that more time is needed to mull matters over, taking the decision "under advisement." Once the judge has made a ruling, one of the attorneys usually will draft a judgment and submit it to opposing counsel and the court for approval. If the two attorneys cannot agree, opposing counsel may also prepare a draft judgment and the court will choose one judgment and may modify it.

When the judge signs the judgment and it has been entered in the record and filed in the county clerk's office, you are officially divorced. In a few states, there is a gap between the time the judge issues a ruling and the date on which the decree is entered, usually three to six months.

The Divorce Judgment

In addition to granting a divorce, a judgment also makes provisions for dividing the marital property, awarding spousal support, awarding child support, and awarding child custody and visitation rights.

DISPUTING THE JUDGMENT If you believe that the court committed an error of law and the final divorce judgment is not acceptable to you, you can ask that an appellate court review the case. If your objection is merely a matter of your feeling that the judge was not sufficiently sympathetic to your situation, your chances of having the judgment reversed or reheard are small.

Note: Suppose you and your spouse reconcile after the judgment has been issued. If a certain amount of time has elapsed since the judgment was issued, you may have to go through the entire process of remarrying, including securing a new marriage license. The states vary as to how much time you have in which to change your mind, with six months about the maximum in any state.

DIVIDING PROPERTY   One of the most difficult aspects of a divorce is deciding which spouse is entitled to what property. Most states agree that property acquired before marriage or received as a gift or inheritance during marriage remains the personal property of that individual. But when it comes to the property acquired through marriage, the states have separate laws. Eight states and Puerto Rico follow the concept of community property, in which property acquired during the marriage is divided equally, virtually by dividing it in half. These states are Arizona, California, Idaho, Louisiana, Nevada, New Mexico, Texas, and Washington. The laws of the remaining 42 states and the District of Columbia support the equitable division of property—that is, that property acquired during the marriage is to be divided in an equitable but not necessarily equal manner. In these states, the court considers a number of different factors to determine how the marital property can be distributed equitably, including:

- age of the partners
- squandering of assets by a partner
- income and property of each partner
- health
- length of the marriage
- need of custodial parent to occupy or own the marital residence
- occupation and income
- loss of inheritance or pension rights
- the contributions each made to the marriage, both economic and noneconomic
- probable future financial situation of each partner

SPOUSAL SUPPORT   Before the 1970s husbands were rarely granted spousal support in the event of divorce. In general, spousal support lasted until death or remarriage. Today, with more than 50 percent of women in the workplace earning a salary and sharing economic responsibilities, the situation has changed; gender is no longer the determining factor when it comes to who requires or deserves spousal support. In 1979 the U.S. Supreme Court ruled that requiring only men to pay alimony violated the "Equal Protection" clause of the Fourteenth Amendment.

Although recent legal terminology has replaced the term *alimony* with *maintenance* or *spousal support*, all three terms are interchangeable. The factors the court examines in determining spousal support include the length of the marriage as well as the standard of living the couple enjoyed; the age and the physical and emotional condition of the person asking for support; the financial situation of both parties; the presence of children in the home of one of the parties; and the reduced earning capacity of a party because of forgone career opportunities.

If the divorce involves complicated issues, litigation can drag on for months or even years. In such cases temporary support is sometimes granted to help one of the spouses financially until the final judgment is issued. At one time permanent spousal support was considered to be just that—permanent. Until an ex-wife remarried or died, the ex-husband was responsible for her sustenance. Now the goal is to urge both divorced spouses to support themselves eventually. Sometimes this can involve one former spouse making payments to the spouse who needs additional training or time to find a job and become partially, if not totally, self-sufficient. In recent years this self-sufficiency test has been criticized because of growing awareness of the opportunity costs of raising children and/or of years out of the workforce.

The following hypothetical situation involves spousal support.

THE PROBLEM

Nancy and Jim have been married for 11 years and have two children, ages nine and six. They are in the process of divorcing. Nancy hadn't completed college when she married Jim. Until the birth of their first child, she worked at a local store, earning very modest wages. She is currently enrolled in nursing school.

Jim is an accountant. Although he earns enough to support the family, he does not feel that his earnings are sufficient to support two households. He is willing to pay child support, but he does not want to pay spousal support to Nancy.

PROBABLE COURT ACTION

The court will probably order Jim to pay child support and spousal support. The child support would be payable until the children are emancipated (no longer considered minors); the spousal support would probably be payable for only a few years, thus allowing Nancy to obtain her nursing degree, reenter the job market, and become financially self-sufficient.

Based on the particular facts of the case, Nancy might succeed in obtaining permanent spousal support. Age of the parties, length of the marriage, years Nancy had been away from the workforce, great discrepancy in earning potentials, and Nancy's contributions to Jim's career (e.g., supporting the family while Jim obtained his master's degree) would all be relevant.

CHILD CUSTODY   Until the nineteenth century, the father was entitled to custody. In the twentieth century, until about 20 years ago, mothers were favored as custodial parents under the "tender years doctrine." Attitudes about what is best for each child are changing. Today, custody decisions are based on the best interests of the child. Several factors are taken into consideration, including:

- the fitness of each parent to care for the child
- the income and financial stability of the parents
- the age of the child
- the sex of the child
- the child's emotional and physical needs
- the child's preference for which parent he or she wants to live with, providing the child is mature enough to make those decisions

Once custody is awarded, court orders provide for the visitation rights of the noncustodial parent, specifying the days, hours, and holidays as well as any other pertinent provisions. Sometimes providing the best situation for a child involves not one custodial parent, but joint custody. Joint legal custody provides that each parent will have some say in how the child is raised. Joint physical custody goes further and provides that the child spends certain specific days, weeks, or months with each parent; the child, in effect, has not one home, but two. In some states joint custody may not be awarded unless the parents can cooperate regarding the children, which is extremely rare when custody is contested.

A court's judgment granting custody to either parent or both is not etched in stone. If circumstances change and the noncustodial parent can prove that she or he is more fit as a parent, the court can alter the original order. Court orders will also provide the visitation rights of the noncustodial parent, specifying the days, hours, and holidays.

Most states now have laws that grant visitation rights to grandparents after a separation or divorce, if this is found to be in the best interests of the child. Should the grandparents demonstrate that the parents are unfit, grandparents can be awarded custody of the children. It should be noted, however, that in a custody dispute between a parent and a grandparent, there is a strong presumption that a parent will be awarded custody unless it is established by clear and convincing evidence that the parent is unfit *and* the best interests of the child dictate that the grandparents receive custody.

The following is a hypothetical situation involving grandparents' custody.

THE PROBLEM

Kenneth and Linda divorced when their son, Max, was a year old. Kenneth was awarded visitation and ordered to pay child support. He moved to another state shortly thereafter and neither he visited Max nor paid child support. When Max was six years old, Linda died suddenly. Kenneth, who had not seen Max for five years, returned to take Max home with him. Linda's parents, with whom Max has a close relationship, initiated an application for custody.

WHAT TO DO

1. Although it is generally very difficult for grandparents to prevail in custody suits against parents, Linda's parents do have a chance to prevail in this case because of Kenneth's failure to support, visit, or otherwise establish a relationship with Max.

2. In order to prevail, Linda's parents must first demonstrate Kenneth's unfitness as a parent. Although there is generally a presumption that a parent will be awarded custody over a nonparent, the parent may lose this right by neglect, disregard, or misconduct.

3. Linda's parents must also prove to the court that they are able to provide a superior environment (compared with Kenneth) for Max. In general, courts may not remove children from their parents merely because another home offers more advantages; however, in a case such as this, where a parent may be adjudged unfit, the availability of a stable, loving home will probably influence the court.

4. It will be helpful for Linda's parents to demonstrate that Max had no contact with Kenneth but did have frequent and loving contact with them. Also, they should show that they live in a suitable home and have sufficient means to provide for him financially, emotionally, and educationally. To this end it will be helpful for them to include the testimony of witnesses such as schoolteachers, mental-health professionals, and others who have seen the grandparent-child relationship.

5. For Kenneth to prevail, he should have cogent explanations for his absence and present the court with specific plans for Max's care and education. He should seek visitation with Max during the pendency of the custody proceeding.

CHILD SUPPORT   Before 1989, child support awards were discretionary. A judge considered the financial resources of each parent, the other expenses of each parent, and the needs of the child. The amount of a child support award was unpredictable, and there was great disparity among judges. Also, awards tended to be on the low side.

The *income shares model* of child support guidelines is applied in 32 states (Alabama, Arizona, Colorado, Connecticut, Florida, Idaho, Indiana, Iowa, Kansas, Kentucky, Louisiana, Maine, Maryland, Michigan, Missouri, Montana, Nebraska, New Hampshire, New Jersey, New Mexico, New York, Ohio, Oklahoma, Oregon, Pennsylvania, Rhode Island, South Carolina, South Dakota, Utah, Vermont,

Consequently, beginning October 13, 1989, the federal government required all states to apply numerical guidelines to promote predictability and sufficiency of child support. The federal government said that judges could deviate from guidelines, but only when application of the guidelines would be unfair or unjust.

Virginia, and Washington) and Guam. Under this model, a total support amount is calculated based on a set percentage of the combined incomes of both parents. Then, the noncustodial parent's share of this amount is calculated based on the proportion of that parent's income to total income. The set percentage is based on family size and may not necessarily apply above a fixed amount of combined parental income.

The following example illustrates that application of the income shares model: Patricia and Joseph have two children and Patricia has custody. They live in a state that applies the income shares model to determine child support. Patricia earns $20,000 a year and Joseph earns $40,000 a year. What is Joseph's child support obligation under child support guidelines?

The precise answer depends on the specific numerical percentages and specific deductions to be taken from income before the numerical percentages are applied. For simplicity, assume that in Patricia's and Joseph's state the numerical percentage for two children is 25 percent and no deductions are to be taken from income.

The combined parental child support obligation in this case would be 25 percent of $60,000 or $15,000. Since Joseph's income was two-thirds of the total, his child support obligation would be two-thirds of the combined parental child support obligation of $15,000. That comes to $10,000 a year or a child support obligation of $192.31 every week.

The *percentage of income model* is applied in 15 states (Alaska, Arkansas, California, Georgia, Illinois, Massachusetts, Minnesota, Mississippi, Nevada, North Carolina, North Dakota, Tennessee, Texas, Wisconsin, and Wyoming) as well as in Puerto Rico and the District of Columbia. This model simply sets child support at a percentage of the noncustodial parent's income. The percentage is determined by the number of children and sometimes by the ages of the children.

The *Melson Formula* is applied in three states (Delaware, Hawaii, and West Virginia). The formula is more complicated than the other two models. It allocates to each parent a poverty self-support reserve, determines total remaining parental income and the noncustodial parent's percentage thereof, applies the noncustodial parent's percentage to obtain the "primary support obligation" based on the number of children, and assesses the noncustodial parent of the income remaining after the primary support obligation is subtracted. This last percentage increases with the number of children being supported.

In most cases a child receives child support until the age of majority: age 18 in some states and age 21 in others. Support can be terminated sooner if the child marries, begins full-time work, or refuses a parent's discipline or control. In certain circumstances a parent is required to support the child past the age of majority. If a child has an illness or disability, for example, the parents usually will be required to provide further support. But the states differ about whether parents must pay for a child's college education. In general, the parents pay for four years of college or trade school after high school.

What if your spouse should die before fulfilling his or her child support payments? Suppose your spouse was ordered by the court to pay for four years of college for your two children, but died before either could complete their educations. Spousal and child support end upon the death of the payor spouse. For this reason courts will often direct the payor spouse to maintain life insurance. In all negotiated agreements, life insurance—at least during the period of the support obligations—should not be overlooked. Since custodial as well as noncustodial parents contribute to the support of children, life insurance for both parents is often appropriate.

What happens when one of the spouses remarries? Let's assume that you (a woman) remarry after your divorce and that your new spouse is quite wealthy. His net worth, generally, should not affect the amount of child support your ex-husband pays for your children. Your new husband is under no obligation to support children that are not his. Since you no longer have to pay a certain monthly rent for an apartment, *your* financial status is changed, and this will be the basis of modifications to your divorce judgment.

MODIFYING A DIVORCE JUDGMENT   The final divorce judgment need not be final; parts of it, especially those that pertain to children, can be changed. If no limits regarding the amount of spousal support or

In a divorce action the court ordered Duke to pay permanent spousal support to Bernadette. Six months after the final judgment, she allowed another man to move into her home with her. Duke called his lawyer, expecting this to be grounds for ending his spousal support payments. However, cohabitation does not constitute remarriage, and unless Bernadette's companion is benefiting from her support payments, the court probably will not consider the change in living arrangements enough to require a modification in Duke's payments. In some states the former spouse must be "holding herself out as the spouse of another," such as having a joint bank account or being introduced as the other's spouse, in order for the court to modify its judgment.

the time in which it was to be paid were placed on the final judgment, these can usually be modified if circumstances change. However, the standard for modification of spousal support provided for in a separation agreement is usually much more rigid than that of an award granted at trial. If you and your ex-spouse agree about the change, your lawyer can file an order spelling out the modification, and the judge will review it and sign it. If you want the judgment modified (perhaps your ex-spouse's salary has increased), your attorney can file a petition for modification with the court. Your spouse will be notified of a hearing, and the court will hear arguments from both sides and rule on it, based on applicable modification standards in your state.

The federal government requires all child support awards to be adjusted every three years to reflect changes in the cost of living.

Enforcing a Court Order
What can you do if your spouse refuses to comply with the court's instructions? Let's assume that the court has issued an order requiring your spouse to pay $300 a month for temporary child support. Your spouse believes the order is unfair and refuses to pay. You have various choices.

If your spouse is employed within the state of your divorce judgment, an income execution can be served on your spouse's employer. You will then be paid child support directly by your spouse's employer, including arrears. The amount you will receive may be as much as 60 percent of your spouse's net income. This is an excellent enforcement mechanism, which is being required for all child support orders issued from January 1994. In other words, child support is being automatically withheld from paychecks just like taxes. Unfortunately, this remedy may not be effective if your spouse is unemployed, self-employed, or employed outside the state.

Alternative enforcement remedies include obtaining a money judgment. This will be effective if your spouse owns assets in his name. It may be worthless if your spouse has no assets or has effectively hidden his assets.

The child support recovery unit in your area may issue an income-tax intercept. If your spouse has overpaid his federal or state taxes and underpaid his child support, his tax refund will be intercepted and paid to you to the extent that arrears are owed. If all else fails, your lawyer may file a petition for contempt of court, requiring your delinquent spouse to explain the failure to pay. If your spouse doesn't respond or has no valid reason, your spouse can be found in contempt of court and be forced to pay a fine in addition to the child support owed and/or spend time in jail.

Theoretically, the spouse who fails to comply with a judgment or order should pay for the attorneys' fees required to force compliance. But if the former spouse has no money or if your case is settled, the burden of paying the attorney may remain yours.

Child support and visitation are separate issues. Let's assume, for example, that your former spouse is three months behind in child support payments, yet shows up every other weekend to visit the children. You believe that it would be fair to deny your former spouse the time with the children because of missed child support payments. Because the courts consider these two issues to be distinct from each other, your only recourse is to petition the court to force your former spouse to pay the child support and to find out if a court order could be issued denying visitation rights.

Similarly, in the absence of a court order suspending support, the noncustodial parent may not withhold child support because he or she has been deprived visitation.

If your former spouse ignores the responsibility of paying child support and leaves the state, enforcement may be difficult, but you have some protection. You can get a court order in your state, and through the Uniform Reciprocal Enforcement of Support Act adopted in most states or the Uniform Interstate Family Support Act adopted in two states, the order can be enforced in the state to which your former spouse fled. With regard to interstate support enforcement, you may retain an attorney in the noncustodial parent's state or work with the child support recovery unit in your state, listed in the phone book under state government.

The following is a hypothetical situation involving child support.

THE PROBLEM

Sharon and her two children, David, 13, and Elizabeth, 11, reside in Florida. The children's father, Lawrence, lives in New York. Sharon has a five-year-old child support order and receives child support of $60 a week from Lawrence. The problem is that $60 a week does not go very far toward the needs of two growing adolescent children. Sharon is a librarian and works for a municipality. Her modest income has not increased significantly during the last five years.

WHAT TO DO

1. If Sharon can discuss her financial problems with Lawrence, she should do this so that he will understand her reasons for needing more child support. Perhaps they will be able to agree on an increased child support payment.

2. If Sharon cannot work out an acceptable settlement with Lawrence, she should go to the child support recovery unit in her county. On Sharon's behalf, the unit will bring an application for upward modification in New York. A lawyer from the child support recovery unit in New York will serve Lawrence with papers and pursue Sharon's claim. Sharon need not appear in court in New York. Since 1989 all states have laws that require application of child support guidelines. If Sharon's five-year-old child support order predated child

support guidelines, Sharon may receive a significant increase in child support.

Tax Consequences

Spousal support, child support, and property settlements are viewed separately in the eyes of the law. The payment of spousal support can be deducted on income-tax returns, while the spouse receiving the support must report it as income. Child support payments, however, do not qualify as a tax deduction nor are they regarded as income.

Other Legal Requirements

Spousal support and property settlements can be worked out and agreed to by the parties, themselves. Property settlements can be discharged by filing for personal bankruptcy, but the responsibility of paying spousal support and child support cannot be discharged. Property settlements are permanent and cannot be modified because of changes in circumstances, but spousal support and child support can be modified. Remember that state laws differ; be sure to find out how your particular situation is affected by the laws of your state.

RIGHTS AND RESPONSIBILITIES OF BEING A PARENT

Parents are required by law to provide their children with proper nourishment, a safe home, clothing, and medical attention. They owe them the duty not to harm or neglect them and to provide them with a proper education. If parents are unfit or abuse or neglect their children, the state has the right to determine whether parental rights should be terminated or whether the child should be placed in foster care. The court may appoint a guardian for the child until the child can return home. The law requires parents to support their children until either of four events occurs:

1. The child reaches the age of majority, ranging from 18 to 21, depending on each state's laws.
2. The child chooses to marry or enter into the armed forces.

3. The child leaves home to live on his or her own.

4. The child is gainfully employed and fully self-supporting.

Children, in turn, have the responsibility of complying with the reasonable wishes of their parents. If they do not, the parents have the right to punish them, short of physical or verbal abuse. In extreme cases, parents may require the intervention of the court to help with discipline. If a minor's behavior amounts to "unruly behavior," such as failing to return home, the court may be able to issue a petition that the child be picked up by the police and be taken home or to a juvenile facility.

Parents should take it upon themselves to obtain two of the most important documents a child will ever need throughout the child's life: a birth certificate and a Social Security card. (At one time, Social Security cards were issued when an individual applied for a job. The new tax laws now require a child to be assigned a Social Security number by the age of two in order to qualify as a deduction on the parents' tax return.) The birth certificate contains the child's legal name and will be necessary when the child wants to apply for a passport or other important documents. If the birth certificate is lost, parents should contact the Vital Records office in their state to obtain a duplicate.

Questions of Paternity

Parents have the same responsibilities to children born outside marriage as they do to children born within marriage. If the father admits that he is the child's biological father, the mother should attempt to have him execute a formal acknowledgment of paternity. If he denies that he is the father, the mother can bring a lawsuit, seeking an order of paternity and child support. Recently developed blood and tissue tests can prove within one or two percentage points that a particular man fathered a particular child. In some states it is considered irrelevant that a husband can prove he is not the father of his wife's child; the law automatically presumes that he is the father. In other states, he has the right to go into court and prove that another man is the legal father. If another man admits paternity, or if it can be proved through blood and tissue tests, witnesses, or other evidence, then the biological father will be responsible for child support rather than the mother's husband, until the child is no longer a minor.

Nonmarital Children

Historically, American law denied children born outside a marriage rights with respect to paternal support and inheritance; however, in recent years the nonmarital child's rights have increased. Today, children born outside a marriage are generally treated the same as children born within one. They can inherit from their mothers and fathers, although the right to inherit from the father may have conditions. In order to prevent fraudulent claims of heirship, most states deny nonmarital children the right to inherit from a father unless there is some proof of paternity. Paternity can be established through judicial proceedings, formal acknowledgment by the father, conduct demonstrating acceptance of the child, or the parents' marriage.

The Uniform Parenting Act, which has been adopted in a number of states and has influenced legislation in others, provides that a parent-child relationship applies to every child and parent regardless of the marital status of the parents.

Over the past decade the Supreme Court, on equal protection grounds, has repeatedly bestowed on children born outside a marriage the same rights conferred to children born within one. These have included the right to recover wrongful death damages for the death of a mother, workers' compensation for a parent's injury, and survivor and disability insurance benefits to nonmarital children under the Social Security Act.

Child custody cases involving nonmarital children are generally governed by the same "best interests" standard as those involving children born within a marriage. In the past mothers of nonmarital children had superior custody rights over fathers, but the current trend is to determine custody on the basis of what is best for the child.

Guardians

The natural guardian(s) of a child is the child's parent(s). But if parents neglect, abuse, abandon, or fail to support a child financially, the court can appoint another guardian. In the event of a divorce, the parent granted custody becomes the guardian. In some states a child over age 14 is permitted to select his or her own guardian. If a minor marries, that child automatically becomes an adult in the eyes of the law, and the court is not permitted to appoint a guardian.

A guardian may be appointed—by the court or through a will—to take care of the child, the child's assets, or both. Sometimes the natural parent will care for the child, but a guardian will be appointed to handle the child's property. A guardian caring for a child provides support, education, and religious instruction, using the income and the interest generated by a child's assets without touching the principal, when possible. When the child reaches the age of majority, she or he will receive all of the assets.

A guardian is responsible for a child's property and is required to use the same care and efforts he or she would if the assets belonged to the guardian. At the end of every year and at the end of the guardianship as well, all investments and transactions that were made on behalf of the child must be accounted for.

RIGHTS OF GRANDPARENTS

Every state has some kind of law granting visitation rights to grandparents in the event of the parents' divorce, death, or declaration as unfit. If a grandparent is denied visitation by a custodial parent in a divorce, the grandparent may have to go to court to convince the judge that the best interests of the child are served by continuing a close relationship.

If the parents die or are determined to be unfit as parents, grandparents may seek custody. Age, physical condition, and financial status are some of the factors considered by the court in granting custody.

RIGHTS AND OBLIGATIONS OF CHILDREN

The rights of a child begin before birth, when it is a fetus. If a parent dies without a will, the state will distribute the parent's property to the child after he or she is born, just as it would have had the parent's death occurred after the child's birth. However, the parent has the right to specify in a will that a bequeath is made only to those children who have already been born at the time of their parent's death, with those born later to inherit nothing.

A child also has the right to sue someone for injuries inflicted upon him or her as a fetus. Suppose a husband and pregnant wife are involved in an automobile accident caused by the negligence of another driver. The unborn child will be permitted to sue the neg-

MAY CHILDREN DIVORCE THEIR PARENTS?

No. Parental rights over their children may not be severed absent abuse, neglect, or abandonment. After a finding by a court of abuse, neglect, or abandonment, a child becomes available for adoption. However, children do not have the right to change parents simply because they find substitutes that they like better or that may be able to provide them with a higher standard of living.

A televised Florida case decided by Florida's appellate court in 1993, known popularly as Gregory K., limelighted these issues. In Gregory K., an 11-year-old child sued to terminate the rights of his natural parents so that he could be adopted by his foster parents. The Florida appellate court said that because of his age, the child could not sue but then allowed the suit because it was also brought by the foster father, a guardian appointed to represent the child, and the state, all having capacity to sue. In Gregory K., the court found abandonment and neglect on the part of the natural mother (the natural father consented to termination of his parental rights), terminating her parental rights and freeing the child for adoption by the foster parents. Despite media distortions, Gregory K. was not about a child divorcing or choosing to change his parents.

ligent driver, if the fetus has sustained injuries or if the injuries incurred by the mother affect the fetus.

SUING AND BEING SUED BY CHILDREN

Children may be sued for negligence if their age, intelligence, and experience reflect that they should have known the danger or risk of their actions. Children have the right to sue someone else, including their parents, whose immunity from lawsuits brought by their children has been abolished in many states. In general, parents may not be sued by their children; however, in some states a child may sue a parent for intentional torts or torts involving reckless conduct that injures the child, such as careless driving or negligently starting a fire.

By far the greatest exception to the parental immunity rule is in cases involving negligent driving, and the reason for this is the existence of automobile liability insurance. This insurance protects the family's assets and therefore minimizes the risk of family disruption, which was what the immunity was designed to prevent.

Some limited form of immunity still exists in cases involving the care, supervision, training, or protection of children, which is based upon family privacy and the assumption that a parent is a better judge of what a child requires than a court.

When a child sues, some states allow the litigation to be brought in the child's own name; others require that the name of a guardian or next friend be used. A "next friend" is an individual who voluntarily brings or defends a lawsuit on behalf of an infant or minor. He or she is neither a guardian, a temporary guardian appointed by the court (guardian *ad litem*), nor a party to the lawsuit.

Entering into a Contract

Children of all ages may enter into contracts, but they have the right to disavow them at any time before they reach the age of majority. If a minor child voids a contract and demands that the other party return the money or goods exchanged in the contractual agreement, the child is required to return what has been received if it is still possessed. However, contracts involving the purchase of goods necessary for day-to-day sustenance, including shelter and food, cannot be disavowed by a minor.

Damages/Debts Incurred by a Minor

Although children are liable for damages caused by their tortious (wrongful) conduct, this is often meaningless because they are usually without the means to satisfy judgments. Accordingly, most state legislatures have enacted parental responsibility laws, which hold parents or legal guardians liable for the willful or malicious conduct of their unemancipated children that results in property damage to another. Approximately one-half of these statutes also allow recovery for personal injuries, and almost all of them have a limit on the maximum amount recoverable.

In general, courts do not recognize lack of parental fault as a defense under these laws. However, because courts do hold parents liable for damages where there may have been no parental negligence, the laws are strictly construed. Courts often decline to hold parents liable where the child's negligent action does not rise to the exact level of malicious or willful conduct or gross negligence required by the law.

In the case of the intact family, courts are loath to interfere with family harmony; therefore, the level of a child's support rights is subject to the parents' discretion. The law provides only that "necessaries" be provided. Necessaries are usually defined as articles or services required for the support of the child, consistent with the parents' means. These have been held to include food, clothing, and shelter as well as medical, dental, and legal expenses. In many states college expenses may be necessaries, depending on the parents' means and educational level and the aptitude of the child for education.

Since parents are not liable for items that are not necessaries, merchants who extend credit to minors for such purchases subject themselves to serious risks.

The following two hypothetical situations involve damages incurred by minors.

THE PROBLEM

Johnny lives in a state where the law provides that parents are liable for a child's malicious and destructive acts. While Johnny is playing near his friend Dennis's house, Johnny's bicycle is broken by a baseball bat, which accidentally slipped out of Dennis's hands. Johnny's parents sue Dennis's parents.

PROBABLE COURT ACTION

The court would probably rule that Johnny's parents cannot recover, because Dennis did not throw the baseball bat with a malicious or destructive intent.

These parental responsibility statutes do not excuse parents for their own negligence. Parents may still be found liable for failing to supervise their children adequately or for entrusting them with dangerous instruments.

THE PROBLEM

Eight-year-old Amanda is playing house at her friend Kimberly's home. Kimberly takes out a kitchen knife and pretends she is preparing dinner. Kimberly's mother is in the room, but does not remove the knife from Kimberly. Kimberly accidentally injures Amanda, causing her to require 20 stitches. Amanda's parents sue Kimberly's parents for negligent supervision and for permitting Kimberly access to a dangerous instrument.

PROBABLE COURT ACTION

A court would likely rule in favor of Amanda's parents because of Kimberly's mother's negligence in failing to supervise her daughter's use of a dangerous instrument.

Owning Property

Minors may purchase and own both real estate and personal property, but they may invoke their right to void the transactions, unless the transactions have been handled by a guardian.

What follows is a hypothetical situation involving a minor owning property.

THE PROBLEM

Jacob, age 16, purchases an automobile with funds he received as a gift from his grandfather. After he drives the car and accrues substantial mileage on it, he decides to return it to the dealer, demanding full repayment. The dealer claims that the car has depreciated in value, and he does not want to repay the full purchase price.

PROBABLE COURT ACTION

Although the result may seem unfair, a court would probably order the dealer to reimburse Jacob the full amount he paid for the car, because he is a minor and may void the contract.

A different result would be reached in states that have adopted a "benefit" rule. In those states, minors may disaffirm contracts, but they are liable in an action for restitution for the benefits they have received.

Drafting a Will

The states differ in this regard, but most require that an individual must be at least 18 years old to draft a valid will. (Wills are discussed in detail in chapter 2.)

ADOPTION

Adoption has always been known as a "creature of statute"—a family relationship created by a court of law. Because of this legal shifting of parental rights and responsibilities, it is critical that anyone adopting a child follow the legal requirements exactly.

Adoption law didn't exist in the United States until the late 1800s. It evolved from a system wherein large governmental agencies were mainly responsible for foster care of children in temporary need. As the number of children in the foster care system rose, private agencies began to spring up. Both types of agency allowed as "policy" only the strictest of "closed" adoptions, that is, both the birth and adoptive parents knew little, if anything, about the other.

The United States adoption sector changed dramatically in the 1970s when the number of babies available for adoption dwindled. Many people were dissatisfied with the way adoptions had been handled in the past. All three sides of the adoption triad—birth parents, adoptive parents, and adoptees—wanted more knowledge of one another. The knowledge was not necessarily identifying information, but rather genetic, medical, and social information. What resulted was a transformation of the process with the establishment of numerous smaller agencies and a new type of adoption called private-placement adoption. Also, as international travel has become commonplace, many adoptions are now taking place overseas.

The Legal Process of Adoption

Adoption law is complex and may be different in every state, but knowing the proper procedures and avenues is vital to negotiating the adoption system successfully. Although all states require that adoptive parents meet certain criteria, laws vary greatly from state to state. Some states have age requirements; some require parents to be married for at least 10 years. Financial requirements are usually not stringent, with the ability to support the adoptive family being sufficient. Information about adoption can be gathered through a number of sources. Under the heading of Adoption Services in your Yellow Pages, you can find agencies, attorneys, and adoptive parent groups. These parent groups have become quite sophisticated in most areas of the country and are an excellent source of information and networking. Members can give you the moral support it may take to get you through what may become a tedious search and a stressful process. Here are three national adoptive parents organizations who can refer you to local groups:

North American Council on Adoptable Children
970 Raymond Avenue
Suite 106
St. Paul, MN 55114-1149
612-644-3036

Adoptive Families of America
3333 Highway 100 North
Minneapolis, MN 55422
612-535-4829

American Adoption Congress
1000 Connecticut Avenue, N.W.
Suite 9
Washington, DC 20036
800-274-6736

Once you have educated yourself by speaking to an agency, attorney, adoptive parent group, or all of the above, you will find that all adoptions have some common legal threads. In every adoption the adopting parent or parents must first undergo a background check, which is commonly called a "home study report." Prior to a child's being placed in the adoptive home, birth parents will sign a consent form. The adopting parents then file a petition to adopt with a court. There are follow-up home studies, and after six to twelve months the adoption is finalized.

HOME STUDY REPORT Depending on the requirements of the country, state, or agency, the evaluation may be rigorous. Most home studies require one to three meetings with a social worker, medical reports, checks on child abuse and criminal histories, letters of reference, and financial statements. If you have any questions about whether you will qualify to adopt, be open about your concerns and talk to the social worker conducting your home study. In most cases the problem you perceive is not really a problem at all.

The following is a hypothetical situation involving adoption.

THE PROBLEM

Janet and her husband Seymour were contemplating adopting an infant; however, they were hesitant because Janet is 42 and Seymour is 44. They were told by many people that you are not allowed to adopt an infant if you are over age 40.

WHAT TO DO

Janet and Seymour finally discussed it with a social worker. After a couple of meetings with the social worker, Janet and Seymour were happy to learn that they had been accepted to adopt an infant.

CONSENTING PARENTS After the adopting parents are approved to adopt and a child is found, the legal process is put into motion when the birth parents sign a consent form approving the placement with the adopting parents. Every adoptive parent's nightmare is that the biological parents will have a change of heart and want their child back. Each state differs in the amount of time that a birth parent is allowed to revoke the consent form and what occurs in that event.

In certain states, if the birth parent revokes consent, the judge will determine what is in the child's best interest; in other states, the child is automatically returned to the birth parents. Depending on the child's age, his or her consent to the adoption may be required. In general, children over age 14 must consent to their adoptions.

While it is uniform that a birth mother's consent to the adoption is necessary, unless her rights are terminated by a legal proceeding, the rights of a birth father to consent to an adoption differ from state to state. In certain states a birth father has the same rights as the birth mother; in others a birth father has no rights, unless he has been involved with or supported the child or the birth mother prior to the placement of the child. It is important for anyone involved in an adoption proceeding to try to find the birth father if he is not involved and to get his consent in writing prior to placement.

What follows is a hypothetical situation involving a challenge to adoption by the biological father.

THE PROBLEM

Helen and Mark had received a child from an adoption agency. Before the placement they were told that the birth mother refused to name the birth father. The social worker at the agency told Helen and Mark not to worry about it. Three months after the child was with them, the agency called and said the alleged birth father, Jim, had come forward, and he wanted custody of his child.

WHAT TO DO

Although the agency recommended that they return the child, Helen and Mark hired an attorney to fight for custody. The first thing they requested was a paternity test. If that test demonstrated that Jim was the father, Helen and Mark could then decide whether or not to return the child. Luckily, the test clearly showed that Jim was not the father. If he had been, and Helen and Mark had continued to fight for custody, the outcome of the matter would have depended on their state's law.

The following three outcomes are based on actual case decisions. A judge in Iowa returned the child to the birth father because his consent to the adoption was necessary. A judge in New York decided the opposite and left the child with the adoptive parents because that was in the child's best interest. A judge in Vermont made a novel ruling and, with the agreement of both parties, left custody with the adoptive parents but gave the birth father visitation rights to the child.

Despite the media preoccupation with adoption disruptions, experts in the field agree that problems arise in less than 0.5 percent of placements. Extensive counseling for the birth parents before placement has proved to be an effective way of helping to prevent problems from happening. An attorney who specializes in adoption law can advise you on the laws within your state.

PETITION TO ADOPT   After the consents are signed and the child is placed in the adoptive home, the legal process continues with the filing of a petition for adoption with the court. This petition includes the request to adopt as well as the adoptive parents' qualifications.

The "new family" will then have a nonthreatening probationary period of six months to one year. This period is used as a test period to see if the placement will work out. During this period there are usually one to three follow-up home visits done by the agency's or court's social worker. If all goes well, the adoption becomes permanent with an informal meeting with a judge, who signs an order that changes the child's name officially, causes an amended birth certificate to be issued, and seals all court files relating to the adoption. All states agree that once the adoption is finalized, unless fraud is committed by the adoptive parents, the adoption cannot be challenged by anyone—including the birth parents.

OPEN RECORDS   Courts will issue an order to open adoption files only when there is a compelling medical reason to do so, such as an organ transplant. However, there is a strong effort by adults who were adopted as children calling for legislation that would help them gain access to their court files, thus acquiring names and other information about their biological parents. One group providing assistance in how to find such information is the Adoptees' Liberty Movement Association, P.O. Box 154, Washington Bridge Station, New York, NY 10033, 212-581-1568. If you or your child decides to search, make sure that the methods you use are legal. Counseling to prepare for a possible reunion is also recommended.

Types of Adoption

INTERSTATE ADOPTIONS Adoption across state lines becomes complicated because laws differ from state to state with residency requirements, the time period before a final adoption order can be signed, and the time when the rights of the biological parents are terminated forever. The *Interstate Compact on the Placement of Children* must be complied with before a child can be taken home. That necessitates the filing of papers in each state capital and a short waiting period in the state in which the child is born. Consult your attorney or agency on each state's requirements and waiting periods.

OPEN ADOPTIONS Adoptions where birth parents and adoptive parents are completely identified to each other are becoming increasingly popular. Although they have always existed among adoptions by close relatives, open adoptions have occurred where birth parents and adoptive parents agree to reveal identifying information about each other. There are some open adoptions where birth parents will continue to have a relationship with the adopted child after the adoption takes place.

AGENCY PLACEMENT Agencies act as intermediaries between the biological and adoptive parents. Whether public or private, adoption agencies must meet certain criteria to be licensed by the state. If you are adopting through an agency, check the state's Department of Human or Social Services. The biological parents sign a formal agreement of surrender, transferring their parental rights to the agency. Today most private agencies will allow the birth parent to choose the adoptive parents; however, the agency is required to conduct extensive background investigations of the biological parents, the child, and the adoptive parents. Some adoption agencies still have highly conventional (and sometimes discriminatory) standards for those who apply to be adoptive parents, including religion, race, age, health, socioeconomic status, and home environment. The home study performed by the agency staff may take a long time, so the agency route may not be the quickest way to arrange an adoption.

Once the home study is completed, the waiting begins while the agency searches for the child. The length of time depends on what kind of child you are looking for. If you only want to adopt a United

States-born, healthy white infant, the wait could be 5 to 10 years. If you are flexible about race, nationality, and physical or emotional disabilities, the adoption could take fewer than 2 years. By law, adoptive children are classified into separate categories as those with special needs and those without. Special needs children include those who are age eight years or older; African-American and older than one year; of any race with physical, emotional, or mental disabilities; and siblings who need to remain together. In 1993 at least 50,000 older children or those with other special needs were available for adoption. If you are interested in adopting a child with special needs, contact your state's Department of Human or Social Services, your local parents group, or a local CAP book source (a photo listing of children available for adoption), c/o Children Awaiting Parents, 700 Exchange Street, Rochester, NY 14608, 716-232-5110.

Although fees for adoption agencies vary widely, it is safe to assume that a private agency fee will be much higher than the public agencies. Some private agencies have been known to charge $20,000 for white, healthy children. To protect yourself, make sure that the larger portion of the fee, or as much money as possible, is paid to the agency *after* the child is placed in your home. If money is required to be paid before that, make sure it is placed in an escrow account and will be returned to you if you are not successful with the agency. A private adoption agency recently went bankrupt, leaving over 100 adoptive parents with no way to recoup over $10,000 each. Adopting a special needs child through a public agency will frequently not only be free, but state subsidies are often available to help with the special needs of the child you adopt.

PRIVATE PLACEMENT   In private adoptions a child is placed directly with the adopting parents, with no agency acting as intermediary. During the pregnancy, birth parents locate the adoptive parents by word-of-mouth networking or by finding them in classified advertisements that the adoptive parents place. After having discussions, during which nonidentifying information is exchanged, and perhaps after meeting each other, the birth parent decides to place the child with the adoptive parents immediately after birth. The process can become very emotional, which can be beneficial in easing each other's concerns—by getting to know each other, both sides learn to trust each other.

The birth parents fill out background forms, which are usually sent to them by the adoptive parents' lawyer, who also requests the birth mother's medical records. These records are kept for the adoptive child. The adoptive parents have had their home study completed. A copy of it with identifying information removed can be sent to the birth parents upon their request. The child is examined by a pediatrician, and the adoptive parents are informed of the health status of the child. As in the other forms of adoption, a consent is signed, and the child is placed with the adoptive parents. In private adoptions children are usually placed with the adoptive parents directly upon their discharge from the hospital. The whole process usually takes about one to two years.

Expenses in a private adoption can range between $5,000 and $20,000, including medical expenses for the birth mother and the child (your insurance or the birth mother's may cover this), attorneys' fees for you and the birth parents, and pregnancy-related living expenses for the birth mother. Private adoptions are not legal in certain states; check with an attorney specializing in adoption in your area before embarking on this adoption route. A list of these attorneys can be found through the American Bar Association, your local state bar association, or the American Academy of Adoption Attorneys, P.O. Box 33053, Washington, DC 20033-0053, 703-759-1560.

INTERNATIONAL PLACEMENT   Adopting a child from a country outside the United States involves complying with many regulations, both American and foreign. To find an American agency or other source that can put you in touch with a foreign agency or source, contact an adoptive parents group in your area. Use one of the national organizations mentioned in this chapter to find a local group, or contact the International Concerns Committee for Children, 911 Cypress Drive, Boulder, CO 80303, 303-494-8333.

Once the home study is done, an extensive set of documents must be filed with the United States Immigration and Naturalization Service, with a request to adopt an unidentified "orphan" from overseas (Form I-600A). The set of documents will include, among others, certified copies of birth certificates, marriage license (if married), tax returns, and FBI fingerprint clearances. All of the documents will have to be translated into the language of the adoptive child's country. Once a child to adopt has been found, some states require the adoptive parents to be preapproved before bringing a child into the state. Check with a local attorney. At that point, the petition to the United States Immigration and Naturalization Service (Form I-600) will need to be amended to have the child classified as an immediate relative. Once INS grants the petition, a visa can be obtained from a United States consulate in the child's country. In most instances, the adoptive parents must go to the foreign country to claim the child and stay there for a few weeks while the paperwork is being processed.

Depending on the foreign country, the adoption may be finalized there or in the state in which the adoptive parents reside. The child will be granted a permanent resident card and can immediately apply for citizenship under the new rules. Many people adopting internationally will also readopt in this country once they are home with the child.

The child who is adopted internationally will usually be at least three months old by the time the paperwork is processed.

The following is a hypothetical situation involving international adoption.

THE PROBLEM

Marie, a single parent, worked with a reputable lawyer with a source for children from Romania. After hearing of a child and deciding to adopt her, Marie went to Romania and took custody of her daughter. After several weeks, her lawyer told her she had a problem because the United States Immigration and Naturalization Service did not consider the child to be an orphan as defined under American law and, as a result, would not issue a visa for the child. Under the present United States guidelines, it is virtually impossible for a child with two parents listed on the birth certificate to be considered an orphan.

WHAT TO DO

Marie contacted her lawyer and had the Romanian court issue a new order declaring the father listed on the birth certificate to be unfit to parent the child. With that and the consent of the birth mother and substantial political pressure from her congressman (who was contacted by Marie's lawyer), Marie was finally issued a visa for the child. Although this worked in Marie's case, it may not in others. To avoid this problem, check your child's parentage before going to the foreign country. Contact your agency or attorney to make sure that the child will be allowed to enter the United States, even if the foreign country says the child can leave.

Because each country has different rules and laws relating to international adoption, the Hague Convention on Protection of Children and Cooperation in Respect of Intercountry Adoption, May 1993, finalized a treaty that will try to streamline adoptions.overseas. As of January 1994, the United States had not signed the treaty, but it had delegates negotiating the treaty and means of implementing regulations were being drafted.

ILLEGAL ADOPTIONS As the apparent pool of adoptable babies dwindles, as adopting parents become exasperated by lengthy agency background investigations and recurring disappointments, and as the media continue to portray legal adoption as hard-to-do or impossible, some people turn to what has become known as the black market. Adoption, like any other business, is subject to unscrupulous individuals who want to make fast money and who prey on the inexperience and desperation of other people. Couples desperate to adopt are particularly vulnerable. So are young women who are deciding whether or not to keep their young children and are being subjected to promises of large sums of money. Unlike private or agency adoptions, black-market placements involve the sale of babies with payments beyond the legal costs of medical expenses, agency or attorneys' fees, and living expenses related to the pregnancy. In most states it is illegal for an attorney to find a child for you. Accordingly, beware of an attorney who is charging an exorbitant placement fee.

What follows is a hypothetical situation involving unscrupulous actions by an attorney in an adoption case.

THE PROBLEM

The Montgomerys began adoption proceedings, retaining an attorney to handle the entire transaction. The attorney said the birth parents' expenses would include payment for the birth mother's medical bills as well as another $8,000 for her "to get back on her feet." He told them knowledge of the $8,000 payment should be kept among the three of them (the Montgomerys and the attorney) and would not be reported to the court.

WHAT TO DO

The Montgomerys immediately reported the abuse to their state bar association. After an investigation, the lawyer was disbarred, and the Montgomerys received back all of the money they had paid to the attorney.

Other Adoption Considerations

WILLS   If the child you are adopting owns property, you should be appointed as legal guardian of the child's estate so it can be properly managed. Inheritance after adoption can become an issue. The child's inheritance rights from the biological parents are almost always cut off after adoption. Some states do not recognize "child" to include adopted children.

What follows is a hypothetical situation involving inheritance and adopted children.

THE PROBLEM

Your grandfather drafts a will and tells you he listed all of his grandchildren as beneficiaries. You are adopted.

WHAT TO DO

Because inheritance laws in some states may not consider adopted grandchildren to be the same as biological grandchildren, ask your grandfather to specify in his will that it does include adopted grandchildren.

Additional Sources of Adoption Information
National Adoption Information Clearinghouse
11426 Rockville Pike

Suite 410
Rockville, MD 20852
310-231-6512

The Child Welfare League of America, Inc.
440 First Street, N.W.
Suite 310
Washington, DC 20001
202-638-2952

CHANGING YOUR NAME

Each state has its own laws and procedures for name changes. In most states it is legal to use any name you wish, without judicial intervention, provided that your purpose in doing so is not misleading, fraudulent, or to deny the rights of others (for example, creditors).

To change a name legally, most states require that a petition be filed, setting forth the current name and address, date and place of birth, and proposed name of the petitioner. Usually, a birth certificate must be filed. To satisfy itself that the name change is for a legitimate purpose, some states require the petitioner to state whether he or she has been convicted of a crime or declared bankrupt, and whether there are outstanding judgments or liens against the petitioner.

Changing the Name of Your Child

To change a child's name, a petition must be filed with the court. If only one parent makes the petition, notice must be served on the other parent or on the child's guardian in order to give the parent or guardian the opportunity to contest the proposed name change. If both parents petition the court to make the change, no notice is necessary.

Courts are often more willing to grant adult name changes than those for children, upon the belief that it is better to wait until the child has reached maturity. To change a child's name, the petitioner must prove that it is in the best interests of the child and that there is a compelling reason to do so. This may require a hearing.

REPLACING A LOST BIRTH CERTIFICATE

Sometimes an original birth certificate is required as identification or proof of one's age. Birth certificates are frequently misplaced and must be replaced. The procedure to obtain replacements varies from state to state. The pamphlets *How You May Save Time Proving Your Age and Other Birth Facts* and *Where to Write for Vital Records: Births, Deaths, Marriages, and Divorces* are available from the U.S. Department of Health and Human Services, National Center for Health Statistics, Rockville, MD 20852; *Guide to Genealogical Research in the National Archives* is sold by the National Archives Trust Fund Board, P.O. Box 100793, Atlanta, GA 30384; *Where to Write for Birth and Death Records of U.S. Citizens Who Were Born or Died Outside the U.S. and Birth Certifications for Alien Children Adopted by U.S. Citizens* is available from Passport Services, Correspondence Branch, U.S. Department of State, Washington, DC 20524.

PROBLEMS WITH PETS

Few pet owners will debate the fact that their dog or cat is an important part of their family. Like any other integral part of our lives, there are laws that apply to pets. Some laws provide pets with certain rights; others place certain restrictions on them. Some laws apply to the people who have taken on the responsibility of owning and caring for pets.

Many laws that govern animals concern health and safety issues. These are usually legislated on a local level and can vary from state to state, county to county, and municipality to municipality. Be sure you understand the law in your particular locality when you purchase a pet or when an issue arises that affects your pet.

Licensing

Virtually every city and county requires a dog to have a license, and some localities require it of cats. Licensing provides one of the best methods of finding a lost pet or the owner of a found pet, and, because a dog usually can't be licensed unless the owner can produce documentation that the dog has received its rabies vaccination, licensing helps reduce the incidence of the disease.

In some locales the veterinarian will provide the license form to send in to the city or county verifying the inoculations; in other locations you may have to get the forms through the government offices. Check the White Pages under city or county government for Animal Control, the health department, or environmental health department for a phone number. They can explain the procedure, the cost, and whether your dog will qualify for a reduced fee, which is sometimes available to a dog after being spayed or neutered or to one serving as a guide dog. You will probably be fined if you fail to have your dog properly licensed.

If you move out of the town or county where the pet is licensed, you'll most likely have to reregister the pet. Most cities and counties give you up to 30 days to get a dog licensed, but it's probably better to do it as soon as you move, especially since the chances of a dog getting lost are obviously greater in new surroundings.

Vaccinations

Rabies vaccinations are usually required when application for the license is made, and then renewed annually. In recent years the incidence of rabies has increased, particularly in southeastern and northeastern states. Dogs and cats contract rabies by being bitten or scratched by a bat, raccoon, bobcat, coyote, skunk, fox, horse, cow, or another cat or dog. An unvaccinated animal will almost always die from a rabid bite or scratch. Humans infected by a rabid animal may die from respiratory paralysis.

Leash Laws

Leash laws will vary, but in general, dogs are required to be on leashes when they are not on their owner's property. Some cities have parks and open areas specifically for dogs to have free rein, but these are clearly marked. Check with your city or county to find out what leash laws apply to you and if there are any special areas for dogs to run free.

There are some places that are off-limits for a dog, even with a leash. Health codes prohibit dogs from entering restaurants, shopping malls, grocery stores, and other public areas. Obviously, guide dogs are an exception, but if you require their services, be sure you know what limitations are provided by local laws.

Finding a Stray Animal

If you find a stray dog or cat, call Animal Control and ask them to come for it. They may be able to find its owner or find someone (including yourself) who wants to adopt it.

If you want to keep a stray dog, call the Humane Society or Animal Control and ask what rights you have in claiming ownership.

Animals that Create a Nuisance

Dogs that have the freedom to roam often stray onto a neighbor's property, sometimes doing damage. A homeowner has no right to use excessive force when trying to remove a stray animal from his or her land, unless it presents a danger to an individual or property. The force used to remove the dog must be reasonable in relation to the extent of danger. If the dog starts to growl at a small child and makes a move as if it is going to attack, you have the right to use any method to stop it, including killing it. But if the dog is merely digging in your garden, you have no right to harm the animal.

When a dog trespasses on your property and causes damage, it's important that you notify its owner. In many states the owner is not liable for damages unless she or he was aware that the dog had trespassed in the past or had destructive tendencies.

If this dog has damaged your property before, you have the right to sue the owner for creating a nuisance. Of course, you should first try to resolve the problem through less aggressive methods than the courtroom. Get other neighbors to join you in convincing the owner to halt the dog's bad habits. Some communities offer mediation services to have an impartial third party guide you and the dog's owner through a more amicable resolution. Animal Control will often intercede if a dog becomes a nuisance, perhaps calling the owner and encouraging more cooperation. If all else fails, consider small-claims court if the amount in damages is relatively small.

Cruelty to Animals

Every state has laws prohibiting cruelty to animals. Some statutes are very specific, such as prohibiting a dog from being left in a nonventilated car or riding in an open pickup truck, or failing to stop when you hit a dog with your car. Some states consider it a criminal offense to "crop" a dog's ears or tail without using an anesthetic, and some states have laws that pertain to conditions in pet shops.

Other laws may be more general, prohibiting cruel treatment or abandonment. Sometimes it is difficult to determine what constitutes cruel treatment. Some individuals may find leaving a dog in temperatures of 35°F to be heartless; someone else may believe that "dogs love the cold." But most would agree that an animal is being treated cruelly if it is neglected for days without food or water, confined to cramped quarters for long periods of time, or severely beaten.

Cruelty to animals is often considered to be a misdemeanor, punishable in many states by imprisonment for up to one year and/or a fine.

Dog Bites

If you've been bitten by a dog and have suffered injuries, there are a few things you should do immediately. Find out who owns the dog, then get the names and phone numbers of witnesses before they walk off.

If you were able to find out who owned the dog, or if it has a tag, call the owner and explain what has happened. Find out if the dog has had its rabies shots.

If the injuries are severe enough that you need medical attention, or if the skin was broken and you're not sure when you had your last tetanus shot, go to a doctor or emergency room. Hold on to all your bills and receipts. Call Animal Control and report the incident. If the dog has bitten someone before and it was reported, Animal Control should have a record of it. The city or county may want to quarantine the dog for about 10 days to be sure it doesn't have rabies.

Depending on the severity of your injuries, you may decide to sue the owner. Some states have laws that automatically make the owner liable when a dog bites someone. If your state doesn't have this type of law, but your neighbor tells you the dog has been vicious in the past, you can sue the owner on the theory that he had reason to know of the dog's dangerous inclinations.

If the dog hasn't attacked anyone in the past, you can still sue the owner if you can show that the owner's negligence caused your injuries. For instance, the dog would have been unable to attack you if the owner held the leash tighter. The owner was negligent and therefore responsible for your injuries, your doctor and hospital bills, time missed from work, and your pain and suffering. If you plan on suing the owner and the amount you are asking for is less than $2,000, consider taking it to small-claims court. Check with the court to see what the maximum limit is on cases that can be brought in that jurisdiction.

If the damages you are requesting for your medical expenses, salary lost from days off work, as well as pain and suffering exceed the limits of the small-claims court, contact a lawyer to handle your case in a state court.

The law doesn't leave the pet owner without any defenses, but they vary from state to state, so you should check with an attorney familiar with "dog bite" cases to determine your best plan of defense. Some valid defenses that may apply in your state and to your situation include: The victim teased or provoked the dog, causing the dog to attack; the victim was trespassing onto the property where the dog rightfully belonged; and the victim knew of the risk involved, but approached the dog or entered the property anyway.

What follows is a hypothetical situation involving a person bitten by a dog.

THE PROBLEM

You and your dog are about to embark on an evening stroll around your neighborhood. As you walk down your driveway with your dog on a leash, your neighbor approaches you to say hello. Your dog unexpectedly lunges at your neighbor, breaking her leash and biting him on the leg. The man's injuries aren't severe, but the skin is broken and he should receive some kind of medical attention. Your state does not have a dog bite statute that automatically makes you liable for the damage your dog has inflicted. Your neighbor sues you in small-claims court.

WHAT TO DO

1. As soon as the dog attacks your neighbor, offer to take the man to an emergency room or to his doctor. Assure him that your dog is current on all her shots.
2. Attempt to settle this dispute amicably, perhaps by paying

his doctor bills. Check with your insurance company and see if your homeowner's policy covers dog bites.

3. If a quick settlement cannot be reached, suggest that your dispute be handled through mediation or arbitration. Many cities have justice centers that provide such services for disputes of this nature.

4. If your neighbor decides to sue you in small-claims court, he has an excellent chance of winning, if he can successfully prove that you knew your dog was dangerous and would attack someone, or if he can prove that you were negligent in not keeping the dog on a sturdy leash.

5. Develop a defense to his case against you. Consider bringing in witnesses that will testify that your dog never attacked anyone before or that you were not negligently leading her on an old and weakened leash. You may be able to defend the claim if you can prove that the neighbor provoked the attack by teasing the dog or that the neighbor knew your dog had dangerous propensities, yet took the risk of getting close to her on your property.

Buying a Pet

Some states have laws that clearly state what your rights are when you buy a sick pet. Other states don't, and they treat the sale of a pet just as if you had bought a bicycle or sofa, with the seller providing certain express and implied warranties.

Suppose you purchase a dog that the seller tells you is a purebred chow. The seller doesn't have the pedigree papers yet, but promises to send them to you as soon as they arrive from the breeder. You pay for the dog. A few days later, the veterinarian tells you that the dog is not only a chow but also a little bit of beagle and a touch of basset hound. You have the right to take the dog back and get a refund, because the seller violated the express warranty that the dog was a purebred chow.

There are also implied warranties that often come along with some sales. The implied warranty of merchantability ensures that the dog you're buying will meet the standard expectations of any other dog you would buy in a pet store. Because the pet store is selling the dog to the general public, you have reason to believe that the dog is in good health. If the dog proves to be sick or impaired, the store owner can't defend a fraudulent sale by arguing that he or she never told you the dog was healthy.

If you are buying a dog for a specific purpose, another warranty comes along with the purchase. Suppose an elderly woman wants to purchase a small, quiet, docile dog to be a companion. The pet store owner recommends a Chihuahua and strongly encourages the sale. The woman knows nothing about dogs, and she is relying strictly on the pet store owner's expertise and good judgment. She takes the dog home, only to find that the dog is totally uncontrollable and anything but docile. The pet store owner has violated the warranty of fitness for a specific purpose, and the woman can return the dog to the store and demand a refund.

What follows is a hypothetical situation involving the purchase of an unhealthy pet.

THE PROBLEM

Jennifer bought a pedigreed dog at the pet store. The dog seemed lethargic when she got him home, but she wasn't concerned until he seemed to get no better the next week. She took the dog to a veterinarian, who discovered that the dog had a serious disease for which treatment would be expensive and possibly unsuccessful.

WHAT TO DO

1. Jennifer should return the pet to the store along with the receipt and the vet's bill and diagnosis. She should demand total reimbursement for the cost of the dog, vet bills, and other expenses necessary to care for the sick animal.

2. If the pet store owner will not refund her expenses, she can take the owner to small-claims court. There may be statutes in her state that require the store to pay her expenses; if not, she may still be able to argue that the pet store owner violated the implied warranty of merchantability by selling a sick animal.

3. If her expenses exceed the limits that qualify her case for small-claims court, she may want to take her case to a state court to recoup the expenses she has incurred. With a lawyer to guide her through the process, she can do some of the work on her own and save attorneys' fees.

2

PLANNING YOUR ESTATE

Human beings don't like to think about the one certainty in all our lives—death. Thinking about death and planning ahead to ensure that your estate is properly distributed are related, but not equally painful or necessary.

If you don't make a will, or if you make one incorrectly and it is considered invalid, you are said to die *intestate*, giving the courts the right to distribute your property in accordance with state statutes and rules, possibly resulting in the distribution of your estate in ways you might never have approved.

Your estate consists of anything and everything you own. It can include houses, cars, boats, insurance, pension plans, savings and checking accounts, stocks and bonds, debts, dogs, and cats. It is important to plan and organize your estate in such a way that you receive full benefits from it while you are alive, and that your beneficiaries continue to do so as well after your death—with as little delay as possible.

TYPES OF PROPERTY

Property is usually described in three categories. The first, *real property*, pertains not only to land, but to any buildings or improvements on it. *Tangible property* refers to possessions, such as jewelry, cars, boats, and paintings, and includes personal effects, such as clothing, furniture, memorabilia, and the like. *Intangible property* includes stock certificates, bonds, cash, and checking accounts.

Your property can be distributed in four ways when you die, and you can use all four methods or a combination in specifying your wishes:

1. a will
2. contractual arrangements with named beneficiaries (for example, life insurance, pensions, and employee death benefits)
3. joint ownership with the right of survivorship (You co-own property, land, and bank accounts that pass directly to the co-owner, not through a will, when you die.)
4. a living trust

THE WILL

The keystone of estate planning is a will. You, as its maker, are the "testator." If you have a valid will when you die, your "executor" (a male) or "executrix" (a female) takes control of your estate, pays your estate's expenses and taxes from the proceeds in your estate, and then distributes the remaining property to your heirs. This process, known as *probate*, requires your executor/executrix to go into court and prove to a judge that your will is genuine and that your estate has been handled properly and according to the terms of your will.

A will sets out to accomplish the above purposes. A testator designates an executor/executrix to carry out the wishes expressed in the will; identifies all property of the testator and names the individual or individuals who are to inherit the property, which includes both specific gifts, such as who will receive a sailboat, as well as the residue, or what is left over after the specific gifts have been disbursed; directs that taxes and expenses be paid; and appoints a guardian to care for any minor children. Some wills go beyond the basics, creating trusts and other mechanisms for distribution.

Who Needs a Will?

Almost all adults should have a will. If you neglect planning for the dispersal of your assets, you could create financial difficulties as well as emotional stress for your inheritors when you die.

Suppose you have a spouse and two grown children. You and

your spouse saw to it that your children were well educated and both are now financially well-off. You have drafted a will, leaving all your property to your spouse should he or she survive you. When you die, your estate is probated, and your spouse is financially secure because of your estate planning. If, however, you, like 70 percent of all adults, didn't bother to make a will, or the one you drafted was lost, destroyed, or declared invalid, the outcome will be quite different for your spouse.

Because you have not left a valid will, the laws of intestacy dictate how your estate is distributed. In many states, instead of your spouse receiving all your property, he or she will receive only one-third to one-half of your estate (depending on the laws of your state). Your two grown children will take the remaining one-half or two-thirds, and if one of your children dies before you do, his or her children will take that parent's share.

The intestacy laws vary from state to state and can be quite complex. You have spent a lifetime amassing equity and possessions. Be sure you don't lose control over them by allowing your state government to decide how they should be distributed. Have a will drawn.

Joint Wills

Many couples believe that because they are going to bequeath their estate to the surviving spouse, they can simply include their joint wishes in one document and create a joint will. This is a common mistake, and a costly one, creating questions about whether the surviving spouse has the right to change the will after the death of the other. Is the will irrevocable? Can the surviving spouse make changes? Joint wills also create tax problems, because the devising of property to a surviving spouse may be seen as a contractual agree-

Remember: Laws governing wills and intestacy differ from state to state. Consult an attorney in your state and prepare a proper will to avoid having your property distributed at your death under your state's intestacy laws.

ment and may not qualify for the marital deduction, which eliminates the federal estate tax.

The best method is for each spouse to make a separate will.

The Legal Capacity to Make a Will

Certain limitations exist regarding who may draft a valid will. In most states you must be at least 18 years old for your will to be considered valid, but if you are an emancipated minor (one who has left home to marry or who is otherwise no longer under the control of parents) or a member of the military, state laws will often permit you to have a will drafted regardless of your age. You must also be of sound mind, a requirement that demands no particular level of intelligence. It refers to your testamentary capacity, determined by your ability to understand that you are bequeathing your property to certain individuals and that you are aware of the nature and the extent of your property.

The Formalities of a Will

The laws in each state vary, but all require certain formalities:

THE WILL MUST BE IN WRITING   A will has to be in writing of some form. As a practical matter, it should be typed or handwritten (there are a few exceptions, noted later in this chapter). Generally, a videotaped will is not valid. Neither are wills that are photographed or recorded on audio tape. The will must be in writing, but the surface it is written on is irrelevant as long as the will is legible.

Without your signature your will is invalid, though some states are flexible, allowing you to make your mark or X instead of providing a signature, even if you know how to sign your name. Your signature need not be legible, spelled properly, or even be your legal name, but it does have to be "complete." In most states, you, as the testator, may direct someone else to sign the will for you ("by proxy") in your presence. Most states require that the signature appear at the logical end of the will.

Although not a requirement, initialing each page of the will is recommended; that way, there is no question that one page was substituted for another fraudulently. Make photocopies of the will before you sign. Only the original should be signed and witnessed.

Courts do not view photocopies as valid, and if you sign copies, you or the court may get them confused.

THE WILL MUST BE WITNESSED   Usually, two witnesses are required for a valid will, but some states require three. Including more than the required number of signatures by witnesses in a will presents no problem, but having too few can invalidate the will.

Witnesses must be competent to understand that you personally signed your will and that you had the necessary mental capacity to do so. The competency of a witness is important only at the time she or he actually witnesses the will; it's immaterial if one or more witnesses die or become senile or blind later. In a few states, if one of your witnesses is named as a beneficiary in the will or is the spouse of a beneficiary, that portion of the will could be declared invalid, and that person would receive nothing.

Usually, witnesses attest to the fact that you signed your will in their presence. But if you sign the will earlier, some states will allow you to announce to your witnesses that it is, in fact, your signature, and their signatures are considered valid as attesting to their having witnessed your will. Both witnesses should sign at the same time in each other's presence and in *your* presence. The witnesses need not know the contents of the will; they are simply witnessing your signing it.

What a Will Contains

THE INTRODUCTION   Most wills begin with a preamble phrase that states your proper name, the county in which you live, that you are of sound mind, and that you intend this document to be your last will. This preamble should leave no doubt that the document is meant to constitute a will, not simply an intent to make a will at some future date. A standard introduction might be "I, Barnaby Butler Brown, a resident of Smithtown, County of Suffolk, State of New York, being of sound and disposing mind and memory, do make, publish, and declare this to be my Last Will and Testament, in the manner and form following, to wit."

THE REVOCATION CLAUSE   The next important element in a will is the clause that revokes any will and codicil you have made prior to this one. Every will should have a revocation clause, regardless of whether you have ever had a will. The clause can be general, such as "I hereby revoke any and all former Wills, Codicils to Wills, and Testamentary Dispositions by me at any time heretofore made." If you plan to revoke a specific will you have made previously, identify it by stating, "I specifically revoke my former Will dated November 8, 1979, executed at Allentown, Pennsylvania."

A DECLARATION OF ALL YOUR RIGHTFUL HEIRS Your "rightful heirs" usually refer to your surviving spouse and children. Such a declaration might read: "I declare that I am presently married and my husband is Kenneth Robert Harris III. All references in this Will to 'my husband' refer exclusively to him. I have two (2) children now living whose names and birth dates are as follows: Kenneth Robert Harris IV, August 9, 1979, and Jeffrey Bennett Harris, February 12, 1982."

Even if you have no plans to leave anything to your spouse or your children, you should mention them in your will. If you fail to name them, they may have grounds for contesting your will later. State laws usually prohibit you from entirely disinheriting your surviving spouse and, in a few instances, children; but in most cases, except for children born after the will was made, you don't have to leave anything to your descendants. To avoid your will's being contested later, it's best to mention by name those you have decided to disinherit, or you may leave them $1 each so it will be clear that you intentionally excluded them.

THE APPOINTMENT OF AN EXECUTOR OR TRUSTEE You should name an executor, an individual you wish to carry out the terms of your will. Executors are often selected because of their relationship to the testator. Although you may get loyalty from a relative or friend, he or she may not be the best choice for an executor. Serving as an executor can be time-consuming and requires some expertise. It also can cause intrafamily jealousies—for example, if one child is selected over another.

A person who is making a will is sometimes advised to name a trust department of a bank to serve as executor; however, be aware that the bank will charge a fee. In many cases, the best method of choosing an executor or trustee is to use a bank trust department jointly in conjunction with a family member or friend, securing both professional expertise as well as a personal connection.

The following is a hypothetical situation involving an executrix's actions with a will.

THE PROBLEM

Joe, who died last year, named his second wife, Martha, as executrix of his estate. Martha has refused to give Joe's children by his first marriage, Steve and Amy, any information concerning Joe's estate. To make matters worse, Steve and Amy believe that Martha has not even probated Joe's will or paid any of the death taxes due at Joe's death.

WHAT TO DO

1. Since wills are public records, Steve and Amy can check at the Register of Wills Office, or Probate Office, in the county in which Joe died in order to secure a copy of Joe's will, if it has been filed.

2. If the will has been filed, Steve and Amy should write either to Martha or to Martha's lawyer (if the lawyer's name appears in the probate proceeding) by certified letter for an immediate reply and a status report on Joe's estate. If the will has not been filed, Joe's children can petition the court for an order demanding that Martha begin probate procedures.

3. If the problem has not been resolved, Steve and Amy should contact a lawyer, preferably a lawyer familiar with the handling of estates in the county in which Joe died. The lawyer, after the will has been probated, should file a petition with the court demanding that Martha immediately file an accounting of what has taken place in Joe's estate. If this accounting is not satisfactory, a further petition should be filed seeking the removal of Martha as executrix and surcharging Martha for any losses to the estate or beneficiaries caused by her failure to act in a timely manner, assuming that Steve and Amy are entitled to a share of Joe's estate.

THE APPOINTMENT OF A GUARDIAN FOR MINOR CHILDREN If you die before your spouse, he or she will become your minor children's guardian. Nevertheless, you should always appoint a specific "guardian of the person" (other than your spouse) in case your spouse predeceases you or is unable to take on this responsibility. For example, your will may state: "If my husband predeceases me, or is unable to act as a guardian of my minor children, then I nominate my friend and her husband, Betty and Barry Stein, to be guardians."

In some states, your surviving spouse is not automatically the guardian of the property left through your estate to your minor children, so it is important to appoint a guardian to handle that responsibility. The person who handles your children's property is called the "guardian of the property" and need not be the same person or persons as the guardian of the person. Because you and your spouse may die simultaneously, particularly if you travel together, nominating guardians in your will is important.

Discuss the responsibilities of guardianship with those you wish to specify as guardians. Once they have expressed their willingness to serve, incorporate their names in your will. You may also give specific directions in your will to the guardians such as: "In the event that my husband and I are both deceased leaving minor children, I direct that my guardian(s) use every effort to have my children admitted and enrolled at the university from which I graduated, or an equivalent school of higher education."

If you have left money or property to your minor child, the guardian of the property will have to make an annual reporting to the probate court and, ultimately, disburse it and account for income and expenses when the child reaches the age of majority. The exact procedure varies from state to state.

SPECIFIC BEQUESTS   You may want to give certain items or belongings to particular individuals. Such an intent might be expressed as follows: "All personal effects, household furniture and furnishings, automobiles, books, clothing, jewelry, and other such tangible personal property owned by me at the time of my death, I give to my husband, if he survives me; if he does not survive me, I give said property to my children equally, or all to the survivors of them."

Specific bequests may be made to anyone who is capable of accepting them. Some people stretch this allowance by bequeathing property and assets to their pets. But state law may not allow direct gifts to animals, so any such disposition might be passed on to the person named next in the will or go to the beneficiary of the residue of the estate. Testators have a way around this by making a conditional bequest. For example: "I leave $40,000 to my friend, Ben Barton, provided he cares for my beloved cat, Zak, for the rest of her life." From the friend's perspective, taking care of a cat for a few years may be a small price to pay for $40,000. If you wish to make such a conditional bequest, be sure to confirm with the beneficiary in question that he or she is willing to abide by the condition you specify. Better yet, if the care of a beloved pet is important to you, talk to your attorney about a trust.

PAYMENT OF DEBTS, EXPENSES, AND TAXES   These items are usually paid by the executor from the residue of the estate, or what is left over after the specific bequests are distributed.

CHARITABLE BEQUESTS   "Rightful heirs" often become upset if they learn that the property they believed would be theirs was left to a church or other institution. Some people who know that their death is near believe that giving to charities will ensure them respect and gratitude once they die. Certain states have laws that restrict the amount of money that can be bequeathed to a charity; some states also require that a will that provides for a charitable gift be executed by a specified time before the testator's death.

THE MARITAL SHARE   Even if your spouse has given you nothing but misery and heartache throughout your marriage, you do not have the right to disinherit that spouse completely. In most states a surviving spouse is entitled to a statutory share in a deceased spouse's estate, so spouses are given the option of rejecting the provisions in the will and electing to take a "forced share." This forced share is a percentage of the estate that state law allows a spouse to elect to take, in lieu of what the deceased has bequeathed in his or her will.

THE SURVIVAL CLAUSE   When you bequeath property to an individual, you must decide whether you want the person's estate to receive it if the person should die before you do. If you do not, each bequest you make in your will has to include the phrase, "if he/she survives me." This becomes complicated when you consider that two people can die within minutes, hours, or days of each other. Even if your beneficiary survives you by two days, the bequest, unless you include a condition, has the same effect as if he or she predeceases you: It goes into the beneficiary's estate. Some testators include a general survival clause that states: "Should any person take under this will, but for this provision, fail to survive me by more than thirty (30) days, such person shall be deemed to have predeceased me for the purposes of construing all the terms of this will."

THE RESIDUE   The estate that is left after the specific bequests have been made is called the residue. Taxes, expenses, and debts are paid from the residue.

An example of the residuary clause you might include in your will is: "All of the rest, residue, and remainder of my property of whatsoever kind and character, real or personal or mixed, wheresoever located, of which I may die seized or possessed or in which I may own any interest, or to which my estate may become entitled after my death, but excluding any property over which I have a power of appointment, I give, bequeath, and devise to my husband, if he survives me."

THE POWERS OF THE EXECUTOR AND/OR TRUSTEE   State laws specify what powers are granted to the executor, but your will can also be very specific in this regard. Powers that are commonly granted include: retaining original property; selling and exchanging property; receiving additional property; investing and reinvesting; continuing business; managing real property; forming a corporation or other entity; paying taxes and expenses; dealing with other trusts; borrowing money; making money advances to immediate family members during probate to protect the estate; voting shares; reducing interest rates; collecting monies owed to the estate; litigating or settling claims regarding the estate; employing and compensating agents; and executing contracts and other instruments.

THE SIGNATURE AND WITNESS ATTESTATION CLAUSES   The signature clause states that you did, in fact, sign the will in the presence of the necessary witnesses. Typical language in a signature clause might specify: "IN WITNESS WHEREOF, I, Caroline Babbitt, hereby set my hand to this, my Last Will and Testament consisting of thirteen (13) pages, including this page, each page of which has been initialed by me, on the 30th day of October, 1993, at Fremont, Nebraska."

The attestation clause might read: "The foregoing instrument consisting of thirteen (13) pages, including this page, was signed by Caroline Babbitt, at the end thereof, in our presence and by her acknowledged to be her Last Will and Testament, and at her request and in her presence, and in the presence of each other, we subscribe our names as attesting witnesses at the City of Fremont, Nebraska, this 30th day of October, 1993."

CONDITIONS Testators can affect a beneficiary long after they themselves have died by bequeathing assets and property with conditions placed on the beneficiary. Courts will uphold wills that include conditions on bequests as long as they are not found to be illegal, against public policy, unreasonable, or impossible to perform. Some of the more common conditions testators have set forth in the past include requiring a beneficiary to give up all alcohol, cigarette smoking, or other "unhealthy habits," or the prohibition of marrying someone of a certain nationality or religion. Prohibiting a beneficiary from marrying at all is considered to be against public policy.

What follows is a hypothetical situation involving a will with conditions.

THE PROBLEM

In his will, George left $50,000 to each of his grandchildren, provided that they receive a Catholic education. George's son, Tom, is in the foreign service, and there is no Catholic school for his children to attend. The priest at the local Catholic church has volunteered to teach religious courses to Tom's children, but Tom does not know whether this will qualify his children to receive the bequest from their grandfather, George.

WHAT TO DO

Tom should consult with a lawyer in the locality in which George's will was probated. He should explain the situation to the lawyer, and the lawyer can either ask the local probate court informally or file a petition with the court, explaining the situation and seeking a determination on whether the church courses will qualify Tom's children for grandfather George's bequest. If the court does not agree, the petition should ask the court to make a recommendation about how to qualify Tom's children for their grandfather's bequest.

Other Types of Wills

The formal, witnessed will is the only will considered valid in all states; however, certain states honor two other kinds of wills: those that are handwritten and those that are made orally. As always, certain conditions prevail.

THE HANDWRITTEN (HOLOGRAPHIC) WILL   The holographic will is not typed or printed; it is handwritten by the person who is bequeathing his or her own property, signed and dated, but not witnessed. Almost half of the states consider holographic wills valid. Maryland, New York, and Rhode Island acknowledge handwritten wills in limited circumstances involving individuals in the armed services.

For a holographic will to be valid, it must be entirely handwritten, from the date to the bequests to the signature, with nothing typed, stamped, or handwritten by anyone else. Fewer than half the states honor handwritten wills, because this type of will presents validity problems. With no witnesses, the courts have difficulty determining with certainty who wrote the will, when it was written, or whether it was, in fact, intended to be a will. For those reasons, the best rule of thumb is for testators to go through the formal will process.

THE ORAL (NUNCUPATIVE) WILL   The majority of states allow wills that have been made orally, or nuncupative wills, under very limited circumstances:

- The will must have been made during the testator's last illness.
- It must have been made in the testator's own home or in the house where he/she has died.
- It must bequeath only personal property, never realty.
- It must be witnessed by two people.
- The testator must have clearly expressed to the witnesses that this oral statement was her/his will, not that he or she intended to make a will later.
- The will must be transformed into a written transcript within a specified amount of time.
- The will must be probated within a certain time, usually six months.

A soldier, during wartime, and sailors, anytime at sea, are not required to follow the normal formalities of an oral will.

Lawrence, a widower and resident of Michigan, conveyed all his property to his daughter-in-law, Hillary, in his will. He drafted the will entirely in his own handwriting and had it properly witnessed and signed. One of the witnesses noted that Lawrence had left out the word "street" in the address of the home he was bequeathing, so she added it for him. Handwritten wills are legal in Michigan, but the fact that the will was not totally in Lawrence's handwriting may invalidate it. Some courts will allow minor notations in another's handwriting if they are considered unimportant to the meaning of the will.

Do You Need a Lawyer to Draft Your Will?

It's not necessary to have a lawyer draft your will in order for it to be valid. But do be aware that the laws from state to state vary, and can have a profound effect on whether a court finds a will properly executed.

You will probably benefit from the guidance of an experienced attorney. If you require a relatively simple will, a general practitioner will suffice, but if you have a good deal of personal and real property, you'll need an estate planner.

Check an attorney's credentials before you seek the attorney's services. You needn't pay the steep hourly rate for an expert in estate planning if a boilerplate document from a general practitioner can provide a good basis for the will you draw. For complex wills, trusts, and estates, the importance of a good attorney—and how much room there is for error—is reflected in the high number of malpractice cases brought each year against attorneys who make serious errors in estate planning.

If your will is going to involve more than bequeathing all you own to your spouse, your state or city bar associations or county estate-planning councils can provide a list of attorneys who specialize in estate planning. If a particular attorney has handled other kinds of work for you, ask for a recommendation to help plan your estate. Friends and associates may be able to recommend an estate planner whom they have used. Call a few of the recommended attorneys and discuss your needs and their experience and fees with them.

Constructing Your Will, With or Without an Attorney

An attorney's office will probably send you a form to fill out, which will simplify and consolidate the information that will eventually be needed if a member of that firm is to plan your estate effectively. You can create such a form yourself, and you might even want to sketch a family tree, showing the names of your children and close relatives, as well as their addresses, ages, occupations, and other important information. This will help not only in selecting your heirs but also in choosing executors, trustees, or guardians.

List your income from all sources, including that of your spouse. Itemize all your assets and their value, including bank accounts, land, homes and furnishings, vehicles, stocks, bonds, and jewelry. List your debts and liabilities, including mortgages, loans, and other obligations. Think about the ultimate goal of your estate planning. Is it to provide assets to your children at the time of your death or to postpone the dispersal of your assets until a number of years later?

Be sure to make your plans based on present circumstances, not on what you believe might take place in the future. For example, don't anticipate that a rich uncle is going to die and leave you $1 million, as he has promised. Create a will and plan based on the fact that you may die tomorrow. Remember that the more thought and work you can do now in supplying accurate information, the less time it will require of an attorney or, eventually, your executor.

If you have decided to use an attorney, take the information you have accumulated to your first meeting. You may learn that there are certain tax consequences that you were not aware of that may change the way you distribute your property. At this meeting, you may also want to discuss executing a "living will" and/or a durable power of attorney.

After you have considered your options and agreed on the proper route to take, it is the attorney's job to prepare the documents that will reflect your wishes. Be sure that the papers are sent to you for your review, and have the attorney explain any information that seems unclear. *Be sure that the documents reflect your wishes.* You may want another person, such as your financial counselor or accountant, to review them. When you are at ease with the finished product, make an appointment to sign the documents. You must follow all the formalities required by your state and noted above, including securing witnesses and observing whatever other requirements are in force. Don't rely on an attorney to see that everything is in order; take the time to review and confirm the final documents yourself, whether or not an attorney has been involved.

Caring for Your Will

You have taken great care to bequeath your property and have executed a valid, witnessed will. But it does you little good if your family, heirs, and executor cannot locate it after your death or if it is destroyed in a fire. Many attorneys will provide a safe place for your will; in some states the probate court offers the same service. A safe-deposit box at your bank is also a possibility, but check to be sure that specified others will be given access to its contents after you die. A fireproof, metal strongbox that contains other important documents in your home is a safe and particularly convenient place. Not only is it the predictable place for your family to find it later, but the will is easily available to you when you want to review it.

If the original copy is not in your immediate possession, be sure you have a photocopy of it. Review your will every three years to update assets and review bequests. Consider your relationship with the named executor and the guardians you have selected to care for your children. If you want to make minor changes, this can be accomplished through an amendment, or *codicil*—an additional document that becomes part of the will and is incorporated by reference.

Revoking or Changing a Will

A will may be revoked in any of three ways:

1. You can intentionally destroy it at any time. The best way to invalidate a will completely is to intentionally burn it, tear it,

cut it, write "canceled" across it, or obliterate some portion of it.

2. In many states a will is automatically invalidated by certain major events in your life, including the birth or adoption of a child, marriage, or divorce. Other changes in your life that may require a new will or amendments include the purchase or sale of a home, a change in your income, the death of relatives, or a move to another state.

3. You can draft a new will that revokes a prior will. The bequests you make in the second document override those in the first.

If the changes you wish to make are significant, destroy the old will and start fresh. Sometimes a will may not need to be revoked entirely; perhaps it simply needs to be amended.

CODICILS   Less significant changes in a will can be accomplished with a codicil, a document that makes the necessary changes without eliminating the entire will. A codicil may be phrased as follows: "I, Bill Smith, of Wilton, Alaska, having made my Last Will and Testament dated February 1, 1992, hereby make this codicil, amending said Will as follows: I hereby delete Article II and substitute the following Article II in its place: . . .

"In all other respects, I hereby ratify and confirm my said Will in its entirety."

A codicil must follow all the formalities of the original will, including the requirement that you sign it and have it witnessed by two or more individuals.

OTHER CHANGES IN A WILL   Some changes unintentionally occur in a will. For example, your father may will you his 1962 Chevrolet Impala, which you have admired for years. Unfortunately, before he dies, he sells the car to a collector. Your father's estate is not required to give you an identical car or to pay you the value in cash. If the estate no longer has the property, whether personal or realty, you have no rights to it. Similarly, suppose that your father bequeaths you $150,000, but only $25,000 is left after taxes and expenses are paid and your mother gets her share of the estate. In this case your

THE WILL • 81

After Frank and Margaret's first two children were born, the couple executed mutual wills, each bequeathing their entire estate to whichever spouse survived the other. Frank died on Monday, August 2, and the next day, their third child was born. Frank's other two children, young adults, contested the will, arguing that the birth of a child automatically invalidated it. Therefore, they argued, their father's estate would be distributed according to the state laws of intestacy, and they would receive part of it. The court could hold that Margaret was entitled to receive the entire estate, because the birth of the couple's third child did not occur until after Frank's death. The court could also find that the child born after the will was made was entitled to a share of the estate, but that the first two children were not. Marriage, divorce, and the birth or adoption of a child may invalidate or affect the provisions of a will in many states.

mother is not required to take from her share to pay you; you'll receive only what is left—$25,000.

Contesting a Will

After you die, your last will and testament will be probated—that is, it will be submitted to a probate court, reviewed, usually determined to be valid, and then recorded. But the possibility always exists that disappointed relatives may contest your will. The only individuals who have legal standing to contest a will are those who have a direct interest in the will or would have some possibility of inheriting from your estate if the will were declared invalid. Creditors have no "standing" to challenge your will.

Some of the possible grounds that, if found to be true, could invalidate a will include:

• You were not of sound mind when you made your will. (For example, you were unable to understand what you were bequeathing.)

- The will was not properly executed. (For example, perhaps there was only one witness instead of the required two or three, or the witnesses did not sign the will in your presence.)

- You made the will under undue influence. (For example, you never would have bequeathed your home to your brother if he had not threatened to publicize a family secret that would harm your son's reputation.)

- Someone committed fraud. (For example, perhaps your disinherited sister destroyed a page of the actual will and replaced it with another.)

What follows is a hypothetical situation involving a contested will.

THE PROBLEM

Estelle was an 85-year-old woman who lived alone. Her only close relative was her son, Arthur, who lived 2,000 miles away and only communicated with his mother infrequently. Estelle had a minor stroke three years ago. One of her neighbors, Vincent, befriended her, helping her with her daily personal and household needs, and has continued to have a close relationship with her. Shortly before her death, Estelle consulted an attorney who prepared a will that left everything to Vincent and nothing to Arthur. Arthur is now contesting the will, and Vincent seeks advice.

WHAT TO DO

1. Vincent should immediately consult an attorney.
2. Vincent should document the duration and extent of his relationship with Estelle, so that the court will be aware of the close relationship and contributions that Vincent made to Estelle's daily life and of the rational basis for Estelle favoring Vincent over Arthur.
3. Vincent and his attorney should contact the witnesses to the will and should present as much documentary evidence as possible concerning Estelle's state of mind, her competency, the fact that she was aware she was disinheriting her son, and that given the circumstances, she had a logical and rational basis for doing so, and her decision was not caused by undue influence on Vincent's part.

AVOIDING A CONTEST   The best way to avoid a contest is to retain an attorney to draft the will for you.

One tactic used to discourage a contest is to include a no-contest clause, which, in effect, says that if any of the beneficiaries contest the bequests you have specified, they take nothing. The "$1 clause" (noted earlier) also can avoid contests, but regardless of your diligence, an unhappy relative may challenge your will.

Going Through Probate

Let's assume that you have been appointed executor of the estate of Ben H., a close friend. He dies, and it is your responsibility to begin the probate procedure. The first step is to locate the original copy of the will. It's best if you planned ahead and found out where the original copy was kept when Ben asked you to become executor.

Once you've located the original copy of the will, take it to the probate court in the county where Ben lived. You'll file a petition for probate with the court, asking that Ben's will be accepted as his last will and testament. The court will provide you with the probate forms. In some states you may be asked to send the notice of petition to everyone mentioned in Ben's will as well as to his rightful heirs (if they were not mentioned in the will). Some states require that you publish a notice in the local newspaper stating that Ben has died, that a petition for probate has been filed with the court by a given date. In those states that do not require such publication, the petition for probate and naming of the executor are done automatically.

In either situation, publication or nonpublication, one or more people may want to object to the will or to you as executor. To make their objections known, they should in most cases retain an attorney or familiarize themselves with local court requirements. They could also write a short letter to the court saying that they object, and the probate court may then give them time to retain an attorney and explain why they are contesting the will. If no objections are made, the court will accept the petition and you as executor.

As executor, you will hold legal title to the property in Ben's estate. His bank account will now be titled "Robert S. (your name),

Executor, Estate of Ben H." You are now faced with the task of developing a complete inventory of all Ben's property, both real and personal, that he owned individually at the time of his death and that will be distributed by probate. Some states give you one month to establish the inventory; others allow up to nine months.

Assuming that Ben had a few debts when he died, it is your responsibility as the executor to see that any known bills are paid, including charge cards, phone bills, attorneys' fees, etc. You are also required to notify Ben's creditors that they have a certain time period in which to make a claim on the estate.

Another important task is filing an estate tax return. First determine if Ben's estate is large enough to require filing a federal and/or state return. If it is, you should consult with a professional (i.e., accountant, attorney) who specializes in estates to prepare the tax return. The proceeds from the estate should not be distributed until the tax returns are accepted by the federal and state governments. If the estate owes money in taxes, *you will be held responsible* for paying them.

The court will require a final report that lists the assets of the estate and how they were distributed, the expenses, fees, and taxes that were paid, and whether the beneficiaries received the bequests to which they were entitled. Upon distributing the inheritances to the beneficiaries, be sure you ask each of them to approve your final accounting, and to sign a document stating that they have received their bequests and that they are releasing you from any further liability or claims.

Once you have completed the final report and have obtained the approval of the beneficiaries, you must submit it to the probate court. If the court accepts the final accounting, the estate is closed, and you are released from your responsibilities as executor.

What follows is a hypothetical situation involving settling an estate.

THE PROBLEM

Twenty-five years ago, Ed prepared a will and named his lawyer and friend, Martin, as his executor. Ed died recently, and Martin, who is now quite elderly, has not communicated with Ed's children. This is especially disturbing to Ed's daughter, Nancy, who is very ill and in need of the funds that she will receive from her father's estate.

WHAT TO DO

Bring pressure, first informally and then formally, upon Martin to expedite the handling of Ed's estate.

1. Nancy should write a certified letter to Martin requesting specific information about the status of the estate and when she might receive her share of the estate. She should request an answer within 10 days.

2. If Martin does not reply to Nancy, she should consult with the Disciplinary Board of the county and state bar association of which Martin is a member and advise them of Martin's failure to communicate with her.

3. If the foregoing recommendations do not solve the problem, Nancy should retain an attorney to take legal action against Martin.

AVOIDING PROBATE   Sometimes the tedious, often costly, and stressful probate process can be avoided. Certain property, "nonprobated," is passed on through means other than a will. This may include life insurance, pensions, employee benefit plans, and trusts. When you die, this nonprobated property will go directly to the named beneficiary, and will not pass through your estate. This clearly has its advantages because it may reduce administrative costs and avoid the delay when the estate would be tied up in probate.

Many couples have joint checking accounts and realty, in which case the surviving partner simply takes sole ownership of all assets when the other dies. Property that you own jointly or co-own with another may not come under the control of your will, depending on whether it constitutes a "tenancy-in-common" or a "joint tenancy with the right of survivorship." If the title of your property states that it is owned by "Joe Doe and Sue Ann Roe," as tenants-in-common, both Joe and Sue Ann each own one-half of the property. When Joe dies, his half goes into his probated estate to be distributed according to his will. But if the title states that it is owned by and is a joint tenancy, the surviving co-owner receives full title upon the death of the other partner. Property in a tenancy-in-common can be bequeathed in a will; property in a joint tenancy cannot.

As you draft your will and plan your estate, be sure to address the status of your property. Don't attempt to make a will without understanding what kind of ownership you have.

Joint Ownership of Property

When married people own property that is titled in both names it is almost always owned by them as joint tenants with right of survivorship—often abbreviated as JTWROS. In many states a joint tenancy with right of survivorship between a husband and wife is called a "tenancy by the entireties," which is a joint tenancy existing between a husband and wife.

The remaining form of joint ownership between husband and wife is as "tenants-in-common." The legal difference is that under the tenancy-in-common, each spouse owns an undivided interest in one-half of the property.

Tax Consequences of Joint Ownership

If the total value of the husband's and wife's estate is less than $600,000, joint ownership of property with the right of survivorship might be the best form of taking title to property. At death, title passes immediately to the survivor without probate and in most cases is not taxable. It also may be the best form of ownership to protect the asset against a creditor of either spouse.

Under the federal gift and estate tax laws, a married person has an unlimited right to transfer as much property as he or she wishes to a spouse without any adverse federal gift or estate tax consequences. Therefore, if property is held as joint tenants with right of survivorship, at the death of the first spouse, the second spouse immediately becomes the sole owner of the property in question without the imposition of a federal estate tax.

If the property is owned as tenants-in-common, then the first spouse to die has the right to transfer (by means of a will) his or her share of the property to anyone. If the property is transferred to the surviving spouse, there would be no tax. If the property were transferred to a third person, and if the total estate of the person dying exceeded $600,000, then there would be estate or gift tax consequences.

For purposes of state inheritance and other death tax laws, some states exempt property owned by husband and wife as tenants by the entireties, while imposing a state death tax on property owned by husband and wife as tenants-in-common. If the husband's and wife's estate exceeds $600,000 and the family estate plan calls for setting up a credit shelter trust, and if all of the family assets are owned jointly by the husband and wife with right of survivorship, no assets could go into the credit shelter trust. This could result in the failure to fund the credit shelter trust properly, thereby resulting in the imposition of large federal estate taxes on the children at the death of the survivor.

Dying Without a Will

If you die without having made a will, you are said to die intestate. Each state has its own laws of "intestate and descendancy," directing who will inherit your property. If you want to research the intestacy laws in your state, visit a law library and check the index of your state code under the subject heading of "intestacy."

The order of who receives property and/or assets first in an intestacy situation is generally as follows:

1. Your surviving spouse, who usually receives one-third or one-half of your estate, depending on whether you have children

2. Your children, regardless of age; if they die before you, their children (your grandchildren) will take their parents' share. Children who have been born outside marriage can usually inherit from their mother and from their father (if he acknowledges paternity or if it has been proved). Adopted children generally inherit from their adoptive parents but not from their adoptive parents' relatives. If an adopted child dies without a spouse or lineal descendants, his or her estate will go to the adoptive parents, not to the biological parents.

3. Your parents, if you have no surviving spouse or children

4. Your brothers and sisters or, if they have died, their children (your nephews and nieces)

5. Your next of kin, which means the nearest blood relative (not relatives by marriage)

Instead of your estate being handled by an executor, as it is when you make a will, an intestate distribution is overseen by an administrator. The administrator might be the surviving spouse, next of kin, a creditor, or a public administrator. All the estate's assets are liquidated, meaning that all property, whether land, jewelry, bonds, or cars, must be converted into cash so that it can be dispersed most efficiently. The only exception might be the "family homestead" in which the surviving spouse and children live.

What follows is a hypothetical situation involving an estate without a will.

THE PROBLEM

Aunt Selma has died and is survived by 3 sisters and 10 nieces and nephews. She never made a will. Before Aunt Selma died, the daughter of one of her sisters was helping Selma with her affairs; after her death, the niece went to the local probate court and filed a petition stating that the only surviving relatives who are entitled to a share of Aunt Selma's estate are her 3 sisters. You are a son of one of Aunt Selma's deceased brothers, and you understand that you may be entitled to part of her estate.

WHAT TO DO

1. Check to determine whether you are entitled to a share of Aunt Selma's estate under your state's intestacy law. In most states the children of a deceased sister or brother of the decedent will be entitled to the share of their parent. This information should be obtainable from the local probate court, by reviewing your state's statutes, or by consulting an attorney.

2. If you are entitled to a share of Aunt Selma's estate, you should contact the person handling the estate directly or the attorney for the estate, whose name should be listed with the probate proceedings, and advise either of them of your position.

3. If he or she refuses to include you in the distributive share of Aunt Selma's estate, you should contact an attorney, who will file a petition with the court to either set aside the petition that was filed or make certain that all persons entitled to a share of the estate will be included in the distribution of that estate.

Power of Attorney

A will gives directions to others for how your estate should be treated after your death. But there are instruments or methods by which you can give decision-making power to others while you are still alive to be used in different circumstances. These instruments include power of attorney, durable power of attorney, durable power of attorney for health-care decisions, and living wills.

A *power of attorney* is a document or written instrument that allows you to appoint someone else as your decision-maker or agent to handle certain transactions, usually relating to business or financial affairs.

If you want to invest in property in another state but are unable to travel and conduct the necessary business yourself, you may execute a power of attorney designating another individual as your agent to conduct the entire transaction. The power you convey can be "once and done," or it can be for a series of transactions. If you become incapacitated, this power of attorney is automatically canceled; to perpetuate the authority, you would require a *durable power of attorney*, which remains valid even if you become disabled. If you don't want to institute a durable power of attorney until such a need arises, some states allow a "springing power of attorney," which does not go into effect until a doctor states that you can no longer take care of your affairs by yourself.

The power of attorney and durable power of attorney are helpful in business transactions, but suppose your concerns involve health care and medical decisions if you become incapacitated. Some states have created a *durable power of attorney for health care*, a written instrument that allows you to select someone to make your decisions for you regarding such matters as surgery or placement in a nursing home. You may also want to give someone a general durable power of attorney to act for you in all matters that you cannot handle yourself.

Care should be taken when you select a person to handle your power of attorney. No special skills are needed, but it should be someone who knows you well and someone you trust. Be sure to make your wishes and directions very clear. Write them down to avoid any uncertainty or confusion. The person you select should want the responsibilities you are offering; it should not be considered a burden. If that person would prefer not to do it, select someone else. If you become dissatisfied with the way that person is handling the responsibility, you have the right to revoke the power of attorney at any time by notifying the person in writing. If you revoke the power of attorney, inform any other parties who may be affected by the power you conveyed.

Each state's laws differ when it comes to powers of attorney, so it's wise to research the proper procedures.

What follows is a hypothetical situation involving power of attorney.

THE PROBLEM

Your widowed mother lives some distance from you and for that reason has given your brother a durable power of attorney to act for her. You have reason to believe that your brother is improperly using the power of attorney to divert your mother's funds to his own bank accounts.

WHAT TO DO

You must take steps to protect your mother's funds for her.

1. Ask your brother, either in person, by phone, or by certified letter, depending on your relationship with him, to furnish for you an accounting of your mother's assets and how they are being handled.

2. Review as many of your mother's records as possible in order to find out whether funds have been diverted for your brother's personal use.

3. If funds are being diverted or if your brother refuses to cooperate with you, then try to communicate with your mother to see if she would be willing to revoke the power of attorney or speak with your brother.

4. If all of the foregoing fail, you should retain the services of an attorney to stop your brother from handling your mother's funds and to compel him to file an accounting of everything that he has handled for her.

Living Wills

A durable power of attorney is often confused with a living will. A living will goes into effect while you are still alive, but only when you are judged by a doctor to be terminally ill. It instructs doctors and health-care providers about what life-prolonging measures you would like them to take, if any, or whether you would like them to employ artificial life-support systems or to disconnect them so you can "die with dignity" if you are diagnosed as being terminally ill.

Each state has its own legislation governing living wills. For information regarding the requirements in your state, contact Choice In Dying, 200 Varick Street, New York, NY 10014; 212-366-5540.

After you have drafted a living will, be sure it has no provisions that are invalid in your state.

The following is a hypothetical situation involving a living will.

THE PROBLEM

Your father is extremely ill, and his doctor has called a family meeting to discuss his present condition. The doctor advises you and the other family members that your father is in a terminal condition, and there is no likelihood of his regaining consciousness or having any normal life functions. The doctor shows you a living will signed by your father, indicating that under this type of circumstance he did not wish to be kept alive. Everyone is in agreement except your sister. Because of her personal religious feelings, she tells the doctor that she believes that it is a sin to do anything to take a human life.

WHAT TO DO

1. Dealing with life and death is always difficult and emotional, but you and the other family members can make it clear that you would like your father's wishes to be respected.
2. Because state and federal law now gives a person the right to make these decisions, your father's decision should be respected by your father's physician, but if there is a problem, you have the right to retain a lawyer and ask the court to enforce your father's wish to "die with dignity."

TRUSTS

A trust is a legal relationship in which property is held for the benefit of another. Trusts are created for many reasons. They can be used to provide financial security to others or to gain a tax benefit. The individual who creates the trust is called the "settlor" or "grantor," and a "trustee" holds the property for the ultimate recipient, the "beneficiary."

There are two kinds of trusts: testamentary and living. A *testamentary trust* is created as part of a will and goes into effect only when the testator dies. The trustee is named in the will and is required to administer the trust funds as the will directs. This type of trust can be used to provide tax savings for children through the use of a credit shelter trust, and can also be used to ensure that college costs are covered for children when they reach their late teens, or that their inheritance is handled responsibly by a mature person until they can be responsible for it themselves.

A *living trust*, or *inter vivos* trust, becomes effective while you, the settlor, are alive. It entails placing assets or property in the hands of a trustee, who manages them, invests them, and pays the trust income to you or the other beneficiaries of the trust, if the trust so provides. A living trust can be designed to provide income to you for life, and on your death all the trust's assets pass on to the beneficiary you have selected. Because the beneficiary may predecease the person who creates the trust, an alternate beneficiary should always be named. Beneficiaries of trusts can be family members, friends, charities, pets, or even strangers, as long as the name of the beneficiary is made specific in the trust documents.

It's no accident that the person who tends to your affairs under a trust is called a trustee; the person you designate must indeed be someone you trust implicitly. If you believe that the trustee is mishandling your assets, consult a lawyer about changing trustees and prosecuting yours for wrongdoing.

What follows is a hypothetical situation involving trusts.

THE PROBLEM

Samuel's father set up a trust before his death, under which Regional National Bank was named as trustee. Under the terms of the trust, Samuel was to receive the income from the trust during his lifetime, and at his death the money was to go to the Society for the Prevention of Cruelty to Animals. Samuel is very unhappy about the amount of income that he is receiving from the trust.

WHAT TO DO

1. Samuel should request an appointment with the investment officer for the trust and find out exactly what investment strategy the bank is using.

2. During the interview Samuel should make certain that the bank's investment policy for the trust is one that attempts to give Samuel, as the lifetime beneficiary of the trust, as much income as possible.

3. If Samuel is unhappy with the result of his meeting with the bank, he should review the trust document and see if there are any provisions for replacing the trustee.

4. If Samuel cannot achieve the desired result on his own, he should contact an attorney, who can attempt to pressure the bank informally into revising its investment policy to provide Samuel with a greater income or, failing that, can bring court action to have the bank replaced as trustee.

Trusts can be either revocable or irrevocable. As the names imply, a revocable trust allows you to change your mind about placing your money and/or property in the trust fund; an irrevocable trust does not. If you specify that the trust is irrevocable and you are not a beneficiary of the trust, you gain the advantage of not being taxed on the trust's assets, because they no longer belong to you; you have made a gift of the trust's assets, and they become the tax liability of the named beneficiary without becoming embroiled in the process of probate court. Gifts to irrevocable trusts and, in many cases, setting up revocable living trusts have the great benefit of executing your wishes relatively quickly and keeping your affairs far more private than the probate process allows.

Revocable Trusts

One of the most common uses for revocable trusts is to provide a vehicle in which to hold your assets during your lifetime, and to pass your assets to your beneficiaries at death, without having your estate go through the probate process.

Another very important use of revocable trusts is to provide an efficient method of protecting your assets and yourself in the event of old age or disability.

A revocable trust can be used when a married person sets up a credit shelter trust for his or her spouse, either in a will or in a separate trust document.

What follows is a hypothetical situation involving a revocable trust.

THE PROBLEM

Shirley is 78 years old, single, and has no close friends or relatives. She is concerned about what would happen to her if she became seriously ill and could not handle her own funds. Shirley wants to set up a trust to make certain that she will be provided for if something were to happen to her.

WHAT TO DO

1. Shirley can consult with the trust department of a local bank and learn the details of how they could administer her funds under a revocable living trust.

2. Shirley should then contact a lawyer to prepare the appropriate trust document. The trust should state that Shirley will transfer all of her assets to the bank, who will hold them for her in a trust, giving her the income from the trust and as much of the principal as she needs. In the event she becomes sick or disabled, the bank, as trustee, can use the funds for her health care, to obtain private-duty nurses, place her in an appropriate retirement community, and otherwise make certain that all of her needs are met.

3. The trust would further provide that at Shirley's death, the trustee would distribute the balance of her estate to those persons and institutions named by her.

4. Because this is a revocable trust, Shirley can always notify the bank that she is no longer interested in its services, revoke her trust, take back all of her funds, and administer them herself.

Irrevocable Trusts

Unlike a revocable trust, once you establish an irrevocable trust, the terms and conditions of that trust cannot be changed. By establishing an irrevocable trust, you are making a gift of whatever property you place in that trust to the beneficiaries of the trust.

People set up irrevocable trusts when making gifts to minor children. These trusts constitute an absolute gift to the children and set up appropriate provisions for the funds to be administered for the children during their minority or until whatever date you choose to turn the money over outright to the children.

Irrevocable trusts can also be used for tax planning purposes, to own insurance policies on your life, or to remove assets from your estate, while providing the terms and conditions regarding how those assets will be administered.

The following hypothetical situation involves an irrevocable trust.

THE PROBLEM

Grandfather Bert wants to give money to his grandchildren, but because they are quite young, he does not want them to handle the money themselves. However, Bert does not want to retain control of the money himself because, if he does, it will be taxed in his estate at his death. He also wants to take advantage of the $10,000 annual gift tax exclusion but does not want to give his grandchildren the right to use the money until they are 21.

WHAT TO DO

Set up an irrevocable trust for the grandchildren.

1. Grandfather Bert should consult an attorney, who can prepare an irrevocable minors trust for each of Bert's grandchildren.

2. Under the provisions of the trust, the trustee, who should not be Bert, will hold and invest the money for the grandchildren and will not give it to them until they are 21, unless the money is needed earlier.

3. The trusts are then set up, are given separate tax identification numbers, and Bert makes out his checks in the amount of $10,000 to the trustee of each trust, which will constitute a gift to each of the grandchildren and remove the total amount from the grandfather's estate.

ESTATES OF $600,000 AND HIGHER

The estate of every taxpayer is subject to the provisions of the federal estate and gift tax. The total value of your assets (this includes life insurance, jointly owned property, pensions, IRAs, your home, stocks, bonds, and bank accounts) will be taxed by the federal government at your death. It is important to understand how this tax works, so that you can eliminate or reduce the tax impact on your family. Since the tax rates begin at 37 percent and go up to 55 percent, tax savings can be significant.

What follows is a hypothetical situation involving federal estate taxes.

THE PROBLEM

John and Barbara are married, and their combined assets, including life insurance, home, pension plan, cash, and securities, total $1.2 million. They have "mom and pop" wills, under which they bequeath everything to each other, and at the death of the survivor, to their children.

There will be no tax when the first spouse dies because of the unlimited marital deduction. When the second spouse dies, their estate will be entitled to a credit equal to $600,000. After deducting the $600,000 credit, the survivor's estate will still have $600,000, resulting in a federal estate tax to their children in the amount of $192,500. The problem is that the $600,000 exemption of the first spouse to die was wasted.

WHAT TO DO

Consult an estate-planning lawyer to set up a credit shelter trust (also called a bypass trust) for John and Barbara. At the first spouse's death, $600,000 would be transferred to this trust, which would ultimately go to their children at the death of the survivor. During the survivor's lifetime, he or she would have the right to the income from the trust, with the assistance of an impartial trustee, and the trustee could use the principal for the surviving spouse if it were needed. The survivor could also be given a limited power to withdraw principal. At the survivor's death, the $600,000 in the trust would go, tax-free, to the children, utilizing the $600,000 tax credit of the first spouse. The survivor's $600,000 would pass to the children using the survivor's $600,000 credit. The children would therefore receive $1.2 million tax-free.

The $600,000 Tax Credit

Every taxpayer who is a citizen is entitled to a unified tax credit of $192,500 (which is equivalent to a tax on $600,000 of assets). If the total of your assets is less than $600,000, your estate will not be subject to the federal estate tax at your death. This credit is allowed to every taxpayer regardless of how that property is left or to whom.

The Marital Deduction

In addition to the $600,000 unified tax credit, every married person is entitled to transfer an unlimited amount of assets to his or her spouse, either during their lifetimes or at death. This is known as the unlimited marital deduction and is available only between a husband and a wife.

Tax-Free Gifts

Gifts made during your lifetime will also be subject to the $600,000 limitation, with one very big exception: Every person has the right to gift $10,000 to as many people as he or she wishes each year without drawing on the $600,000 lifetime exemption. A husband and wife together can gift $20,000 to each child or any other person, and a husband and wife are permitted to give $20,000 to a person, if the other spouse formally joins in the gift. By use of the $10,000 annual exemption, it is possible to reduce the size of your estate and the amount of federal estate taxes that would otherwise have to be paid at your death.

There is a further exemption for gifts to recognized charities. If you make a gift to charity in your will, that gift will not be subject to the federal estate tax. There are also methods to reduce the size of your estate by making gifts to charities during your lifetime through the use of charitable remainder trusts and charitable lead trusts. (Ask an estate planner for an explanation of these trusts.)

The Generation-Skipping Tax

In addition to the federal estate tax and gift tax, there is a generation-skipping transfer tax, which is imposed when you skip a generation and leave assets directly to your grandchildren or other persons in their generation. This tax is subject to a $1 million exemption for each recipient.

PLANNING YOUR FUNERAL

Unpleasant as it may be, part of estate planning includes making decisions regarding your funeral and burial/cremation. The law gives you the right to decide how your body is to be treated after your death.

These decisions should not be left to your loved ones to make after you have died. It's best that you formally draft instructions before the fact. First, you must decide whether you want to be buried or cremated or whether to donate your body to a medical institute or university. If you choose either burial or cremation, specify whether you want this to be preceded by a ceremony; specify whether the ceremony is to be religious (specify) or nonreligious, with or without the body on view; or whether you prefer an immediate burial or cremation followed by a memorial service or other ceremony later.

In addition, you can also designate the funeral home that you would like to handle the arrangements and where you would like to be buried.

Such choices are personal, of course, but finances are often a consideration. If cremation is your choice, the expenses of a casket, embalming process, flowers, and many other funeral costs, will be eliminated.

"Pre-Need" Plans

Not only can you instruct your survivors about what funeral home and cemetery you prefer, but you can also pay for your funeral before you ever need it. Some funeral homes provide "pre-need" plans, allowing you to pay the entire amount in advance; others arrange for you to pay in installments over a specific period of time. The payments are to be placed in an interest-bearing trust fund or savings account, so that, theoretically, by the time you die, the accumulated interest will compensate for the inflated prices of your funeral.

Each state has laws governing pre-need plans, and a state official, such as the comptroller or secretary of state, is designated as the watchdog of the system. But not all state laws are the same: Some don't require that the entire payment amount be placed in an account; others allow funeral homes to keep the interest. Even in states that have strict legislation, these matters are often difficult to monitor and control. Some unscrupulous funeral homes fail even to open a trust fund or account with the payments they receive. Some pre-need plans are sold by sales representatives who go door-to-door to take advantage of unsuspecting senior citizens. The Federal Trade Commission's Cooling-Off Rule applies to this kind of sale, allowing the purchaser three business days to change his or her mind. But the contracts that are involved in door-to-door purchases can be complicated and may not protect an individual's rights.

While most pre-need plans are legitimate, they may have liabilities. In some cases the individual dies before all the payments are made, or because of inflation, all the expenses are not covered, and the burden of making up the difference falls on the shoulders of the survivors. If the survivors cannot absorb the expenses, they may decide to rearrange your funeral plans after your death.

Memorial Societies

Memorial societies are nonprofit, volunteer organizations that serve as advisers to consumers in preplanning their funerals, helping to find low-cost services in their vicinity. Funeral homes often offer lower costs to society members, knowing that a lesser profit will be made up in the long run by the larger number of customers. Some societies encourage their members to enter into formal contracts with specific funeral homes to ensure relatively inexpensive services. To find a memorial society in your city, look in the telephone book's White Pages under "Memorial Service of [city]," or under "Associations" in the Yellow Pages.

Your Rights of Protection Against Funeral Fraud

Because the American funeral industry was once rife with abuses, the Federal Trade Commission created the Funeral Rule in 1984 to protect bereaving consumers from deceptive practices. The Rule requires funeral homes to provide consumers with certain information, including the prices of different services and products, over the phone to facilitate comparison shopping. When you consult funeral

If you are interested in a "pre-need" plan, check with the Better Business Bureau to be sure the funeral home you choose is well established and reliable. Be certain that you understand what services you will receive in return for the dollars spent. Have the firm's representative explain what percentage of the money you pay in installments (if that is the option you choose) will be placed in an account, and who will receive the interest or the overage if money is left in the account after your funeral. Be sure that these matters are specified in the contract, and consult with a local senior citizens support group before you sign it. (Senior citizens' groups are often familiar with these plans.) Another safeguard may be to join a memorial society.

home representatives in person, they are required to give you lists and prices of all the services and products they provide, specifying which funeral and burial items are required by law.

Funeral home representatives must also provide information regarding embalming and cremation.

EMBALMING They must state, in writing, that embalming is not required by law except in certain situations. If they embalm a body without permission, they are not permitted to charge for this procedure unless the law requires it. They must state that if a funeral and viewing are desired, embalming probably will be necessary; embalming is not necessary in an immediate burial or cremation.

CREMATION Since a metal casket will not be necessary for an immediate cremation; the funeral provider must inform consumers that they have a right to purchase an unfinished wood box or something similar, and the funeral provider must have these boxes available for purchase.

The Funeral Rule also requires providers to present you with an itemized bill of all the services you have selected and to inform you of any extra fees being charged for advance purchases, such as obituary notices or flowers.

Your Funeral Instructions

Regardless of what type of funeral or cremation you desire, set down your wishes in writing. Without prior instructions to anyone, your funeral may not be what you had in mind, and your survivors may feel impelled to spend beyond their means for a ceremony you would have disdained. Even though funeral and burial instructions are not legally enforceable, specifying them usually helps your survivors at a difficult time and gives you the best assurance that your wishes will be respected.

Unlike a will, little knowledge is required to draft funeral instructions. They can be as simple as the following:

Funeral Instructions for Burial

I, Jane Pole, hereby direct the disposition of my remains upon my death as follows:

1. It is my wish to be buried in plot #12 of Shady Rest Park, in the City of Omaha, Nebraska. The deed to this plot is with the original of these funeral directions.

2. It is my desire that all funeral arrangements be handled by the Gregory Funeral Home, 1234 Spring Street, Omaha, Nebraska; [telephone number].

The original of my last will and testament is in my safe-deposit box at the Fidelity Mutual Bank, Forest Street branch, 5678 Forest Street, Omaha, Nebraska (or at the Law Offices of Jeremy Jenkins, 9999 White Street, Suite 400, Omaha, Nebraska). My daughter, Anne Zelnick, has a copy of the key.

DATE: January 30, 1994

_____ Jane Pole

Funeral Instructions for Cremation

I, Jane Pole, hereby direct the disposition of my remains upon my death as follows:

1. It is my wish to be cremated, and that the cremation and all other arrangements be handled by Gregory Funeral Home, 1234 Spring Street, Omaha, Nebraska; [telephone number].

2. It is my wish that after cremation, my remains be disposed of as follows: taken to the top of Lookout Mountain in Omaha, Nebraska, and scattered over the rocks.

The original of my last will and testament is in my safe-deposit box at the Fidelity Mutual Bank, Forest Street branch, 1234 Forest Street, Omaha, Nebraska (or at the Law Offices of Jeremy Jenkins, 5678 White Street, Suite 400, Omaha, Nebraska).

DATE: January 30, 1994

Jane Pole

Be sure *not* to put your funeral instructions with your will for safekeeping. By the time your will is read, your body may already be in the ground, your survivors having been unable to read your cremation request and your request concerning the disposal or retention of your ashes.

If you fail to instruct someone regarding your wishes, your surviving spouse or next of kin will be required legally to make those decisions for you. Courts may have to become involved if a dispute arises about which "next of kin" is closest.

Remember, scattering cremains is restricted in some states. Laws should be checked before finalizing instructions.

Organ Donations

You can bequeath your healthy organs to medical science when you die. Donation is a simple procedure and is made possible in all 50 states and the District of Columbia through the Uniform Anatomical

---

Rachel wanted her body to be cremated when she died. She wrote out her funeral and cremation instructions formally, directing her sister, Karen, to scatter her ashes in the woods at her favorite lake. Upon her death, Karen arranged for Rachel's cremation but thought her additional instruction too time-consuming and dispersed her ashes in Rachel's backyard. Rachel's family was very upset and attempted legal action against Karen. Unfortunately for the family, they have no legal recourse. Funeral and burial instructions are not legally enforceable.

Gift Act. Go to your local Department of Motor Vehicles and ask for a donor card. Fill it out, have it witnessed, and have it laminated to the back of your driver's license. The Living Bank, a national non-profit organization in Houston, can also provide you with a Uniform Donor Card. Send a self-addressed, stamped envelope to The Living Bank, P.O. Box 6725, Houston, TX 77265.

In addition to attaching the donor card to your driver's license, be sure to tell your family, your doctor, and any estate-planning adviser that it exists and where it is located. A standard donor card might read:

I hereby make an anatomical gift effective upon my death
____ Kidney ____ Eye ____ Any Organ

_____
Signature of Donor

_____
Witness

_____
Witness

Sale of Organs for Transplants

Attempting to sell your organs for transplant purposes is against the law. It is a violation of federal law to sell or receive an organ for money, punishable by a fine of $50,000 or a prison sentence of five years. All states have similar laws.

3

CONTRACTS

For better or worse, many facets of our lives are dictated by contracts. As a result, contract disputes are quite common. Buying a home, a car, and even an appliance necessitates your entry into an agreement to make payments in return for a product that may provide certain warranties. You know that employment and services are often covered by contracts, but you may not be aware that you are entering into a contract when you order a hamburger at a fast-food restaurant, hop the bus to go downtown, or hire a baby-sitter.

Moreover, contract disputes are governed by two sources of law. Traditional contract law developed from the common law and covers many types of contracts, such as contracts for services. However, contracts for the sale of goods are covered by the Uniform Commercial Code (UCC) as it has been adopted in the various states. Generally, it is much easier to make a contract under the UCC than under the common law.

Finally, many elements of contract law are the same under both the common law and the UCC. However, in other cases, the law may be very different. It should also be noted that both types of contract law may vary from state to state.

DOES IT HAVE TO BE IN WRITING?

Both common law and state laws protect you against breach of contract. Valid contracts are often made orally, but certain contracts are required by law to be in writing. These include:

104

- contracts for the sale of land
- contracts for the sale of any goods priced at $500 or more
- contracts in consideration of marriage (such as prenuptial agreements)
- contracts that are incapable of being performed within one year
- agents' contracts
- promises to discharge or answer for the debts of another

The law that governs oral contracts, the Statute of Frauds, has a number of exceptions. The best general rule to follow is that if a contract involves something you cannot afford to lose, *get it in writing!* A written contract provides the best evidence if you need to go to court to enforce it.

Contracts don't have to be in formal, legal language, but this doesn't necessarily mean that you can easily draft one yourself. A well-drafted contract should spell out in exact, detailed terms what each party expects from the other and should cut down on the possibility of expensive or time-consuming legal procedures in the future. It's usually a good idea to use an attorney to either draft an agreement or review one that has been sent to you, particularly if it involves large sums of money.

THE ELEMENTS OF A CONTRACT

A valid contract must contain three necessary elements: the offer, acceptance, and consideration (payment).

The Offer

A contract begins with one party making an offer or proposal to another to enter into an agreement. To be valid, the offer must satisfy three requirements: (1) There has to be serious intent to enter into the contract; (2) the terms of the contract must be definite; and (3) the offer must be communicated to the person being offered the contract (the offeree).

THE INTENT OF THE OFFER   The offer has to be made with the intention that the deal be made then and there, not sometime in the future. Statements such as "I'm asking a hundred dollars" or "I won't take anything less than a thousand dollars" indicate that there is a present intent to enter into a contract. But phrases such as "I'm hoping to get a hundred dollars" or "Are you interested?" leave doubt as to whether further negotiations are needed or whether the offer is complete.

But if a joke is judged to have been made in such a way that a reasonable person could believe the statement was made in good faith, a court could consider it valid.

> *Suppose Jerry bought a new convertible, and that on a rainy evening the convertible top got stuck and refused to go up, resulting in a soaking for Jerry and his passengers. Feeling frustrated and a little embarrassed, he told his friend Millie that he'd "unload this clunker for $20." Millie pulled out a $20 bill and said "I'll take it off your hands."*
>
> *Jerry's comments were obviously meant as a joke, said in frustration, and they do not constitute a legally binding offer.*

ADVERTISEMENTS AS OFFERS   Commercials and advertisements on television or radio or in print are generally not considered to be valid offers but merely invitations to make offers. Such advertisements are not usually specific enough to meet the requirements of an offer, because they do not state who may accept, how many may accept, how one accepts, or the time limitation in which one may accept. Therefore, under traditional contract law, retailers are generally not under an obligation to sell a product at an advertised, but mistaken, price, for instance.

Remember: Deceptive advertising practices, such as "bait and switch," are generally prohibited by state consumer protection laws and not by contract law. Customers who think a store or retailer may be engaged in deceptive advertising practices should complain to their state attorney general.

If you read in the newspaper that microwave ovens are on sale at the appliance store for $99, and you are told when you arrive at the store that the newspaper misprinted the ad and the actual sale price is $299, the store is *not* required under contract law to sell the product for the advertised price.

Some advertisements may be specific enough to constitute an offer. A store should be required to honor an advertisement that states: "Compact disc player Model XL 402 will be sold for $150 to the first five customers who come into the store on Saturday, June 2." The specificity of this advertisement would make it a valid offer. By the specificity of the terms, it is clear what one must do to accept the offer.

OFFERS AT AUCTIONS   At an auction the auctioneer is not making an offer to sell to the highest bidder, but is actually inviting offers from the bidders. Most auctions are "with reserve," which means that the auctioneer has the right to withdraw an article before it's sold. Bidders may also withdraw a bid before the auctioneer accepts it; the auctioneer accepts a bid only when the hammer falls.

During an auction "without reserve," the auctioneer must sell the article to the highest bidder and cannot withdraw an article. The bidder, on the other hand, may withdraw the bid at any time before it is accepted.

THE TERMS OF THE CONTRACT   The court won't enforce a contract if the terms are not clear or if they leave undefined areas for interpretation. Generally, an offer has to include:

the names of the parties entering into the contract
the subject matter of the contract
the price of the article or service
time for performance

For example, Rosalie told her neighbor, Claire, that she'd like to sell her three acres of farmland for a fair price. Claire quickly responded that she'd be glad to pay "a fair price" for the land. But Rosalie's vague statement was too indefinite to be considered an enforceable offer.

Sometimes a court will enforce a contract despite the fact that a specific price or time for performance is not spelled out in the contract. For instance, Fred's Landscaping Company offered to till and seed five acres of Pete's property, but the two didn't specify price.

Once the job was completed, Pete refused to pay what he considered an exorbitant bill, and the matter eventually went to court. Rather than void the contract, the court may eventually decide that Pete should pay Fred the equivalent of the fair market value of the services he provided.

AN OFFER MUST BE COMMUNICATED   An offer is not an offer until it is received directly from the person making the offer, but offers can be implied. For instance, if you went into a hair salon for a haircut and didn't ask the price or look at the price list posted on the wall, you can't legally refuse to pay the posted price, because your behavior indicated your acceptance of the offer being made.

TERMINATION OF OFFERS   An offer can be terminated in a number of different ways. If you are not interested in an offer, you can reject it, thereby officially terminating it. If you change your mind later and want to accept it, you can only hope that the offer will be made again, because your original rejection has terminated the offer.

If you are making the offer and want to terminate it, you can do so at any time before it's accepted, and its revocation is effective as soon as the person considering the offer receives notification.

But if the person making the offer has already started performing his or her end of the bargain, it's too late for the offer to be revoked.

Suppose Bernard offered to pay Ernie $50 to rake the leaves from his front lawn. Ernie begins raking and is halfway done when Bernard decides to do the work himself. Since Ernie has already started the job, Bernard is not legally entitled to revoke the offer.

In order to revoke an offer that has been made to the general public, the person making the offer must do so in the same manner in which it was made. For example, Lisa places an ad in the newspaper, offering a $200 reward for anyone who finds her lost watch. Lisa later decides that such a large reward is beyond her means. She then runs a similar announcement in the same newspaper a few days later revoking the reward offer. Sarah finds Lisa's watch and returns it. Not having seen the revocation, she asks for the reward. Lisa is not legally required to pay Sarah, because she has revoked the offer in the proper manner.

Sometimes the person making the offer will set a time limit on

> Daniel is shopping for a new car and sees a car he likes at his local dealer. Daniel and the salesman discuss the price of the car, and the salesman states, "If you buy this car today, you can have it for $12,495." Daniel doesn't like being pressured by salesmen and says no, he doesn't want to buy a car today. The salesman again states, "This price is only good if you buy the car today." Daniel again says, "No." Daniel's rejection has terminated the offer. If Daniel later decides that he wants to buy that particular car, the salesman is under no obligation to offer it to him for $12,495.
>
> However, salesmen often state that an offer is good only if you accept it that day. This is a negotiating tactic that increases stress and is designed to get you to make a purchase before you are ready to do so. You should usually refuse such an offer—at least for a while—so you can reflect on whether the offer is really a good one and whether you are ready to make a purchase. In many instances the same offer will be made again if you decide you want the product.

how long the offer will remain open. In such cases failing to meet the deadline automatically terminates the offer. If no fixed time period has been stated, the offer will usually end after what is considered a reasonable time. For example, if the product offered is perishable (such as vegetables or flowers) or if it fluctuates quickly in price (such as commodities or stocks), a reasonable time may be only a few days, hours, or even minutes.

What follows is a hypothetical situation involving an offer.

THE PROBLEM

At a yard sale, Jill offers to sell a rowing machine to Jennifer for $20. Jennifer makes no response and leaves the yard sale. Jennifer's departure terminates the offer, because it is not reasonable to require Jill to wait before offering to sell the rowing machine to another party; therefore, Jennifer cannot return to the yard sale and demand the same offer. However, if Jill and Jennifer are friends and Jill offers to sell her rowing machine to Jennifer for $20 and no time limit is stated for the offer to remain open, a reasonable limit would probably be several days, unless someone else buys it first or unless Jill indicates she will hold it for Jennifer until Jennifer decides whether she wants it.

WHAT TO DO

In considering whether to accept an offer or in making an offer, it is a good practice to set a time limit for acceptance. Since Jill and Jennifer are friends, Jill could set a definite time limit on the offer to Jennifer, such as one week. Both parties are then clear on the time for acceptance.

If the terms of an offer become illegal before they are accepted, the offer is automatically terminated. For instance, Howard, a Michigan resident, agreed to buy and send five lottery tickets every month to Elaine in Pennsylvania, charging her the cost of the tickets plus a $20 monthly service fee. Before Elaine could take him up on his offer, the Michigan legislature voted to eliminate the lottery. The termination of the lottery terminated Howard's offer.

An offer is also terminated if it becomes impossible to fulfill before it's accepted. Suppose a cleaning service offers to clean an office building on a daily basis for $500 a month. If the building burns to the ground before the building's owner can accept the offer, the offer is considered terminated.

Acceptance

The next step in creating a valid contract occurs when the offer is properly accepted. Proper acceptance requires that:

- The offer may be accepted only by the person to whom the offer has been made.
- The acceptance must be identical to the terms of the offer.
- The acceptance must be communicated to the person to whom the offer was made.

WHO MAY ACCEPT THE OFFER   Only the person to whom the offer has been made may accept the offer. Suppose Maria offers to sell Jack her personal computer for $800. Jack isn't interested but tells Carol about Maria's offer. Carol contacts Maria and asks whether she can buy the PC. The original offer is not valid, because Maria's offer to Jack is not transferable to a third party.

THE ACCEPTANCE AS "MIRROR IMAGE" Under traditional common law, the acceptance must be identical to the offer, that is, a "mirror image" of the offer. The person making the offer must completely understand the terms without qualifications. For example, Nate offers to build a garage for Eileen for $1,500. Eileen accepts the offer but adds a provision that Nate will also build a shed next to the garage. Since this provision is an additional term to the original offer, it is not a valid offer. Eileen's proposal is a counteroffer, which Nate is free to accept.

Under the Uniform Commercial Code the acceptance does not have to be identical to the offer. Acceptance occurs even if the acceptance contains terms different from or in addition to the offer, subject to certain restrictions. For example, B.G.D. Wholesalers offers to ship to Albert, a filmmaker, five camcorders at a total cost of $6,000. Albert accepts the offer but stipulates that the camcorders must be sent within four days. B.G.D.'s offer has been accepted under the UCC, and the delivery date is an additional term that is considered a proposal for the contract. The proposal becomes part of the contract unless the offer limited acceptance to the original terms or the party making the offer objected to the added term within a reasonable time.

COMMUNICATING ACCEPTANCE The person to whom an offer has been made must let the person making the offer know that the offer is being accepted. Acceptance may be communicated face-to-face, by telephone, mail, telegraph, or fax.

When an acceptance is sent through the mail, it becomes legally effective when it is properly stamped and dropped into the mailbox.

SILENCE AS ACCEPTANCE Under traditional common law, silence doesn't usually constitute acceptance. But silence may mean acceptance if the parties agree to it ahead of time or if their prior conduct indicates that silence affirms a contract:

Suppose Laura mows Rob's lawn once a week for the whole month of May, as she has been doing every spring for the past three

Suppose Lee offers to sell Andy a parcel of lakefront property for $200,000. Andy receives the offer and immediately responds by letter that he would like to buy the land for the asking price. Andy's acceptance gets lost in the mail, reaching Lee several weeks later. In the meantime Lee had agreed to sell the parcel to someone else. Andy has a valid contract, effective when he mailed his acceptance, and should contact Lee to make his case and/or contact an attorney if he still wishes to buy the property.

years. When she sends her bill to Rob, Rob refuses to pay it, claiming that he had not contracted for the work *this* spring and had intended to hire someone else to do the job. Because Rob had remained silent for an entire month while the job was being done, his silence would probably be considered legal acceptance of Laura's work, and he would be responsible to pay the usual mowing fee.

Under the Uniform Commercial Code, offers may be accepted in any reasonable manner, including silence if that is reasonable under the circumstances. Suppose that you receive notice that your daily newspaper rate is increasing to $.50 per day for delivery. If you do not cancel your subscription, your silence would constitute acceptance of the new rate.

Payment (Consideration)

It's not enough that both parties agree to the terms of the contract. There must be payment—"consideration" or "bargained-for exchange." The consideration may be an act (such as a statement that you will sell your friend your car for $5,000), a forbearance to act (such as a statement that you forgive a debt), or a spoken promise to act (such as "I'll give you $25 tomorrow if you mow my lawn"). The act or promise must involve each of the parties giving something up; it cannot be something they were already obligated to do. Ralph agrees to wash Alan's car for $20, a job he had done often in the past. Halfway through the task, Ralph tells Alan that he'll finish the car for another $10. Since Ralph is already obligated to do the job for $20, the additional $10 would not be valid consideration since Ralph was not giving up anything he wasn't already required to give up.

Another example of this situation occurs if you have already agreed to purchase something for a set price, and when you arrive to pick up your purchase, the seller tells you that you can take the goods only if you pay an additional amount for them. This retroactive price increase would not be enforceable.

THE PAROL EVIDENCE RULE   Parol evidence is evidence of agreements that are not included in the written contract. Under traditional contract law, once a contract has been signed, it's presumed to include all the oral agreements and details that have been discussed and agreed to prior to the drafting of the formal contract. The parol evidence rule prohibits the parties from coming back later and arguing that despite what is written on paper, certain oral agreements were made and not included in the final agreement.

For example, Jessie and Andrew meet with a carpenter to discuss the remodeling of their kitchen. Jessie explains that the remodeling must be completed by February 6, and the carpenter states that the work can probably be completed by that date. However, the contract previously signed by the parties on January 3 and intended by them

Something given or performed in the past is not valid payment. Suppose Stephen was put through college by his wealthy Uncle Oscar. Upon graduation, Uncle Oscar demands that Stephen come to work for him because he has paid for Stephen's education. Stephen is under no obligation to comply with his uncle's request, because no contract or bargain had been made between them. The cost of his education was a gift, not payment in advance for services.

as a final and complete agreement on all aspects of the project states that the work will be completed within a reasonable time but no later than February 15. Jessie and Andrew cannot require the contractor to complete the project by February 6, because that date was not included in the final agreement.

This traditional rule is usually not applicable to contracts for goods that are covered under the Uniform Commercial Code (UCC). Under the UCC, the rule has two parts. First, if the parties intended that a written contract was the final agreement on certain terms, neither party can contradict those written terms with evidence (parol evidence) of agreements made and not included in the final written contract. For example, Dan and Debby agree to buy a car from Tom for $2,500. They agree to that price in writing, and they intend the document to serve as the final agreement on the price of the car. Under the parol evidence rule, neither party can use other evidence to show that there was an earlier agreement concerning the price. However, the final agreement on the price of the car would not keep one party from introducing parol evidence regarding what kind of warranty came with the car.

The second part of the rule states that if the parties to a contract intend the written agreement to be final for their entire agreement, the parties cannot use evidence of earlier agreements to add to the contract. In this case, the written agreement is the complete statement of the agreement between the parties, and nothing else can be added to the agreement. This part of the rule, for example, would permit parol evidence of a warranty on the car Dan and Debby purchased from Tom, unless the written agreement on price was intended to be their final and exclusive agreement on all terms including warranties. The parol evidence of a prior agreement might still be allowed, however, to show that the parties did not intend the contract to be a complete expression of their agreement.

Remember: Because the parol evidence rule may restrict or limit parties to the terms of the written agreement, you should carefully review any contract before signing it and make sure that all of the terms and conditions are correct. Also, make sure that any oral agreements are in the written contract.

UNENFORCEABLE CONTRACTS

Even when you have an offer, acceptance, and consideration, you may not always have an enforceable contract.

Incompetent Parties

Not everyone is capable of entering into binding contracts. Someone who lacks the mental capability or is too drunk or drugged to understand the nature, the purpose, and the result of the contract is considered incapable of entering into a valid contract.

Minors, usually children under the age of 18, may refuse to comply with a contract if they so choose. For example, 17-year-old Bart agreed to pay Don $800 for the use of his resort condo in Panama City, Florida, for a week. Bart signed the lease and promised Don he would send him a check for the rent. After Bart spent the week in the apartment, he refused to pay Don the $800. Unfortunately, Don can't sue Bart and force him to pay. Bart is a minor, so he's not required to hold up his end of the bargain, although he has the right to enforce a contract against an adult.

Exception: If the contract involves the "necessities of life," including food, shelter, clothing, and other essentials, a minor may be required to comply with the contract.

Illegal Contracts

A court will not enforce a contract that involves a violation of the law. If Beth agrees to sell Eric cocaine for $100, the contract would be void since the parties are contracting to engage in activities that are against the law.

Contracts Induced by Fraud or Duress

Jodi bought a sedan from Hardly Used Cars but later discovered that the dealer had rolled back the odometer. Because the dealer misrepresented the product and fraudulently induced her to enter into the contract, Jodi can return the car and get her money back.

Contracts induced by duress, either physical or financial, are also voidable.

Annette wanted a stamp in Marjorie's collection that was valued at $50,000. Marjorie refused to sell Annette her prized stamp at any price. Annette then threatened to reveal that Marjorie had been arrested 20 years ago for shoplifting. Marjorie, afraid of the bad publicity, agreed to sell the stamp well below its known value. She was induced by duress and can ask the court to void the contract.

Unfulfillable Contracts

Not all valid contracts can be fulfilled. Even those that meet all the qualifications—offer, acceptance, consideration, competent parties, and legal subject matter—sometimes fall short of completion for a variety of reasons and are considered "discharged."

Impossibility

You agree to buy a car and to exchange money and title next Wednesday. On Tuesday the car catches fire and explodes. In most jurisdictions the contract would be discharged because there was an inability to perform the contract the next day.

Rescission

Bill promises to wash Alice's car on Friday morning, but the weather forecast calls for a 100 percent chance of rain in the afternoon. Both parties agree that washing the car that morning would be a useless exercise, so they mutually rescind their agreement.

Rescission and restitution occur when mutually rescinding the contract is not enough because the parties will not be restored to their previous positions. Restitution is necessary because one party has already received a benefit from the contract and will be "unjustly enriched" if the contract is only rescinded. Building on the example above, when Bill promises to wash Alice's car, Alice pays Bill the $20 in advance. When they rescind the contract because of the expected rain, Bill will have to make restitution to Alice by returning the $20. Otherwise, it would be unfair for Bill to keep the money now that he doesn't have to wash the car.

Substituting a New Contract

Alice still wants her car washed, so she calls Bill and says that although Friday is not a good day to wash her car, Sunday would suit her better. If both agree, the old contract is thereby revoked, but a new one has been created.

Novation

Jack has agreed to rent his house to Bertha for $1,000 a week. At the last minute, Bertha comes down with the flu but informs Jack that her friend Rita would like to rent it in her place. The contract is discharged, but a new one takes its place with different parties. This creates a "novation."

DISSATISFACTION

Dissatisfaction can occur for many reasons that do not relate specifically to the agreement itself. For example, after delivery of a carpet the buyer decides it is not the right color for the room, although the color of the carpet is the color the buyer ordered. Where a product or service has been warranted to be of a certain type or quality, that warranty establishes a standard for the goods or services that becomes part of the contract. In these circumstances, if the goods or services fail to reach that standard, the seller of the goods or provider of the services has breached the contract by breaching the warranty.

What can you do to help ensure that you receive the quality of goods and services you expect when you agree to a contract? First, be as specific as possible. Clearly state what you want in the goods or services. Also, make sure the seller or provider knows what you are expecting and for what purpose you are using the goods or services. If possible, make certain that the contract explicitly states the warranty you expect to receive for the goods or services.

If you receive goods or services that are not at the level you expected, ask the seller to take back the goods, if possible, or to reduce the price of the goods or services you received. If the seller refuses, try to arrange for mediation or arbitration. You may also file a complaint with the local Better Business Bureau and the state office

Gary takes his car to Stan's Brake Shop and asks Stan to install new brakes on all four wheels. Stan installs the brakes and tells Gary, when he picks up the car, that he installed new front and rear brakes. As Gary is driving away from the shop, he realizes that the brakes aren't working as well as he thought they should. Upon investigating this matter, Gary discovers that Stan installed used brakes instead of new ones. Stan has breached the warranty by stating that new brakes were installed rather than used ones. By installing used brakes, Stan has not met the standard of the goods required under the contract.

In another situation, Charles contracts with a catering service to cater a reception for his parents' anniversary. Charles approves a menu that includes crabmeat salad, his mother's favorite dish. At the reception, Charles discovers the crabmeat salad contains chopped celery, the one food his mother dislikes. Charles is very disappointed with the salad, but there has been no breach of contract, because there were no specifications pertaining to the ingredients in the salad. If the contract had specified crabmeat salad without celery, the contract would have been breached. Even without specifications, if the crabmeat had been spoiled, that would have constituted a breach of contract because the contract assumes the food is edible.

of the attorney general. Finally, you may file suit for breach of contract in small-claims court.

BREACH OF CONTRACT

To breach a contract is to fail to fulfill one's responsibility under it. If you believe that someone has breached a contract, it's up to you to prove both that the other person has breached it and that you have performed your obligations or were excused from them. In contract cases the person bringing the action (the plaintiff) may ask for payment to compensate for losses resulting from a breached contract. In deciding such an action, the court attempts to place a successful plaintiff in the same position that person would have been in had the other party (the defendant) not broken the agreement. This is accomplished by the awarding of compensatory damages.

The law provides a standard formula for determining damages, depending on what kind of contract is involved—for example, an employment contract, a construction contract, or a land sale contract. If an individual breaches a contract for the sale of land, the standard measure of damages is the difference between the price specified in the contract and the fair market value of the land.

Suppose Lucy agrees to buy a plot of land for $20,000 from Ron. Realizing that the land is worth much more, Ron sells it to another party for $30,000, the fair market value of the land. Lucy can sue Ron for breaching the contract and demand $10,000, the difference between the contract price and the fair market value determined by an appraiser.

In addition to the standard measure of damages, a plaintiff may also recover *consequential damages*. This is possible when both parties were aware at the time they entered into the contract that if it were breached, the nonbreaching party would suffer economic loss beyond the standard measure.

If an award of monetary damages will not sufficiently compen-

A ballet company hired Lenny to build a set for an upcoming performance. The contract stated that "time is of the essence" and that the construction had to be completed by January 2. Costumes were made, tickets were sold, and the ballet company expected to net about $10,000. The set was not completed by the January 2 deadline. The ballet company can sue Lenny for breach of contract. They are entitled not only to recover what they already have paid him but also to receive "consequential damages," the cost of costumes and the profits they would have made had he not breached the contract.

sate the injured person, a court may require the breaching party to comply with the contract; that is, it may demand "specific performance." Suppose you enter into an agreement with your neighbor to buy a strip of land between your two properties. You hire a contractor to build a garage on the property, but before you can break ground, your neighbor changes his mind and offers to return your money. At this point, neither money nor another parcel of land will help you, only the land that borders your property. You can request that the court demand "specific performance," in this case, the conveyance of that particular parcel of land. Punitive damages are generally not awarded in contract cases (as they often are in personal injury cases). Also be aware that there may be a tort without personal injury.

Remedies to Breach of Contract

Not all problems of breach of contract end up in the law courts. There are many informal steps you can take to settle disputes to your satisfaction. In addition, there are alternative dispute procedures such as arbitration and mediation that can be considered for aid and guidance.

What follows are hypothetical situations involving breach of contract.

THE PROBLEM

Darlene purchased a portable dishwasher from an appliance store. The dishwasher worked fine for five weeks, but in the fifth week the spraying wand in the top of the dishwasher fell off its track and onto the heating element, where it melted. Since the dishwasher came with a warranty on all parts and labor for one year, Darlene called the store, told them what happened, and asked when they could come out to repair it. The manager told her the spraying wands come off their track only if the customer overloaded the dishwasher, and the warranty did not cover this abuse.

WHAT TO DO

1. Darlene should contact the manufacturer of the defective appliance at the phone number and address listed on the warranty. She should explain when and where she bought

the appliance, what the problem is, and when it occurred. She should also record the date of the phone call and write down the name of the person she spoke with. If there is a resolution of the issue agreed to on the phone, she should write a letter to that person repeating what she told them on the phone and what the resolution was. She should be sure to keep a copy of this letter for her files.

2. If the manufacturer does not resolve this matter on the phone, Darlene should send a letter explaining the problem again and asking for a resolution. This letter should be sent by certified mail—return receipt requested—to the manager of their customer service department. If this letter does not resolve the issue, she should send another letter and ask the company to agree to an alternative dispute resolution process, such as arbitration or mediation.

3. If none of these tactics works, Darlene should report the problem to the attorney general's office in her state, describing the situation and giving them copies of the letters sent to the manufacturer. She may also decide to file a claim in small-claims court. Each jurisdiction has different rules and procedures that govern its small-claims court, so check with your local small-claims court to find out its requirements.

THE PROBLEM

Judy wants to convert her screened porch to a family room. She calls a local contractor, Henry, and he looks over the porch and tells her it will cost around $3,000. She is pleased with that price and tells him to do the work. Henry spends several days on the project, and when it is completed, he gives Judy a bill for $5,000. Judy is flabbergasted and asks why the bill is so much

Although arbitration can be useful to consumers, it is not always preferable to litigation. For example, consumers generally must pay part of the arbitrator's fee. If the manufacturer has the right under the contract to select the arbitrator, the consumer may be faced with a decision-maker who depends upon the manufacturer for a large share of his or her business.

higher than his original estimate. Henry tells her it just cost more than he had thought.

WHAT TO DO

First, Judy should explain to Henry why she believes she has been overcharged. She and Henry might be able to resolve the matter between them. If not, Judy can file a complaint with the Better Business Bureau and with her state's attorney general's office. If her state requires that contractors be licensed, she can file a complaint with the licensing authority. (Such an authority may also have a procedure for resolving fee disputes.) Finally, Judy may have a right to sue Henry for violating the state's consumer protection statute, if his conduct is considered to be unfair and deceptive.

Remember: Whenever you want someone to do work in your home—repair work, remodeling, electrical, plumbing, etc.—you should get several written estimates for the work that clearly state what work is covered by the estimates. Compare the estimates. If one estimate is much cheaper than the others, be certain it includes the same work. Even if this low bid is for the same work, beware of such offers, as they might be a sign of an unscrupulous contractor. Ask the repairman, contractor, etc., to supply references. Call the references and see if they were satisfied with the work.

Once you have decided to accept one of the estimates, ask the contractor to agree, in writing, that the estimate is the price for the work. Make the estimate binding. If there are unknown contingencies, spell out how those issues will be dealt with. For example, the contractor may state that the estimate assumes the porch floor is solid underneath, but if it is not solid, it will cost an additional specific amount to convert the porch into a room.

Always check with any appropriate licensing agency and the Better Business Bureau *before* contracting for any work in your home. Any special arrangements suggested by the contractor, such as a discount for payment in cash, might be an indication of an unscrupulous contractor.

4

WRONGFUL INJURY

Under common law, which is unwritten law based on custom and handed down to the United States from England, every person is responsible for his or her own wrongdoing.

In addition, both state and federal statutes protect certain personal rights, including the right to enjoy freedom and property without undue interference from others. If these rights are violated and the violation causes injury to you or your property, you can remedy the violation either by entering a mutually agreed upon settlement or by bringing a lawsuit against the person(s) who caused the damage. There are three types of harms for which you can recover damages:

1. those caused by *negligence*
2. those caused by *intentional acts*
3. those caused by *products and goods* that have entered the stream of commerce (discussed in detail in chapter 9)

NEGLIGENCE

A surgeon has just removed your right large toe because it was the source of circulation problems. Unfortunately, it was the left large toe that was causing the problem.

You're eating lunch at the corner diner. As you take the last bite of your sandwich, you feel glass crunching between your teeth.

123

You find that your mouth is cut, and you fear you have swallowed some crushed glass.

You're driving your two children to school when a cab driver goes through a red light, plowing into your car and injuring your children and causing you fright.

You've just spent a considerable sum of money having your hair colored and permed. Unfortunately, the hairstylist left the chemicals for these procedures on your hair too long; three days later, your hair becomes brittle and begins to break and fall out.

Injuries resulted in all four cases, not from intentional conduct, but because an individual did not exercise that degree of care under the circumstances that was expected; that is, the individual failed to meet a certain duty or standard required for the specific activity. In each of these cases, someone's negligence caused injury.

The surgeon's responsibility was to use the best judgment and exercise reasonable care in performing the surgery competently. Removing the wrong toe of a patient during surgery was irresponsible and negligent.

The restaurant's duty was to provide patrons with safe, uncontaminated food. The presence of glass or any material foreign to the substance on your plate may make the restaurant operator liable for your injuries.

Driving a car requires a duty to use care and common sense. If a driver fails to stop for a red light, not only has a traffic violation probably been committed, but a duty has been breached. If the driver causes an accident resulting in serious injuries to your children, you probably have a strong negligence case to take to court.

You may not always like your new hairstyle when you leave a salon, but the stylists' actions only become negligent when they burn your hair with chemicals or cause other such injury. Hairstylists are trained and licensed professionals who are expected to meet basic standards of care.

The mere fact that someone was negligent doesn't automatically give you the right to sue. Three elements are necessary before you have a chance to win a legal action:

1. You must be able to show that the negligent person has failed to meet an accepted standard of care. The common law has created a standard based on how a "reasonable man" would act in the same circumstances. Statutes, rules, regulations, and ordinances also set standards of care.

2. You must be able to show that your injuries are measurable, that is, that some significant damage was done.

3. You must be able to prove the other person's negligence was a substantial cause of your injuries.

Suppose the cab driver's negligence caused an accident, but nobody in your car was hurt. You can't sue the driver simply because the driver was negligent and should be reprimanded. If the law was broken, it's up to the police to charge the driver with a traffic violation. You can sue in a civil matter only if you have suffered measurable damages.

Intent is not an element in negligence. The cook or waiter probably didn't intentionally put glass into your food; the cab driver didn't plan to pass a red light and run into your car; the hairdresser wasn't attempting to burn your hair; and the surgeon did not intend to amputate the wrong toe. Instead, each made mistakes, and the mistakes were significant enough to cause harm, such as pain and suffering, to others; these "mistakes" make them liable for damages.

Defenses to Claims of Negligence

Let's assume that although the cab driver negligently went through the red light, you could have put your brakes on in time to avoid the accident had your vision not been blocked by your poodle riding in your lap. Your own negligence is said to be "contributory" and might prevent you from recovering a full award for the cab driver's negligence. A few states prohibit recovery of any award if the injured person was also contributorily negligent.

Instead of contributory negligence, some states follow the rule of comparative negligence. In comparative negligence cases, the plaintiff can recover damages even if he or she was negligent. Most jurisdictions allow the injured person to recover damages based on reduction in the amount of his or her own percentage of negligence.

Remember: *Laws differ from state to state. Check the relevant laws in your area and/or consult an attorney before pursuing legal action.*

Suppose you were involved in an auto accident and you suffered $20,000 in damages. The jury could decide that the other driver, the defendant, was 60 percent at fault; therefore, you would recover 60 percent of the damages, or $12,000. Some states require the injured person to prove the defendant at least 50 percent negligent before they permit any recovery.

Another aspect of negligence cases concerns the known risks the injured party might have assumed (assumption of risk). Let's say that you go to an indoor hockey game and choose to sit in an area where there is no Plexiglas separating you from the playing area. A flying puck hits your face, lacerating your eyelid and causing blurred vision. Bringing a successful negligence suit would be difficult, because you know that hockey pucks travel at significant speeds and you assumed the risk of being hit when you chose to sit in an unprotected area.

In addition, the admission ticket you purchased may have a disclaimer printed on the back that releases the stadium owner and/or operator from liability when an injury occurs. The disclaimer may also be posted on a sign near the entrance. In some states, if the language on a disclaimer is easy to understand and large enough to be conspicuous, it may protect the owner/operator. In other states, such disclaimers are not valid, and the owner cannot disclaim liability if he or she is clearly negligent.

Even in jurisdictions that permit disclaimers on tickets for sporting events, the owner/operator of a stadium may still be held responsible for negligent injury that does not arise out of the event itself. The following is a hypothetical situation involving negligence.

THE PROBLEM

Red sits in the bleachers in a stadium that is not kept in good repair, and the floorboards become weak and rotted. Red's foot goes through the rotted wood when stepping down on a slat on the bleacher, resulting in a serious leg injury. Despite the fact that a disclaimer was printed on the ticket and posted on the wall, the owner's negligence and failure to provide safe facilities in a public place can make him or her liable.

WHAT TO DO

Red should write a letter to the stadium explaining that his leg was injured when it went through a rotted slat in the bleachers. He should give the date and time of the accident, and send a copy of his admission stub if he still has it. Also he should describe the medical treatment he has received, if any, and what his doctor said about future medical treatment. In all likelihood Red will receive a call or letter from the owner of the stadium and/or the stadium's insurance carrier, asking for additional information concerning the accident and Red's injuries. Red may receive an offer to settle the matter. At that time it might be advisable for him to consult with a lawyer to see if the offer is a fair one. If the attorney advises Red to reject the offer and begin a lawsuit, he must take into account how much the attorney's fees would be in such a case if he won, and what the reasonable costs would be if he were to go to court. The offer he's advised to refuse may be reasonable after he takes into account all of the expenses and risks of litigation.

Your Liability for Someone Else's Negligence (Imputed Negligence, Vicarious Liability)

In certain instances one may be held responsible for someone else's negligence. Suppose the driver of a company truck causes an accident while on the job. The injured party may sue not only the negligent driver but the employer as well. This principle of law, called "respondent superior," makes an employer responsible for the acts of his or her agents if the injury was caused while the agent was acting within the scope of his or her employment. However, if the employee was on his or her way home at the time of the accident, the principle doesn't apply.

Similarly, in some states the owner of an automobile is responsible for the negligence of a driver who is a member of the owner's family or household, if that driver was given permission to drive

Roger went to the Grand Prix Raceway to drive go-carts. Before he began, he was required to sign a document releasing the raceway's owners and employees from liability for injuries or death, even if they were negligent. Roger signed the release and slid into a car to be the first driver of the day. As he came into the first curve, his tire hit an oil slick, sending the car into a cement wall. Roger suffered severe injuries and sued the raceway owners for negligence.

Despite the fact that he signed the release, a court found the owners liable. Roger proved that they were negligent for having failed to check the track for oil or obstacles before his drive. Their defense, that Roger assumed the risk of the go-cart ride, was not valid because, although Roger assumed risks normally associated with go-cart racing, he did not assume the additional risk of a foreign substance on the track. In some states agreements that release persons from their own negligence have no force if a lawsuit is eventually brought.

("family purpose" doctrine). Some jurisdictions make the owner of a car liable if the car is loaned to a driver the owner knows is inexperienced, irresponsible, or frequently drunk ("negligent entrustment" doctrine). In most jurisdictions a statute provides that the owners of automobiles are responsible for the negligence of any operator driving with the owner's permission, express or implied. These laws, usually known as financial responsibility statutes, also require the owner and/or registrant of a car to purchase insurance before the car is driven.

Professional Negligence

A professional, such as a doctor, is required to perform professional work according to the best judgment and a degree of competence expected of persons in that specialty. Professional negligence, whether by a doctor, lawyer, engineer, or accountant, is usually known as malpractice. For example, if a physician removes the wrong toe of a patient, the doctor is probably responsible for doing so. The doctor failed to properly identify the part of the body upon which to operate, a task that the community would expect of a surgeon. However, if an emergency arises during the course of an operation that requires the surgeon to end the operation quickly and bring the patient out of anesthesia, the doctor would not be held responsible for leaving sponges or an instrument in the patient. Under normal circumstances a surgeon is expected to count carefully the sponges and instruments used before closing a patient, but in this case a life-threatening emergency did not permit the surgeon to perform this procedure with the necessary care. This does not mean the surgeon did something negligent.

INTENTIONAL ACTS

Although negligence is the more common tort, another category of claim often made in a lawsuit is willful torts or intentional wrongs, which cover a wide range of injuries from assault to invasion of privacy. Intent means the desire to bring about a result or acting in a way that is almost certain to bring about a particular result. Intentional torts usually have a shorter statute of limitation, or time in which to sue, than negligence actions. In many states intentional torts have limitation periods of one year.

What follows is a hypothetical situation involving an intentional wrong.

THE PROBLEM

Rick lives in a building on a cobblestone-lined street in a historic district. A gas company lineman begins to dig up the cobblestones with a jackhammer. When Rick asks whether or not the lineman has a permit and intends to replace the cobblestones, the lineman pushes Rick, who falls and breaks his wrist. This is an intentional tort.

WHAT TO DO

Rick should first report the incident to the police and give accurate information about the accident to his physician. He should then write a certified or registered letter to the gas company identifying the lineman, explaining the circumstances, and describing his injuries. If Rick cannot come to an agreement with the company, he should retain an attorney to file suit.

Assault and Battery

Assault occurs when someone who has the apparent ability to cause imminent bodily harm intentionally commits an act that threatens a person. If someone points an unloaded gun at you and threatens to shoot, that person can be sued for assault, even though there were no bullets in the gun. It's enough that you believed you were about to be harmed. To constitute assault, there need be no contact or harm, but threatening words are not enough for an assault. For instance, it's not sufficient that someone says, "I'm about to kill you." But if a hand is moved toward a weapon or sharp object, this movement will probably qualify the action as an assault.

Battery involves actual and intentional physical contact without a person's consent. Being struck with a weapon, for example, or having a chain yanked from your neck is battery. The police may bring a criminal action against someone who commits assault or battery, and you may bring a civil action to recover medical or other expenses arising from your injuries.

Intentional Infliction of Emotional Distress

The intentional infliction of emotional distress is a willful tort involving outrageous conduct that causes severe emotional pain or discomfort. You have the right to sue a person who intentionally causes you extreme emotional distress. For example, suppose your neighbor tells you he's going to shoot your dog. You are very attached to the dog, and you start losing sleep, can't concentrate, stop eating, begin losing weight, and become nervous. You have a cause of action against your neighbor for the intentional infliction of emotional distress.

As a general rule, the negligent, unintentional infliction of emotional distress does not give rise to a cause of action for damages unless accompanied by physical injury, physical impact, or some other physical manifestation. Some states have recently begun to reject the physical impact rule and permit recovery of damages in cases based solely on emotional distress.

For example, suppose Marsha is walking with her 17-year-old daughter Miranda when a car mounts the sidewalk, misses Marsha, but hits Miranda. Marsha, who sees the whole accident, can sue for the negligent infliction of mental distress.

Marsha must sue the driver on behalf of her daughter, Miranda, because children under age 18 cannot sue in their own names. Such suits by "infants" cannot be settled without the permission of a judge. For this reason it is better if Marsha seeks the advice of an attorney for Miranda's case as well as her own.

False Imprisonment/False Arrest

False imprisonment or false arrest is the intentional detainment of someone by a person without authority. False imprisonment does not mean you were in prison for a crime you didn't commit; it means your right to freedom of movement was unjustifiably denied.

Suppose a store security guard suspects you of shoplifting and detains you in the store's offices for five hours before determining that you have not taken anything. You have an action for false imprisonment, because the guard kept you detained for an unjustifiably long time. If the person detained is found to have items that were unpaid for, the detention is usually justified; also, if a person is only momentarily detained, the period of time may not suffice to claim false imprisonment. But if you were detained for five hours and had not stolen anything, you may have a case not only against the guard but also against the store by which the security guard is employed, as well as the agency, if the guard works for one, on the theory of respondent superior. (This is a legal doctrine that places the liability on the employer for acts committed by an employee while performing his or her job responsibilities.)

You would be entitled to compensation for your loss of time, for physical discomfort or inconvenience, and any injury to health, as well as damages for emotional distress and humiliation. If the false arrest has been carried out by the police, you would also be entitled to compensation for any harm to your reputation as well as reimbursement for your attorney's expenses. Punitive damages may also be recovered if it can be shown that the guard or policeman acted with reckless disregard of your interests.

In such a case you should write a letter (with a return receipt) to the store and send a copy to the security agency, if you know its name. Explain the circumstances and state that you would like to talk to their representative as soon as possible. A good question to ask is "What do you intend to do about this?" If you cannot reach agreement with the store or the agency, you should consult an attorney.

Trespass

Your personal property and land are protected by law against infringement or damage. Trespass is any unauthorized entry to land. If your neighbor comes onto your land and chops down your sycamore tree, that neighbor can be sued for property damage as well as for trespassing—entering your property without permission or invitation.

Trespass to personal property occurs when someone, without justification or consent, damages, destroys, or physically interferes with another's use of goods. This tort is also known as *conversion*. Suppose Herbert, a local sheriff, mistakenly seizes Andy's car because Andy's finance company mistakenly gave Herbert the wrong license plate number. Andy has an action against Herbert for trespass as well as an action against the finance company for negligence.

Andy should contact Herbert and send him a copy of his bill of sale showing the origin and financing of his car. If this does not clear up the problem and if Andy cannot get the car back from Herbert, he will have to seek an order from the court, first to show he is not in arrears and then to show that the finance company made a mistake. He can later sue Herbert for trespass.

Nuisance

A nuisance is any inconvenience caused to another. Some nuisances relate to property, some are intentional, and others result from negligence. Nuisances can be public or private. A nuisance is an invasion or interference of any kind in a person's use or enjoyment of his or her personal property. A public nuisance is one that interferes with rights of the public to use, have access to, or enjoy property.

Suppose your next-door neighbor has landscaped his property in such a way that runoff from a heavy rain washes onto your lawn, damaging the grass. This is not a trespass, because no one came onto your property, but it is a nuisance. If the neighbor refuses to correct the damage, you can bring a nuisance action against him because he is interfering with your use and enjoyment of your land.

The following is a hypothetical situation involving a nuisance.

THE PROBLEM

Norm and Cliff own an attached house. Norm has a central-air-conditioning unit, which was installed on his roof. When in use, the unit's vibrations shake Cliff's roof. Cliff has spoken to Norm about it, but Norm claims the installer followed the appropriate procedures in installation and nothing can be done about the vibration.

Cliff has a case against Norm because Norm's air conditioner is interfering with Cliff's enjoyment of his land. Cliff can seek damages as well as an injunction against Norm to prevent him from using the unit.

WHAT TO DO

First, Cliff should write a letter to Norm, sending a copy to the installer if he knows who it is. Cliff should outline the problem and explain that the vibrations began only after Norm had the air conditioner installed. If Norm cannot get the installer to remedy the problem, Cliff will have to sue Norm to attempt to get a satisfactory resolution and is best advised to retain a lawyer.

Interference with Personal Property

The law creates a relationship called a "bailment" with another person from whom you borrow, lend, lease, or to whom you leave personal property. The person given temporary custody of the personal property in a bailment is required to care for it. If the property left as a bailment benefits the person who has temporary custody of it, that person will be required to treat it carefully and return it to you in the same condition it was in prior to the transfer.

Suppose your friend Madge needs to trim the foliage in her yard and asks to borrow your hedge trimmer. This loan is solely for her benefit; you receive nothing in return. Under the law, she is required to use the tool only for trimming her foliage. If she lends it to a friend or decides to start her own landscaping business using your trimmer, you can sue her for conversion (the unlawful appropriation of one's personal property). A person given temporary custody of property is required to use ordinary care and diligence in caring for it. It is that person's legal responsibility to return the property in the same condition in which you lent it. If Madge leaves the trimmer lying in her driveway and a car drives over it, or if she tries to cut down a tree with it and breaks a blade, she's required to replace it.

The law is different if you have given up temporary possession for your own benefit. Suppose your laptop computer has been malfunctioning and a friend offers to take a look at it free of charge. She is doing this solely for you, receiving no benefit herself, and is therefore responsible only for gross negligence—that is, she cannot leave it out in the rain or allow her two-year-old nephew to play with it.

If the transaction involves both parties receiving a mutual benefit, then the individual with temporary custody is legally required to use ordinary care while keeping it. Let's say you leave your antique grandfather clock at a repair shop. As long as the proprietor has a skilled person working on the clock and doesn't allow the potential for its misuse—for example, letting a child play with it—the proprietor is not liable if it malfunctions.

The following situations are common bailments in which the individual holding temporary possession has certain responsibilities.

DRY CLEANERS   Your dry cleaner is required to clean your clothing without damaging or losing it. If you're dissatisfied with the cleaning job, return the item and ask that it be recleaned. If the garment is damaged beyond repair by the cleaner, the owner is required to reimburse you only for the value of the clothing just prior to cleaning, not what it would cost you to buy a new one. If the item was two years old, you'll get the depreciated value, not the present purchase price. If you cannot reach an acceptable resolution with the cleaner, you may have to go to small-claims court to get satisfaction.

A dry cleaner is permitted to limit its liability for damage to clothing by printing a disclaimer on the claim ticket, stating that management will not be responsible for damages exceeding a certain dollar amount or the cost of cleaning. The same disclaimer is usually posted on a wall or other visible place in the dry-cleaning establishment to put the customer on notice of limited liability.

Although some of the transactions that occur between dry cleaners and customers are annoying, they are not necessarily legally negligent actions. Suppose you're told that the dress you'll need for an important business meeting on Friday afternoon will be ready on Friday morning at 7:00. When you go to pick it up, you find out that the dry cleaner had equipment problems and the dress won't be ready until Saturday. Despite the fact that the dry cleaner failed to meet its obligations, there's nothing you can do to be compensated for your inconvenience. The fact that the dry cleaner sends your garments out to be cleaned by a cleaning plant makes no difference.

CAR MECHANICS   An auto mechanic is required to use ordinary care in handling a vehicle you leave for repair. If the car in the mechanic's temporary custody is damaged because of negligence—for example, fire or water damage that occurred in the garage—you have the right to recover the present value of the car. If you drop your car off for a minor repair, informing the mechanic that you'll need to pick it up in three days because you have an important business trip ahead of you, and the mechanic fails to have it ready on time, you can sue the mechanic. But don't expect to recover substantial damages; at best, you may be entitled to the cost of renting a car until the mechanic completes the work, assuming you can prove the mechanic agreed to have the car ready for your trip.

If you do rent a car, after you pick up your car, send a copy of the car rental bill to the garage (via return receipt mail) explaining why you had to rent a car. If the garage refuses to pay for the rental, you should write to the home office of the garage, if it is a national company, and explain the problem. If you still receive no satisfaction, you will most likely have to sue in small-claims court.

Suppose the car is repaired, but you don't pick it up because you can't afford the repair costs. The mechanic has the right to hold on to the car (called a "mechanic's lien") until you can come up with the money. If it remains at the garage for some time and the mechanic is tired of waiting for payment, the mechanic has the right to get a court order to sell your car and recover the money you owe him, plus interest, storage costs, and the expense of holding the sale. If the selling price exceeds the incidental expenses, the mechanic is required to return the remaining amount to you.

PARKING LOTS   There will probably be a disclaimer of liability printed on the back of your claim ticket and posted at a conspicuous place when you park your car in a public parking lot. The disclaimer will state that the parking lot owner will not be held responsible for the theft of or damage to your car or any personal belongings left in the car. Courts will usually honor these disclaimers if the parking lot owner was not obviously negligent.

If the parking lot attendant takes your car keys, parks your car, and implies that the lot will be supervised in your absence, liability for any damage done to the car will rest with the parking lot owner. If the lot is left unattended or if the attendant leaves your keys in the car or someplace where they are accessible, you can sue the owner.

The owner will be liable for any damage caused to your car while parking it. And if the attendant fails to lock your car and something is stolen from inside the car, the parking lot owner will be held responsible.

If your car is damaged while in a parking lot or garage, you should first send the lot or garage a return receipt letter with a copy of the itemized list of damages. If you have had the damage repaired, you should include copies of the paid bill and canceled check. If something was taken from the car, you should try to locate the sales receipt showing the date when purchased and the price. You should also contact your insurance company if you have theft or collision insurance. Your company may pay you only a portion of your loss if you have a deductible policy; however, if your company later recovers from the insurance company of the garage or lot, you will then get back a portion of your deductible. If you have no theft or collision insurance, you will probably have to sue in small-claims court for the damages.

If you park your own car in an unattended lot, lock it, and take your keys, any damage done to your car becomes your problem because you're not paying for parking services. You're paying only for the use of the space, and this is not a bailment.

HOTELS   Hotels are usually liable for any theft from your room, unless you've left your door unlocked or are found to have been negligent in some other way. Hotels usually limit their liability to a certain dollar amount and suggest that all valuables be placed in the hotel safe, then, it's up to the hotel management to decide if they want to take on the liability of keeping large amounts of cash or valuables in their safe.

CHECKROOMS AND LOCKERS   The checkroom is required to treat your property carefully and return it to you in the same condition it was in when you left it.

Under common law, a hotel is responsible as an insurer for loss of a guest's property; therefore, if the checkroom is operated by a hotel, automatic liability follows for losses. Many states have statutes that limit the responsibility of establishments having checkrooms. These statutes usually require that notice be given to the public that liability is limited. For example, if a restaurant or theater posts a sign limiting its liability to $100, as long as it's clearly visible to the patrons, it is probably valid.

What follows is a hypothetical situation involving a bailment.

THE PROBLEM

Alicia leaves her mink coat with the attendant of the coatroom of Joe's Restaurant. No fee is charged, but there is a conspicuous sign saying the restaurant's liability is limited to $50 for lost property. When Alicia returns, the attendant can't find the coat and claims someone must have stolen it while she took a break. Joe's is liable to Alicia, but only for $50.

WHAT TO DO

Alicia should keep her receipt and send a copy of it to the restaurant together with an explanation of the circumstances. If the restaurant refuses to pay Alicia the $50, she can file suit in small-claims court for the full amount of the value of the coat. The restaurant will have the burden of proving there was a valid limitation posted.

Invasion of Privacy

Everyone has the right to privacy, without unreasonable intrusion into his or her personal affairs. In order to support a legal action that claims invasion of privacy, one of four types of activities must have occurred:

1. an unreasonable intrusion upon the plaintiff's solitude, such as eavesdropping by illegal wiretapping or peering into the windows of a house

2. the public disclosure of private facts, such as a department store posting notices around town that you owe it money, even if the facts are true

3. the appropriation of someone's name or appearance for the benefit of the user, for instance, if a company uses your photograph in an advertisement without your permission

4. any activity that places you in a "false light" in the public eye, such as a statement that you have an alcohol problem (whether or not the statement is true is irrelevant)

What follows is a hypothetical situation involving invasion of privacy.

THE PROBLEM

The *Local Dispatch*, a newspaper, accepts an advertisement for publication from Lebedeu Furniture. The ad has a picture of Roz wearing a bathing suit and sitting in her backyard on a Lebedeu chair. Roz sees the ad, which says "Relax on Lebedeu's." Roz did agree to have her picture taken when the chair was delivered, but she was never asked if she would approve of its use in an advertisement. Roz has a cause of action against Lebedeu Furniture for invasion of privacy, because they used her photo for commercial purposes without her permission. The *Local Dispatch* has done nothing illegal.

WHAT TO DO

Roz should write a return receipt letter to Lebedeu, claiming she did not authorize her photo to be used in their ad. She should ask someone to contact her immediately about the incident. If Lebedeu refuses to pay Roz a reasonable fee for the ad or make compensation for the invasion of her privacy, she should consult an attorney to pursue a lawsuit.

Defamation—Slander and Libel

Untrue spoken or written statements that damage a person's reputation are grounds for bringing a legal action. Libel is defamation of character through the written word. If the defamatory statement is spoken rather than written, it is called slander. A defamatory statement is not actionable unless the statement is "published," meaning that it is read or heard by a third party. The statement has to be found to be false. Truth is an absolute defense in most cases.

For example, if a co-worker tells a colleague that you are embezzling funds from the company, you can bring a slander suit against the co-worker if the statement is false and another person agrees to testify to its having been made. If someone writes a postcard that falsely accuses you of infidelity and sends it through regular mail, this can give you the right to sue for libel, if you can prove the statement false.

Public personalities are given less protection and have a greater burden of proving libel or slander. A celebrity or person in the public eye must do more than show that a newspaper's statement was false in order to recover damages. A public figure has to prove that the falsehood was made with the knowledge or suspicion of its falsity in order to recover damages.

What follows is a hypothetical situation involving slander.

THE PROBLEM

Leon has worked for the Acme Shoe Company for 10 years. Sid, his newly appointed manager, falsely tells his supervisor that Leon is a child molester. As a result, Leon is fired. Leon has an action against Sid for slander.

WHAT TO DO

Leon can first write a letter to Acme explaining that Sid lied about him and asking to be rehired; however, in such a serious case, retaining a lawyer as soon as possible is probably the best route to take.

Malicious Prosecution

Sometimes people use the legal system to carry out their own vendettas. Anyone who brings an unfounded criminal prosecution against an innocent party can be charged with malicious prosecution.

If you prove in a civil lawsuit that a person intentionally brought criminal proceedings against you for a malicious purpose, and charges against you were dismissed, you for a malicious purpose, and attorneys' fees, court costs, and other expenses involved in defending yourself against the criminal proceeding. In addition, you may be able to receive compensation for the damage done to both your personal reputation and your career or business, as well as compensation for embarrassment and mental anguish.

Strict Liability

A person who conducts an ultrahazardous activity that is extremely dangerous can be held liable for injuries suffered by a participant even though the harm was not intentional or negligent. For example, explosives, such as firecrackers, are considered to be ultrahazardous, and if someone is injured during their use, the person conducting the activity may be held strictly liable.

Your Liability for the Acts of Others

CHILDREN   Some states have statutes that make parents liable for the willful or malicious acts of their children. If no statutes are on the books, you, as a parent, probably have no liability unless:

- you are aware that your child has committed destructive acts in the past, yet you do nothing to stop your child
- you consent to or participate in wrongful acts
- your child was acting as your agent when the act was committed
- you negligently allowed your child to play with or have access to a dangerous instrument

Suppose a playmate of your 10-year-old son gives him a cigarette lighter. The boys play with it together and start a fire in your neighbor's garage. If your state has no parental liability laws, you would most likely not be held responsible, because your son had never committed such an act before, you were not aware that he had a lighter, you never gave your consent, and he was not acting as your agent.

What follows is a hypothetical situation involving liability for the acts of others.

THE PROBLEM

Sarah was given a moped by her parents for her twelfth birthday. The first time she used it, she had no mishaps. She invites Elizabeth to take a ride on it, and Elizabeth is seriously injured when Sarah, who is driving, crashes into a parked car. Even though the jurisdiction in which Sarah lives has no parental liability law, her parents may be held liable for Elizabeth's injuries because they might be found to have been negligent for entrusting Sarah with a dangerous instrument.

WHAT TO DO

Elizabeth's parents should have the police investigate the accident and make an official report. If Elizabeth's injuries are not severe, her parents can write a claim letter to Sarah's parents, asking them to forward the claim to their insurers. If an agreement cannot be worked out or if Elizabeth's injuries are severe, a lawyer should be retained to represent Elizabeth and her parents.

Dogs

Your liability for damage done by your dog or any injury it inflicts is governed by whether the dog has caused such damage in the past, whether you knew about it, or the type of dog you have. For example, if you knew the dog had a propensity for digging under your fence and damaging your neighbor's garden or if you were aware that the dog had attacked children in the past, you can be held responsible for doctor bills, lost wages, repairs to property damages, and other such costs.

RECOVERING DAMAGES

An injured party in personal injury cases may be entitled to demand both general and special damages. Suppose you suffered extensive injuries as a result of slipping and falling at a grocery store. General damages would include compensation for the pain and suffering you experience, past (from the time of the injury) and future, as well as

The Stetsons bought a two-month-old German shepherd puppy and were told that Shep (the dog) was gentle and loved children. Shep bit the first child who attempted to pet him. The child's parents threatened to sue the Stetsons, but because the dog was not known to have attacked anyone in the past, the Stetsons weren't liable. If they keep the dog and Shep bites someone else, they can be held liable because the standard of their knowledge has been established by the first incident. If the Stetsons' dog were a mature German shepherd, there may be responsibility even if the dog has never bitten anyone before. If such a dog exhibited aggressive traits, the owners can be held responsible.

for any resulting disability or disfigurement. Special damages consist of compensation for past and future medical bills and lost wages.

Sometimes, in addition to compensation for injuries, a judge or jury will award "punitive" damages to punish the responsible party if they believe the actions were malicious or willful. In negligence cases, punitive damages can seldom be recovered, because the negligent action was usually unintentional.

In cases such as a continuing trespass, the injured party cannot expect to be made whole with money. Instead, he or she should ask the court to issue an injunction to halt the infringing activity.

If the party responsible for causing damage is not receptive to your plight, the next step is to contact a lawyer.

5

CARS AND DRIVING

From deciphering sticker prices and dealer advertisements to being at ease with practices of salespeople, buying a car requires knowledge and preparation. In addition to securing good value, you need to know how to protect yourself from fraudulent practices and to understand your legal responsibilities to others.

BUYING A NEW CAR

The Contract

When you buy a new car, you need a contract of sale, which must include everything you and the salesperson/dealer have agreed upon verbally. If the salesperson promised you a free undercoating but failed to include it in the contract, it is indeed unlikely that it will be provided. A car dealership usually works with standard contracts that contain paragraphs of boilerplate provisions, but you have the right to make the additions and changes that reflect whatever agreements you and the dealer made together. To alter the standard contract, cross out the incorrect language, add the change(s) with either pen or typewriter, and be sure both you and the person signing on behalf of the car dealership initial the changes. Be sure you understand everything in the agreement, and don't sign it until you do. The contract should include the following:

• the names of the buyer and seller
• a description of the car, including the make, model, color, year,

engine size, and vehicle identification number, as well as additional equipment, such as power windows, tilt steering wheel, and CD player

- the price you have negotiated for the car and the financing terms, including the total amount to be financed, the annual percentage rate (APR), the length of the loan, and the total amount of interest to be paid

- a provision that the sale is contingent upon finding appropriate financing if you are not financing the car through the dealership

- the amount allowed for any trade-in you are making to offset the price, including identification of the car and its mileage. Unless you have taken the car across country or otherwise damaged or altered it since the dealer's initial appraisal, the dealer should not attempt to lower the trade-in amount offered to you originally.

- a cancellation provision that allows you to change your mind within a certain period of time and have your deposit refunded

- whatever warranties you have agreed on, both full and limited

Once you sign the contract, you are committed. This is true even if the car is not yet available to be delivered to you. Be sure to read the entire contract before you sign it, and be sure you understand each of its provisions.

Canceling the Contract

Suppose you put down a $1,000 deposit on a new car on Monday, planning to return the following Saturday to sign all the paperwork. In the meantime the dealer is having the car you want brought in from a neighboring state. On Friday you decide that you cannot really afford a new car and that you want to cancel the purchase. Since you have not entered into a written contract, you should not have much trouble canceling the deal and getting a refund.

The situation might be different if all the paperwork has been signed and the dealer has gone to a lot of trouble in locating and transporting the car. You have legally committed yourself to buying the car, but you would be protected if you had the dealer include a

> Steve and Martha fell in love with a 1994 convertible and were told by the dealer's salesperson that if their credit checked out, they could finance the car at 11 percent. The salesperson went to the phone, came back a few moments later, and told them that their credit was "no problem." The salesperson instructed them to sign some "insurance documents" that would enable them to drive the car home that night before the official paperwork was completed. They dutifully obeyed the salesperson. It was three weeks later when they discovered that what they had signed was a contract, obligating them to a loan with a 20 percent interest rate, not 11 percent. The dealer had apparently engaged in this unscrupulous practice with a number of unsuspecting consumers, who eventually took the dealer to court in a class action lawsuit.

cancellation provision in the contract that allowed you to change your mind within a certain time period without losing the deposit. There is no standard cancellation provision included in contracts for the sale of a car. If you do not insist on adding such a provision to the contract, you will not have this right. If you wait a lengthy period of time and then cancel, the dealer has the right to take you to court, asking for damages such as the profits lost or the time involved in locating and transporting the car, including even the time any salespeople spent with you.

If you are a minor (younger than 18 or 21, depending on the state), a car dealer cannot hold you legally responsible for a contract. Theoretically, you are too young to make such a large purchase and should not be held to such a commitment. Chances are that no dealer will sell a car without an adult involved in the transaction, signing the contract and making the obligation.

Title

A title is the legal document that shows car ownership and the right to sell or convey the car to another person. States vary on how legal title is passed to a new owner, but generally the process simply means that the former owner endorses the title over to the purchaser. When you borrow money to buy a car, the lender will usually hold on to the certificate of title until the loan is paid off.

Financing a Car

Most new-car buyers finance the purchase, paying the loan off over a period of several years. Dealerships frequently offer financing, but be sure to investigate other sources, including your own bank or credit union. Comparison shop before choosing the lender that best suits your needs and budget. The Truth-In-Lending Act, or TILA, simplifies matters because it requires lenders to reveal certain information in writing, including:

- the amount being financed
- the length of time allowed to repay the loan
- the amount of the monthly payments
- the finance charge
- the annual percentage rate (APR)
- the total number of payments

The APR relates the total finance charge to the length of time you have to repay the loan and the amount of credit you are receiving. The total finance charges will be lower on shorter loans because your monthly payment will be larger. Be sure to consider all the factors, not just the APR, when you finance a car.

Leasing Versus Buying

Car leases are of two kinds: closed-ended and open-ended. The open-ended lease, the less common type, requires lower monthly lease payments because it is based on what the residual value of the car is expected to be at the end of the lease period. If the estimate is inaccurate, the person leasing the car will have to make up the difference at the end of the period between the estimated and the actual residual value. (If the model has acquired a poor reputation or has otherwise lost its appeal to the buying public, the residual value may be lower than expected.) Closed-ended leases require higher monthly payments because the person leasing is not responsible for making good at the end of the lease if the residual value falls. You pay more, but there are no surprises at the end.

Leases generally require payment of a deposit as well as one or two months' payments in advance. You enter into a contract to lease the car for a certain period of time, usually three to five years. There may be certain details in your contract that are negotiable, so be sure the contract clearly states who pays the sales tax, license fee, title fee, and insurance, and who is responsible for repairs and maintenance, wear and tear of the vehicle, and mileage.

In your leasing agreement, be sure to cover options to renew or extend your lease, to terminate it early, even to purchase the vehicle. Keep in mind that in the event that you "total" your leased car in an accident, the insurance company will pay you the "blue book" value of the car, not the residual value due under the lease. You may find the leasing company looking to you to make up the difference between the two.

The Consumer Leasing Act (CLA) was passed in 1976 to protect consumers who lease a car (1) for personal, family, or household purposes; (2) for more than four months; and (3) if the total obligation is less than $25,000. The CLA requires the leasing company to provide written information specifying payments, sales tax, title, license fees, and insurance. The company must also state who will have to pay for repairs and maintenance, what warranties are provided, and how a purchase price will be computed if the lease has an option-to-buy provision. For more information about your rights under the CLA, write to:

The Federal Trade Commission
Credit Practices Division
Pennsylvania Avenue and Sixth Street, N.W.
Washington, DC 20580

What follows is a hypothetical situation involving paying for repairs of a leased car.

THE PROBLEM

Five months after Glenda leased a new car, it developed serious transmission problems. She called a towing company for help, but she had no idea who was responsible for the repairs—the leasing company or her.

WHAT TO DO

1. Glenda should check her lease to determine if her car is covered by the manufacturer's new-car warranty or if the company leasing the car to her is providing its own warranty. She must be certain that the warranty covers the transmission.

2. If the car is no longer under warranty, she will still need to refer to her lease to see whether the leasing company is responsible for after-warranty repairs or whether she'll have to pay for them. According to most lease agreements, the person leasing the car usually pays for repairs and maintenance after the new-car warranties expire.

PROBLEMS WITH YOUR NEW CAR

Forty years ago, new-car buyers were at the mercy of the dealer and manufacturer when they had problems with the car. Today, new-car purchases are protected by warranties, "lemon laws," and other laws to prevent unfair and deceptive practices. Not all remedies are available in every state.

Warranties

Every new car comes with warranties, both express and implied. Express warranties can be full or limited; full warranties are seldom given on the entire car, but rather on a particular part or group of parts. For example, if there is a *full warranty* on the car's drive shaft, the warranty will list four guarantees:

1. The drive shaft or a part of it will be replaced free of charge if it develops problems within a reasonable time of delivery.

2. Anyone owning the car during the warranty period can make use of the remedies the warranty offers.

3. If the dealer can't repair the problem after a certain number of trips to the service department, the buyer is entitled to a refund or to a new part plus installation.

4. The dealer will provide easily accessible service to the consumer.

If one of the four guarantees is missing, the part most likely carries only a *limited warranty*. An *express limited warranty* guarantees that the description and promises made about the car are accurate at the time of purchase.

If you buy the car from a dealership or any other merchant, the car also carries with it an *implied warranty of merchantability*, which basically guarantees that the car meets certain standards of quality and is suited to the purposes for which it was purchased. An *implied warranty of fitness for a particular purpose* is a little different, stating that the vehicle you purchased is suitable to be used for the special purpose you require. For example, if you need a four-wheel-drive vehicle to negotiate steep hills and mountains, and the salesperson assures you that Model XE will be powerful enough to do so, the implied warranty of fitness for a particular purpose should enable you to return the car if it fails to fulfill the promised tasks.

What follows is a hypothetical situation involving implied warranty of fitness for a particular purpose.

THE PROBLEM

Josh told the car salesman that he needed a family car that would have the capability of towing a boat. Acting on the advice of the salesman, Josh bought a particular utility van and was pleased with it until a few weeks later when he backed it up to his boat for the first time and realized it wasn't designed to tow something that heavy.

WHAT TO DO

1. Josh should drive the vehicle back to the dealership and speak with the salesman and the manager or owner, explaining the problem. He should tell the manager that he informed the salesman that this van was purchased to tow his boat, and that he was assured that the van could perform that particular function. Josh can attempt to rescind the sales contract and hope that the dealer refunds his money or works out an arrangement where he can get a vehicle

that can tow his boat. If the dealership refuses, he should go on to step 2.

2. Josh should contact the state attorney general's office and file a complaint. The salesman may have violated the state's unfair and deceptive practices laws. If this does not resolve the problem, Josh should consider going on to step 3.

3. Josh can bring a civil action against the dealership, but he must continue making car payments and attempt to be reimbursed later. The problem Josh will probably run into in getting a refund or an award in court is that the new-car contract he signed probably voided all implied warranties. His success would have been greatly increased had he demanded that the standard contract be amended to contain the implied warranty that the car be capable of towing a boat.

In 1975 Congress passed the Magnuson-Moss Warranty Act, making the manufacturer directly responsible for fulfilling new-car warranties. Other laws require manufacturers to develop informal dispute resolution methods, primarily arbitration, to settle conflicts with disgruntled car buyers.

HOW WARRANTIES WORK   Suppose that you've signed all the paperwork, consummating the car deal with the salesperson. You slip behind the steering wheel and shift into forward, only to find the gear shift in your hand! In some states you have legally accepted the car as soon as you leave the car lot; other states give you a little more time to reject the car. You now have a choice: You can require the dealer to fix the problem, or you can decide you just don't want the dangerous and defective vehicle and ask for a refund.

REVOKING THE CONTRACT   If you discover a defect two weeks after you have taken delivery of a new car, or if you have been driving the car despite its problems, it is probably too late to reject it. But you may still be able to revoke the contract if the defect is major, and you should put the dealer on written notice of the problem and return the car. If you have already put down a deposit or made any payments, you should be able to get your money back if the car is truly defective.

The following hypothetical situation involves getting a full refund after finding a defect in a new car.

THE PROBLEM

Sylvia bought a new car from a reputable dealer. Two days after driving it off the car lot, and on her way to Florida, the power steering made a screeching sound. Too far from the dealership to return it, she had to go to a mechanic in another city for repairs. Two days later the problem reoccurred, and the car had to go into the shop once again. Apparently, Sylvia bought a defective car. She has two problems: getting a refund back on a defective car, and being reimbursed for the out-of-pocket repair bills she paid.

WHAT TO DO

1. Sylvia should save all the receipts from the repairs done to the new car by independent mechanics. (If she had been vacationing in a locale that had a dealership that serviced the make of her car, she could have had it repaired there instead of by an independent mechanic.)

2. As soon as she returns from vacation, she should take the car back to the dealership and explain the problem, producing the repair bills. She may get no satisfaction from the dealer, because this is apparently a defect that should be remedied by the manufacturer.

3. The dealership may offer to help by contacting the manufacturer and serving as the mediator between Sylvia and the company.

4. If the dealership leaves it up to Sylvia to contact the manufacturer, it can provide the address and phone number of the zone office. A factory representative may be sent by the zone office to look at Sylvia's car.

5. The zone office may not be willing to do anything about the problem, so Sylvia might want to use the arbitration program provided by the manufacturer. An arbitration program can be successful, but if it is not in this case, Sylvia might want to find out if her state offers a state-administered arbitration plan.

6. In addition to all the efforts Sylvia is making to resolve her problem, she should file complaints with the state attorney general's office (or consumer affairs office) and Better Business Bureau.

7. If all else fails, Sylvia may want to hire an attorney and sue the manufacturer in court. She should look into her state's lemon laws and determine if her situation qualifies.

Lemon Laws

After manufacturers gave consumers the protection of warranties, many new-car owners were still faced with the problem of cars that functioned improperly. In 1982 Connecticut became the first state to pass a lemon law, which requires manufacturers to either replace a car or refund the cost of the car if it has not been satisfactorily repaired in a reasonable time period or within a certain number of visits to the repair shop. All 50 states and the District of Columbia have some sort of lemon law, although they vary in the remedies they provide and the coverage they offer.

For a car to qualify as a lemon under the New York lemon law, it must meet the following requirements:

1. The car must be used for personal, family, or household purposes. A car used for delivering flowers does not qualify; a car used for going to and from work does.

2. The car must be sold, leased, or registered in New York State. The car is covered by the lemon law for a specific period of time: two years from the original date of delivery or 18,000 miles on the odometer, whichever comes first.

Barry purchases a new car in New York from a local car dealer. He drives it to and from work for a few weeks without a problem, but, without warning, it starts to stall frequently, often in congested traffic. He returns it to the service department at the dealer and has it checked over and repaired under warranty. Two days later, the problem returns. In a period of six months, Barry's new car has been in the dealer's shop six times without the problems having been resolved. The dealer and the manufacturer have not refused to honor the warranty; nevertheless, Barry is still faced with a car that not only does not perform properly but is a hazard.

Under the New York lemon law, Barry has legal recourse because he and his car meet all the qualifications.

3. The problem must continue despite four or more repair attempts, or the car must be out of service for a cumulative total of 30 or more calendar days for one or more problems.

4. The defect must substantially impair the value of the car, but it cannot have been caused by the owner's or driver's abuse, alteration, or negligence.

Buyers in New York, for example, must follow a certain procedure to get relief under the state's lemon law:

1. The relief must be sought within four years of delivery of the car.

2. The buyer must give notice of the problem to the manufacturer, its agent, or the dealer, providing the year/model, vehicle identification number, date of purchase, mileage, servicing dealer, and a description of the problem, documenting each visit to the service department or repair shop with copies of receipts or service reports.

3. The buyer must be willing to go through an informal dispute resolution procedure created by the manufacturer or through a state arbitration board.

4. If that fails, the buyer has the option of taking the manufacturer to court, filing a civil suit in state court.

If the buyer's argument is convincing and the arbitration board rules in his or her favor, two options are available. The buyer can either accept a comparable replacement vehicle or secure a refund of the original purchase price, plus sales tax, license, registration, and other miscellaneous fees. The manufacturer can demand that the refund be reduced by a certain formula (mileage multiplied by contract price divided by 100,000) if the car has 12,000 miles or more on the odometer.

The individual state laws vary, but all are based on the premise that consumers buy a new car for enjoyment, dependability, and performance, and that the offer of free, unlimited trips to a car repair shop is not an acceptable remedy for a manufacturer's failure to provide these.

Remember: Lemon laws differ from state to state. Check the dealership or has been test-driven by prospective buyers. But any driving relevant laws in your area and/or consult an attorney before pursuing legal action.

BUYING A USED CAR

A car is still considered new if it has been driven back to the dealership or has been test-driven by prospective buyers. But any driving beyond that turns a new car into a used car.

The Federal Trade Commission created the Used Car Rule to protect consumers from unscrupulous car salespeople. But if you buy a car privately, perhaps through a friend or an advertisement, the Rule does not apply; private transactions are usually "as is," relieving the seller of any responsibility for a lemon or repairs once the papers are signed. If you buy a used car in this way, protect yourself by insisting that the contract include some recourse for you should the car fail to function shortly after you drive it away. Ask the seller if the car is covered by any manufacturer's warranties or service contracts that may still be in force when you become the owner, and take possession of them.

If you buy a used car from a dealer, the rules change. The Used Car Rule requires all such used cars to have a "Buyer's Guide" sticker displayed in the window, clearly disclosing important information about the car and the responsibility of the dealer.

The sticker carries information about all of the following matters.

Available Warranties

About 50 percent of all used cars are sold "as is," meaning that you are responsible for paying all future repair costs. Despite any comments or claims the dealer makes about the vehicle, he or she does not legally assume any responsibility for the repairs. In most states a car sold as is does not carry the implied warranties mentioned above, such as a warranty of merchantability or warranty of fitness for a particular purpose. But Kansas, Maine, Maryland, Massachusetts, Mississippi, New York, Vermont, West Virginia, and the District of Columbia prohibit as-is sales and require implied warranties. If the dealer is providing implied warranties, he or she will check the appropriate box on the Buyer's Guide sticker. This means that the dealer does not make any specific promises to fix things that need repair when you buy the vehicle or after the time of sale. But state law implied warranties may give you some rights to have the dealer take care of serious problems that were not apparent when you bought the vehicle.

If the car is not being sold as is, the Buyer's Guide sticker will indicate whether the warranty is full or limited. If limited, it will specify what percentage of labor and parts the dealer will be required to pay, as well as what systems are covered and for how long.

Get It in Writing

The Buyer's Guide sticker warns buyers to ask the dealer to put all promises in writing because "spoken promises are difficult to enforce."

Inspection

The Buyer's Guide sticker suggests a "prepurchase" inspection by your own mechanic, either on or off the dealer's lot. For insurance reasons, some dealers prefer that the mechanic makes the inspection on the premises of the dealership.

Possible Major Defects

The Buyer's Guide sticker contains a list of major defects that could possibly affect your used car, including 52 items within the 14 primary vehicle systems.

Service Contract

If the dealer will sell you a service contract, the dealer will check the box that reads "A service contract is available at an extra charge on this vehicle. Ask for details about coverage, deductible, price, and exclusions. If you buy a service contract within 90 days of the time of sale, state law 'implied warranties' may give you additional rights."

Before you purchase a service contract, be sure that the parts covered by the service contract are not already protected by warranty; you don't want to pay for something you already have. Second, consider whether it is likely that the car will need repairs, and if so, how much they will cost. Evaluate the reputation of the dealer who is providing the service contract, and also determine if the length of coverage is appropriate for you. Some states don't require the dealer to mention a service contract, so you might want to ask about its availability.

Protection Against Unfair and Deceptive Practices

Despite the diligence of automakers, the possibility of buying a lemon or a new car that needs repairs will always exist. But sometimes the problem is created by the deception of a disreputable car dealer or salesperson who lies or otherwise fails to disclose important information about the car. Each state has separate laws that define certain acts as unfair or deceptive. Most states consider the following actions to be illegal:

- failing to disclose hazardous defects in the car
- failing to inform the consumer that the former owner used the car for excessively wear-incurring purposes (such as hauling lumber)
- charging the consumer more than the advertised sale price
- odometer tampering

Rolling back a car's mileage on the odometer is a common practice by unscrupulous dealers. Professionals can chisel thousands of miles off a used car, leaving the consumer with a vehicle that has undergone far greater use than the odometer reveals.

What follows is a hypothetical situation involving deceptive practices of a used-car dealer.

THE PROBLEM

Mary Lou bought a late-model used car that had low mileage and appeared, at least to the untrained eye, to be in good condition. The salesman told her it was owned by a woman who only used it to drive back and forth to work. A month after purchasing the car, scratched-off paint revealed that it had been previously used as a taxi. The contract did not state that this was an as-is sale.

WHAT TO DO

1. Since the car dealership may have violated the unfair and deceptive acts or practices statutes in her state, Mary Lou

should report the possible criminal actions to the state attorney general's office, state department of consumer affairs, if any, and the Better Business Bureau. In addition, she should immediately contact the used-car dealer and demand her money back.

2. If step 1 does not resolve her problem, she may want to sue the dealer under the state's unfair and deceptive practices statutes, the Federal Motor Vehicles Information and Cost Savings Act, or other state and federal laws. She will need help from an attorney in her state.

You can take the following five steps to avoid being a victim of odometer fraud.

1. Drive the car for a certain distance to be sure the odometer is working and that the mileage is being properly reflected as you drive.

2. Check the wear on the brake and clutch pedals, the carpet, door handles, and driver's seat, comparing it against the mileage on the odometer.

3. Look at the car's warranty documents, inspection stickers, and maintenance records to see whether they legitimately track the mileage on the odometer.

4. Examine the odometer, looking for marks, scratches, misaligned numbers, or any other evidence that tampering has taken place.

5. Have a mechanic look over the engine, the transmission, and other parts of the vehicle to determine whether the visible wear corresponds with the odometer reading.

If anything looks out of the ordinary or if the odometer reading seems rather low after conducting the five comparisons, ask the seller to provide you with the odometer disclosure statement from the prior owner. (This may also be an indication to start over with another dealer.) Federal statutes require the seller of a passenger vehicle to provide the buyer with a written document stating the odometer reading. Dealers must keep these statements for at least four years so that potential buyers can verify that the odometer is working as it should. If the dealer has no odometer statements on file, ask for the names, addresses, and phone numbers of the previous owners so that you can contact them.

Suppose all your best efforts are in vain, and you buy a used car only to find out later that it has had its odometer rolled back. Check with your state's consumer affairs office to find out what your rights are in suing the seller under not only state law but also the Federal Motor Vehicles Information and Cost Savings Act and other statutes. Odometer rollback is a federal criminal violation subject to prosecution by the U.S. Department of Justice.

CAR REPAIRS

America's number one consumer complaint is car repair fraud. In addition to the standard complaints of highly inflated bills, final bills that far exceed verbal estimates, and incompetent workmanship, charges of unfair and deceptive practices abound. These include performing work that was unnecessary or never authorized and claiming that certain repair work or service was performed when it never was.

Some municipalities and states have laws meant to prevent these violations, such as requiring repair people to provide written estimates. In states that have no such requirement, the consumer must take certain precautions: Confirm the credentials of the mechanic or garage with the Better Business Bureau or the state bureau of automotive repair, if any; always ask for a written estimate that separates the cost of parts from labor; initial anything you authorize and leave the mechanic a phone number where you can be reached if it appears that the costs will exceed the estimate; and ask the mechanic to save any damaged part removed.

If, despite all your efforts, you believe you have been taken advantage of, contact the state attorney general's office (consumer protection division) and report the experience to the Better Business Bureau.

The following hypothetical situation involves auto repair rip-off.

THE PROBLEM

Philip pulled into a gas station for a routine oil change. While looking under the hood, the mechanic told Philip that he needed a new water pump. Knowing nothing about cars, Philip told him to replace whatever part was needed. One month later Philip's car developed problems and he was told by another mechanic that his water pump was getting old and was leaking. It was apparent that the first mechanic doing the oil change charged him for a new water pump plus labor but never did the work.

WHAT TO DO

1. Philip should contact the attorney general's office and any state licensing agency for mechanics and report the repair rip-off, because the crime of theft was committed.

2. Philip should speak to the manager or owner of the gas station that conned him, in an attempt to get an explanation and refund.

3. If the problem is not resolved, Philip can sue the gas station owner and mechanic for the amount paid plus punitive damages, because this was an intentional violation of state and federal statutes.

RENTING A CAR

Car rentals range widely in price and other terms, and you should be aware of hidden costs, such as the costs for unnecessary insurance coverage.

The Collision Damage Waiver (CDW) and Other Insurance Coverage

Insurance coverage is perhaps the most misunderstood of all elements in a car rental agreement. Consumers are always asked about—and sometimes pressured into purchasing—the collision damage waiver (CDW), primarily because it can cost another $10 to $13 a day. Because car renters are frequently in a hurry, they often don't take the time to find out exactly what is being offered and whether it duplicates coverage they already have. More than 20 states have laws that govern CDW costs, and Congress has considered legislation that would prohibit the sale of CDW.

If you purchase CDW, the rental company will take care of any physical damage caused to the car during your rental. But contrary to what many car renters believe, CDW does not cover bodily injury or personal property damage.

The rental company will also offer you personal accident insurance (PAI) and personal effects coverage or protection (PEC or PEP) for your luggage. Before going to the rental company, check your personal automobile, homeowner's, and health insurance policies to see whether you are already covered for property damage or loss as well as personal injuries sustained in a rental car. Other sources of coverage may include your motor club membership, your credit card companies (if you plan to charge the rental), and your employer's insurance (if the rental is a business expense). Be sure that you are not already covered under another policy before you pay for the costly coverage the rental companies want to sell you, but do make sure that you are covered in one way or another.

Refundable Charges

Some rental companies ask you to put down a deposit when you rent the car, which is refundable when you return it. Because renters usually use credit cards to pay for this transaction, which isn't processed unless they fail to return the car, many consumers reason that this deposit is really no money out of their pockets. Nevertheless, keep in mind that it does shrink, at least temporarily, the credit limit on your credit card. If you are planning a long, expensive trip, it may be advisable to charge the rental car on one credit card and carry a second card for purchases or travel expenses.

Other Fees

OUT-OF-STATE FEES   You may be charged extra if you travel to another state.

DROP-OFF FEES   If you don't return the car to its original pickup location, the company may charge you an additional fee.

AIRPORT SURCHARGE   If a car rental office is located at an airport, a fee may be levied for using airport property.

GASOLINE COSTS   Companies use different methods to charge for gasoline. Some give you a car with a full tank, and charge you nothing if you return it with a full tank. But if you return it less than full, you will be charged at inflated gasoline prices. Other companies give you gas and just tack on the cost to your bill, deducting the fuel in the tank upon your return. Some companies offer you an option to purchase gas in advance at a reasonable price, but you have to buy a full tank regardless of how far you intend to drive the car. Be sure to ask who pays for the gas before you drive out.

MILEAGE FEES   Some rental agencies charge you per mile if you drive over a set number of miles. For example, a car rental company may charge you nothing for mileage if you don't exceed 50 miles per day. But any mileage beyond that will cost you $.21 per mile. Depending on how far you plan on driving, you might want to consider a rental agreement that has a higher daily or weekly cost but provides unlimited mileage.

TAXES   As a rule, car rental taxes are higher in large cities than they are in the suburbs. If you can, look for the offices in the more rural areas.

ADDITIONAL DRIVER CHARGES   The base cost of a rental car usually covers only the primary driver; another fee may be added for each additional driver. Sometimes younger drivers will be charged extra. Be sure to ask about this policy.

CAR SEATS OR BIKE RACK FEES   Be sure to request any needed extra equipment, such as child car seats or bicycle racks, days in advance of your trip—and expect to pay a little more for it.

As in any contract, make sure everything you have agreed to is in the contract and that you understand it completely before you sign it.

TRAFFIC AND TRAFFIC VIOLATIONS

What to Do When You're Stopped by the Police

If a police officer signals for you to stop your car, always pull off the road on the right, never the left. If you are at an exit on an interstate highway, go to the end of the ramp and find a safe place to stop. When an exit is not close by, pull over onto the shoulder of the road. You should never attempt to evade an officer once you have been signaled or told to pull over. After you bring the car to a complete stop, stay where you are. During daylight hours police officers prefer to get out of their cars and walk to yours; it's safer for them to do so. Keep your hands on the steering wheel where the officer can see them. Roll down your window only when the officer tells you to, but put your hands back on the wheel once you do. The best thing for you to say at this time is "Hello, officer" and nothing more, because you may not be sure why you are being stopped.

The officer may ask you to step out of your car and walk just behind it, in front of the police vehicle. Keep your hands where the officer can see them. The officer will most likely ask you first for your driver's license, registration, and insurance card. You should be carrying this information "on your person," as the law requires in many states. Such a requirement is to simplify identification in the event that you are in a severe accident and are thrown from your vehicle. But if your license and other papers are in the car, inform the officer of this before you move to locate and produce them. Police officers are trained to establish the identities of anyone they detain immediately, in case the detainee should try to flee or to pull a gun.

If you are directed to pull over at night, the officer may follow a different procedure. Possibly with a spotlight and the help of a microphone, the officer may ask you to step out of your car while the officer stays in the police car. When the officer has had a chance to observe you and believes that you present no threat, you'll be approached and told why you have been stopped. The officer expects a response from you, and you should make sure that your response is calm and reasonable. Don't argue with or insult the officer. Be polite, and if you were speeding and there were extenuating circumstances, explain them. Such an explanation doesn't alter the fact that you were violating the law, but the officer might be more lenient if your explanation is considered reasonable. If you have to go into court later on the charge, remember that the officer will be there testifying against you.

Suppose you do everything correctly when the officer pulls you over for speeding: You follow proper procedure and you are polite and apologetic, but the officer writes you a ticket anyway. In some states the procedure is that you will be asked to sign the ticket—

merely to show that you received it, not as an admission of guilt. You may also be asked to surrender your license, which then becomes the court's assurance that you will appear for your hearing. The ticket serves as your substitute license until your court date. If you tell the officer that it's important that you have possession of your license, perhaps for identification purposes, you may be permitted to go to court in advance of your court date and post bond.

Your Protection from Illegal Search and Seizure

One of the fundamental safeguards provided by the United States Constitution is the right to privacy and protection against illegal searches and seizures. If you are stopped for a routine traffic violation, the police don't have the right to search your car or rifle through your trunk or glove compartment.

In general, police officers are limited to certain conditions under which they may search your car or arrest you for what they may find.

- If you have drugs or a gun in "plain view," the police officer has the right to search your vehicle, seize the contraband, and arrest you.

- If an officer suspects you of having committed a crime or believes that you are about to commit a crime, he or she has the right to stop you and ask your name, address, and what you're doing. If the officer believes that your behavior is suspicious and that you may be armed, he or she has the right to "frisk" you. If the officer suspects you have a weapon, he or she is permitted to search you fully.

- If the officer arrests you for any reason, he or she has the right to conduct a search of your vehicle to be sure you have no firearms, but the search is limited to the area immediately around your "person."

- If an officer has probable cause to believe that you have drugs or illegal firearms in your car but does not have the time to obtain a search warrant, he or she has the right to search without it. Such situations are called "exigent circumstances," because the likelihood is great that the evidence will disappear if the officer waits to get a warrant.

- If your car has been impounded or moved to a police facility or lot, the police are allowed to conduct an inventory search of everything in the car. If illegal drugs, firearms, or other evidence of a crime is found, these may be seized.

- If the police set up roadblocks to randomly ask that drivers show their driver's licenses and proof of insurance or to check for drivers who may be intoxicated, these stops are constitutional as long as certain drivers are not specifically singled out for no apparent reason. The officers in roadblock searches are required to stop each and every car or to conduct the search according to another specific, nondiscriminatory pattern, such as stopping every sixth vehicle.

Losing Your License

When a court takes your driver's license away, it may be suspended for a set period of time or revoked until proper application is made to have it reinstated. Licenses can be suspended for two categories of offenses. The first involves your committing certain serious violations, including failure to stop and render aid, hit-and-run, leaving the scene of an accident, driving under the influence of alcohol or drugs, refusing to submit to a Breathalyzer test, failing to report an accident that caused damage, and driving without proof of insurance. The second category of offense is through the accumulation of "points." Most states assign a certain number of penalty points to each traffic violation. As you receive a citation, the prescribed number of points for that violation goes on your driving record. If you accumulate a predetermined number of points during a specific time period, the state will suspend your license. In Georgia, for example, if you unlawfully pass a school bus, you will be penalized 6 points; illegally going through a traffic light causes 3 points; and reckless driving carries a penalty of 4 points. In Georgia, if you accumulate 15 or more points in a 24-month period, your license will be suspended.

Just as each state has its own point system, each jurisdiction—whether city, county, or state—has its own system of fines. This is why you may be fined $50 for "failing to yield" in one town and $75 in a neighboring locality. Be aware that traffic fines are a major source of revenue in some of the smaller jurisdictions.

Traffic Violations

Most traffic violations are considered misdemeanors. Some, such as going through a stop sign or passing improperly, are considered relatively minor and involve little more than the embarrassment of your appearing in traffic court and paying a fine. Other misdemeanors, such as a first- and second-time "driving under the influence" charge, can be more serious and involve fines, driving school/rehabilitation, license suspension, jail time, or a combination of those. Traffic violations that constitute serious crimes are classified as felonies and include driving while a habitual violator (three or more citations for driving under the influence), homicide by vehicle in the first degree, or causing serious injury. If you are convicted of a felony, a judge can sentence you to more than a year in jail and/or a large fine.

Driving Under the Influence

Whether your state calls it DUI (driving under the influence) or DWI (driving while intoxicated), driving after having consumed a specific amount of alcohol or drugs is against the law. Each state has its own criteria regarding how much alcohol must be in your blood before you are presumed to be intoxicated. The alcohol in your blood—the BAC or blood alcohol content—is indicated by a percentage. In most states, if your BAC measures .10 percent, you are automatically considered to be intoxicated. Many states are considering or have implemented BAC limits of .08, .06, or even .04 percent. No distinction is made concerning what you were drinking: 12 ounces of beer, 5 ounces of table wine, and 1½ ounces of 80-proof liquor all contain the same amount of pure alcohol.

The number of drinks that it takes for you to reach a BAC of .10 percent depends on your weight, how quickly you drink, and the amount of food in your stomach. For example, after four drinks, a person weighing 100 pounds generally has a BAC of .20 percent. Someone who weighs 200 pounds and consumes four drinks will probably register .09 percent on a Breathalyzer test—just below the level of presumed intoxication in most states. Of course, this does *not* mean that you should drive a vehicle after consuming *any* amount of alcohol.

What are the legal guidelines and procedures that cover DUI situations? If a police officer considers your driving to be a bit erratic or if you are stopped at a police roadblock (usually set up on a weekend when heavy drinking is expected), the officer will pull you over and ask for your license, car registration, and proof of insurance. During this procedure, the officer will be looking for evidence of the odor of alcohol or marijuana on your breath or in the car and listening to your speech to see if it is slurred or confused. If the officer decides that you are impaired in some such way, he or she may ask you to get out of the car and to undergo a few physical dexterity tests, recite the alphabet, or walk a straight line. Some officers administer a Breathalyzer test on the spot to confirm their suspicions that a driver has had too much to drink, although these preliminary tests are often not admissible in court and are not mandatory. If a police officer believes that your blood alcohol content is close to .10 percent, or the required BAC for presumed intoxication, the officer has the right to arrest you and have you tested.

The officer is required to read "implied consent warnings" to you. The exact language varies from state to state but usually informs you that you are required to submit to a state-administered breath, blood, or urine test to determine if you are under the influence of alcohol or drugs. The warnings also inform you that you have the right to ask for an additional test at a facility of your choice at your expense. You are also advised of the penalty for refusing the state-administered test.

The officer must now get you to the closest testing facility to obtain an accurate BAC level. The officer probably will request a breath test for you if alcohol intoxication is suspected or a blood or urine test if drug use is suspected. If a Breathalyzer test is administered at the police station and the results are negative for alcohol, yet the officer believes you to be intoxicated, the officer has the right to take you to another facility, often a hospital, for a urine or blood test. If you, not the officer, believe that a second test should be administered, most states will allow it if you pay for it.

Remember: Do not consider refusing to submit to the test, because the officer has the right to suspend or revoke your license on the spot if you refuse.

If an officer arrests you on a DUI charge, the officer has the right to search you and the passenger compartment of your car. If you are alone or cannot make arrangements quickly to have your car removed from the site of the arrest, the police may take possession of it and conduct an inventory search. In this situation all parts of the vehicle can be searched, and if the car is found to contain illegal drugs, alcohol, firearms, or contraband, these can be used as evidence to convict you. The district attorney will look at the results of your tests, the evidence found on you or in the car, and the testimony of the police officer to determine whether to prosecute the case.

What to Do If You Face a DUI Charge

Be aware that whether this is your first DUI or your fourth, the charge is serious. Don't attempt to save money by handling the matter alone. Consult an attorney who handles such cases on a regular basis. The attorney will be able to gain access to your test results and determine how strong a case the state has against you by consulting with the prosecutor.

Pleading guilty to a DUI will have a few automatic results. The conviction will go on your driving record and is likely to be available to job interviewers and to those who process applications for military service. Insurance companies may cancel your coverage or raise your rates after such a conviction because you are considered a bad risk.

NOLO CONTENDERE   Sometimes a driver has no valid defenses. Many states allow a *nolo contendere*—no contest—plea on a first-offense DUI. This is not an admission of guilt, nor does it absolve you of the charge. Making such a plea usually requires the help of an attorney, who may charge anywhere from $200 to $800 to represent you. You must convince the judge that this is your first DUI, that you have a good driving record, and that you will never commit the offense again. If your plea is accepted, you will have to pay a fine to the court and attend a "defensive" driving school.

If you are lucky enough to be granted the *nolo contendere* plea, this will be the last time it will be accepted; any subsequent DUI arrests can cost you stiffer fines, revocation of your license, and possibly a jail sentence.

Keep in mind that alcohol-related violations can have a legal impact on people who never drink alcohol. Many states have passed "dram shop" laws that allow injured parties to sue a host or hostess who served the drunk driver too much alcohol. In some states, if a person lends a car to an intoxicated driver, the lender can be held liable.

Carrying Alcohol and Weapons in a Vehicle

Many states have open-container laws that prohibit anyone from driving while having a container in his or her possession from which alcohol can immediately be consumed or where the seal has been broken. Such a container is considered to be in the driver's possession except when it is being held by a passenger or is *locked* in the glove compartment, the trunk, or another nonpassenger area of the vehicle. Remember that each state has its own motor vehicle laws, and they will vary.

Brett went to Helene's college graduation party where a great deal of beer was being consumed. Brett decided to leave at about midnight, and Helene's mother said good night to an obviously highly intoxicated Brett. Two miles down the road, Brett lost control of his van and ran into a car being driven by Abby. Brett suffered only a few minor bruises, but Abby was killed. Abby's father brought a wrongful-death action not only against Brett, but against Helene and her parents. Many states have enacted such "dram shop" laws that hold bars, clubs, and even private individuals liable when they allow others to drink and drive.

The same applies to possession of weapons in your car. Loaded pistols and other firearms, knives, metal knuckles, and other weapons can be transported in a vehicle if they are in open view or in the glove compartment. They cannot be concealed on the person or concealed within reach, such as under the seat.

Other Violations

No matter how responsible a driver you are, you may face certain common traffic violations. One out of every four accidents is caused by speeding. Whether you exceed the speed limit by 5 miles per hour or 50, you may still be punished with a fine and penalty points. The fine you pay and the points you accumulate will vary, based on whether you exceed the speed limit by 14 miles per hour (two points in Georgia) to 35 or more miles per hour (six points in Georgia).

Speed detection is becoming more sophisticated, so what used to be a driver's word against the judgment of a police officer is now a driver's word against radar or another mechanical tracking device. Opposing a machine's recording is difficult. This is not to say that you cannot take issue with charges that you were speeding. State laws have strict guidelines about radar devices being calibrated at certain times during their use, and require that the officers operating them receive special training. If you can prove that the radar device was not calibrated properly, or that the officer was not trained in its operation or read your speed incorrectly, you may succeed in having your citation dismissed—a relatively unlikely outcome.

Twenty percent of all accidents are caused by a driver's failing to yield the right-of-way and driving into the path of traffic. One out of every 10 accidents is caused by a driver's following another car too closely, usually rear-ending it as a result. Going through traffic lights and stop signs as well as failing to signal properly are other common offenses that cause accidents. Most states have laws requiring seat belts, at least for the driver and front-seat passenger. Car seats for infants and young children are mandatory in many states, as is, increasingly, the requirement to use headlights for visibility during rain and snow.

KEEPING UP-TO-DATE   A police officer who finds that you are driving without a license or driving with a suspended license will give you a ticket. State laws require your car to be registered and your tags to be renewed each year. Certain inspections are also required, including testing emission control and other parts of the car. Failing to conform to such state regulations can result in serious penalties.

Appearing in Traffic Court

If you have been cited for a traffic violation, the ticket will note a date, time, and court location where you must report. Never ignore a ticket; if you have a schedule conflict, you should try to change your other appointment. If you have a legitimate reason for postponing your appearance—asking for a *continuance*—such as being committed to appear in another court or serving on jury duty, call the clerk's office and see what can be done to have your appearance rescheduled. The clerk may ask that you come down to the court and file for a continuance in person. But don't attempt to delay your court date in order to get enough money together to pay your fine; judges look harshly at repeated requests for a continuance. Failing to appear for a hearing (without being granted a continuance) can result in the suspension of your license; in some jurisdictions, a bench warrant will be issued for your arrest.

Appearing in traffic court will not resolve other issues that may be involved in your citation, such as damage to your car or a civil lawsuit that another driver has filed against you. These are handled in a different proceeding in a different court.

If you have been cited with a minor traffic violation, you probably don't need the services of an attorney; by the time you pay an attorney's hourly fee, you may well be exceeding the fine you'll have to pay if you are found guilty. But consider retaining an attorney if the violation involves the possibility of having your license revoked, a jail sentence, or the prospect of exorbitant car insurance rates.

The first step in going to traffic court is to be prepared. Police officers cannot remember the details of every incident or accident they investigate or every traffic citation they issue, so they refer to reports to refresh their memories. Get a copy of the report by calling the court clerk's office; the clerk will tell you the cost (usually only a few dollars) and the procedure by which you can get a copy. It's important that you review the report so you know how the officer perceived the incident or accident and you understand what to expect in court when the officer testifies.

If you believe that the report works against you and is inaccurate, be prepared to take issue with it and explain where it's in error. Many drivers hesitate to contradict a police officer's testimony, working under the misconception that a judge will always take an officer's word as truth. This is not the case. Most judges realize that officers can't possibly be correct all the time. If you honestly believe that the officer was mistaken, stand your ground. But do so calmly and politely. Remember the distinction between not challenging an officer at the site of the alleged violation and asserting your difference with the officer in court.

As you prepare your case by reviewing the report and the citation, outline the facts of your case. If you were involved in an accident, decide what you need to prove your innocence and what evidence, facts, and witnesses will help to prove it. Plan what you want to tell the judge, and prepare your presentation in the clearest and most concise way. Be thorough. You may want to do a little legal research in the local law library. The librarian can show you how to find the code section and appropriate statute relating to the offense with which you are charged.

Read the statute to determine if you have violated it. Compare the code section with the one noted on the citation. If the officer used the wrong citation, you may have grounds for having the ticket dismissed. Look over the cases cited at the end of the code section and copy those that help support your defense. Prepare any evidence that you gathered for your case, including photographs or affidavits from witnesses.

Before you go to court, talk with any friends who have had similar experiences in the same jurisdiction. Some counties or cities hold the trial on the initial appearance, allowing defendants to plead guilty or not guilty and proceeding until the judge delivers a verdict. Other jurisdictions have "arraignment hearings" in which defendants are allowed to enter a plea, then a trial is scheduled at a later date if the plea is not guilty. Before you appear on the appointed date and time, find out what kind of proceeding you are facing by calling the clerk of the court.

ENTERING YOUR PLEA   When you arrive in court on the date set for your appearance, you will be asked to enter a plea. Although not all courts are the same, generally, you will plea to one of the following:

Guilty: A guilty plea admits that you committed the offense for which you are being charged. The liability of a guilty plea is that you will most likely automatically be fined and your admission goes on record, which can be entered into evidence later if you are sued in a civil action arising from the matter. The advantage of a guilty plea (if you are guilty) is that it is the fastest way to resolve the charge against you.

Not Guilty: A plea of not guilty denies that you committed the violation, and states that you want a chance to defend yourself. The judge may hear your case the same day, or another court may be assigned to hear it at a later date.

Guilty, with an Explanation: Sometimes there are extenuating circumstances for committing a violation, and you want to explain them. Do so. You might tell the judge, for example, that you know you were speeding, but that you were on your way to the hospital where your father had been taken after suffering a heart attack. Your explanation may not change the judge's mind about finding you guilty, but it is worth submitting on the chance that it might or that the fine may be reduced.

Nolo contendere: A plea of *nolo contendere* (no contest) is neither a guilty plea nor a plea of not guilty.

Suppose you have been stopped for reckless driving and have been found to have a blood alcohol level high enough to be charged with driving under the influence. This is your first DUI and you have an otherwise clean driving record. If the court accepts your plea of *nolo contendere,* you will most likely be allowed to keep your license and probably will not have to serve any jail time. Most states do require, however, that you attend a defensive driving school and pay a fine. "Nolos" are the legal system's way of giving defendants a second chance—a chance to right a wrong. Pleas of *nolo contendere* are not available to those with more than one DUI violation.

IF YOU PLEAD NOT GUILTY Suppose you've pleaded not guilty to the charge. The bailiff will eventually call your case, and you must now prove that you were unjustly charged. If the violation you are charged with is serious—for example, if the offense occurred during an accident or if several witnesses were present—the procedure can be relatively complicated; sometimes, a prosecutor or solicitor will argue the state's case, and witnesses will be cross-examined.

For minor traffic violations and infractions, the process is simple and usually involves only you, the police officer, and the judge. Keep in mind that the entire hearing might be over before it starts if the arresting officer doesn't show up. Because the officer is such an important part of the state's case against you, you may ask the judge to dismiss your case if the officer fails to appear without a good excuse.

The police officer will explain to the judge why you were cited, what was observed, and how you violated the law. When the officer completes the testimony, it's your turn to tell your version of the events. If you disagree with the police report, be sure to tell the judge. Present any evidence you may have, including photographs and written reports from witnesses. Answer any and all questions the judge asks you.

Suppose you went through a stop sign because shrubs along the road completely hid it from view. If the officer was unsympathetic and gave you a ticket anyway, submitting a photograph of your view as you came upon the intersection and how the shrubs hid the sign will be very supportive as evidence in your case. Make sure the date of the photograph is indicated. If you know of other motorists who have had the same problem at that intersection, ask them to come to court as witnesses, or to submit a letter to the court. If you have such a legitimate reason for your actions, the judge may dismiss the violation; however, if the matter becomes your word against the officer's, your chances of prevailing are slim.

Suing the Other Driver in an Accident

In order to sue someone for negligence committed during an auto accident, three elements must have been present. First, the other driver must fail to meet the basic standard of having observed due care. Second, the plaintiff must have suffered significant injuries. Some states require a "threshold" or minimum total of medical costs that reflect injuries before the case can be taken to court; this is to prevent frivolous "fender bender" cases from being brought to court for undeserved compensation. Third, the other driver's negligence must have been the cause of the plaintiff's injuries. (If a driver's injuries were the result of personal carelessness, he or she has no right to sue another driver.)

You and another driver, Charles, were involved in an automobile accident. He misjudged your speed and distance and made a left-hand turn directly in front of your car. The ensuing impact sent you through the windshield, causing three broken ribs, a fractured arm, and a lacerated forehead. Since the accident, you have been experiencing dizzy spells and excruciating headaches. You have had to miss six weeks of work and have months of physical therapy ahead of you.

Charles was cited for an improper turn and was fined in traffic court. Your insurance company paid for your medical expenses and time missed from work. Charles's insurance company covered the cost of replacing your car, which was destroyed in the accident. But none of this compensates you for your pain and suffering, the lack of companionship or consortium you can provide your spouse, and any punishment for Charles's careless driving. In this case you may have grounds to sue Charles for personal injury.

Many legal matters can be handled without a lawyer, but an automobile personal injury case is not one of them. Consult an attorney who specializes in automobile personal injury cases. Do careful research to find a good one (see chapter 11). Most auto personal injury or "PI" attorneys charge a percentage, or "contingency," of the plaintiff's settlement, often 33 percent of the amount awarded by a judge or jury. If no settlement is won, no fee is charged.

If you are the driver being sued, be sure to contact your insurance company. The company will usually handle the case and use its own attorneys. Any award or settlement against you will be paid by your insurer up to the limits of your policy. If you are underinsured, the other driver can sue you personally for the remainder if the award exceeds your coverage.

What to Do at the Scene of an Accident

If you are a driver involved in an accident with another vehicle or a pedestrian, you have certain legal responsibilities. First, if you are not already standing still, stop your car immediately. No matter how minor the damage to the cars involved, get out of your car if you are not injured (being careful to avoid any moving vehicles) and be sure the other driver and passengers are not injured; then assess the damage. Next, immediately write down the tag (license plate) number of the other driver's vehicle in case the driver decides to flee. If your vehicles are causing traffic problems and have the potential of creating other accidents, each of you should make a mental note or draw a diagram of where the cars impacted and came to rest before moving them off to a safer place. Then, call the police. If possible, don't move the cars until the police can be contacted and arrive to note the situation.

Check again with the other driver and passengers to be sure no one is injured. You have a duty to render aid to the injured; your failing to do so can result in suspension of your license or even a charge of vehicular homicide if someone dies. If the injuries seem serious, don't try to move an injured person. Cover the person with a blanket or something warm until an ambulance arrives. If the injured person needs CPR (cardiopulmonary resuscitation), you may administer it if you have been trained in providing it. If the injuries are less severe but still require medical attention, offer to take the person to a doctor or hospital.

Be sure to exchange all necessary information with the other drivers involved in the accident. Get full names, addresses, phone numbers at both home and work, birth dates, car descriptions, and insurance information, including the name of the insurance company and the driver's policy number. Don't reveal your own insurance policy limits and coverage to avoid being targeted with exaggerated claims in the future.

Take the time to look at the other driver's license carefully. Does it list any restrictions, such as corrective eyeglasses? If so, check to see if the driver is wearing any, either glasses or contact lenses. Make sure the picture on the license looks like the person standing before you.

If any witnesses have stopped and can testify that the accident was not your fault, ask for their names, addresses, and telephone numbers, but be aware that many such witnesses would prefer not to become involved. If you are a witness to an accident that results in serious injury or death, many states require that you stop at the scene and provide your name.

Remember that leaving the scene of an accident is a serious violation that can result in the suspension of your license. Even if you

Beware of the unscrupulous ploy that begins with a motorist stepping from his or her car, assessing any damage, and telling you that it's not worth reporting to the police. Unsuspecting, you may fail to take down his or her name, address, or insurance information, only to find out a few days later that the accident was reported to the police and that the driver's insurance company and that the other driver has charged you with causing damage to his or her car. Be sure to get all information, no matter how insignificant the "bump" seems.

run into a telephone pole and no other vehicle or person is involved, you are obliged to report the accident to the police. If another driver is involved, be sure the other driver has all your vital information and understands where you are going when you leave to call the police and that you will return immediately.

If you have been involved in an accident, be careful about what you say to the others at the scene. No matter how bad you may feel, even if you made an improper turn and caused the accident, don't admit fault to anyone. Any such expressions of fault may be used against you in the court and may also affect your insurance rates. If the other motorist involved admits guilt, remember that this story may be altered after attorneys and insurance companies advise the driver.

After you have notified the police, immediately contact your insurance company if any injuries or deaths have taken place. If the accident was minor, notification can wait until later. Check your policy for the reporting requirements; if you wait too long, your company may waive coverage. Likewise, your company representative can advise you about having your car repaired. Be sure to have the company representative inspect the damages and give you an estimate before a mechanic begins any work.

PREPARE FOR POSSIBLE FUTURE LITIGATION   After you have called the police, think about how the accident occurred and what you want to say to them. Keep in mind that what you say and how you say it may have a profound effect on how the police report will be written.

DOCUMENTATION   If you want to be well prepared, carry a form for such contingencies in your glove compartment; sometimes these are provided by insurance companies. Another helpful tool in documenting an accident is a camera. Some drivers carry a small, inexpensive camera in their glove compartments. "Disposable" cameras are perfect for this purpose because they do not require a large investment. If you have one, use the camera to take pictures of the cars, the accident scene, any physical damages, and anyone with personal injuries. Photographs can serve as evidence when you go to court or file a claim with an insurance company.

When the police arrive, they will ask you and the other driver for identification and for your accounts of what happened. If someone was seriously injured or killed during the accident, it's best to wait until you have a lawyer present before answering questions. But if the accident is relatively minor, discuss it with the officer honestly and concisely. Be sure not to leave out important details. If a traffic light malfunctioned and caused the accident, for example, make sure you alert the officer. Describing it to a judge weeks later in a courtroom might be too late.

RESPONSIBILITY   Never accept any responsibility or liability at the scene of an accident. If you have filled out an information sheet, show it to the officer. After the officer has conducted an investigation at the accident site, the officer might cite you and/or the other driver with a traffic violation. If this is a minor infraction, such as charging you with going five miles over the speed limit, the officer will probably ask you to give up your license until you appear in court. Your ticket serves as the substitute license. If the officer charges you with a more serious infraction, such as drunk driving or leaving the scene of the accident, you may be arrested and booked. If you cannot make bail, that is, post some kind of security such as cash or property, you may have to remain in jail until your hearing.

THE REPORT   The police officer will write out the accident report at the scene of the accident. It will document the details of the accident: who was involved, driver's license numbers and insurance information, how the accident occurred (with a diagram), if any citations (tickets) were given, if any injuries were incurred, and who witnessed the accident. Sometimes, the officer will record this information and complete the report at the police station. If you want to know what the report contains, check with the clerk's office of the appropriate court a few days later and find out how you can get a copy.

AFTER LEAVING THE SCENE   You may leave the scene only when all information has been exchanged and the police officer has gathered the necessary information for the accident report—never sooner. If you have not notified your insurance company from the scene of the accident, do it as soon as possible. If you have any aches or pains resulting from the accident, call your doctor. What may seem minor at the time could turn into major problems later. Notifying your doctor and having a medical examination will make any injuries you may have received easier to substantiate to an insurance company or to the other driver, whom you may end up suing later on.

THE SETTLEMENT   Expect a call from the other driver's insurance company. If the accident was clearly the other driver's fault, the company may offer to settle quickly. Be careful. You may end up settling for far less than what you need to recover. For example, your injuries may turn out to be more serious than you expected and may cause you to lose time from work. Before you agree to a settlement or sign any release, wait a few weeks to see what effects, if any, the accident may have on your health. Any release that you sign with an insurance company accepting recompense for your injuries is considered final. If you accept $3,000 as final settlement, for example, this is the most the company will ever pay you, even if you later develop chronic back pain that causes you to miss six months of work.

What follows is a hypothetical situation involving an automobile accident.

THE PROBLEM

As Byron approached an intersection on a green light, another car driven by Ruth cut in front of him, causing a collision.

WHAT TO DO

1. Assuming Byron is not injured, his first responsibility is checking the severity of Ruth's injuries and getting medical attention for her if necessary. While waiting for an ambulance, Byron should make Ruth as comfortable as possible. If Byron fails to care for Ruth's injuries, he could have his license suspended under the laws of some states.

2. If the cars are blocking traffic and create a dangerous situation, Byron and any bystanders should try to get the cars off to the side of the road.

3. Byron and Ruth should exchange names, addresses, phone numbers, driver's license numbers, tag (license plate) numbers, and insurance information.

4. Byron should try to find witnesses to the accident. He should take their names and other information so that if he needs to go to court, they can be called to verify his version of the

story. He should ask if they can stay long enough to talk to the police.

5. Byron should contact the police, and both parties must wait until they arrive.

6. While waiting, Byron should be gathering information by talking to the other driver, taking photos of the accident scene (if he has a camera), and organizing his recollection of what happened just before the collision.

7. When the police arrive, Byron should cooperate fully and not leave until the police tell him they no longer need him.

8. Byron should contact his insurance company. Some companies require that they be notified right after calling the police. Others are willing to wait until the insured gets back home. Byron should know the procedure prior to an accident so he can comply with it. If he doesn't, his claim may be denied.

AUTO INSURANCE

Be sure you know exactly what kind and how much insurance you have on your car or cars. Being overinsured is a waste of money, but being underinsured can ruin you financially if you are found to have caused injury to someone in an accident.

Categories of Auto Insurance

Most states require drivers to carry certain types of insurance, but the categories can be confusing.

BODILY INJURY LIABILITY COVERAGE If you have caused an accident and you are found to have been negligent, you are financially responsible for the injuries or death of other drivers, passengers, or pedestrians. When the injured parties file a lawsuit, your insurance company will have its attorneys handle your defense. If a judge or jury "finds" for the injured parties or if a settlement is reached, your insurer will pay the award up to your policy limits. You are personally responsible for any damage costs, including medical bills, over and above your insurance coverage. Be sure you carry enough coverage so that any damages you unwittingly cause are covered by your insurer.

PROPERTY DAMAGE LIABILITY   Medical expenses are not always your only problem if you cause an accident. You must contend with the damage to the automobiles as well as to lawns, houses, signposts, fences, or other property damaged by the accident. If your property damage insurance coverage is insufficient, you might have to pay for the damage yourself.

MEDICAL PAYMENTS COVERAGE   This type of insurance covers any medical expenses you incur as a result of an accident, regardless of whose negligence caused it. If another driver caused the accident and your insurance company pays for your doctor and hospital bills, your company has the right to sue the other driver's insurance company, or to "subrogate" it. Your policy limits dictate how much your company will pay in benefits.

PERSONAL INJURY PROTECTION (PIP)   This is a broader medical coverage offered in states with no-fault auto insurance. Like medical payments insurance, it pays medical and hospital expenses and some funeral bills. But it also reimburses injured persons for a portion of their lost wages and pays for essential services, such as housekeeping, that they can't perform. In some states motorists can buy both PIP and medical payments coverage if they want more medical coverage.

If you have a good health insurance plan, you're probably already covered for any medical expenses your family might incur as the result of an auto accident. Keep in mind, though, that without these coverages, nonfamily members injured in your car are unprotected, except by their own health policies, if any. If they are hurt in your car, they would have to sue you or the other driver to collect.

UNINSURED MOTORIST COVERAGE   If another driver collides with your car or otherwise causes an accident but has no insurance, your uninsured motorist insurance will cover the repair costs. In addition, if, for example, your car is sideswiped by another car but the driver never stops, your uninsured motorist insurance will cover the costs if you can somehow prove that it was another driver's negligence, not yours, that caused the accident.

UNDERINSURED MOTORIST COVERAGE   Many drivers have some but not enough insurance. To protect yourself against exposure to others who don't carry enough insurance, you can buy underinsured coverage in some states. It fills the gap between the inadequate coverage of the underinsured driver and your own damages up to your policy limits.

COLLISION COVERAGE   This is the coverage that pays to have your car repaired or replaced if it has been damaged in an accident. Most policies contain a deductible—the portion of the expenses you pay yourself before the insurance company's responsibility begins. The higher the deductible, the lower your premiums. Some deductibles are as low as $50; others can be as high as $500. If the damage doesn't exceed the amount of the deductible, the insurance company isn't required to pay for any of it.

COMPREHENSIVE COVERAGE   Collisions can destroy your car, of course, but so can floods, fires, falling rocks, vandals, or a collision with deer in the roadway. Comprehensive insurance covers the cost of replacing your car if you are faced with any of these unfortunate occurrences.

OPTIONAL COVERAGES   Some drivers like to plan for the possibility that their car will be out of service should they be involved in an accident. Certain insurance covers the towing of your car or repair required on the road. Other coverage provides the use of a rental car if yours is in the repair shop for a few days or weeks.

NO-FAULT INSURANCE   Some states have instituted various versions of no-fault insurance to speed up the process of compensation for those injured in auto accidents. This means that an insurance company will pay PIP, or Personal Injury Protection, payments up to a certain limit

Jeff purchased a $45,000 car with a five-year bank loan. Three years into the loan, Jeff was in a serious accident and his car was "totaled." Jeff was shocked when the insurance company gave him a limited cash amount for the value of his three-year-old car: $18,000. He still owed $20,000 on the car loan. Jeff, like many car owners, didn't understand that it's not the value of the loan that's insured, but merely the value of the car, which depreciates quickly.

for an insured person, regardless of who is at fault. The payments go toward paying doctors, hospitals, and wages lost from missed work. No-fault coverage grew out of a concern that those who suffered injuries had to wait for unconscionable periods of time for medical attention while insurance companies litigated about who was at fault and who should have to pay.

No-fault States (as of 1993)

Arkansas	Maryland	Pennsylvania
Colorado	Massachusetts	South Carolina
Connecticut	Michigan	South Dakota
Delaware	Minnesota	Texas
Florida	New Hampshire	Utah
Georgia	New Jersey	Virginia
Hawaii	New York	Washington
Kansas	North Dakota	Wisconsin
Kentucky	Oregon	

What follows is a hypothetical situation involving collecting a claim from an auto insurance company.

THE PROBLEM

Sharon's car was hit broadside by an unknown motorist, causing extensive damage. She filed a claim with her insurance company, which had a reputation as a "slow pay." Weeks passed, with the insurance company ignoring her phone calls and avoiding her demands for resolving the problem.

WHAT TO DO

1. Sharon should report her insurance company to the state insurance commissioner or government agency that oversees insurance issues in her state. The agency will most likely contact Sharon's insurance company and investigate the situation. If this does not resolve the problem, she should go on to step 2.

2. If the amount of the claim is small, she might want to file a lawsuit against the company in small-claims court. The company would then be forced to respond to her claim and explain why it has failed to act in good faith. If her claim is too large for small-claims court, she should go on to step 3.

3. Sharon should talk to a lawyer about intervening. Sometimes just the initial contact by a lawyer will prompt an insurance company to respond, but sometimes it requires that a bad-faith claim be filed in court.

WHERE TO GO WITH CAR COMPLAINTS

Consumers with complaints that relate to an automobile have several options. If the dealership that sold you your car fails to satisfy your complaint about a new car, look to the car manufacturer. Most have national or regional offices that handle consumer complaints. If this proves fruitless, consider using a state-sponsored third-party dispute resolution program, or mediation. For information on mediating car disputes, write:

Automotive Consumer Action Program (AUTOCAP)
8400 Westpark Drive
Mclean, VA 22102

The effectiveness and fairness of such programs is questionable because the members of the arbitration panels are often selected from among auto dealers.

Two organizations that mediate disputes for certain makes of cars are the Better Business Bureau (BBB Auto Line) as well as the American Automobile Association (AUTOSOLVE). State-sponsored arbitration programs should also be contacted. Check your phone book for their local offices.

If your complaint involves car repairs or used cars, contact your state consumer affairs office as well as the local Better Business Bureau. If the problem has broader ramifications, such as your wanting to report a series of odometer rollbacks, write:

Federal Trade Commission
Bureau of Consumer Protection
Washington, DC 20580

or

Center for Auto Safety
2001 S Street, N.W.
Washington, DC 20009
202-328-7700

If you have experienced a safety problem with your car, write:

The National Highway Traffic Safety Administration
400 Seventh Street, S.W.
Washington, DC 20590

Or, you can call its safety hotline at 800-424-9393; in Washington, D.C., call 202-366-0123. The NHTSA also provides information on auto recalls and defects.

For complaints about car rentals, including deceptive advertising or fraudulent practices, contact your state consumer affairs office, the attorney general's office, or the Better Business Bureau. If you have a problem with a large car rental company, call its national headquarters; some have consumer complaint officers.

For complaints about car insurance, begin by consulting your local insurance agent. Keep in mind that some of the major insurance companies maintain consumer affairs offices to handle your complaints. If what you need is simply more information about how car insurance works, contact:

Insurance Information Institute
110 William Street
New York, NY 10038
212-669-9200

If you have questions about the laws in your state that govern licensing, registration, or titles, contact the Department of Motor Vehicles, listed under State Government in your phone book.

6

CIVIL RIGHTS AND PERSONAL FREEDOMS

Civil rights laws, which affect the quality of our lives on a daily basis and govern so many of our personal interactions, are often taken so much for granted that we may never notice them until a problem arises. We know we have freedom of speech, but we rarely consciously think about it, unless, for example, a public speaker offends us by a speech filled with racial slurs. We know we have freedom of religion, but we probably don't examine this freedom until it is somehow threatened. For instance, what if our local public school doesn't excuse our children for their religious holidays?

Have any laws been broken? Have any rights been violated?

Questions and challenges to civil rights are encountered so frequently in everyday life that it is very important to understand the most problematic issues and how they are currently interpreted.

Neither the Bill of Rights (the first 10 amendments to the U.S. Constitution) nor the additional 17 amendments mention segregation, abortion, education, or even privacy, leaving it up to the justices of the Supreme Court to interpret our rights in light of the social and political climate of the times.

Some of our rights are spelled out clearly, such as the legal voting age, while others are implied in the amendments or interpreted by the courts, such as our right to privacy or right to travel.

THE FREEDOM OF EXPRESSION

The First Amendment prohibits governmental interference with freedom of expression, which includes the right to free speech, press, assembly, and petition. The definition of speech goes beyond the spoken word; it also includes language on bumper stickers, license plates, and tee-shirts. Although these rights are inalienable (cannot be taken away), they're not absolute or unlimited. It's the judicial system's job to maintain a balance between the free exchange of ideas and philosophies and the protection of its citizens against violence and other antisocial behavior it deems injurious.

The use of profanity and lewdness is protected by the First Amendment, but through the years the Supreme Court has wrestled with the issue of whether and what expression should be limited as obscene. In 1973 the Court established a definition of obscenity that applies a three-criteria test: For expression to be judged obscene, it has to appeal to the "prurient" or lewd interest in sex; portray sexual conduct in an obviously offensive way; and be judged to have no serious literary, artistic, political, or scientific value. The three criteria, said the Court, were to be evaluated in light of the standards of the

Two weeks before Election Day, a newspaper published a front-page story stating that the town's mayor was a member of a neo-Nazi group. The reporter based his story on an anonymous phone call. The mayor is entitled to sue the publisher for defamation of character, even though a celebrity or other individual in the public eye must prove that the person committing the defamation—in this case libel—either knew that the statement was false or had a "reckless disregard" for its truth. Failing to confirm a story of that kind with reliable sources and having entertained serious doubts as to the truth constitutes such disregard; thus the mayor can recover damages for defamation. The right to free speech is not unrestricted.

average person in the local community, as opposed to those of the country as a whole.

In addition to expression judged to be obscene, two other types of speech do not enjoy First Amendment protection because they are considered to go beyond the mere expression of ideas. They include the use of statements judged to be libelous and expressions that present a "clear and present danger."

Libel law is based on the principle that an individual's reputation is considered valuable and so should be protected against any false spoken or written word that unjustly impairs it. Because they have allowed themselves to be in the public eye, public figures and officials are granted less protection than the average citizen; they are required to prove that a falsehood was made with malice, that the individual knew or should have known that it was untrue.

What follows is a hypothetical situation involving libel.

THE PROBLEM

Anne, a schoolteacher, moved with her family to another state, where she applied for several teaching positions. In spite of her extensive experience and outstanding academic qualifications, she was turned down for every job for which she applied. She was told by one of the schools that her previous employer had given her a very negative recommendation based on her high rate of absenteeism and lack of involvement in school governance. In fact, Anne never missed a day of class and was as involved as any of the other teachers in various school committees.

WHAT TO DO

1. Anne should call or write her previous employer and ask what information they are providing to the schools to which she has applied for employment. If they acknowledge the mistake, she should confirm this acknowledgment in a letter to them and request that they write to each of the schools to which she applied, giving them the correct information along with an apology for the mistake. Anne should ask to receive a copy of each such letter that is sent.

2. She should also ask her previous employer for a copy of her personnel file. Many states require employers to make such

files available to employees for inspection and copying. If there is inaccurate information in the file, she should request that it be changed.

3. If the officials at her previous school refuse to acknowledge that the information is inaccurate or refuse to take corrective action, Anne should appeal to the superintendent of schools for remedial action. Such a letter should include all of the relevant information and the names and phone numbers of people who can confirm the accuracy of Anne's account. If the superintendent does not respond, she should send a follow-up letter with a copy to the state board of education.

4. If none of these steps gets results, Anne should consider filing a lawsuit, possibly in small-claims court, where she could handle the case herself without an attorney. If the stakes are sufficiently large and her reputation has been indelibly harmed, she should consult an attorney. Defamation cases, like other personal injury claims, are often handled on a contingency fee basis, which means that the client does not pay for the attorney's time; instead, the attorney receives a percentage of the settlement or judgment recovered in the case (usually 33 percent).

The second kind of unprotected expression is when language is judged to incite or cause serious harm intentionally—when it presents a "clear and present danger." In the famous example offered by Justice Oliver Wendell Holmes (*Schenck v. United States*, 1919), the U.S. Supreme Court offered as a standard the act of shouting "fire" in a crowded theater"; the Court ruled that the danger created to the public good outweighs the shouter's First Amendment right to free expression. Under this standard, expression judged as inciting to riot against the government is generally not protected.

Symbolic Speech

During the height of the Vietnam War and the heated emotions that surrounded it, antiwar demonstrators often wore black armbands. The Des Moines school system attempted to ban its students from wearing such armbands, but in 1969 the Supreme Court ruled that students had the right to wear them because wearing them apparently was not interfering with discipline in the school. The armbands were protected as "symbolic speech."

In 1989 the federal government passed legislation that prohibited the misuse or defacing of the American flag. The following year, the Supreme Court found the law unconstitutional, holding that although state and federal governments can create symbols, they cannot dictate or prohibit actions surrounding them (*United States v. Eichman*, 1990). In an earlier case (*Texas v. Johnson*, 1989), the Supreme Court said: "If there is a bedrock principle underlying the First Amendment, it is that the Government may not prohibit the expression of an idea simply because society finds this idea itself offensive or disagreeable."

But the Court looked at the burning of draft cards differently. In 1968 it determined that draft cards were an integral part of the Selective Service system, and that their destruction hindered the system's process. The Supreme Court held that draft card burning was not protected symbolic speech.

Freedom from Compelled Speech

Just as the First Amendment provides Americans with the freedom to speak, it extends the freedom to abstain from speech completely. For example, the Supreme Court has held that a citizen cannot be forced to pledge allegiance to the American flag. And in 1977 the Court held that a person has the right to cover up the (New Hampshire) state motto "Live Free or Die" on a license plate, because it was counter to a person's religious beliefs.

What follows is a hypothetical situation involving freedom of speech.

THE PROBLEM

The town library committee has recently learned that the town's public library collection includes a book questioning whether the Holocaust actually occurred. The committee believes such a book is not only offensive but also ludicrous from the standpoint of historical accuracy. They decided that it is unworthy of inclusion in the library collection and ordered the librarian to remove it. Simon, a civil libertarian, believes that the book should stay, even though he himself lost several relatives in the Holocaust. He believes that exclusion of the book on the basis of its content is a dangerous precedent and that banning the book may even give it greater credibility in the eyes of some people.

WHAT TO DO

1. Simon should ask the library committee to schedule a public meeting to discuss the issue and to reconsider its decision.

2. If the committee refuses to reconsider its decision, Simon should bring the issue to the attention of the mayor, board of selectmen, or other officials with responsibility for the library. He should ask for consideration of the issue and possibly for a meeting involving the librarian, library committee, and interested citizens.

3. Simon should consider writing a letter to the editor of the local newspaper, encouraging fellow citizens to express their views on the subject to the library committee.

4. Although filing a lawsuit is expensive, the local office of the American Civil Liberties Union (ACLU) or an association of librarians might be willing to find a lawyer to handle the case on a *pro bono* basis. (Lawyers have an ethical obligation in most jurisdictions to do a certain amount of work each year *pro bono publico*, i.e., for the public good, without charge or at a reduced rate.)

FREEDOM OF THE PRESS

Despite the fact that the First Amendment mentions the press specifically, the truth is that the news media, whether print, radio, or television, have no special rights over and above that of the average American. Nevertheless, the question of prior restraint, or censorship, usually concerns the press more specifically than it does others. In 1931 the Supreme Court stated that the government had no right to censor something before it was published, holding that the public was entitled to the free flow of information and ideas.

What follows is a hypothetical situation involving freedom of the press.

THE PROBLEM

A group of local high school students calling themselves High School Students for the Environment (HSSE) has begun publish-

One of the nation's most important prior restraint cases involved the Pentagon Papers, classified government documents regarding Vietnam War policy. The information in the Pentagon Papers was embarrassing to the Nixon administration, and after two newspapers began publishing portions of it, the federal government asked the Court to prohibit further publication. The Supreme Court, much to the dismay of the government, held that prior restraint in this circumstance was a violation of First Amendment rights.

ing a monthly newspaper that it would like to sell in newspaper distribution boxes around the city. HSSE asks city officials for permission to place the distribution boxes in locations where there are already such boxes containing daily or weekly general interest newspapers. The city refuses HSSE's request on the ground that space on the public sidewalks is limited, and therefore some line has to be drawn concerning the use of such space for distribution boxes; the city claims that drawing the line at daily and weekly newspapers is defensible. HSSE believes that it has been refused permission primarily because of the content of the newspaper.

WHAT TO DO

1. HSSE should find out who has the last word on decisions of this kind in the city—is it the mayor, the city council, or some other body or official? HSSE should ask for review of the official's decision.

2. If HSSE does not receive a favorable response, it should look for allies in challenging the city's ruling. There may be a trade association of newspaper publishers that would be willing to help. Likewise, the ACLU might be interested.

3. If those organizations cannot negotiate a solution (such as setting distribution boxes in a few selected locations), HSSE should consult an attorney, perhaps someone from the ACLU, and a lawsuit could be filed. Since HSSE will be asking for injunctive relief (an order requiring the city to permit HSSE to install distribution boxes), the claim cannot be brought in small-claims court, but must be brought in the state or local trial court.

FREEDOM OF ASSEMBLY AND PETITION

The First Amendment also prohibits governmental interference with "the right of the people peaceably to assemble and to petition the Government for a redress of grievances." Simply put, Americans have the right to conduct peaceful demonstrations, protests, and rallies.

The Court often uses the "clear and present danger" test in determining whether First Amendment protection is extended to gatherings, demonstrations, and protests. In 1982 National Association for the Advancement of Colored People (NAACP) spokesman Charles Evers warned a group of African-Americans in a rally that if they ignored a boycott against white store owners, they would be punished. The white merchants sued the NAACP for interfering with their livelihood, arguing that the First Amendment did not protect Evers's speech. The Supreme Court disagreed, holding that his words did not incite lawless conduct or violence. His speech and the right to assemble were protected.

What happens if the speaker is not attempting to induce violence but his or her words nevertheless create unrest or dissatisfaction? What if the crowd becomes hostile toward the speaker? The First Amendment protects the speaker, and the police must control the crowd, not arrest the spokesperson. Verbal assaults that inflict injury or incite an immediate breach of peace, called "fighting words," are not protected.

What follows is a hypothetical situation involving freedom of assembly.

THE PROBLEM

In two weeks the town of Ashford will be the site of a march by the Ku Klux Klan, which has asked for and received a parade permit from the town. The Klan chose Ashford because of its large African-American population and because it recently elected an Asian-American mayor. An ad hoc committee of citizens plans to line the parade route to protest the Klan march, but the mayor has announced that because of the strong sentiment against the Klan in Ashford, she will not permit anti-Klan protesters to be in close proximity to the march. The citizens committee believes that its right to assemble peacefully is being infringed.

WHAT TO DO

1. The citizens committee should ask for a meeting with the mayor and, if necessary, the town counsel. The mayor is understandably concerned about keeping the peace and the political repercussions of a violent clash between the Klan and the protesters. The town counsel may be more attuned to the First Amendment implications of limiting the protesters' right to assemble.

2. If those discussions are not fruitful, the citizens committee should consider approaching the city council or legislative body for the town to seek a resolution of this dispute. The city council may have the power to override the mayor's decision or may, by adopting a resolution, persuade the mayor to reconsider.

3. It may be worth consulting the state attorney general's office. In most states, the attorney general has the responsibility for enforcement of state law, including laws pertaining to civil rights and civil liberties, even if such enforcement pits the attorney general against a municipality. The ACLU and other civil rights/civil liberties organizations might also be willing to assist the citizens committee.

FREEDOM OF RELIGION

The First Amendment provides that "Congress shall make no law respecting an establishment of religion, or prohibiting the free exercise thereof." Theoretically, the amendment (which applies to any governmental action) creates a separation of church and state.

The freedom of religion guaranteed by the First Amendment is made up of two parts: the Establishment Clause and the Free Exercise Clause.

The Establishment Clause

The first clause of the First Amendment prohibits the government from promoting religion. The Supreme Court has determined that three issues must be addressed before the government can become involved in a religious matter. First, what is the government's reason for involvement? A strictly nonreligious legislative purpose must be served. Second, the main effect of the government's action cannot be the advancement of religion. And third, the action cannot "foster excessive government entanglement with religion."

A wide range of Establishment Clause issues have been tested in the courts:

- Prayers, daily Bible reading, reciting the Lord's Prayer, and posting of the Ten Commandments in public schools are prohibited. Prayer in schools has been a volatile controversy since 1962. But an opening prayer for Congress is permitted, with the Court holding that the founders of this country did not perceive it as violating the Establishment Clause, since the first Congress paid a chaplain to provide an opening prayer.

- Assistance to religious schools is permitted in some circumstances, such as paying bus fares for students and lending secular textbooks to parochial and private schools. But direct grants to religious schools, including supplementing salaries, have generally been held to violate the First Amendment.

- Property and other tax exemptions to religious organizations have been upheld as constitutional.

- Blue laws, or Sunday closing laws, have been upheld on the basis that they were created to provide a day of rest, not for religious purposes.

- Nativity scenes and religious displays on government property are protected by the First Amendment if used in conjunction with the secular celebration of religious holidays.

The Free Exercise Clause

The second part of the religious freedom guarantees in the First Amendment prohibits the government from interfering with a person's right to have and practice certain religious beliefs. In some cases the Supreme Court has been called on to determine whether the "free exercise" of religion interferes with the welfare of the public.

- The Court held that the Amish, a religious group, are required to pay Social Security taxes despite the fact that they oppose a system of public insurance. Yet in a separate case the Court ruled that Amish children were not required to attend public school, a practice that violated their religious beliefs, if they received the proper education at home or in their private community.

- The right of a Seventh-Day Adventist to refuse to work on a Saturday, her Sabbath, was upheld by the Court on the ground that requiring her to do so violated her right to freely exercise her religion.

- An Orthodox Jew maintained that the air force's insistence that its members not wear hats or headwear indoors was interfering with his religious right of wearing a yarmulke. In this case the Court ruled in favor of the military, which claimed uniformity was important in maintaining order.

What follows is a hypothetical situation involving freedom of religion.

THE PROBLEM

Marshall, an observant Jew, was recently fired from his position as a salesclerk at a department store. On his tenth day of employment at the store, Marshall informed his supervisor that he would not be available to work on Jewish holidays, and he provided his supervisor with a list of those holidays for the coming year. The supervisor was alarmed to discover that Marshall was not planning to work on several of the store's busiest days because of his observance of those holidays. The next day, Marshall was fired. When Marshall asked the supervisor why he was fired, the supervisor informed him that the personnel office was cutting back on staff because of budgetary problems, and he was the first to go because of his lack of seniority.

WHAT TO DO

1. Although it may seem apparent that the reason for Marshall's termination was his religion, he should try to get as much information as possible before considering legal action. For example, he should ask the supervisor's manager about the reasons for his termination, and he should request a copy of his personnel file from the company.

2. If the company has a personnel manual or policy concerning employee grievances, Marshall should initiate a complaint and follow the procedures for processing a grievance.

3. If Marshall is not able to resolve this matter within the company, he should promptly consult the state or local antidiscrimination agency or the federal Equal Employment Opportunity Commission (EEOC). Staff investigators at such an office will most likely investigate Marshall's claim and make a determination regarding whether state and federal laws barring discrimination on the basis of religion have been violated. (It is important to take this step promptly because of the short statute of limitations on most discrimination claims.)

4. Marshall can also proceed with a lawsuit if the antidiscrimination agency fails to act on his complaint, or if he asks for and receives a "right to sue" letter, which the agency will issue on request after a certain period of time has elapsed. Antidiscrimination lawsuits are complicated, however, and in most cases legal representation will be necessary. In Marshall's case the Anti-Defamation League or the American Jewish Congress as well as the ACLU and civil liberties organizations might be able to either provide counsel or make a referral.

DUE PROCESS RIGHTS

The Fifth and Fourteenth Amendments guarantee that no one shall "be deprived of life, liberty, or property without due process of law." There are two types of due process rights. *Substantive* due process requires that laws be written so that the governed understand their obligations—that is, comprehend what is illegal and what are the penalties—and that the laws apply equally to everyone. *Procedural* due process refers to how the government carries out proceedings, such as a hearing or trial, in which an individual's life, liberty, or property are at stake. The individual must be given proper notice, an opportunity to prepare, a chance to be heard and respond, and the opportunity to have a fair hearing before an impartial panel.

The deprivation of liberty means more than simply imprisonment, and the term *property* goes beyond land or personal belongings. These words are far-reaching, say the courts, and the right to a fair hearing prior to the withdrawal of Social Security benefits, before the garnishment of wages, or before a parent is stripped of the right to care for a child are all implicit in the Due Process Clause of the Fifth and Fourteenth Amendments. These due process guarantees also provide us with the rights to privacy, to marriage and a family, and to travel.

THE RIGHT TO PRIVACY

Americans consider privacy to be one of their most precious rights, and in the age of computers and the stockpiling of personal information by government and private agencies, the loss of privacy is a growing concern. Records are readily available concerning your physical health, your financial circumstances, and even your preferences in books and rental videos.

Legal Protection

The word *privacy* is not mentioned in the Constitution, but several amendments imply the privilege. The First Amendment grants us the right to associate with whomever we wish. In prohibiting the quartering of military troops during peacetime without our consent, the Third Amendment protects the general sanctity of our homes. The Fourth Amendment protects individuals against unreasonable searches and seizures, and the Fifth Amendment gives us the right to refuse to testify against ourselves.

In addition to these constitutional protections, you have the right to sue anyone who

- uses your name or photo for commercial use without your permission
- trespasses or intrudes on your private property, including your house, apartment, boat, hotel room, or office
- publicly discloses private facts about your life
- places you in a "false light"

These intrusions are known as "torts."

Americans are entitled to private communications, and federal and state laws prohibit the opening of, reading of, or tampering with mail belonging to others. Eavesdropping and the unauthorized wiretapping and recording of telephone conversations is also illegal, but controlling these abuses becomes more difficult as cellular and cordless phones facilitate easy surveillance of the airwaves. In addition, the phone companies quite legally keep records of whom we call, both long distance and local.

What follows is a hypothetical situation involving the right to privacy.

THE PROBLEM

Hillary was astonished when she picked up the daily newspaper and saw her photograph on the front page. The photo accompanied an article about a crackdown on people with dozens of unpaid parking tickets whose cars had been "booted." The caption under the photo identified the individuals in the picture as scofflaws waiting in line to pay their long-overdue parking tickets. Hillary, however, was not in line to pay parking tickets; she was in line to renew her driver's license.

WHAT TO DO

1. Hillary should call the newspaper, ask for the news editor, and insist on an immediate retraction or correction, prominently located on page one. She should follow up on her phone call with a hand-delivered letter that same day confirming the substance of the phone call.

2. If the news editor does not agree to print a retraction or correction, Hillary should call the editor or publisher of the newspaper immediately, and, if neither is available when she calls, send a fax or hand-deliver a letter demanding a correction.

3. If the retraction is printed, Hillary should take the further step of requesting that the newspaper either discard the photograph or, if they intend to keep it for their files, attach a note to it indicating that she was merely waiting to have her driver's license renewed at the time the photograph was taken.

4. If the newspaper fails or refuses to publish a retraction or correction, she should consult an attorney about the possibility

of filing a lawsuit. Since the photograph was used without her permission, she will probably have no difficulty establishing the newspaper's liability. In order to recover a judgment, however, she will have to show that she suffered monetary injury to her reputation and/or emotional distress as a result of the invasion of her privacy.

Privileged Communications

Communications between doctor and patient, lawyer and client, and clergyperson and parishioner are considered to be "privileged," or protected; such professionals cannot be compelled to reveal to the courts or others information that was given to them in confidence. But as businesses become more computerized and office personnel have increasing access to privileged information, private information is readily obtainable.

The following hypothetical situation involves privileged communications.

THE PROBLEM

After 14 years of marriage, Harvey and Sheila are in the midst of a bitter divorce. They have not been able to resolve the issue of custody of their only child, Ellen, who is six years old. Harvey's lawyer has hired a private investigator, who is looking for evidence that Sheila has mistreated their daughter. Sheila recently learned that the investigator paid a visit to the minister of the church in which Sheila is active. Sheila suspects that the investigator may have been asking the minister whether she had ever confided in him about difficulties in caring for Ellen.

WHAT TO DO

1. Sheila should ask her minister whether he has been asked about her conversations with him. If her conversations were private (no third parties were present), they are considered privileged and, in general, cannot be used in any legal proceeding. (In some states, however, laws permit the disclosure of otherwise privileged information if it pertains to child abuse or neglect.)

2. If the minister has been interrogated by the investigator, Sheila (or her attorney) should send a letter to her husband, the investigator, and her husband's attorney protesting this infringement of her privacy. Sheila should also remind her

minister that she considers any conversations she has had with him to be confidential and privileged.

3. If the incident is repeated, Sheila should consider reporting it to the state bar or other attorney licensing body, report the conduct of the investigator to the state attorney general's office, and request that the court in which her divorce action is proceeding issue an order barring such intrusive inquiries.

Freedom of Information Act

As technology expands, additional legal safeguards are needed to protect our privacy. Until the mid-1960s the federal government and all its agencies maintained a policy of secrecy around the records it had amassed about government operations and the private lives of United States citizens. In 1966 Congress moved toward changing this by passing the Freedom of Information Act (FOIA), which required government agencies to release their records under specific conditions on request, with certain exemptions, such as information relating to national security. Agency refusals to provide information requested under FOIA are subject to judicial review.

In addition the Privacy Act of 1974 requires the government to disclose what personal information it retains in its files in regard to individuals, and specifies that these records be used only for their original lawful purpose. People are permitted to request copies of their files and are able to correct them if inaccuracies are found. If you decide to apply for government records—whether from the Internal Revenue Service, the Securities and Exchange Commission, or the Social Security Administration—you can consult the *United States Government Manual* (found in most libraries) to determine where to address the Privacy Act officer of the respective agency. Ask the officer what information and personal identification you will need to supply in order to receive a response to your written request for information. Many states have their own Fair Information Practices statutes, which make information held by state agencies available upon a proper request.

Fair Credit Reporting Act

Perhaps the single federal privacy statute that affects most Americans is the Fair Credit Reporting Act of 1970. It sets out guidelines for the reporting of consumer credit histories: who has access to them, how they are to be used, how to get a copy, and how to have errors corrected. (See chapter 9.)

Other Privacy Issues

Aside from matters of access to and disclosure of government records, the courts have been faced with other privacy matters that involve such issues as marriage, sexual relations, and procreation. In 1965 the U.S. Supreme Court held that the state of Connecticut had no right to prohibit the sale of contraceptives to married couples. Justice William O. Douglas reasoned that "the very idea [of such a ban] is repulsive to the notions of privacy surrounding the marriage relationship. . . . We deal with a right of privacy older than the Bill of Rights." Seven years later, the Supreme Court ruled that unmarried couples should have the same right to use contraceptives in the privacy of their own homes.

In *Roe v. Wade* in 1973, the Supreme Court held that a woman's right to privacy includes the right to abort a fetus during the first three months of pregnancy; however, during the second trimester the states may intercede to regulate abortions, and during the third trimester abortion can be prohibited unless the woman's life is found to be threatened by the pregnancy. Since the 1973 decision, a woman's right to have an abortion has been challenged in the courts by those who have sought to either eliminate the ability to obtain a legal abortion, place limitations on conditions under which abortion would be legal, or limit or eliminate government financial aid to those seeking an abortion and/or to health facilities where abortions are performed.

What follows is a hypothetical situation involving the right to privacy and housing discrimination.

THE PROBLEM

Albert and Victoria have been on a waiting list for public housing for over one year. When their names reached the top of the list, they were called in for an interview with the Housing Authority director, who gave them an application to fill out and asked them several questions, including "Are the two of you married?" Albert and Victoria said that they did not consider such a question appropriate. The director then told them that the Housing Authority has a policy against renting units to unmarried couples of the opposite sex. The director admitted that the Housing Authority would rent the unit to them if they were both male or both female. Albert and Victoria believe that, since both of them are over 21, what they do in the privacy of their apartment is their own business.

WHAT TO DO

1. Albert and Victoria should (a) inform the director that they object to the policy and (b) request that the Housing Authority refrain from renting the apartment for a reasonable amount of time while they try to determine the legality of the policy. This request should be confirmed with a letter to the director.

2. Albert and Victoria should try to determine whether the director was carrying out the actual policy of the Housing Authority or merely imposing her own values. A call or letter to the chair of the Housing Authority should enable them to get an answer to that question.

3. If the Housing Authority stands behind the director with regard to the policy, Albert and Victoria should lodge their protests with the mayor, town counsel, and counsel for any state or federal agency that provides funds to the Housing Authority (such as the U.S. Department of Housing and Urban Development).

4. If these protests do not produce results, Albert and Victoria should contact an attorney and consider filing a lawsuit requesting an injunction against the Housing Authority's restrictive policy. A legal services office that handles landlord-tenant matters might be able to provide legal representation.

THE RIGHT TO EQUAL PROTECTION

The Equal Protection guarantees of the Fifth and Fourteenth Amendments assure that every citizen has the same rights and obligations as those of any other. Federal, state, and local governments are prohibited from treating groups or classifications of individuals differently on the basis of characteristics such as race, national origin, religion, age, and gender. Many of these rights were established only after those who suffered discrimination engaged in long and costly legal battles to secure them.

Equal Access to Public Accommodations and Facilities

The Civil Rights Act of 1964 prohibits racial discrimination in any public accommodation—that is, any facility within the realm of interstate commerce that provides food, lodging, or entertainment. This includes any facility that uses out-of-state products, hires employees from out of state, or is located close to an interstate highway. In other words, virtually all restaurants, hotels, gas stations, bars, movie theaters, video stores, doughnut shops, etc., are prohibited from discriminating on the basis of race, religion, ethnicity, and gender. Public facilities, which include those owned, managed, or operated by or for a state, local, or the federal government also are prohibited from discriminating against anyone. Only private clubs that have a limited selective membership have the right to deny admission or use of their facility to others, and even some of those clubs have recently been ordered to halt discriminatory practices.

What follows is a hypothetical situation involving racial discrimination and public accommodations.

THE PROBLEM

Phil, the vice president for marketing of a large electronics firm, frequently takes business prospects to lunch at a fancy restaurant in a local hotel. Each time Phil has gone there, he has been given a table at the back of the restaurant in spite of his request for a table by the front window. Each time he has been told that the tables at the front window are reserved, but he has often seen them remain empty throughout his meal there. Phil, who is African-American, suspects that the restaurant is making a concerted effort to seat nonwhite patrons in out-of-the-way corners of the restaurant. He has noticed that nonwhites who eat in the restaurant are almost invariably seated by the maître d' at the rear of the dining room.

WHAT TO DO

1. Phil should call or write a letter to the hotel management, outlining the problem and asking for a response.

2. If the problem persists, Phil should contact the state antidiscrimination agency or a local civil rights organization. Such agencies and organizations often use "testers" to determine whether racial discrimination is being practiced—that is, they send white and nonwhite people (who are otherwise similar) to the restaurant to see how they will be treated. The results often determine if there is a basis for legal action.

3. Phil might consider contacting civil rights and other civic organizations, asking them not to patronize the hotel or restaurant until they change their practice of seating nonwhites at the back of the restaurant. Such a boycott could lead to legal action by the restaurant or hotel to stop the boycott; however, Phil has the right to disseminate truthful information about the restaurant.

Education

Although nothing in the Constitution guarantees a public education, civil rights laws have made it illegal to provide members of one race with a lesser quality of public education than those of another. Civil rights acts prohibit discrimination based on race, color, national origin, and age in programs or activities funded by the federal government. This includes admissions, financial aid, academic programs, grades, discipline, and athletics.

In 1954 the Supreme Court in *Brown v. Board of Education* struck down intentional school segregation as a violation of equal protection and held that racially segregated school systems have a duty to desegregate "with all deliberate speed." In 1971 the Court held that busing was constitutional to eliminate segregation and that federal courts have the authority to supervise the desegregation process and compliance with desegregation orders.

In an effort to correct the inequality of the past, affirmative action programs sometimes relied on racial quota systems, which drew charges of reverse discrimination. The most publicized such case, the *University of California Regents v. Bakke* (1978), involved a white man, Allan Bakke, who was refused admission to the University of California at Davis Medical School. The school had set aside 16 percent of its student positions for members of minority groups. Bakke sued the school, arguing that he was a victim of discrimination because the minority quota prevented his acceptance. The Supreme

Court held that race could be used as a factor in deciding who should be admitted, but that the use of quotas in affirmative action programs was discriminatory.

What follows is a hypothetical situation involving racial discrimination in education.

THE PROBLEM

George and Grace are Hispanic-American parents of Carmen, a very bright 14-year-old who will be starting high school next fall. George and Grace would like their daughter to be enrolled in the college prep "track" at the high school, but they have discovered from talking with other parents that the high school rarely assigns Hispanic-American students to the college prep program, in spite of the fact that a significant percentage of the high school's students are Hispanic-American. They are also concerned because the high school has never hired a Hispanic-American teacher. George and Grace fear that if they wait until the fall to see what program Carmen is assigned to, it will be more difficult to change her placement.

WHAT TO DO

1. George and Grace should speak with the principal and, if necessary, the superintendent of schools to express their concerns.

2. If George and Grace are unable to resolve this matter at the local level, they should consider contacting the state board of education. Most state education departments have an office in charge of compliance with civil rights laws and carrying out affirmative action mandates.

3. As a last resort, George and Grace should consider contacting an attorney and filing a lawsuit; in connection with the lawsuit, they would have access to information about their school system's failure to hire Hispanic-Americans and failure to assign Hispanic-American students to the college preparatory program. Although school officials are almost certain to deny any intentional discrimination, the record of their past decisions with respect to hiring and placement may demonstrate a pattern of discrimination.

Education and Religion

The Supreme Court has ruled that the public education system cannot violate a person's right to practice his or her religion. For example, students may choose to attend private or religious schools instead of opting for a public school education. Students are permitted to be absent from public schools on religious holidays without penalty.

Housing

The Civil Rights Act of 1968 prohibits racial discrimination in housing. It applies to all dwellings sold or rented through a real estate agent, multiple-unit buildings with more than four units, single-family homes sold in developments not privately owned, and dwellings constructed with financial assistance from the federal government.

THE RIGHTS OF WOMEN

Women won the right to vote in 1920, when the Nineteenth Amendment was ratified. Discrimination against women by governmental agencies was declared a violation of equal protection rights by the Supreme Court in 1971. Women have also gained the protection of other legislation, including laws that prohibit discrimination against them in education, housing, employment, and the granting of credit.

> *The debate team at Jefferson High School has traditionally been all male. Monica, one of the better orators in the school, wants to join but is told the team is restricted to boys. If they are found to have discouraged her from joining the team, the school administrators are violating federal civil rights legislation, which prohibits discrimination based on sex in any federally funded program or activity. Monica's parents can file a complaint with the Education Department of the Office of Civil Rights.*

What follows is a hypothetical situation involving discrimination based on gender.

THE PROBLEM

Rose, a loan officer at a local bank, has served on the finance committee for the town for eight years. The five-member committee has never had a woman chairperson, and Rose believes that her professional experience and long service on the committee amply qualify her for the position. The chair of the finance committee (like the other members) is appointed by the mayor. When Rose called the mayor and requested that she be nominated for the chair position, he told her that, although he would never discriminate against women, he thought that the town was not yet ready to have a woman in charge of town finances and that her nomination would erode the credibility of the finance committee and impair its ability to function. In the end the mayor appointed a man less qualified than Rose as chair of the town finance committee.

WHAT TO DO

1. Because there were no witnesses to the conversation between Rose and the mayor, Rose should promptly document the conversation by sending a letter (certified mail, return receipt requested) to him, recounting her recollection of his statement about the town being unwilling to accept a woman as chair of the finance committee. The letter should ask the mayor to let her know if his recollection of the conversation differs in any way.

2. Since the mayor cannot legally use the excuse of acquiescence to the prejudices of others, his decision constitutes sex (gender) discrimination if it was based primarily on Rose's gender. If the mayor's appointment needs to be confirmed by the town selectmen or another governmental body, Rose should consider challenging the appointment in that arena. Alternatively, Rose could ask the mayor to give her some assurance that the appointment will be made the following year in a gender-neutral manner.

3. If Rose is not able to correct the problem in the political arena, she should consider legal action against the mayor and the town. Legal assistance might be available from organizations such as the American Civil Liberties Union, National Organization for Women, and other women's rights organizations.

THE RIGHTS OF THE DISABLED

Legislation protecting the rights of disabled Americans is a relatively new phenomenon. The Rehabilitation Act of 1973 was the first major law that gave disabled persons protection from discrimination. In 1975 the Education for All Handicapped Children Act was passed. This law requires that children with special needs—the disabled, the mentally retarded, and the emotionally disturbed—have the option of a free public education, either in regular public schools where they would receive special attention or in special schools.

In 1990 Congress passed the Americans with Disabilities Act (ADA). ADA is such a sweeping piece of legislation that it was designed to be phased in over a 25-year period, with most of the changes to be in place by 1995.

A disabled person, as defined by law, is someone who has a mental or physical impairment that substantially restricts one or more major life activities, such as walking, breathing, working, or caring for oneself. The categories covered include disabilities resulting from cancer, AIDS, multiple sclerosis, diabetes, heart disease, and schizophrenia.

What follows is a hypothetical situation involving discrimination against a disabled child concerning education.

THE PROBLEM

The local public school system has just refused Julia's request to enroll her son, Lyle, in the regular kindergarten program. Instead, Lyle, who has epilepsy, has been assigned to a school for special needs students. Julia wants Lyle to be "mainstreamed," because she thinks that his attending a school for special needs students will impair his self-esteem. Lyle's epilepsy is controlled by his taking an antiseizure medication, and Julia has explained to school officials that Lyle's teachers would only need to be aware of certain very simple precautions in the event that he has a seizure. The school officials have expressed concern about the effect that Lyle's seizures may have on his fellow students. In addition, they are concerned about the long hours Lyle will be at the school and the school's after-school program, because Julia is a single mother with a full-time job.

WHAT TO DO

1. Julia should find out whether Lyle's physician would recommend mainstreaming Lyle in an ordinary public school classroom. If the answer to that question is yes, Julia should get a letter from the doctor, addressed to the elementary school

principal and superintendent of schools, explaining the reasons why Lyle does not need to be in a special school.

2. If the state department of education has a "special needs" office, Julia should contact that office and ask for assistance.

3. If there is an association or society of people with epilepsy, or an association of parents of special needs children, Julia should look to them for advice and support in negotiating with the school system.

4. As a last resort, Julia might consider contacting an attorney and litigating to assert Lyle's right to be in a mainstream classroom. Federal law requires school officials to make reasonable accommodations for Lyle to obtain an appropriate education.

The most significant changes brought by the ADA are in the area of employment, where discrimination in hiring, promoting, and dismissing people with disabilities is now prohibited. An employer cannot inquire about an individual's disability in a job interview unless the applicant raises the subject first. An interviewer cannot ask whether an applicant has filed previous health insurance or workers' compensation claims, or whether he or she has had problems with drugs or alcohol. Once the individual has been offered a job, the employer can inquire about disabilities for the sole purpose of making reasonable accommodations. Employers are required to make physical alterations in the workplace to accommodate disabled employees as long as this does not create an "undue hardship." (Building a ramp for a wheelchair, for example, is not considered an undue hardship; buying a specially equipped computer might be.) Until July 26, 1994, these ADA requirements apply only to employers with 25 or more employees. After that date, those with 15 or more employees will be covered by the Act.

What follows is a hypothetical situation involving discrimination against the disabled.

THE PROBLEM

The town hall in Ainsworth is over 200 years old and is completely inaccessible for people in wheelchairs. There are no ramps that would permit access to the first floor, where the town offices are located; likewise, the stairs to the second floor, where board meetings are held, create a barrier. Joe, who is paralyzed from the waist down, has asked the town whether it plans to make the town hall wheelchair-accessible, and he has been told that there is no money in the town budget to do so. Now that he is retired, Joe wishes to get more involved in town government, and he is frustrated by having to rely on others to move him in and out of the town hall.

WHAT TO DO

1. Joe should ask whether the town has compiled a list of citizens with mobility impairments or if there is a local association of people with disabilities. Joe's request stands a better chance of being honored if he joins with others in making it.

2. Even if there are no other similarly disabled people in Ainsworth willing to join with Joe in this effort, he should ask the town to make a reasonable accommodation by installing a ramp to the first floor of the building and conducting board meetings in wheelchair-accessible locations, such as schools.

3. If town officials will not make such accommodations, Joe should bring the matter to the attention of the town meeting, board of selectmen, or other town legislative body. He should also consider soliciting support by means of a letter to the editor of the local newspaper.

4. If the town will not make a reasonable accommodation, Joe should consider legal action. A complaint to the state or local antidiscrimination agency is one option. Another is to seek legal assistance for the filing of a lawsuit; the state attorney general's office, the American Civil Liberties Union, or a statewide organization of people with disabilities might provide legal representation.

The ADA also prohibits discrimination in public transportation, including buses, trains, taxis, and limousines. This includes the requirement that new buses be equipped with wheelchair lifts, and commuter rail services must have at least one car that can accommodate mobility-impaired passengers. Places of public accommodations, such as restaurants, offices, zoos, and grocery stores, must remove any physical barriers and adopt policies and procedures that avoid discrimination against the disabled.

THE RIGHTS OF OLDER AMERICANS

Discrimination against older Americans has been most obvious in the workplace, where employers justified forced retirement at age 65 by maintaining that people of this age were less efficient and less productive than younger workers. Such discrimination is no longer permitted; state legislatures and Congress have enacted laws that prohibit age discrimination by employers. The Age Discrimination in Employment Act (ADEA) protects Americans between the ages of 40 and 70, prohibiting discrimination in hiring, promotions, benefits, pensions, salaries, terminations, or other employment-related decisions because of age. (See chapter 8.)

Older Americans have also been victims of more subtle discrimination in housing, voting rights, and accommodations to the disabled.

What follows is a hypothetical situation involving age discrimination.

THE PROBLEM

Daniel and Deborah, a married couple in their sixties, wanted to move. They responded to an advertisement for an apartment, but when they arrived to inquire about the vacancy, the building manager said that the unit was no longer available. When they saw the same ad in the newspaper the following week, they returned and asked the manager about the apartment. He told them that he would be willing to rent the apartment to them, but the building's owner had instructed him not to rent to "older people" because they need more services from the building's management. Also, there has been a rising number of robberies and beatings of older people, and the owner is worried about being sued.

WHAT TO DO

1. Daniel and Deborah should contact the owner of the building and ask if the policy described by the manager is, in fact, the owner's policy. If the owner denies that such a policy

exists, they should ask the owner to instruct the manager to rent the vacant apartment to them.

2. If the owner admits that apartments in the building are not available to "older people," they should insist on a change in the policy, because discrimination on the basis of age is unlawful. The owner's fear of lawsuits because of possible criminal activity by others is not a legal justification for such discrimination, nor is the concern that older people might need assistance.

3. If the owner refuses to change the policy or denies having such a policy, Daniel and Deborah should report the incident to the state or local antidiscrimination agency and the U.S. Department of Housing and Urban Development for investigation. Those organizations have the legal authority to pursue litigation against the building owner and obtain an order requiring the owner to rent any available apartment to Daniel and Deborah if they are otherwise qualified to be tenants.

SOCIAL SECURITY RIGHTS

Congress granted qualified Americans the right to Social Security benefits in 1935, and through the years the system has changed to adjust to the needs of those who receive assistance. In addition to providing retirement income for those who qualify, other categories of Social Security benefits include Old Age, Survivors', and Disability Insurance (OASDI).

Your eligibility for retirement benefits and the amount of Social Security payments to which you are entitled are determined by the number of quarters of coverage (three-month periods) you've been employed and how much you have paid into the system, as well as by how much you've earned.

Old Age or Retirement Benefits

To the federal government, 65 is retirement age, the time when you'll receive full Social Security benefits if you've accumulated enough quarters and are otherwise eligible. You can receive benefits if you retire as early as age 62, but you'll collect only 80 percent of full

> *Check with your local office of the Social Security Administration to find out how many quarters you've accumulated and how that translates into benefits. Be sure the records are accurate by checking them against your own. If your name has changed, remember to let your local Social Security office know so that your quarters are properly credited to you.*

benefits. Your benefits decrease for each month before age 65 that you retire and increase for each month after 65 that you continue to work.

If you decide to come out of retirement and return to work at age 70 or later, you won't lose any of your benefits. But if you are younger than 70, benefits may be affected, depending on your income. Returning to work also adds "quarters" and income to your record and may increase the benefits to which you are entitled later.

Others who are eligible to receive benefits as a dependent because an immediate family member already receives retirement benefits include:

- a husband or wife at age 62 (If he or she applies at age 65, benefits amount to one-half of the spouse's; earlier application, such as at age 62, will lower the monthly payments.)
- a divorced spouse at age 62, if the couple had been married for a minimum of 10 years
- dependent children in elementary or secondary school, who can collect benefits up to age 18
- dependent children regardless of their age, if severely disabled before the age of 22

Survivor Benefits

The dependents or former dependents of a deceased employee are eligible to receive Social Security benefits regardless of whether the employee reached retirement age before his or her death.

- A surviving spouse and dependent children of a deceased employee are entitled to survivor benefits.

- A divorced spouse who was married to the deceased for a minimum of 10 years can collect benefits at age 60 or, if disabled, at age 50.
- A widow or widower who retires can receive benefits at age 60 or, if disabled, at age 50.
- A parent who received at least half his or her support from an adult child also may claim benefits at age 62.

Disability Benefits

You can collect Social Security disability benefits before retirement age if you have a disability that prevents you from working for a year or more or if you have a terminal illness. To qualify you'll be required to prove the extent of your disability to a panel of Social Security Administration evaluators, and you won't be eligible if it is decided that treatment would significantly improve your illness. If you are turned down for benefits, you can request a hearing before the Social Security Administration. If this proves fruitless, you may file a lawsuit in federal district court.

Supplemental Security Income (SSI)

Supplemental Security Income (SSI) is a program administered by the Social Security Administration that provides monthly benefits if you meet certain requirements, including: *age or disability* (if you are a low-income person who is 65 or older, *or* have corrected vision of 20/200 or less, *or* you meet the Social Security benefits disability requirements noted earlier) and *adjusted income and resources* (if you have an adjusted income and resource level—cash and other liquid assets—below a certain ceiling).

In order to apply for SSI, you must first apply for another type of benefit, such as a pension, general Social Security benefits, or workers' compensation.

Appealing a Decision for Social Security Benefits or SSI

The Social Security Administration will make an initial decision about your eligibility, about any reduction of benefits, and other such issues. You'll be notified in writing of the decision, and you'll have 60 days in which to contact your local Social Security Administration office and ask that it be reconsidered. Most people conduct the appeals process themselves, but the elderly or others who want assistance can ask local advocacy groups to recommend an adviser or a specialist in Social Security procedures.

The Social Security Administration will reconsider its determination and respond with another letter. If you're turned down once again, you have 60 days to request a hearing before an administrative law judge (ALJ). If the ALJ refuses to hear your case, or hears it but doesn't give you the decision you were looking for, you have another 60 days in which to file an appeal with the Appeals Council of the Social Security Administration. If the Appeals Council won't hear your case or comes back with a negative decision, you can file your appeal in a federal district court within 60 days of the council's notice.

Supplemental Security Income (SSI) appeals follow the same route, but if you don't want your SSI benefits to be reduced while you go through the lengthy appeals process, you have only 10 days to request reconsideration, not 60.

If it's determined that you've received more than you're entitled to in Social Security benefits or SSI, the government has the right to collect those overages by stopping your benefits or, if the benefits are necessary for your living expenses, by gradually taking the overages out of your future payments unless fraud was involved.

MEDICAL PROGRAMS

Medicare

Medicare is a federal medical program for people age 65 and older, regardless of income or employment status. Medicare includes a hospital plan as well as an elective insurance plan for nonhospital medical expenses. The cost of the hospital plan, which requires you to pay only a calendar-year deductible amount, is defrayed by the Social Security payments you have made through employment, but if you haven't worked enough quarters to qualify, you can enroll at age 65 by paying monthly premiums. If you are younger than 65, you can receive benefits if you've been entitled to Social Security benefits for 24 months or more. Anyone 65 and older can elect to pay monthly premium payments for the medical insurance part of the Medicare program.

If you receive Social Security benefits, you are automatically enrolled in the hospital insurance portion of Medicare, but a monthly payment is required in order to be enrolled in the medical portion of the program. This provides such services as visits to the doctor, outpatient hospital care, and physical therapy. Medicare does not cover categories such as private hospital rooms, dental services, pharmaceuticals, and routine checkups.

If you do not receive Social Security, you should enroll in Medicare at your Social Security office at least three months before your sixty-fifth birthday.

Medicaid

Medicaid is a federal and state program that provides medical care to low-income people regardless of age—those who already receive Supplemental Security Income (SSI) or Aid to Families with Dependent Children (AFDC) or have an income and assets that fall below a certain level. Medicaid requires no premium payments or deductibles.

Appealing a Medicare or Medicaid Decision

Both Medicare and Medicaid claims are administered through local and state agencies, so any appeal must be made through that office, not the Social Security Administration or another federal agency. If

Nursing homes may attempt to convince the children of nursing home residents that they have a financial obligation to pay the bills. Not so. The only family member legally responsible is the spouse of the person who lives in the facility. But Medicare and Medicaid can also provide some assistance. Hospital social workers are good sources of information about negotiating the nursing home system, as are independent social workers who specialize in such counseling.

a hospital informs you that Medicare will not cover the remainder of your hospital stay, or if you have any other problem with a claim or benefits, talk to the program's representative at the state agency about appealing the decision or call on your local neighborhood advocacy agency for help in how to do so.

PENSIONS

Some employers, although under no legal obligation, establish pension plans to contribute to the support of their retired former employees. The Employee Retirement Income Security Act of 1974 (ERISA) establishes minimum standards for the plans and a method of administering them. Under ERISA plan administrators must make sure their employees understand the benefits to which they are entitled, must issue an annual report, and upon request must provide updated plan descriptions and personal benefit statements. The pension plan must also provide a claim and appeals procedure. If the employee makes an appeal and gets no satisfaction from the company's appeals system, the employee can file a lawsuit in state or federal district court. Employees who suspect ERISA violations should contact the U.S. Department of Labor.

HOUSING

Most cities provide some public housing for older Americans or disabled citizens, although applicants usually must join a long waiting list. The rent in these facilities (sometimes including utilities) cannot be more than 30 percent of a resident's family income, and fluctuates as income is raised or lowered. For those living on a fixed income, the rent should probably be reviewed annually.

The government also provides "Section 8" housing, in which residents pay 30 percent of their income as rent and the government subsidizes the rest. To qualify, you must be age 62 or older, disabled, or live with family members, and your income must be beneath a certain level (an amount that varies from community to community).

A third type of housing available to older Americans offers lower rent as a result of government subsidies to certain landlords, though there is no legal cap on how much rent the landlord can charge. Check with your local housing authority to find out what types of housing are available in your community.

UTILITIES

The public service commissions in many states have rules that protect the elderly from having their electricity, gas, or phone disconnected, and some state agencies help defray the cost of heating and air-conditioning for senior citizens. Check with your state or local agency on aging for the availability of such benefits in your location.

WHAT TO DO WHEN YOUR CONSTITUTIONAL RIGHTS HAVE BEEN VIOLATED

If you believe you have been denied your constitutional rights, you can get help from certain government agencies as well as private organizations. Before you file a grievance with one or more federal agencies, be sure to obtain information from a public interest group or other advocacy organization that works to limit infringements of your constitutional rights.

If you find that a federal or state law is unconstitutional, you will need to go to court to challenge the law.

But we don't automatically have the right to challenge a law in court. Those who wish to do so must have "standing"—have a direct stake in the outcome. For example, a young man of draft age has standing to challenge the constitutionality of conscription into the armed services because the law affects him directly. Before a challenge can be brought, a bona fide dispute between two parties must also be present. It's not enough to have some hypothetical question or a dispute that was resolved a year ago. If you feel you have standing and a "present controversy" (a case liable to trial in a court of justice), talk with a lawyer or a representative from an agency or association that shares your concern.

WHERE TO GO FOR HELP

Sometimes the federal agency system can seem like a maze, with no indication about which office has enforcement powers over what violations. If the following list doesn't contain what you need, call the Federal Information Center in your state, listed in the phone book under the heading of Government Offices—U.S. Government. A representative will direct you.

Organizations

CIVIL RIGHTS VIOLATIONS
Commission on Civil Rights
624 Ninth Street
Washington, DC 20425
800-552-6843

The Commission on Civil Rights acts as a clearinghouse for discrimination violations. Send your complaint to the address above. The commission will refer it to the appropriate federal agency: Department of Justice, the Department of Health and Human Services, or another office.

The National Association for the Advancement of Colored People
(NAACP)
Call your state or local chapter.

American Civil Liberties Union
132 West 43 Street
New York, NY 10036
212-944-9800

National Organization for Women (NOW)
Call your state or local chapter.

DISCRIMINATION AGAINST OLDER AMERICANS
State Office of Aging
Check the state government listing in phone book.

American Association of Retired Persons
601 E Street, N.W.
Washington, DC 20049
202-434-2277

National Council on the Aging
409 Third Street, N.W.
Washington, DC 20024
202-479-1200

American Association of Homes for the Aging
901 E Street, N.W.
Suite 500
Washington, DC 20004

Social Security Administration
800-SSA-1213

DISCRIMINATION IN EDUCATION

U.S. Department of Education
Office for Civil Rights
400 Maryland Avenue, S.W.
Room 5000
Washington, DC 20202
202-205-5413

The Office for Civil Rights within the U.S. Department of Education also has regional offices in Boston, New York, Philadelphia, Atlanta, Chicago, Dallas, Kansas City (Missouri), Denver, San Francisco, and Seattle. (This is part of the former Department of Health, Education and Welfare.)

HOUSING DISCRIMINATION

Office of Fair Housing and Equal Opportunity
U.S. Department of Housing and Urban Development
451 Seventh Street, S.W.
Room 5100
Washington, DC 20410
202-708-4252
800-424-8590

DISCRIMINATION AGAINST THE DISABLED

The provisions of the Americans with Disabilities Act are enforced by several federal agencies. If the violation involves employment, contact the Equal Employment Opportunity Commission (EEOC, see below). If public transportation fails to comply with the ADA, the U.S. Department of Transportation should be notified. If you're denied adequate accommodations in public facilities, such as restaurants and malls, write to the United States Attorney General's Office.

EMPLOYMENT

Equal Employment Opportunity Commission (EEOC)
1801 L Street, N.W.
Washington, DC 20507
202-663-4900
800-669-4000

Pension and Welfare Benefits Administration
U.S. Department of Labor
1730 K Street, N.W.
Washington, DC 20006
202-254-7013

IMMIGRATION

Center for Immigrant Rights
48 St. Marks Place, 4th Floor
New York, NY 10003
212-505-6890

Immigration and Naturalization Service
U.S. Department of Justice
425 I Street, N.W.
Washington, DC 20536
202-514-4316

National Network for Immigrant and Refugee Rights
310 Eighth Street, No. 307
Oakland, CA 94607
510-465-1984

7

BUYING OR RENTING A HOME

BUYING A HOME

From the moment you decide you would like to buy a house or an apartment, you begin a chain of events governed by a number of legal procedures—all of which will vary from state to state. When you find the right home at the right price, the legal process will begin when you sign a binder (a document guaranteeing performance of a contract) and put down an escrow deposit (money held in trust by a third party) confirming your right to buy the property. The seller or the seller's agent or attorney will draw up a sale and purchase agreement—the contract—agreeing to convey (transfer) the property with "marketable title," free and clear of any liens, mortgages, or other claims. The contract will also establish all the terms of the sale, including the price, any financing involved, and the obligations of both the buyer and seller. At this point you (the buyer) may be required to put down an additional deposit to be held in escrow until the formal transfer of the property, or closing. These are procedures that occur in many states but not all.

Meanwhile, you will have much to do before the day of the closing arrives. First, you'll probably have to find a bank or another lending institution to finance the mortgage. You'll have to arrange for a termite inspector to give the house a clean bill of health, and you should retain an inspector to check over the plumbing, the electrical wiring, and the general structure. At the closing you'll be required to show proof of having obtained homeowner's insurance to protect the lender in the event that the property suffers a fire or other damage. You will have to arrange for a title search or "abstract," providing proof that you hold title to the property without any defects or "cloud of title."

Once these matters are accomplished, the closing can take place, and ownership changes hands.

Brokers and Agents

Most prospective buyers work with one or more real estate brokers or agents, simply because these real estate professionals provide listings of available homes and can show you properties on a schedule that will save you time. Be aware that while the broker works with both the buyer and seller, the broker's fee (a certain percentage of the purchase price) is paid by the seller. The broker represents the seller, no matter how helpful the broker is to you. However, some states have held that a broker may represent the buyer even if the broker is not paid by the buyer.

An agent's responsibilities to the seller usually include suggesting how the house can be improved to bring a higher price, helping to determine a reasonable asking price, providing information on homes similar to those of the seller and what they are selling for, marketing the property and advertising it in the local newspapers, having it listed on the local multiple-listing services (computer compilations of every house available in the area), showing it to potential buyers, participating in negotiating the sale, and helping to arrange for the closing.

Remember: *Laws differ from state to state. Check the relevant laws in your area, and/or consult an attorney before pursuing legal action.*

The Real Estate Listing Agreement

If you decide to sell your home and retain the services of a broker, you'll be expected to sign a real estate listing agreement, which specifies the obligations of both you and the broker. The broker will present you with a standard boilerplate contract, usually with terms favorable to the broker.

The contract will specify that the seller will pay the agent a commission, usually a percentage of the final sale price of the home. Average percentage rates vary depending on the type of the house and the region of the country and are negotiable, but they are usually about 6 or 7 percent of the sale price of the home. If the sale price turns out to be $100,000, at 7 percent you will be paying $7,000 for the broker's services, an amount that will be due from you at the closing.

Real estate commissions are of two kinds: the *listing* commission and the *selling* commission. Suppose Homer and Marge want to sell their house and they sign an agreement with Acme Realty to handle the sale; Acme places their house on the Multiple Listing Service. You, a potential buyer, look at homes with the help of the Royal Realty Company. A Royal agent shows you the home, and you decide to buy it. Your Royal Realty agent assists in negotiating the deal and helps arrange for the closing. Acme Realty will receive the "listing commission" because Homer and Marge entered into a contract with them, and it was through Acme's efforts in listing the home that it was sold by your Royal broker. Royal Realty will receive the "sales commission" because it was Royal's agent who ultimately closed the deal.

Although the broker's commission is commonly paid by the seller, sometimes buyers retain their own agents to represent them. This arrangement is usually done on a flat-fee basis rather than on a percentage of the selling price of the home.

About 30 states require that the broker make it clear at the first meeting with a potential buyer that the broker has entered into a contract with the seller and is working for that party.

TYPES OF LISTINGS The real estate listing agreement should also clearly state whether the listing with the broker is "exclusive" or "open." An *open listing* means that the seller can list the home with a number of brokers and that only the broker who actually closes the sale gets the commission. An *exclusive listing* entitles the listing broker to a commission no matter who arranges for the sale of the house—even if you sell it. If you want to reserve the right to sell your house yourself, you need to make this exemption clear in the agreement with the broker who has the exclusive; if this is not done, the agent will be entitled to a commission even if you sell the house yourself. Exclusive listings usually last for 60 to 120 days by agreement and may be renewed.

If you are attempting to sell your house in the fastest way possible, a broker may suggest a "net listing." Beware of such suggestions. Here the broker promises the seller that the house will be sold at a "guaranteed" price—the price the broker quotes is often well below the home's market value—and the broker's fee will be the difference between the actual selling price he/she obtains and the "guaranteed" price. Not only can the seller lose a great deal of money under such an arrangement, but net listings are illegal in many states.

OTHER CONTRACT TERMS   Some listing agreements favor brokers by allowing them to collect their commissions if they deliver a bona fide offer regardless of whether the sale closes. Avoid this pro-broker provision. Include language in the agreement that the broker earns the right to a commission only when all of the following take place:

- A contract reflecting acceptable terms to the owner is signed.
- The executed contract is the result of the efforts of the broker (not in an exclusive listing).
- The purchase price agreed to by the seller is paid.
- The deed conveying title is delivered according to the terms of the contract.

The broker should not be entitled to take a commission if either the seller or buyer backs out of the sale, unless the seller intentionally defaults to avoid having to pay a commission. And the commission should not be paid until the closing, when the payment for the home and the title change hands.

The listing agreement should also include a clause stating that the seller has the right to raise or lower the price of the house without affecting the percentage of the broker's commission, that the seller is not responsible for any expenses the broker incurs in marketing the property, and that the seller may withdraw the house from the market.

BREACH OF LISTING AGREEMENTS   Implicit in a real estate listing agreement is that your broker will work hard to sell your house, using all the tools at the broker's disposal to bring in prospective buyers and close the deal for a price and terms to your liking. Even if you have an exclusive right-to-sell contract, you can terminate the agreement if you believe that the broker is doing a poor job. Express your grievances about the broker's failure to seek prospects, and allow a chance for explanations about what effort has been put forth. It is best to document your grievances in writing through letters to the broker. If the broker has clearly breached your contract, find another broker.

BROKER MISREPRESENTATIONS AND DISCRIMINATION   It is illegal for a broker or an owner to make false representations about a house or apartment. This includes not only intentional misrepresentations but also those caused by negligence.

It is the duty of the broker to inspect a home carefully before making claims about its quality and to provide the buyer with accurate information. Otherwise, the broker is guilty of misrepresentation. Omitting important facts can be considered fraud, and this includes such matters as failing to tell a prospective buyer that a six-lane highway is proposed for the area.

If you are a buyer and you believe that a broker is guilty of mis-

Suppose you are the seller, and neither you nor the broker can establish the exact age of the furnace in the house you are selling. Rather than revealing ignorance or doing the homework involved to find out, the broker tells the buyer that the furnace is 3 years old. Later you and the broker find out that it is actually much older—say, 10 years old. That's misrepresentation.

Bonnie, a real estate agent, showed a home to Carl and Hilda but failed to mention to them that recent construction in the neighborhood had unearthed a toxic waste dump. She hoped to rush the sale along so that it was consummated before the news reached the press. Bonnie succeeded, but as soon as Carl and Hilda learned of the discovery, they sued her for fraud and reported her actions to the state Board of Realtors.

The sellers can also be held liable for the fraudulent sale.

representation or another breach of ethical conduct, file a complaint with the local Board of Realtors, your state real estate licensing board, the real estate commission, and/or the Better Business Bureau. You may also have the right to sue the agent/broker and recover damages. Consult a lawyer who specializes in real estate property law.

What follows is a hypothetical situation involving misrepresentation by a real estate broker.

THE PROBLEM

Steve purchased a home in a suburban community for $200,000. He was shown the house by Sandra, a broker. He asked Sandra about the school district in which the house was located. She told him that it was in the Tenth District, which is the best in the area. In fact, the house was in the Ninth District, and the broker was aware of that.

WHAT TO DO

Sandra committed a blatant misrepresentation. She would be liable to Steve for any damages that he may have sustained as a result of this misrepresentation. If the value of the house would be greater had it been in the better school district, Steve could recover damages for the difference in the value. In some states Steve might be entitled to punitive damages, which are in the nature of a civil fine paid to a claimant for an intentionally wrongful act. Steve should also report Sandra to the state agency that licenses real estate brokers.

Steve should retain a lawyer to sue Sandra in state court for his damages.

Sellers and brokers are prohibited from discriminating against anyone because of race, religion, national origin, color, or gender. Such discrimination is present if an agent refuses to show you a house in a certain area or attempts to discourage you from seeking one. It is illegal for a seller to instruct a broker to exclude clients because of their race, religion, national origin, color, or gender. If you believe that you have been a victim of housing discrimination, contact:

The Department of Housing and Urban Development
451 Seventh Street, S.W.
Room 5100
Washington, DC 20410
202-708-1422
800-424-8590 outside DC

What follows is a hypothetical situation involving discrimination by a real estate broker.

THE PROBLEM

Andy was looking for a home in a predominantly white neighborhood. He went to Mark, a local real estate broker. Andy is African-American. Mark told him that there were no homes available in the white neighborhood that were in his price range. Mark did suggest that there were homes in his price range in the adjoining predominantly African-American neighborhood. There *were* some homes available in Andy's price range in the white neighborhood, and Mark was aware of those listings.

WHAT TO DO

Andy should file charges against Mark with the fair housing commission in his state or county and with the licensing agency for real estate brokers. Andy should also contact an attorney in order to seek monetary damages for Mark's discriminatory actions.

The Binder and Deposit or Escrow

When you come to an agreement, the seller or broker probably will ask you to sign a binder, which states the names of the potential buyer and seller, the address of the property, the price of the home, and, if a broker is involved, the percentage of the commission. The binder also states that this document is temporary until after the seller or the seller's attorney has had a chance to draft a sales contract. Depending upon the state, you may be asked to draft a sales contract. The seller may ask for a binder payment of as little as $100 or as much as a few thousand dollars. Put down as little as the seller is willing to accept. And be sure the binder states clearly that if a sales contract is not drafted and signed by a certain date, your deposit will be refunded in full. Both buyer and seller must sign the binder.

Home Inspection

Don't sign a contract without having the house inspected from top to bottom. Have a structural engineer examine the foundation, the plumbing, the hot water heater, electrical system, the furnace, air-conditioning, and the roof. Be sure the house is free from termites and termite damage.

If you can't get the house inspected before signing the contract, include a clause stating that if a problem is discovered during inspection, you can void the contract. If you like the house despite a problem, you may want to proceed with the sale if the seller agrees in the contract to repair it before you move in or close on the house, or you may want to renegotiate the sales price.

The Purchase and Sale Agreement

Once you negotiate the price and other terms, it is time to put the entire agreement in writing. If there are disputes later about what price and conditions were agreed upon, this contract will serve as the legitimate instrument in which the agreement was recorded. At this point, you will probably want to hire a real estate attorney, who should make sure that the agreement is in order. A purchase and sale agreement (contract) should contain the following information:

- the full names of the buyer and seller
- a legal description of the property
- an inspection clause
- the purchase price and the amount of the deposit (Payment in full for the selling price will be required at the closing; if you will be financing the home with a mortgage, specify the deposit, the amount being borrowed, the interest rate, and the length of the loan.)
- proof of marketable title (The seller must provide a certificate of title or a title insurance policy proving ownership of the home and that there are no claims or liens against it; if there are any title restrictions, these must be revealed in the contract. This varies throughout the country. The seller must have a good title, but it does not always provide proof. In many states the buyer must order his or her own title search.)
- the date on which the buyer will take possession (A provision could be included in the contract that allows the buyer to charge the seller rent if he fails to make the house available as soon as the title has been transferred.)
- specification of which party will pay expenses up to the closing, including property taxes and utility bills, or how these are to be divided
- who will be responsible for any damage to the property before the closing (If you include a clause in the sales agreement [contract] specifying that you, the buyer, are responsible for any damages that occur before closing, you must buy insurance that covers the home as soon as you agree in writing to the purchase.)
- a listing of the personal property or fixtures that are to be conveyed with the house (For example, you knew that the sellers were taking their furniture with them, but you were surprised to discover that the draperies and wall-to-wall carpeting were missing when you took title to the house. The contract should specify what personal property as well as fixtures attached to the house will remain. How about the refrigerator, washing machine, chandelier? Get it in writing.)

You've had the house inspected from attic to basement, and you are happy with its condition. You sign the sales agreement and pay the amount due on contract. Four days before closing, an electrical storm causes a fire in the house, gutting the living room. Without a clause in the contract specifying who is responsible for fire or other hazards before closing, there may be a question about who will pay for repairing the damage and whether you have the right to back out of the contract. In some states the house will be technically yours because you have signed the sales agreement and paid escrow. Other states put the burden on the seller because the house is not officially sold until the closing. The risk should be with the person who controls possession of the house, and the contract should state this.

- a clause that allows you to cancel the deal if the inspections reveal serious problems (Suppose you cannot get a structural engineer or termite inspector to examine the house before you sign the contract. If repairs turn out to be necessary, you can handle them in several ways. First, you can agree in this clause to take care of the needed work yourself if the cost of the house is reduced by the amount of your expenses. Or, if the seller is to make the repairs, be sure the contract specifies that these be completed prior to closing.)

- a mortgage contingency clause (Even if you have prequalified for a loan with a lender, there is no guarantee that you will be able to obtain the financing you need between the time you sign the contract and the day you close on the house. A mortgage is contingent on a clause in the agreement that makes the purchase contingent on your being able to find, for example, a loan for $150,000 at 8.5 percent interest within 45 days after signing the contract. A seller usually will agree to such a contingency. The clause also protects you from the seller's bringing a breach of contract suit against you later if you fail to secure the financing you want; if you are paying cash, you will not need this clause.)

- a clause that assures you that your deposit will be refunded if you cannot obtain financing or if the title is not marketable after the title search is completed (Remember that when you sign the contract, you'll be paying the seller a down payment, sometimes 10 percent of the sales price you have negotiated.)

The following is a hypothetical situation involving removal of a fixture before a closing.

THE PROBLEM

Marcy entered into a contract to sell her house to Tina. The contract did not make any references to the personal property included with the house. Prior to closing, Tina inspected the house and discovered that the hot water heater was missing.

WHAT TO DO

Tina should refuse to close unless Marcy installs a comparable hot water heater. In most states, a hot water heater would be considered a fixture and included with the sale of the house unless specifically excluded.

Be sure you do not agree to a closing date that does not allow you proper time to get the financing you need or, alternatively, one that is so far in the future that it threatens the stability of the contract or the time period of your mortgage commitment.

Mortgages

Several different financing options are available to home buyers. Regardless of what kind of loan you're seeking, shop around to compare interest rates, discount points, origination fees, and application fees. Also determine whether the lenders will "lock in" a certain interest rate (agree to honor the approved interest rate even if rates rise before your closing date).

OWNER-FINANCED LOANS   When interest rates are high and the housing market is difficult, sellers are sometimes willing to finance a mortgage personally. Such an agreement presents pros and cons for both parties. If you are the seller, you may be able to sell your home more quickly than otherwise, but because you are not a lending institution, you will have difficulty checking on the buyer's creditworthiness. If the buyer defaults, you will have to foreclose on the loan and may end up in possession of your house again. If the buyer had been able to obtain financing elsewhere, you would have already received the full purchase price.

If you are a buyer who is financing through an owner, you should have the advantage of paying a relatively low interest rate, as well as saving on the cost of a bank's loan origination fee and any points that would have been payable at the closing. The buyer should use an attorney to verify such a transaction and must obtain title insurance.

Buyers sometimes find that foreclosures are brought relatively quickly if a home is being owner-financed and no reputable mortgage company is handling the default in payment. In states that do not require judicial proceedings before a lender forecloses, an owner can take the house from under a buyer if only a single mortgage payment is missed, without notice and without offering a chance to "cure" the default. To prevent this, the buyer should negotiate a default notice provision in the mortgage.

FIRST AND SECOND MORTGAGES   In the case of a homeowner's undertaking two mortgages for the same property, the first mortgage is determined by which was recorded first in the county clerk's office. This mortgage has superior claim over the second.

Suppose, for example, that you own a home that was financed by a $100,000 mortgage through the New Mortgage Company. Ten years after you buy the house, you want to add a garage/apartment, so you obtain a second mortgage of $30,000 from your bank to finance the renovation. (Second mortgages are sometimes referred to as "home equity loans" because the equity that has accumulated in the house becomes the collateral.) Now suppose that you suffer financial reverses and are unable to make your mortgage payments, both mortgage holders foreclose, and the ensuing sale of the property generates only $100,000 in proceeds. The New Mortgage Company, which holds the first mortgage, will be permitted to satisfy the total amount you still owe to it. If any proceeds remain, the bank that holds the second mortgage can attempt to satisfy the debt. Those who hold mechanic's liens (see the information about title searches, pages 236–38) on the property will receive their due amount only if enough proceeds remain. Real estate tax liens have first priority over *all* mortgages even if the taxes become a lien after the mortgages are recorded.

Applying for a Mortgage

THE LOAN APPLICATION   The Equal Credit Opportunity Act prohibits lenders from discriminating against an applicant because of race, color, religion, national origin, sex, or marital status. But a loan application can ask just about anything else short of infringing on those protections. Be prepared to lay out your financial past and present, from your income to your assets, liabilities, and credit history, all with documentation. At the end of the application, you will be asked to sign a release allowing the lender to contact employers, creditors, and credit bureaus.

Don't attempt to hide a bankruptcy you may have filed in the past or any other blemish on your credit record. Not only will your misrepresentation be easily discovered and your loan denied, but you will be committing a federal crime.

The application also contains a statement that your signature indicates your agreement to comply with all bank rules and regulations. Be sure you sign only when you understand what you are agreeing to.

CO-SIGNING A LOAN APPLICATION   Sometimes a loan applicant knows that he or she won't qualify, perhaps because of credit history or income level, and asks another person to "co-sign" in order to guar-

Dean agreed to partially finance the sale of his home to Anne. Everything went well for the first two years; then Anne stopped sending her mortgage payments, both to the bank, which held the first mortgage, as well as to Dean. If the bank forecloses, it will take the full value of its loan from the proceeds of the sale. Dean will receive his money, or a portion of it, only if the equity in the house exceeds the bank loan.

antee payment of the loan. Be aware that such co-signing means that if the buyer is unable to make the payments, the cosigner becomes fully responsible for making them. Consumers should co-sign loans for others only if they are prepared to repay the entire loan in case of default.

LENDER MISREPRESENTATION   The Truth-In-Lending Act prevents lenders from misrepresenting the terms of a loan. The lender is required to provide, in writing, the full amount of the loan and how it will be disbursed, that is, how much of the loan goes to the seller, how much goes into escrow, and so on. The lender must disclose the loan's annual percentage rate, the total amount of interest charged over the life of the loan, the payment schedule, all insurance and escrow requirements, and any penalties that will be charged for late payments or prepayments.

Unless you negotiate with the lender that there will be no prepayment penalty and the mortgage agreement states this, the lender will levy a penalty if you prepay the entire balance or a portion of it within the first few years of the mortgage. Such a penalty usually amounts to 1 or 2 percent of the entire mortgage.

ATTORNEY'S FEES   Drafting the sales contract, searching the title, and representing you at the closing will almost always require the services of a lawyer. This expense usually becomes the responsibility of the buyer. Before you retain the attorney, be sure to negotiate a fee or at least a specific range of payment should the purchase become more complex than contemplated. (See chapter 11.)

Title Searches and Title Insurance

When you own property "free and clear," it means that no one else has any claims on it. Some consumers believe that title to real property is something tangible, a piece of paper. Not so. Title refers merely to your legal ownership of a property; the piece of paper that represents the title is called the deed.

The general assumption when a house is put up for sale is that the seller owns the property and has the right to convey it to you. This can be a dangerous premise. One way to prevent surprises later is to have an attorney or title company perform a title search and

Be aware that the lure of guaranteed mortgages for individuals with poor credit histories is used as a common basis for fraud. Many consumers who have been turned down by conventional lenders abandon all caution when the prospect of obtaining a mortgage is offered to them.

Some advertisements, for example, offer guaranteed loans if the buyer will first pay an advance fee of several hundred dollars. Buyers are instructed to call an 800 number from which, in turn, they are directed to call an expensive 900 number for more information. Some such perpetrators offer a money-back guarantee if the loan fails to materialize, while others claim that the fee the buyer pays will be applied to the "loan" upon its approval. But once the consumer pays the fee, the money disappears along with the "lender." No reputable lender will extend a loan to someone with a poor credit history. Rather than risk such an outcome, it's best to attempt a rehabilitation of your credit through the Consumer Credit Counseling Service. (See chapter 9.)

Over three-fourths of the states have ceilings on how much interest a lender can charge. If the rate offered you seems considerably higher than what you have seen advertised by local banks, check with your state office of banking. Lenders found to be engaging in usury (lending money at exorbitant interest rates) are committing a criminal act, which may result in a prison sentence or in being barred from receiving the interest or even the principal of such a loan.

prepare a title abstract. This entails researching back through the chain of ownership to ensure that the present seller does, in fact, hold title to the property and that there are no liens on the property by others.

A lien is a claim made against a property for the payment of a debt. The most common lien is a mortgage; the person or lending institution that provided the mortgage is the lienholder and has the right to sell the property in case the borrower defaults. Taxes, utility assessments, or judgments awarded by a court that go unpaid also create liens, and a thorough title search includes checking tax and other such records.

MECHANIC'S LIEN   Failing to pay for improvements on a home can create a "mechanic's lien." Suppose a homeowner has hired a home improvement company to add a deck to the house. The contractor completes the work to the homeowner's satisfaction, but the homeowner doesn't have the cash to pay the contractor. The contractor has a right to place a mechanic's lien on the property for the outstanding payment, recording it with the county clerk or registry for deeds. If the homeowner sells the home, a thorough title search by the buyer's attorney will reveal the contractor's mechanic's lien. The buyer should expect the seller to pay off the indebtedness; otherwise the selling price should be adjusted accordingly. If the buyer fails to have a title search conducted and buys the home, the contractor's lien stays on the property until it is satisfied by the new owner.

What follows is a hypothetical situation involving a mechanic's lien.

THE PROBLEM

Warren had central air-conditioning installed in his house but never fully paid the contractor. He subsequently sold his house to Brandon. The contractor filed a mechanic's lien a week after the closing, which was within the statutory period for filing.

WHAT TO DO

If Brandon had obtained title insurance at the closing and the title policy omitted all exceptions for mechanic's liens, then he could require his title company to remove the mechanic's lien. If Brandon did not obtain title insurance at the closing, he will have to sue Warren to force him to pay the contractor; otherwise Brandon may be forced to satisfy the mechanic's lien.

EASEMENTS   Easements work in the same way as mechanic's liens. If the homeowner has granted a neighbor an easement, perhaps one allowing the neighbor to place half the neighbor's driveway on the homeowner's property, the easement should be recorded with the county and the record of it will turn up in a competent title search when the home is put up for sale. The buyer will be required to pay for the property "subject to" that easement. If a title search shows a lien or other encumbrance, you might want to consult an attorney to find out how serious a defect there is.

What follows is a hypothetical situation involving an easement.

THE PROBLEM

Kirk was interested in buying a secluded house in the country. He entered into a contract to buy a house that was subject to good title. Kirk's attorney ordered a title search and discovered that an adjoining property owner had an easement right-of-way to cross the property to get to the public road.

WHAT TO DO

Kirk could cancel the contract and get his deposit back, or he could negotiate a reduction in the sales price. Kirk could also renegotiate with the adjoining property owner.

TITLE INSURANCE   To protect yourself beyond the title search, many attorneys will recommend that you purchase a title insurance policy, which most lenders require. The title insurance company will search the title of the property and issue a policy ensuring that the property is free and clear of any other claims. If this has been done and you are notified six months after moving into your new home that a previous owner's relative was willed the property and is suing you for possession and title, you are protected; if you purchased title insurance, the company that issued the policy will go to court with you to defend your right to the property and will pay any settlement involved in resolving the dispute.

The Deeds

When you buy a home, the property will most likely be conveyed to you by a *general warranty deed*, guaranteeing that the property is being conveyed free and clear. The seller also promises to protect you from any other people who might stake legal claim to your property, either by defending your title in court or by compensating you if someone does successfully prove to be the rightful titleholder.

A *grant deed* provides the same guarantees of ownership and lack of claims or encumbrances as does the general warranty deed, but it doesn't promise to actively defend your right of possession and title. A *bargain and sale deed* assures the buyer that the seller has done nothing to affect title. A *quitclaim deed* is the least beneficial to the buyer because it merely conveys whatever rights and title the seller has; the seller does not guarantee that no assessments are outstanding or that a previous heir to the property will not come forward to make a legal claim.

Homeowner's Insurance

Homeowner's insurance will help pay to replace or repair your home and its contents if they are damaged or destroyed. A basic bare-bones policy covers you against fire, smoke, windstorms, hail, lightning, volcanoes, explosions, riots, aircraft crashes, damage by vehicles belonging to others, theft, vandalism, and broken glass. If you want more than this kind of basic protection, you can take out a more expensive policy to include coverage of damage from pipes freezing; hot water heaters bursting; falling objects; the weight of snow, sleet, and ice; earthquakes and floods; and electrical malfunction. An even more comprehensive and expensive policy can protect your home and its contents from almost every unforeseen damage, except nuclear accidents and wars.

Homeowner policies also protect you if certain personal property is stolen or destroyed. This includes theft from hotels and from your car, and it applies to the homeowner and family members. If you share a home with people who are not legally related to you, their names should appear on the policy, otherwise their property will not be covered. Certain items, such as jewelry, are only covered in small amounts in basic policies, but special policies called *floaters* can be purchased to protect your valuables if they are stolen or lost.

Be sure not to overinsure your home and its contents. If your home is valued at $150,000, for example, you can probably manage with $120,000 of coverage, because the land and at least the foundation will most likely remain. If you carry $150,000 worth of protection and it costs only $100,000 to replace your home and its contents, the insurance will pay only $100,000 at most. Insurance must be based on replacement value, not market value. It is conceivable that replacement value may be higher than the market value. In such instances the home should be insured for at least 80 percent of replacement value. In areas that have experienced rapidly increasing real estate values, it is especially important to avoid underinsuring the home. Your safest bet is to buy a guaranteed-replacement-cost policy.

Homeowner's insurance also provides liability coverage, which protects you if someone is injured or dies on your property. For example, suppose you invite Bud to your home for a cookout. You forget to put the garden hose away, and it lies coiled in tall grass. Bud doesn't see it, his feet get tangled in it, and he falls, hitting his head on the cement sidewalk. The accident causes a concussion and serious neck injuries. Bud's medical bills will most likely exceed the liability coverage you would normally have in a basic homeowner's policy. For this reason you might want to consider purchasing an "umbrella" policy as well, raising your protection to as much as a million dollars. One source of information about homeowner's insurance is this industry-sponsored organization:

Insurance Information Institute
110 William Street
New York, NY 10038

What follows is a hypothetical situation involving a liability claim made against a homeowner.

THE PROBLEM
Kathy invited Frieda to her house. When Kathy was bringing tea from the kitchen to where Frieda was sitting, she inadvertently dumped the hot teapot on Frieda.

WHAT TO DO
Frieda asserted a claim for the damage to her clothing, for her doctor bills, and for her pain and suffering. Kathy should immediately contact her home insurance carrier; it will provide her with a legal defense and pay the claim up to the limits of the policy.

The Appraisal

That you (the buyer) and the seller agree on the value of the property you are buying is irrelevant to a potential lender; the lender will want a professional appraiser to give an opinion of what the property is worth. The lender's appraiser will compare your home with others in the local area that have been sold recently and that have been similarly financed. If all goes well, the appraiser will come in with an appraisal that is close to what you and the seller think is fair. If you disagree with the appraisal, ask your lender to show you a copy. Check it over with the help of your real estate agent, and if you find errors or problems, talk to your loan officer about it.

The Closing

When all the advance work has been completed and you have received a mortgage or other financing, the title has been searched and has been found to be marketable, the house has been appraised and has passed termite and structural inspections, and you have taken out homeowner's insurance, you are ready to "close the escrow" or "close on the house." This process usually requires a meeting attended by the buyer and seller, the real estate agents involved, a representative from the lender as well as the escrow company, and the attorneys for both buyer and seller.

First, the lender will be shown the title search as proof that the seller has clear title to pass to you. The buyer must also exhibit proof that the property is insured, usually in the form of a binder issued by the insurance company. When the lender is satisfied, it will provide you with the loan. (In some cases these proofs can be done prior to the closing. Check your state's requirements for closing procedures.) You, in turn, will pay the seller the outstanding balance on the purchase price and accept the deed. At this time the seller will be required to pay off any remaining mortgages, and you may be asked to reimburse the seller for any taxes or assessments that have been made in advance on the property, including fuel payments. The deed will be recorded in the county courthouse, and returned to you. A copy of the deed is maintained in the recording office as evidence to others that the property has been conveyed.

Restrictions that May Interfere with Property Rights

Certain restrictions on the property may interfere with its use or sale. These include the following.

EASEMENTS These are rights given to others by an owner to enter the property for a specific reason. Easements must be recorded in the office of the county recorder.

COVENANTS Covenants are certain promises that may have been made about the property and which appear on the deed. They can be promises to perform an activity, such as keeping the sidewalk free from snow, or to refrain from an activity, such as not building a fence around the property. Like easements, covenants must be put in writing and recorded in the office of the county recorder; unless properly recorded, neither will pass with the land when it is sold.

ZONING Cities, counties, and states divide areas into districts, and place certain restrictions on the type of buildings that can be constructed and on how the land may be used. In certain zoning areas, for example, a house may be required to be a certain height or set back a certain number of feet from the road. Zoning restrictions may preclude any multifamily or commercial use. Sometimes the zoning of a particular area can be changed through a hearing process, with variances being granted in certain cases. But buyers should not count on obtaining variances after the fact of purchase. Be sure to become familiar with any zoning restrictions before you buy. A gravel mine being legally installed across the road from your tranquil country home could be an unpleasant surprise.

What follows is a hypothetical situation involving zoning regulations.

THE PROBLEM

Glenn bought a suburban home. He and his wife had one child and purchased the small home with a view toward expanding it in the future. A few years passed, and Glenn and his wife had two more children and needed to expand the home. He hired an architect to design an addition to the house. The architect checked the local zoning regulations and determined that the house could not be expanded because it was the maximum size permitted by the zoning laws.

WHAT TO DO

Glenn will have to apply to the local zoning board for a variance to enlarge the house beyond its current size. He will have to convince the zoning board that this variance will not cause any problems for the adjoining neighbors or to the services provided by the local town. Each of Glenn's neighbors will have to be given notice of his application and will have an opportunity to object. The variance is totally within the discretion of the zoning board, and there can be no assurance that it will be granted. (Of course, this situation could have been avoided if Glenn had checked the zoning laws *before* he purchased the home.)

CONDEMNATION   The government (local, state, and federal) has the power to condemn your property. By offering you what they determine is the fair market value of the property, the government can force you to sell it to them so that an airport, a freeway, or an office building, for example, can be constructed on the site. Your only redress is going to court, either to challenge whether the government had the right to take your property or to demand that they pay you more than they are offering for it.

TRESPASS   A trespass is an intentional civil wrong. It is entering upon property of another without the owner's permission. It may also constitute a criminal wrong if it can be established that the trespasser (the one who enters the property of another without the owner's permission) enters the property knowingly in violation of the rights of the owner.

What follows is a hypothetical situation involving trespassing.

THE PROBLEM

Linda purchased a home with a large tract of land. A week after Linda acquired the property, she saw Jason strolling through her property. Jason did not possess an easement or other right to cross Linda's property. Linda confronted Jason and told him that this was her property and he had no right to cross it. On another occasion Linda saw Jason crossing her property. Linda posted "no trespassing" signs at the borders of her property to alert others not to enter her property. Regardless, Jason persisted in entering Linda's property.

WHAT TO DO

First, Linda should notify the local law enforcement authorities and file a charge of criminal trespass against Jason. This will probably be the most expedient way to keep him from entering her property. In addition, Linda can contact an attorney and bring a civil action against Jason to enjoin him from entering her property and to seek damages for his wrongful entry.

NUISANCE   A nuisance is a condition or conduct that interferes with an occupant's quiet enjoyment of property. For example, a neighbor who cuts the lawn with a power lawn mower at three in the morning on a regular basis would be guilty of nuisance. Adjoining neighbors would have the right to sue the inconsiderate grass-cutter, enjoining this behavior with a court order and seeking damages. An "attractive nuisance" is a condition on a property that would generally attract the interest of children and is likely to cause damage to those children. For example, an unfenced swimming pool might be deemed to be an attractive nuisance, and the failure by a property owner to exercise due care to protect children from that attractive nuisance could result in liability on the part of the homeowner. This liability would arise even if the children were trespassing.

What follows is a hypothetical situation involving trespassing and an attractive nuisance.

THE PROBLEM

Lester owns property that contains some very interesting trails. The local children built some jumps on the property to take their mountain bikes over. Lester was aware of their use but failed to take any action. Allison took her mountain bike into Lester's property, attempted to jump over one of the jumps, and fell and broke her arm. Allison's parents are now suing Lester for negligence by allowing an attractive nuisance, the jumps, to exist and taking no steps to protect the children from injury.

WHAT TO DO

Lester should notify his insurance company of the claim. They should argue that Allison was a trespasser and that he had no obligation to protect her from her own wrongful acts.

Allison's attorney would assert that this was an attractive nuisance because it drew young children into a dangerous situation and Lester was aware of it. Under these circumstances, it would be argued that Lester was negligent in failing to eliminate the attractive nuisance.

WATER RIGHTS   In most states landowners have certain rights (known as *riparian rights*) to water that passes over their property. As a result of these rights, a landowner could bring an action against an upstream property owner for actions that may materially alter the flow or quality of the water.

What follows is a hypothetical situation involving water rights.

THE PROBLEM

Betty owns property that has a lovely stream passing through it. One day she noticed that the volume of the water in the stream had decreased dramatically. She conducted an investigation and determined that Barry, the owner of property about two miles upstream from her property, decided that a pond would be a significant asset on his large tract of land. Barry hired contractors to dam the stream, forcing the water to accumulate into a large pond on his property.

WHAT TO DO

Betty should retain a lawyer, who would bring an action against Barry for both injunctive relief and damages. The action would be based upon Barry's unlawful interference with Betty's riparian rights (water rights) to that stream. Barry would have the right to draw water from the stream but could not draw water in such a volume as to materially affect the downstream landowners. Barry's actions are clearly material and would entitle all downstream landowners both to injunctive relief (an order compelling Barry to restore the stream to its original condition) and to damages for the loss of the benefit of the stream for the period that the water was diverted.

REAL ESTATE TAX ASSESSMENT   The local governmental body in which property is located has the power to assess the real estate for tax purposes based upon its value. A homeowner who believes the assessment to be excessive may challenge that assessment. A homeowner can either hire an attorney who specializes in these challenges or may challenge the assessment without an attorney, as is most often the case. Many local governments have a simplified procedure for challenging assessments. The homeowner will have to do some research to determine the assessment of the house relative to that of comparable houses, complete the required forms, and make arguments substantiating why the homeowner believes that the home has been overassessed.

Problems with the Lender After the Sale

Your monthly mortgage payment usually includes not only payments on the principal and interest on your loan but also installments on your property taxes and homeowner's insurance premiums, which the lender holds in escrow; it's the job of the mortgage company (or its servicing company) to send your tax payment to the city and/or county and to send your premium payments to the insurance company. The lender may notify you that your escrow is getting low and may increase your monthly mortgage payments "to get you caught up." Federal law prohibits a mortgage lender from holding on to more than two months' worth of insurance and tax payments at a time in your escrow, but some lenders do so nevertheless.

To determine how your lender is handling your escrow payments, check your annual loan statement, which reflects the monthly balance. Find the month that had the lowest amount held in escrow. If that figure is higher than two months of required escrow, the lender is hoarding more of your money than is allowed by law. If you find that this is the case, write and call it to the lender's attention. If the lender fails to respond or fails to lower the escrow requirements, report the exchange to the state attorney general or the state office that oversees banking, and supply copies of the pertinent correspondence.

Another common problem with home mortgages is that the servicing companies retained by banks to process your monthly mortgage payments, taxes, and insurance payments sometimes fail to do so on time. Some lenders tend to change servicing companies frequently, and in the shuffle your property taxes may be paid late or not at all or your insurance may lapse because the premium payment arrived too late. For mortgages obtained after June 1991, Department of Housing and Urban Development (HUD) rules provide some protections, including:

- The lender must provide a loan applicant with written information stating what percentage of its accounts has previously been moved to other servicing companies, as well as the likelihood of yours being transferred.

- If your lender is going to transfer your loan, it has to give you at least 15 days' notice. After the new company takes over, it has up to 15 days to notify you of the change and provide you with its address and telephone number (so that you can call either toll-free or collect). You will not be penalized or reported late if you send your payment to the old service company's address within the 60-day period after the loan is moved, providing the payment was not late. If you discover that your loan has been transferred after the 15-day notice period, notify the new company that the first lender failed to notify you on time.

HUD rules also require servicing companies to respond when you, the borrower, have questions about your loan. The lender has 20 business days to respond to your correspondence regarding the servicing of your loan and has 60 business days to correct problems and provide an explanation in writing. (During that 60-day period, the lender cannot report your disputed payment to a credit bureau as delinquent.)

CONDOMINIUMS, COOPERATIVES, AND TOWNHOUSES

Some forms of home ownership refer to units within apartment buildings or housing complexes: condominiums, co-ops, and townhouses. The difference among them lies in precisely what portion of the property is being conveyed to you when you purchase it.

CONDOMINIUMS   Unlike buying a freestanding house, wherein you purchase the entire structure—the walls, the ceilings, the land under and around it, and the airspace above it—buying a condominium normally entitles you to own only the area within a unit's walls. In some cases, depending on the deed and other documents, you may own the inside of the walls of your unit while the homeowners' association owns the property, the buildings, the lobby, and any recreational areas.

COOPERATIVES If you buy a cooperative, or "co-op," all you own is stock (shares based on the size of your unit) in a corporation. The corporation owns the building and the land and leases the unit to you.

TOWNHOUSES In the relatively new kind of arrangement known as townhouse ownership, you actually own the land under your unit as well as the inside and outside of the walls, with the exception of walls that are shared with another townhouse owner. A homeowners' association owns the rest of the property.

Rules and Regulations of Condominiums and Cooperatives

Condominiums and cooperatives are operated by owners of units who are elected to the board of directors or, in the case of a condominium, the board of managers. These entities have bylaws and other rules and regulations that govern the use and operation of the units. They also determine the expenditures to be made by the condominium or cooperative for repair and capital improvements and set the maintenance fees for each unit. In the case of cooperatives, they usually have the right to approve sales of units or subleases of units.

What follows is a hypothetical situation involving purchasing a cooperative apartment.

THE PROBLEM

Alan found a purchaser for his cooperative apartment and submitted the purchaser for approval by the cooperative board. The purchaser had more than sufficient financial means to make the purchase and make the monthly maintenance fees and had supplied excellent character references. Nonetheless, the board rejected the purchaser's application.

WHAT TO DO

Alan or the purchaser would have no recourse against the cooperative board unless it could be established that the sole reason for rejecting the proposed purchaser was race or religion. Other than discrimination, cooperative boards usually have absolute discretion in rejecting potential purchasers.

If Alan or the purchaser suspects that the board turned down the purchaser as a result of discrimination (racial, religious, gender, etc.), the local governmental fair housing agency should be notified. Alan should also consult an attorney to determine if he has a basis for a lawsuit against the cooperative.

AVOIDING THE PITFALLS OF TIMESHARES

Timeshares represent the rights to limited, preplanned use of a vacation home. Of the two types of timeshare plans, deeded and nondeeded, buyers who purchase *deeded* timeshares actually own part of the property; *nondeeded* timeshares give buyers only a license to use the vacation home for a certain amount of time each year for a predetermined number of years.

Before deciding to purchase a timeshare, consider all the costs it will involve—not only the monthly mortgage payments but also the maintenance fees and necessary travel expenses. Check with other owners, consumer groups, and the Better Business Bureau to make sure that the management company is reputable. If you are satisfied, find out what opportunities are available to exchange with other timeshare owners in other areas.

Be sure the timeshare contract protects you from any potential default by management or its contractors. Your contract should include a "nondisturbance" clause that guarantees you the right to continue using your timeshare even if the developer or management company defaults and lenders or other third parties make legal claims against them. In addition, including a "nonperformance" protection provision will protect you against losing your ownership rights even if a lender or a defaulting builder or management company attempts to buy out your contract. Check to see if there is a "cooling-off" period, which gives you a chance to reconsider the purchase and cancel the agreement, if you choose to, within a few days. Some states have laws that require a cooling-off period.

If you are considering buying into a timeshare where the community is not yet completed, proceed with special caution. Get a written commitment specifying the date when the facility will be ready. Have a portion of your investment placed in escrow, which will enable you to recoup some of your money if the project defaults. Be wary about the prospect of living in an unfinished community that has been taken over by the seller's bank.

Each state's Real Estate Commission usually oversees the sale of timeshares. If you need more information, contact that office. The FTC has the power to investigate timeshare companies that are thought to be engaging in illegal practices or fraud. Write to the Federal Trade Commission, Division of Marketing Practices, 96 Pennsylvania Avenue, N.W. Washington, DC 20580. If you believe you have been defrauded by a timeshare company, consult an attorney.

AVOIDING LAND SALE SCAMS

Consumers often buy land for its potential value as an investment rather than for their personal use. Because of the uncertainty of future value, potential land investors need to be especially cautious before making a purchase.

The Interstate Land Sales Full Disclosure Act was passed in 1968 to protect consumers from land sale scams. The law requires devel-

Because HUD does not check the land to verify the accuracy of property reports, buyers cannot rely on the report alone. You must research the value of the property by talking to real estate professionals in the area, checking tax records for appraisals, looking into the county's development plans for surrounding property, familiarizing yourself with any zoning restrictions, and determining your responsibilities for providing sewerage, water, and electricity to the undeveloped land. You must also investigate the company selling the land, checking with HUD and the Better Business Bureau and looking at appropriate court records to determine if the company has been sued.

opers who are selling or leasing 100 or more unimproved lots through interstate commerce to file basic information about their properties with the Department of Housing and Urban Development (HUD). Before you sign a contract to buy land, the developer is required to provide you with this information in the form of a "property report."

Be sure your cancellation rights are spelled out in your contract. If the land is subject to the Full Disclosure Act—that is, if the developer is selling or leasing 100 or more unimproved lots through interstate commerce—you'll have a 7-day cooling-off period in which to change your mind. If the contract fails to state that you will be provided with a warranty deed within 180 days of executing the agreement, the cancellation period may be extended up to two years. If the land is not subject to the Act, be sure the contract contains such a cancellation clause.

What follows is a hypothetical situation involving land sales.

THE PROBLEM

Maurice entered into a contract to buy a plot of undeveloped land in Texas with the intention of building a new home on it. Maurice later discovered that a major warehouse distribution center was going to be constructed across the road, which would have very heavy tractor-trailer traffic.

WHAT TO DO

Maurice would have the right to cancel the agreement within seven days if the sale was subject to the Land Sales Full Disclosure Act. (If not, he should have negotiated a period of time to terminate after he conducted due diligence with respect to the land.)

If more than seven days have elapsed and there is no due diligence period, then Maurice will probably be bound to the contract to purchase the property.

If you believe the seller misrepresented the property or if any part of the agreement is breached, you have the right to take the seller to court. Contact the Federal Trade Commission if you believe any laws have been violated, and if you have complaints about a developer who is subject to the Full Disclosure Act, notify HUD.

HOME IMPROVEMENTS

The Contract

Making improvements on your home requires exercising just as much caution and legal protection as buying one. When you select a contractor, be sure to check references carefully and compare bids. You can contact the Better Business Bureau to find out how long a contractor has been in business and whether any complaints have been lodged against the company. Find out if the contractor is a member of a professional organization that has a code of ethics and whether the contractor has agreed to arbitrate contract disputes. Be sure to ask what type of insurance the contractor carries as well as the amount of coverage, including property damage, personal liability, and workers' compensation; then verify this information with the insurance carrier. States and cities often have licensing and bonding requirements for contractors. Find out what is required in your locale, and check to be sure your contractor holds the proper license and is sufficiently bonded.

As is the case when buying a home, your contract (in this case with the contractor) dictates the terms of the agreement, regardless of what was promised verbally. It should include:

- the contractor's name, address, phone number, and professional license number
- detailed description of the work to be done, including the materials to be used and their quality (The material descriptions should include quantity, weight, brand names, and model numbers.)
- the fact that the materials and labor are covered by a full warranty, guaranteeing that any problems will be corrected at no cost to the homeowner (If the warranty is limited, the contract must specify this and explain what is covered and under what conditions.)
- the assurance that the work is to be performed in compliance with building code and zoning regulations
- the starting and completion dates (If the job is to be finished by a certain date, try to write in a clause that will impose a

penalty on the contractor if the contractor fails to meet the deadline.)

- the total cost of the project, listing separate breakdowns of labor and building materials costs
- the payment schedule (Ideally, you should avoid making any payment in advance. As a compromise, you may agree to pay a deposit for special-ordered or custom items or one-third of the total fee upon signing the contract and the remainder upon completion to your satisfaction. Remember, you should never pay in cash.)
- the contractor's responsibility to remove materials and debris after completion at no extra cost to you

In addition to the standard clauses, if you're having a significant amount of work done by subcontractors, include a release-of-lien provision. This prevents a lien from being placed on your home if the contractor fails to pay his subcontractors or suppliers. The other alternative is to pay a percentage of the cost into an escrow account, which is not to be released until the job is satisfactorily completed and the contractor provides evidence that the subcontractors have been paid.

You may want to consider adding an arbitration clause to the contract stating that if there is a dispute about payment or the quality of the work, the dispute will be submitted to arbitration instead of the parties having to enter into expensive litigation.

Although arbitration can result in a speedier and less costly resolution of a dispute, it does have its disadvantages. For example, arbitration typically excludes the right to discovery of documents in the other party's possession, documents that you may not possess but would strengthen your case. Also, arbitration decisions usually are not appealable and there is no official record made of the proceedings.

In some states consumers have a three-day cooling-off period in which to change their minds and cancel the agreement after they sign a home improvement contract. The contractor has the legal responsibility to inform you of your rights to cancel and to provide you with the proper forms by which to do so. If you decide to cancel, be sure to send the forms by certified mail, return receipt requested, so you have proof of the contractor's receipt of your notice of cancellation.

If the Contractor Defaults

You'll be asked to sign a completion certificate when the work is done. Don't sign a completion certificate until you've inspected the job and have determined that it meets the specifications of the written agreement. If you're not pleased with the finished work, notify the contractor by certified mail, return receipt requested. If you get no satisfaction, contact the state consumer affairs office or the attorney general's office and ask them to conduct an investigation. Clearly state what has occurred, and include documentation, such as your written contract, invoices, canceled checks, and photographs of the work completed.

You still have the option of filing a lawsuit with the small-claims court, providing that the damages you claim are small enough to qualify there. If not, you may want to hire an attorney and go through the state court system. You should also file a complaint with the Better Business Bureau.

What follows is a hypothetical situation involving a problem with a home improvement contractor.

THE PROBLEM

Jessie hired a contractor to build an addition to her home. She and the contractor entered into an agreement for the construction of the addition, which provided that the payments for the work were to be made on a periodic basis as the work progressed and a 10 percent total cost was to be held back until the entire construction was completed. When the job was approximately 85 percent complete, the contractor filed for bankruptcy and walked off the job.

WHAT TO DO

Jessie should locate another contractor to complete the work and utilize the funds from the 10 percent that was withheld and the unpaid balance of the contract price to pay for the completion of the work. If this amount is insufficient to complete the work, she should file a claim in the bankruptcy court for the shortfall.

If the contractor had not filed for bankruptcy but still failed to complete the work, the only means of recovery would be to sue the contractor for the additional costs incurred to complete the work.

RENTING AN APARTMENT OR A HOUSE

The relationship between landlords and tenants goes back to feudal days, a time when the landlord always wielded the power. Although some tenants may believe that this is still the case, the law has gradually moved toward giving tenants equal footing.

A lease is a contract between two parties, the tenant and landlord. Like all contracts, a lease gives each party rights as well as obligations. The amount of time you plan on staying in the rented premises and the commitment you are willing to make in writing will determine what kind of lease you should sign.

Discrimination

In certain circumstances a landlord is legally entitled to refuse to rent an apartment to you. Turning you down as a tenant on the basis of race, national origin, gender, or religion are illegal under the Federal Fair Housing Act, and if you believe that you have been discriminated against, contact the Department of Housing and Urban Development. But if you are destructive or if you are a poor financial risk, the landlord may be able to refuse you legally.

What follows is a hypothetical situation involving discrimination against an apartment renter.

THE PROBLEM

Angela responded to an advertisement in the local newspaper placed by the landlord offering an apartment for rent. Angela called about the apartment, and the landlord asked her to come to the building and fill out an application. Angela has been employed in the same job for five years, her salary is sufficient to pay the rent, and she has excellent references from her present and former landlords. Upon meeting Angela, the landlord informed her that the apartment had just been rented. Angela is Asian. In fact the landlord had not rented the apartment.

WHAT TO DO

Angela should file a complaint with the local fair housing agency in the city or county where she lives. In most states they will provide legal counsel for her to bring a claim against the landlord not only to compel the landlord to rent Angela the apartment but also to recover damages from the landlord's wrongful act.

Leases

Leases are of two basic kinds, depending on the commitment you wish to make and the landlord's willingness to furnish you with the type you prefer.

"PERIODIC TENANCY"   In this kind of lease, the periodic tenancy can be month-to-month or week-to-week. Either you or the landlord can terminate it by giving 30 days' notice on a month-to-month lease or 7 days' notice on a week-to-week tenancy. These leases are your best bet if you prefer not to be committed for longer periods. The disadvantage is that the landlord can terminate the lease or raise your rent with only 30 days' notice.

"TENANCY FOR A DEFINITE TIME"   This kind of lease is designed to end automatically within a certain number of days, weeks, months, or years. When that time period ends, you will have to move out with no advance notice necessary unless you and the landlord decide to renew the lease. You have an advantage in this type of tenancy because the landlord has no right to remove you or to raise your rent before the lease expires, as long as you've complied with all its requirements.

Understanding the Lease

Ask for a copy of the lease before you decide to rent the house or apartment. Unlike a contract to purchase a house, where you'll most likely retain an attorney, a lease is an agreement you will probably be reviewing on your own.

Some leases will use the terms *Lessee* and *Lessor* instead of *Tenant* and *Landlord*. Others will refer to the "party of the first part" and the "party of the second part." These terms are usually self-explanatory. A popular phrase in some leases is "said Lessor does hereby demise and let unto Lessee." Contrary to the connotation of death, this simply means that the landlord is leasing the property to the tenant. Fortunately, most states have laws that require residential leases to be in "plain English" as opposed to legalese.

THE DEPOSIT   Many first-time renters are unaware that more than one month's rent may be required to secure an apartment. Some landlords ask tenants to pay not only the first and last months' rent upon signing the lease but also an application fee, a security deposit, a cleaning deposit, or a "pet fee." Be sure you ask for the total amount that will be necessary for you to secure a lease for the unit you want. The lease should specify that the landlord keeps the deposits in a segregated interest-bearing account that is refundable to you when you leave—minus any damages the landlord might have the right to withhold.

POSSESSION   One of the basic duties of the landlord is to deliver possession of the premises. When the landlord signs the lease, the landlord is guaranteeing that the tenant has the legal right to occupy the property. Be sure there is a clause guaranteeing that the landlord will pay you damages if you are prevented from taking immediate possession.

Beware of leases that totally absolve landlords of any liability if the unit is not available for you to move into on the date specified in the lease.

RENT   Leases establish a monthly rent as well as when and where it is to be paid. The lease may also include an "escalator clause," a provision that allows the landlord to increase your rent. In some locations rent increases are determined by a state or local government agency. If possible, try to eliminate the possibility of a rent increase for the term of your lease. If you have a three- or six-month lease and the building or community has several vacancies, the landlord may be willing to freeze the rent for you. (Remember, if you have a month-to-month lease, the landlord is required

Suppose you sign a lease that states that you can move in on April 1, but the present tenant refuses to move out, forcing you to search for another apartment. You find one, but it costs you $200 more per month than the one you had originally rented. The landlord has breached the lease, because the landlord was obligated to "deliver possession" of the apartment to you on the contract date, regardless of fault.

If the landlord breaches the lease in this way, you have the right to sue and attempt to collect damages for the difference between what you agreed to pay and what it actually cost you for a different apartment. If the delay is short and you choose to rent a room in a hotel or boardinghouse until you can move into the landlord's unit, the landlord may have to reimburse you for the difference in rent and for possible storage of furniture and belongings. Such reimbursement is easier to recover if a "damages" clause is included in the lease.

to give you 30 days' notice before raising your rent.) The phrase "without demand" means that the landlord will not send you a monthly statement or bill for the rent; it's your responsibility to remember your rent payment and to pay it within the time specified in the lease.

LATE PAYMENTS AND RETURNED CHECKS The landlord may penalize you for late payments; the lease should specify the amount of the penalty and also spell out what fee will be charged if the bank returns your checks.

RENEWAL TERM Some leases include the institution of a monthly fee in addition to the rent if the initial term of the lease expires without renewal, turning the arrangement into a month-to-month tenancy.

ASSIGNMENT AND SUBLETTING An assignment refers to having another person take over your lease. If assigning the lease is not prohibited, the person(s) to whom the lease has been assigned becomes responsible for fulfilling the lease's obligations, and you are without further responsibility. If the new tenant fails to pay rent or otherwise breaks the lease, the landlord must deal with the new tenant directly, not with you. You, however, remain "secondarily" liable for any rent not paid and any damage caused to the apartment by the new tenant. If the landlord is unable to recover unpaid rent or payment for damages from the new tenant, the landlord would be permitted to sue you for the unpaid rent.

If the lease gives you the right to sublet and you sublet your apartment instead of "assigning" the lease, matters are quite different. If the sublesee does not pay the rent, your landlord can sue you. Since the sublesee never entered into a contract with the landlord, all the responsibility still rests with you, the original tenant.

UTILITIES   Some leases cover payment for all utilities in addition to the rent; others require you to pay for some or all of them directly to the utilities companies. Be sure you understand who is responsible for the electricity, gas, water, and trash removal, and how much these services will cost.

THE RIGHT TO ACCESS   The landlord might sometimes need access to your unit, such as when making necessary repairs or when showing the apartment or house to a prospective tenant, but you have a right to "quiet enjoyment" of the premises. For the landlord to come in unannounced or without your permission is considered trespassing and invasion of your privacy. Try to get the landlord to agree in the

---

Lynne's lease specifically states that she cannot sublet or assign the lease on her apartment to anyone. But when she is offered an excellent job in another city, her friend Yvonne offers to take over the lease on her apartment. Without informing the landlord, Lynne moves out and Yvonne moves in. Lynne has violated the terms of her lease, and her landlord is legally entitled to evict Yvonne and demand that Lynne pay the rent for the remainder of the lease.

lease to give you 24 hours' notice before either arriving at your door or entering with a passkey, and be sure to define "reasonable hours" for such access.

USE OF PROPERTY   Since the building in which you live is probably zoned as residential, not commercial, local ordinances prohibit you from opening a commercial enterprise in your home. The landlord has grounds for evicting you in the event that you violate any laws, whether city, county, state, or federal. If inconsiderate neighbors create excessive noise or other intrusions and the landlord fails to remedy the situation after you complain, the landlord has failed to provide you with the right to "quiet enjoyment." If so, you have the right to move out before your lease expires and to sue the landlord.

PETS   Landlords who permit pets often request a "pet fee," which is sometimes refundable. If you bring a pet into a "no-pet" complex or if you fail to secure prior approval, the landlord has the right to evict you.

INDEMNIFICATION   The indemnification clause in your lease means that the landlord is attempting to be relieved of any liability for injuries to anyone coming into your apartment or onto the grounds, regardless of fault. For example, suppose the landlord has failed to fix a broken step leading to your unit; your brother comes to visit you, trips, falls down eight steps, and ends up in the hospital with a broken leg. The landlord may include a clause in the lease attempting to make you, the tenant, responsible for such liability, despite the fact that it is legally the fault of the landlord for failing to keep up the premises. You should avoid signing a lease with such a clause.

NONWAIVER   The nonwaiver clause means that the landlord's waiving certain requirements of the lease does not constitute a precedent on his or her part. Suppose, for example, that you buy a parakeet, despite the fact that your lease prohibits pets. Your landlord finds out but neither requires you to remove the bird nor threatens to evict you. Your parakeet dies, and you automatically assume that you can replace it with a second bird. Because your landlord did not enforce the pet prohibition the first time around does not mean the landlord waived the right to enforce it or any other violation in the future.

ATTORNEYS' FEES   Some leases state that if either party sues the other, the prevailing party will receive reasonable attorneys' fees as well as any court costs from the other party.

Landlords sometimes attempt to include a clause stating that "the tenant shall pay and discharge all costs, expenses, and attorneys' fees which shall be incurred and expended by the landlord in enforcing the covenants and agreements of this lease, whether by the institution of litigation or in the taking of advice of counsel, or otherwise." In other words, no matter which side eventually prevails, the landlord wants you, the tenant, to pay for the landlord's attorneys' fees. In some states such a provision is illegal and would not be enforced in court.

An acceptable, middle-of-the-road approach to attorneys' fees in a lease allows for the party that "prevails," or wins, to have his or her legal fees and costs paid by the other party. Another approach is a written agreement that each side cover his or her own legal fees.

REPAIRS   Some leases require the tenant to accept the apartment "as is," a boon for the landlord but not for you. For example, if you move into an apartment and discover that it is overrun with cockroaches, that the windows don't close properly, and that the air conditioner is broken, many judges would agree that the apartment is uninhabitable. The landlord is responsible for making sure that the apartment is livable.

You are required to put the landlord on notice if such conditions exist in your apartment, allowing sufficient time for appropriate action to be taken. If the landlord fails to make such repairs, you have two choices. You can move out and sue the landlord for the rent, deposits, and fees you have already paid, or you can stay in the premises and demand damages for the difference between what your monthly rent is and what the true value of the apartment is in its present condition.

Before you sign the lease, discuss with the landlord any damage or problems you might have found in the apartment and ascertain that they will be taken care of before you move in. Enumerate the problems in a written list, often called a "punch list." Have the landlord sign it, and obtain a statement confirming that the repairs will be done quickly.

The responsibility for the upkeep of the premises usually falls on the landlord, with the exception of damages created by the tenant, the tenant's family, or the tenant's guests (lease provisions shift this burden to the tenant). Upkeep is more or less an extension of the landlord's responsibility to make the premises habitable. If the landlord ignores your complaints about a leaky roof, a toilet that is backed up, or broken burners on the stove, you can either end the lease, move out, and sue for damages, or you can notify the landlord of the problem and of your intention to have the repairs done yourself, deducting the cost from your rent.

What follows is a hypothetical situation involving a landlord withholding services.

THE PROBLEM

Roy leased an apartment to Adrienne in an apartment building. The lease was for three years. A year after Adrienne moved in, Roy decided he wanted to raise the rent but had no basis for increasing the rent or for terminating the lease. The heating system servicing Adrienne's apartment stopped working in the middle of February. Adrienne immediately reported this condition to Roy, who claimed he was trying to repair the system, but was, in fact, delaying in an attempt to force Adrienne to vacate the apartment. Adrienne found the apartment uninhabitable and moved out to temporary quarters.

WHAT TO DO

Adrienne should contact an attorney and consider suing Roy for actual damages based on the costs of moving out of the apartment and finding a temporary place to stay. In addition, because Roy's actions were intentional, Adrienne should seek punitive damages against Roy, which could be fairly high given the fact that Roy intentionally refused to repair the system in order to force Adrienne out of her apartment.

In some cities and counties, a governmental agency will make repairs to apartments and to the structures in which the apartments are located if the landlord fails to make the repairs in a timely fashion. The governmental agency will then recover the amount spent from the landlord.

Some landlords welcome tenant improvements, such as painting or wallpapering. Others completely prohibit any alterations, and still others will allow certain alterations if written requests for permission are submitted. If such alterations are permitted, clarify who pays for the materials and who retains ownership of "fixtures," such as bookshelves or chandeliers, that are attached to the property. Laws in some states allow the landlord to keep fixtures, regardless of their value, if they have been screwed into the wall or ceiling. Some landlords will insist that the apartment be restored to its former state (before the tenant moved in) before the tenant moves out.

SUBORDINATION Some leases include subordination clauses, which specify that the lease is subject to the mortgages others hold on the property. Under such a clause, if the landlord fails to make a mortgage payment, for example, the bank or mortgage company can foreclose, force the sale of the property, and evict you with no appeal on your part and without refunding your deposits. If you can eliminate this clause, be sure to do so.

SEVERABILITY The severability clause in a lease merely reinforces what is already the law in most states: that if a portion of the lease is found to be illegal, that part will be stricken but the rest of the lease will stand. Suppose, for example, that the lease prohibits the tenant from allowing any children to live in the leased premises. This was once a landlord's prerogative, but no longer. Should you challenge this clause in court and win, you are still committed to all the other obligations to which you previously agreed.

ENTIRE AGREEMENT Leases usually contain a clause stating that the lease is the total agreement made between the parties regarding the leased house or apartment. This is simply a statement that you should not count on any verbal agreement you may have made with the landlord to be honored if it does not appear in the written lease. Make sure that any such agreement is added to the lease and signed, no matter how a landlord may persist in assuring you that this is unnecessary.

SPECIAL STIPULATIONS Find out what extra amenities you may be entitled to as a tenant at the apartment. If the landlord tells you that you will have access to a heated swimming pool, indoor gym, laundry facilities, and garage parking, be sure these are spelled out in the lease. Should the landlord decide that the upkeep of the pool is too expensive, for example, and closes it, getting such amenities noted in writing will allow you to demand that either the pool is open and properly maintained or that you receive a rent reduction. If the landlord does not comply, this could be a basis for cancellation of the lease.

EVICTION   Failure to pay the proper amount of rent or other fees on time is the most common cause of evictions. Suppose you believe that your landlord has unjustly raised your rent. Don't ignore the increase by paying the lesser original amount or by not paying the rent at all. Pay the full amount, but protest in the form of a letter, and then take the matter to court; the other two actions can constitute grounds for your eviction.

Many landlords start eviction proceedings when a lease expires and the tenant refuses to move out. In the case of month-to-month leases, the landlord has the right to evict a tenant after the tenant is given the proper 30-day notice. A tenant who remains on the property after the lease expires is considered a "holdover tenant" and can be taken to court. If your lease has expired yet the landlord accepts the next month's rent, in many states you remain a tenant on a month-to-month lease basis and cannot be evicted until the landlord gives you the 30-day notice the lease requires.

The landlord also has the right to evict you "for cause," that is, a violation of your lease, perhaps keeping a pet in a "no-pet" complex, conducting illegal activities on the leased premises, or failing to pay your rent.

To evict you, the landlord must first put you on notice, in writing, of the intention to evict you (unless the term of the lease has expired, in which case no notice is necessary), citing the parties involved, the address of the leased unit, the date of notice, the amount of rent or fees overdue, or another explanation of the violation.

States vary concerning what constitutes the tenant's legitimate receipt of the notice; some states require personal service, some require registered or certified mail, while others allow delivery by regular mail or merely dropping off a notice at the door or mailbox of the tenant's apartment. After sufficient notice has been made, the landlord has the right to file a complaint in court, to actually sue you. If you fail to appear, the judge will automatically grant the eviction to your landlord.

If you have a defense to not paying, such as the landlord's refusal to maintain the premises, be prepared to prove it in court. As noted, when a landlord rents an apartment, the landlord implicitly warrants that the unit and the surrounding property will be habitable. When you go to court, bring photographs, neighbors as witnesses, and, if applicable, reports from the health department to prove to the judge that the landlord failed to maintain the premises.

What follows is a hypothetical situation involving eviction proceedings.

THE PROBLEM

Howard, the landlord, brought an eviction proceeding against Ann because Ann did not pay the rent. Ann stopped paying rent because Howard refused to repair the collapsed ceiling in her bathroom. The condition was very dangerous and rendered the bathroom unusable.

WHAT TO DO

Ann should defend the action (not paying the rent) in court on the grounds that the landlord breached the lease's warranty of habitability by failing to make the necessary repairs to make the apartment livable. Ann should bring photographs of the condition to court, together with copies of notices written to the landlord demanding the repairs. Ann should also document any expenses she incurred as a result of the problem. If Ann is successful, she will probably receive an abatement (or reduction) in her rent for the period of time that her bathroom was in a state of disrepair. She might even recover additional damages for the inconvenience caused by Howard's failure to act promptly.

8

THE WORKPLACE

Employment is a matter of contract. An employer who has a job to fill enters into an agreement with an employee who agrees to fill it. Each party has certain rights in return for privileges.

Historically, the employer has had the upper hand, with employees working "at will," or at the pleasure of the employer. State and federal law is moving toward giving the employee more protection, but many employees who work without written contracts, regardless of the level of their employment, are often at the mercy of their employers in many states. However, employees do have many rights, as the following material indicates.

EMPLOYMENT DISCRIMINATION

Discrimination in employment based on race, national origin, gender, religion, age, or disabilities is prohibited. Title VII of the Civil Rights Act of 1964, the Age Discrimination in Employment Act, Section 504 of the Rehabilitation Act of 1973, and the Americans with Disabilities Act of 1990 all make this clear. These protections apply to every aspect of employment, including classified advertisements that an employer runs, the job interview, wages, promotions, the job environment, termination, and retirement. With certain exceptions, if an employer asks questions in an interview or on an application that imply that these factors will carry any weight in the employer's hiring decision, the employer is vulnerable to a lawsuit.

SOME EXCEPTIONS: BONA FIDE OCCUPATIONAL QUALIFICATIONS (BFOQS)
There are certain conditions under which national origin, sex and religion, or age may be genuine considerations in hiring. Such considerations are known as bona fide occupational qualifications, or BFOQs.

The sex of a person can be considered in a job description if the job requires privacy (such as a changing room or restroom attendant). Sometimes BFOQ also applies if the job is only capable of performance by one gender—a wet nurse or clothing model, for example.

Advertising and Recruiting

Employers and newspapers are no longer permitted to use headings such as "Help Wanted, Male" or "Young, Attractive Receptionist Wanted." Any reference to sex or age in Help Wanted advertising is considered discriminatory. Employers are expected to include phrases in their ads suggested by the Equal Employment Opportunity Commission. For example, "Dinah's Diner does not discriminate on the basis of race, color, national origin, sex, age, or handicap."

Interview and Application Questions

Employers and applicants alike are faced with the dilemma of what questions are proper to ask and which should be answered in an interview or on a job application. Some common sensitive areas include:

HEIGHT AND WEIGHT   Height and weight requirements that disproportionately qualify women or members of racial or ethnic groups must bear some relationship to a potential employee's ability to do a job.

PHOTOGRAPHS   Employers may not request that a photograph be included in a job application. A photo reveals an applicant's sex, race, age, height, and weight, which may not be considered on most job applications. (An exception would be requesting a photograph of an applicant for a modeling job.)

MARITAL STATUS AND PLANS FOR A FAMILY   Marital status is irrelevant to the job, as is the occupation and background of one's spouse, and therefore it is usually inappropriate for employers to inquire whether an applicant is married, single, divorced, or living with another person. If such inquiries are made only of candidates of one sex, they would ordinarily be prohibited by Title VII. Employers are allowed, however, to have applicants "check" the title he or she prefers to use, including Mr., Mrs., Miss, Ms., Dr., Ph.D., or "other."

Some employers prefer not to hire pregnant women to avoid the possibility of maternity leave or the demands of child care. Nevertheless, refusing to hire a woman because she is or may become pregnant, asking if an applicant is pregnant, or inquiring about whether she hopes to start a family is illegal.

ENGLISH LANGUAGE   Asking if an applicant can speak English may discriminate on the basis of national origin, and the question may be asked only if the ability to communicate in English is necessary to job performance.

RELIGION   Questions about an applicant's religion are usually illegal because they are ordinarily without relevance to job performance. Employers are permitted to ask whether an applicant will be available to work on Saturdays, Sundays, or evenings, if that is a legitimate job requirement. Religious institutions are, however, exempt and are permitted to hire only persons of a particular religion to carry out their activities.

UNION MEMBERSHIP   Employers are prohibited from asking applicants whether they have participated in union activities in the past or whether they would join a union if hired.

ARRESTS AND CONVICTIONS   Asking whether an applicant has ever been arrested is unwise and inappropriate for two reasons. First, arrest records provide no information concerning actual criminal activity, and are of no legal significance. Second, the inquiry itself can have racially discriminatory impact on minority applicants, who would be disproportionately disqualified if arrest records were considered in making employment decisions.

An employer is not usually permitted to turn down an applicant because he or she is enrolled in a drug or alcohol rehabilitation program. Addiction to drugs or alcohol is considered a disability, and those who are addicted are disabled and protected by federal laws, including the Americans with Disabilities Act.

> Rena applied for a job as an administrative assistant in a large corporation. During the interview, the personnel manager asked her if she had any plans to raise a family. If Rena is denied employment based on her response and can prove it (by proving that men were not asked the same question), she can file a complaint with the Equal Employment Opportunity Commission, charging sexual discrimination in hiring, and can later sue in court if she chooses to.

PHYSICAL CONDITION AND DISABILITIES   An employer is permitted to ask a prospective employee to submit to a physical examination as a final step after being offered the job, if this is standard procedure for all acceptable applicants. But it is illegal to ask detailed questions about an applicant's medical history. (See page 283 for drug testing.) The Americans with Disabilities Act limits the types of questions that an employer can ask a disabled applicant during a job interview.

CREDIT RECORDS   Refusing employment on the basis of an applicant's poor credit history is discriminatory. An employer may make such inquiries only if a bad debt or a history of garnishments has any bearing on the available job, for example, such as working for a lending institution or bank.

An applicant must be notified if an employer runs a credit check and must be told which credit bureau was contacted. If the applicant is denied a job because of the report, the applicant must be permitted to defend any negative results.

EMPLOYMENT CONTRACTS

Every time an individual takes a job, an employment contract has been created. Whether it's spelled out explicitly in writing or merely implied, an employment agreement establishes the wages the worker will receive, the work that is to be performed, the place of performance, and the length of time that the work is available. If

COPING WITH ILLEGAL QUESTIONS

Be sure to review all employment applications and forms to check for discriminatory questions, and be aware of improper questions during the interview. If you believe that you were denied a job based on a refusal to answer discriminatory questions or if you gave an answer to a discriminatory question, because you feared that failure to do so would jeopardize your chances of employment, you can file a complaint with an appropriate agency to protect your rights. This includes the state or local human rights office, or a regional office of the Equal Employment Opportunity Commission. Private lawyers, as well as organizations such as the NAACP or ACLU may be able to assist in filing discrimination charges.

It is always a good idea to first document your complaint by writing a letter. (See sample letter, Appendix D.) Follow up the letter by contacting the agency to confirm that action is being taken to protect your rights. Speak to a lawyer to determine your rights and options if you are not satisfied with the progress of the investigation. You should also consider filing a formal discrimination lawsuit through either a private attorney, after an investigation by the state agency, or the EEOC if you were denied a job because of refusing to answer discriminatory questions or because of answers to illegal questions. Sometimes these agencies will sue on your behalf.

these elements are not clear and a conflict arises, a court may be required to interpret the intentions of the parties.

Working without a written contract means you're "working at will," the will of the employer. A written contract may spell out your rights and obligations and reduce your chances of having to litigate to get what was promised to you. It binds both parties, however, and may prevent you from leaving a job you do not like. A well-drafted agreement should reduce the likelihood of misunderstandings between an employer and employee by spelling out clearly the terms of employment. In certain circumstances it may reduce the employer's prerogative to fire an employee at will, to confiscate benefits, or to lower salaries.

A good contract requires more than the basic elements of wages, place of employment, job requirements, and length of employment. It should spell out matters that seem trivial but may become major conflict points later, such as the number of sick days, weeks of paid or unpaid vacation, bonuses, advances, a description of disciplinary and grievance systems, and termination policy.

Oral contracts may be valid, but they are often difficult to prove in court. The Statute of Frauds requires that a contract be in writing if it cannot be performed within one year. Many states will not enforce an oral contract if its obligations extend beyond one year.

Terminations

Written employment contracts should contain a clause that restricts the conditions under which an employer can terminate the employment. Ordinarily, contracts will provide that termination can only occur "for good cause."

What follows is a hypothetical situation involving breach of an employment contract.

THE PROBLEM

Gwen, a fashion designer, was given a written contract by her employer when she began work. The contract stated that she was hired for a minimum initial period of one year, from January 1 through December 31, at an annual salary of $48,000 ($4,000 per month). On August 15, Gwen was suddenly terminated with no explanation. She had been doing a good job and had received compliments about her performance. She had even received a small raise of $200 per month on July 1 of that year.

WHAT TO DO

Gwen should contact an employment lawyer. She should immediately write her ex-employer a certified letter (return receipt requested) documenting her contractual right to compensation through the contract year. Since she had not been fired for cause (i.e., for a good reason such as insubordination, misconduct, etc.), she is entitled to receive the full amount of pay as called for in her contract through December 31, less what she earned from any unemployment benefits or another job.

STIPULATED DAMAGES   When a contract is breached, it's often difficult to determine how either party should be compensated. Some contracts include a "stipulated damage" clause that spells out what each party will receive if the other fails to uphold the contract. Others state that if an employer fires the employee without cause, the employee will be entitled to the full salary that would have been received through the remainder of the contract term had the job not been terminated.

RESTRICTIVE COVENANTS   Some employers will attempt to prevent you from working for their competitors after you leave their employ by using a "restrictive covenant" in employment contracts. Such a clause often sets type of industry or business, time, and geographical restrictions on where an employee can work after leaving the current job. Neither federal nor state law spells out what limitations are unfair to employees or not protective enough of employers, so deciding whether a restrictive covenant should be upheld is often left to a judge. A restrictive covenant must have *reasonable* limits on time and geographical area, limits that can vary from state to state. In general, a one-year prohibition from working in the same state or surrounding counties is considered reasonable.

Arnold works as an executive for the Rubber Tire Company in Omaha, Nebraska. His employment contract prohibits him from working for another tire manufacturer in the midwestern United States in any capacity for a period of 10 years after leaving Rubber. A court would most likely invalidate the restrictive covenant because its geographical and time limitations make it virtually impossible for Arnold to earn a living in the field of his expertise.

Signing an Employment Contract

Before you sign a contract, particularly one that includes a restrictive covenant, it's advisable that you consult an attorney who specializes in employment law. When you are ready to sign it, be sure the person executing it on behalf of the employer has the authority to do so. Make sure, too, that any employee handbooks or company rules/regulations are attached to the contract if they are incorporated by reference. Put your copy of the agreement (with the original signatures) in a safe place.

If Your Employer Is Unwilling to Give You a Written Contract

Many employers are not willing to enter into written contracts. If your employer is one of them, you can still take certain steps to protect your rights.

LETTER OF AGREEMENT   After the employer has committed to hiring you for a definite period of time and you have agreed to all conditions, including wages and hours, write the employer a letter of agreement, spelling out your understanding of the terms of employment. Include a statement that you expect the employer to let you know if the letter contains an error or if something is unclear. Send the letter certified mail, return receipt requested.

Courts may view the letter as a valid contract if your employer has either signed it or failed to respond and repudiate it. Be sure to keep the evidence that the employer received the letter. Many employers will initiate this procedure by sending you a letter of agreement or will do so if asked to by a newly hired employee.

EMPLOYEE HANDBOOKS AS CONTRACTS   The law differs from jurisdiction to jurisdiction about whether employee handbooks are valid contracts that can be upheld in a court of law; some states uphold them while others do not. Some require that in order for such a handbook to hold legal significance, the employee must have read it. Other questions the courts have considered include whether the employer can write a disclaimer in the booklet itself stating that it is not a contract and whether the employer has the right to change the contents of the handbook after the employee has been hired. If you are relying on an employee handbook to protect your rights or if your written contract contradicts the information provided in the handbook, consult an attorney about the laws in your state.

YOUR RIGHTS ON THE JOB

Once you are hired for a job, regardless of what the contract covers, you are entitled to certain rights provided by federal and state laws as well as the United States and state constitutions.

Protection Against Discrimination

Just as it does during the recruitment and interview stages, the law prohibits employers from discrimination in the workplace on the grounds of race, national origin, gender, religion, age, or disability. Discrimination is illegal in terms and conditions of employment, including without limitation: assignment, promotions, transfers, evaluations, raises, and fringe benefits. Employers are sometimes required to make affirmative accommodations for certain groups of individuals.

AGE DISCRIMINATION   The Age Discrimination in Employment Act protects people between the ages of 40 and 70 from age discrimination in employment. This offers protection to individuals against adverse practices or policies based on bias or stereotypical notions about the characteristics or capabilities of workers based on age. Nonetheless, workers in this age group, like all other workers, are subject to neutral performance-based standards and rules. Older workers who fail to fulfill the requirements of their job have no more special protection against losing their jobs than a younger person with the same work habits and/or performance.

Employers are permitted to offer incentives for early retirement to older workers, but it is illegal to force workers over age 40 into early retirement or to terminate, threaten to terminate, demote, or reduce their salary or benefits.

SEX DISCRIMINATION   The Equal Pay Act, passed in 1963, requires employers to provide equal pay for work requiring equal skill, effort, and responsibility performed under similar conditions. Title VII offers broader protection by prohibiting sex discrimination in all terms and conditions of employment, including without limitation

Boris, 62 years old, often took "cat naps" at his desk in the afternoon on company time. After warning him on several occasions that his napping would have to end, his supervisor fired him. Boris appealed his termination to the EEOC, claiming age discrimination. An EEOC attorney explained to him that being an older American does not guarantee him special privileges on the job even though his rights are protected. The employer has the same right to fire Boris for napping as he would have to fire a 25-year-old for the same offense.

wages and compensation, hiring, assignment, promotion, training, the availability of job opportunities, and fringe benefits.

An employer is prohibited from allowing pregnancy or the fact that a woman is fertile or married and in her child-bearing years to influence any employment-related decisions so long as the woman is capable of performing the job effectively. Pregnancy is to be treated as a temporary disability. As a result of the passage of the federal Family and Medical Leave Act, employees who work for companies with more than 50 full-time employees are allowed to take up to 12 weeks of unpaid leave for temporary medical reasons, including childbirth or to care for a newborn or newly adopted child, a sick dependent, spouse, or an elderly parent.

Sexual harassment is another prohibited form of sex discrimination. Sexual harassment can range from an employer's or supervisor's pressuring an employee to participate in sexual activities in return for promotions, salary increases, or special favors on the job to employers creating a "hostile working environment."

Employers are responsible for acts of managers, but you must put the employer on notice if the sexual harassment resulted from acts of a co-worker or low-level supervisor. If other women have experienced similar problems, proof of such a pattern may strengthen your claim.

Speak to an experienced labor lawyer immediately if the matter is not resolved satisfactorily. An experienced lawyer can tell you

Danielle had been working as an administrative executive for a large company for more than 25 years. In the past few years, she observed that some of her closest friends at the company had been laid off and younger workers (under 40) were hired in their place. Danielle did not believe that the reason for the firings was due to legitimate, nondiscriminatory, rational business reasons. She also feared that her job might be in jeopardy, because an executive had recently asked her, "Haven't you considered retiring?"

Danielle sent a letter to the vice president of personnel stating that she had no intention of retiring. She also informed management of the liability-sensitive question put to her and the fact that under state and federal law it was illegal to impose compulsory retirement or force her into taking early retirement.

whether it makes sense to file a claim in court or with an appropriate agency such as the EEOC or if it's more desirable for him or her to contact the employer and try to settle the matter out of court. In any event a course of strategy should be implemented and followed *immediately* to prevent you from suffering more abuse and to protect your rights in this area.

The number of sex discrimination cases against employers has increased in recent years as employees become aware of this protection, and, as a result, the courts will be defining clearer guidelines in the future about what constitutes a violation of a worker's right to be protected against sexual harassment and other forms of sexual discrimination.

In November 1993 the Supreme Court announced a broad definition of sexual harassment in the workplace that will enable workers to win suits without having to prove that the offensive behavior left them psychologically damaged or unable to do their jobs. The Court rejected a standard adopted by several lower federal courts that required plaintiffs to show that sexual harassment made the workplace environment hostile enough to cause them "severe psychological injury."

DISCRIMINATION BASED ON RACE OR NATIONAL ORIGIN Any discriminatory employment practice relating to promotions, salary increases, training, or day-to-day treatment violates civil rights laws. Some overt forms of discrimination create a hostile work environment, while other forms of racial discrimination are more subtle, including neutral practices that have an adverse impact on some groups or different treatment that appears to be based on race.

Employers who require that employees have United States citizenship or fluency in English may be acting illegally if they single out a particular nationality or if the requirement has no relationship to the job being performed.

RELIGIOUS DISCRIMINATION Employers must make accommodations for an employee's religious beliefs if they don't create an undue hardship for the employer.

Most religious accommodations involve the employer permitting an employee to schedule work time around particular religious holidays, after sundown, or on weekends. An employer must be willing to make these accommodations unless it can prove that doing so will cause undue hardship. Employers must also be flexible when an employee's religious beliefs require the employee to engage in prayer breaks, certain styles of dress, or opposition to unions or physical exams.

What follows is a hypothetical situation involving religious discrimination on the job.

THE PROBLEM

Hilda was hired by an auto manufacturer to work on an assembly line. She was a devout member of a religion that prohibited her from working from sunset Friday to sunset Saturday. When the company required mandatory overtime on Saturday, Hilda refused based on religious grounds and because her employer had excused other workers for personal reasons. She was fired after missing a series of Saturday work shifts.

WHAT TO DO

Hilda should contact a lawyer, file charges with the EEOC or an appropriate state agency, and possibly file suit in federal court

> Carlos was a dedicated and long-time worker with 24 years of experience who felt he was unfairly denied a promotion. Carlos believed that management failed to give him a promotion and raise because he was of Puerto Rican descent. The promotion was given to a white worker with 4 years experience at the company. Carlos noticed that this was the third time in 4 years that a promotion was not offered to him but was given to a nonminority worker with less experience and skill.
>
> Carlos spoke to his supervisor, who said he would investigate his complaint. After hearing nothing, Carlos decided to find out if he had been a victim of race discrimination. He contacted a local EEOC office and scheduled an appointment with an investigator, who prepared a complaint form that Carlos signed, which was forwarded to the company. After an investigation, the EEOC found that Carlos had good reason to believe he had been discriminated against. Several weeks later the company offered Carlos a promotion and raise, and he dropped his charge.

alleging the company violated Title VII of the 1964 Civil Rights Act that makes it unlawful to fire or discriminate against anyone on the basis of his or her legitimate religious beliefs.

DISCRIMINATION AGAINST THE DISABLED   The Americans with Disabilities Act of 1990 prohibits discrimination against disabled workers by employers with 25 or more employees (15 or more after July 26, 1994), employment agencies, and labor unions. Just like religious accommodations, an employer must make accommodations for otherwise qualified disabled workers as long as doing so doesn't create an undue hardship for the employer. If the demands of a job can be restructured, or a piece of equipment altered in a way that is not prohibitively costly, the employer is expected to accommodate. (Chapter 6 details the rights of the disabled in the workplace.)

What follows is a hypothetical situation involving discrimination against the disabled in the workplace.

THE PROBLEM

In an unfortunate hunting accident, Mel, a comptroller, suffered gunshot wounds that caused him great pain and discomfort. When he was ready to return to work, Mel required a wheelchair because he was unable to walk more than a few feet without assistance. However, he could still competently perform his job, which did not require him to be on his feet.

Because of the expense and delay involved, Mel's company chose not to install ramps and other accommodations to enable Mel to maneuver his wheelchair into the building and around the office.

WHAT TO DO

Mel should inform (in writing) the company that pursuant to the Americans with Disabilities Act it is required to make existing facilities accessible to disabled employees, provide personal assistants to help a qualified individual with a disability perform an essential job function, and, in general, offer reasonable accommodations for persons with disabilities regardless of how the disability was acquired.

If Mel's employer does not make reasonable accommodations within a reasonable period of time, he should contact the Equal Employment Opportunity Commission.

Enforcing Your Rights Against Discrimination in the Workplace

If you believe you have been the victim of discrimination, report it to your employer; perhaps the employer was unaware that the discrimination was taking place and will take measures to remedy it. If you get no satisfaction, you can file a formal complaint with either the Equal Employment Opportunity Commission (EEOC) or the state agency in your region that handles employee discrimination complaints. If you have a discrimination complaint, check the filing procedure with the EEOC or agency that handles employee grievances in your state before you take further action.

The speed with which you file a complaint with the EEOC is important because a statute of limitations (180 days; less for federal government employees) applies. You should contact the EEOC for further information.

Using the address at the end of this chapter, obtain and fill out a copy of an EEOC "Charge of Discrimination" form, providing your name, address, and the other requested information. You will be asked for the "particulars," including the date, time, individual(s) who discriminated against you, the names of others who have had the same experiences, and what actions you took. Your description need not be lengthy, but keep in mind that it should be informative enough for the EEOC to conduct an investigation.

The EEOC will send your employer a copy of your complaint along with a request for a written answer to the charges. The EEOC will usually try to resolve the complaint through conciliation even before investigating. If, after an investigation, the Commission finds that no discrimination took place, both parties will be notified and the employee still has the right to file a private lawsuit against the employer. If the EEOC investigation determines there is probable cause to believe that the employer discriminated against the complaining party, the Commission will attempt to persuade the employer to correct the wrong. This can include reinstatement to the job, payment of lost wages and benefits, and the restitution of other financial losses. Damages are sometimes available to compensate for future financial losses, pain and suffering, or egregious conduct.

If the company chooses not to settle the case out of court, the EEOC may decide to file a lawsuit on your behalf or intervene in a lawsuit you may file. In any event, the EEOC is required to issue the employee a right-to-sue notice, either at the conclusion of its proceedings or any time after 180 days upon the employee's request. The right-to-sue letter entitles the employee to file a personal lawsuit within 90 days.

YOUR RIGHTS TO PRIVACY IN THE WORKPLACE

The workplace does not offer the same rights to privacy as those you have in your home, primarily because it belongs to your employer. That employer has the right to protect the property and the enterprise through inspections and searches, if there is sufficient reason (probable cause) to believe an employee is involved in illegal activities.

Employers occasionally believe they need to conduct "pat-down" searches because they suspect that an employee is embezzling funds or stealing office supplies or merchandise. Pat-down searches are sometimes permitted if they are done with probable cause, out of view of other employees, and no aggressive behavior is used. But if you have been singled out randomly, searched and embarrassed in front of other employees, or pushed or shoved in the process, and the employer had no good reasons to suspect you, contact a lawyer to determine whether state law provides you any remedies.

Employers who suspect wrongdoing will often interrogate employees. If you are questioned, you have the right to know whether you are a suspect, to refuse to sign anything, to decline answering questions, to have a lawyer present, and to walk out of the interview at any time. If your employer wants to tape the interview, the employer must first get your permission.

If you discover that your employer has wiretapped your business or home telephone with electronic devices and is eavesdropping on your business or private conversations, you can bring a civil lawsuit and file criminal charges against the employer. It's also illegal to look in your windows, but an employer can follow you to public places without violating any laws.

What follows is a hypothetical situation involving invasion of privacy at the workplace.

THE PROBLEM

While in her office, Nina received a phone call from a friend advising her about a job opening in another organization. Nina's employer, who had a well-known policy of monitoring business calls in the offices, overheard this conversation and fired Nina the next day.

WHAT TO DO

Nina should contact a lawyer and commence a lawsuit for invasion of privacy, unfair discharge, and other legal causes of action. She should seek to have the court reject the employer's probable argument that Nina's knowledge of its monitoring policy constituted consent; arguably, Nina consented only to monitoring of out-going business calls, not in-coming personal calls.

Drug and Alcohol Testing

Some states allow employers to test their employees for alcohol and illegal drugs and to make hiring and firing decisions based on the results. Other states restrict drug testing to employees who are in positions where safety is a major issue. Still others permit testing only if there is a reasonable belief that the use of alcohol or illegal drugs is preventing an employee from adequately performing a job.

No general consensus exists concerning how much privacy an employee can expect or what rights an employer should have to investigate and take action against employees who abuse alcohol or drugs. If you have questions about these rights, consult a lawyer who specializes in employment law.

Polygraph (Lie Detector) Tests

Polygraph test results are not admissible in a courtroom, yet some employers fire employees and bring criminal charges based on these results. More than half the states have laws that prohibit or restrict the use of polygraphs, and even in those states without such laws, the courts sometimes prohibit polygraph use. The Employee Polygraph Protection Act passed by Congress in 1988 provides that in order for an employer to administer a polygraph test to an employee, the employer must prove that economic loss will result without the

Suppose your employer decides to search your desk or locker. Do you have the right to sue him for invading your privacy? That will depend on how much privacy you legitimately expected to have. If your employer announced that the company had a policy of searching desks, lockers, and other areas in the workplace, you can't expect much privacy and won't get much help in court from a judge if those areas are searched. But if no policy existed and you kept your locker or desk locked and only you had the key or the combination, you could reasonably expect those areas to be protected from an employer and might be able to prevail in a lawsuit.

use of the test. Nevertheless, the employee can still refuse to submit to the test and cannot be punished for filing a grievance. Violation of this law can result in a fine against the employer, and the employee has the option of filing a lawsuit.

YOUR RIGHT TO JOIN A UNION

The National Labor Relations Act gives workers the right to join labor unions and to engage in collective bargaining. In order for a group of workers to be represented by a union, a majority vote of all employees in an election held by the National Labor Relations Board is required.

Unions negotiate a collective bargaining contract with the employer, addressing issues such as wages, working hours, hiring, layoffs, promotions, and benefits. These contracts also create a grievance procedure that provides a system for the union to represent individual workers in negotiations. In some cases there are provisions for binding arbitration.

Employers are prohibited from asking job applicants if they have participated in union activities in the past or whether they would join a union if they are hired. Employees cannot be fired, laid off, demoted, or punished in any way for participating in strikes or other protected union activities. Activities that are not protected include destruction of property, physical violence, or work slowdowns.

If you believe that your employer is violating your right to join a union or participate in union activities, talk to your union representative or contact the Department of Labor in your state.

IF YOU ARE WRONGFULLY DISCHARGED

Illegal terminations include those based on:

- discriminatory grounds, such as race, religion, national origin, age, gender, or disability
- pregnancy
- an employee's refusal to commit illegal acts

- "whistle-blowing," or reporting an employer for violating a law, governmental regulation, or important safety violations affecting the public welfare
- joining a union
- participating in group protests against unsafe or unhealthy job conditions
- performing a governmental obligation, including jury duty
- an employee's eligibility for accrued benefits such as pensions or commissions
- an employee's filing of a workers' compensation claim or other statutory right

Whether or not an employee has a right to sue an employer for wrongful discharge is often determined by what has been agreed upon in the employment contract. If your employer breached your contract by demoting or firing you without cause, you may have the right to file a lawsuit. The court will seldom require an employer to give you your job back, but it can direct that employer to pay you monetary damages based on lost wages since the day you were fired to the time of trial. You will be expected to "mitigate" your damages—that is, attempt to find another job or source of income after you have been fired.

If you are the party who breaches the contract by quitting or forcing your employer to fire you because of your behavior, the employer may have the right to sue you. The employer is also required to mitigate its damages by hiring someone else to replace you, but a court can direct you to pay the employer's costs in finding your replacement (such as the fee to a job search firm). You may also be asked to pay the difference between what your employer has to pay the new person and what the employer would have paid you, had you not quit. In very rare circumstances, when an employee with unique or special talents quits and cannot be replaced, causing irreparable damage to a business—a movie star, for example—the employer can ask for significant "consequential" damages.

If there is no written employment contract in place, an employee is usually considered to be working "at will" and has little recourse if fired, unless discrimination took place. But if the employee has performed acceptable work, the employer is required to pay that employee the value of services rendered regardless of whether an enforceable contract existed. This legal theory is called *quantum meruit*.

What follows is a hypothetical situation involving a *quantum meruit* claim.

THE PROBLEM

For more than a year, Bernard, a sales representative earning a salary and commission incentives, worked diligently to locate a customer interested in making a large purchase of his company's products. Bernard had discovered the customer and had met with key employees on several occasions to implement this large initial sale. Bernard told his company what he had done and even introduced management to the customer. Just before the customer was about to place an initial order for 50 machines (costing $20,000 each), Bernard was suddenly terminated without notice or cause.

WHAT TO DO

Bernard should immediately send a letter (certified, return receipt requested) to his former employers, advising them that he was the soliciting, procuring cause of the order, and that he should be entitled to receive commissions for his efforts if the order was consummated.

If the company failed to respond to Bernard, he should contact a labor lawyer to collect any commissions due him.

SAFETY IN THE WORKPLACE

Before the 1970s employees who worked at unhealthy or unsafe job sites had little recourse but to tolerate the danger or quit. The federal government stepped in during the early 1970s, creating the Occupational Safety and Health Administration (OSHA) and legislation that requires employers to meet certain standards. OSHA's responsibilities include:

- developing and issuing regulations on worker safety and health
- inspecting work sites to be sure employers are complying with laws and regulations

- investigating complaints made by employees
- issuing citations and imposing penalties for noncompliance

Employers are required to keep records regarding any injuries, illnesses, deaths, or exposure to toxic chemicals that take place in the workplace. If an accident kills an employee or results in more than four employees needing hospitalization, the employer must report the incident to OSHA within 24 hours.

Employees have the right to walk off a job site only if it presents an imminent and very serious threat to their health. They have the right to complain about dangerous and unsafe conditions in many ways, for example, by reporting the conditions to OSHA and requesting an inspection. If an employee is fired or punished in any way by the employer for these actions, the employee should contact an OSHA office within 30 days of the punishment, asking the agency to investigate and intercede to reinstate that person.

If an employer violates the Occupational Safety and Health Act or any of its regulations, OSHA has the power to impose a small fine. If the employer fails to correct the problem, that employer can be fined as much as $1,000 a day. Additional fines can be imposed for other infractions, including the making of a false statement to an OSHA inspector, warning an employer of a future OSHA inspection, or the death of an employee because of an employer's willful violation. If an employer believes that an OSHA citation and penalty were in error, the employer has the right to appeal.

What follows is a hypothetical situation involving safety in the workplace.

THE PROBLEM

Several workers at a company believe they got sick after inhaling stagnant air at a plant, and they asked management to look into the matter. Initially, despite several requests, management did not actively address their complaints.

WHAT WAS DONE

The workers then formed a committee and took several steps on their own. First, they gathered the facts. They documented the environmental condition of the workplace site to support their position. They inspected ventilation, physical arrangement of ducts, etc. Next, they sought medical proof to determine if their illness could have been caused by noxious fumes or air. They saved reports about their medical conditions and drug prescriptions and visited the employer's medical department as well as private physicians to document their conditions and possible causes of illness.

Then they spoke to management and presented management with letters from their personal physicians stating the need to work in a safe environment. Finally, they confirmed all of their grievances in writing after the meeting.

When the company failed to act promptly in this area, one of the workers met with a lawyer. The lawyer advised that the workers had several options, including presenting demands directly to the employer, contacting a representative of OSHA and instituting an investigation, and filing a formal complaint under OSHA.

GUIDELINES FOR WAGES AND HOURS

The Fair Labor Standards Act of 1938 created much-needed guidelines for minimum wages, overtime pay, and the prohibition of child labor. The Act also set 40 hours as the length of a workweek, with overtime to be paid for every hour over that at one and a half times the usual wages. With a few exceptions that allow children to begin working at a younger age (such as newspaper delivery at 14) or later (hazardous jobs at 18), 16 is the minimum age for employment.

If you believe that an employer is violating the Fair Labor Standards Act by not paying minimum wage or proper overtime, contact the U.S. Department of Labor. You also have the option of suing the employer in state or federal court, but that can be expensive.

What follows is a hypothetical situation involving an employee not receiving proper compensation for overtime.

THE PROBLEM

Jack was hired as an hourly worker. He did not receive benefits such as medical insurance or vacation pay. Typically, he worked a 40-hour week. His job consisted of performing many odd jobs, such as transporting company workers, performing maintenance and cleaning services, and in general being available to do whatever was requested of him.

One Friday he was informed that he was supposed to transport the boss's daughter to college. Jack left his home the next morning at 7:00, picked the boss's daughter up at her home, drove to the college, and moved her belongings into her dormitory room. He arrived back home at 11:00 that evening. Jack expected to receive 24 additional hours of pay. The following Friday, he was paid for 8 additional hours and was told that he would not have to work the following Monday but would be paid for that day.

WHAT TO DO

Jack should advise management that this arrangement is not proper, because nonexempt employees who work more than 40 hours per week are not supposed to be compensated at straight time only. He should also state that the company cannot give him a day off at its discretion, even though he would be paid for that day.

If Jack does not receive satisfactory compensation, he should contact the local office of the Department of Labor (Wage and Hour Division).

Workers' Compensation

The workers' compensation system was created in an attempt to provide a sure, fair, and predictable remedy for work-related injuries and illnesses, although the success of this compromise has been questioned.

Workers' compensation (once called workmen's compensation) laws were created to make the system more equitable; although each state's version differs, all accomplish the same ends. They permit employees to receive compensation for job-related injuries, regardless of who was at fault, and the employee gives up the right to bring a personal injury lawsuit in court—a suit which, if successful, could be a more lucrative award than workers' compensation benefits.

Most employers and employees are covered by workers' compensation laws. Exceptions include farm laborers, domestic servants, employers with fewer than three regular employees, and independent contractors. Employers are required to carry workers' compensation insurance through a company or to be self-insured.

Under workers' compensation laws, most states define compensable injuries as those that "arise out of and in the course of employment." The employee must prove that the injury was caused by a condition associated with employment, and the injury, in most states, must be work-disabling. In other words, the injury or illness must have been caused by the job and must have occurred while performing employment duties. An employee isn't covered during a meal break unless it was required for the job—a business lunch, for example. If a delivery person is on company time, but is making a quick detour to go to a newsstand, the delivery person is not covered by the law.

States differ about whether heart attacks and psychological disorders are compensable.

Workers' compensation benefits usually include:

- disability benefits paid weekly, the amount based on whether the employee's injuries are temporary or permanent, total or partial (Benefits are computed by taking a percentage of the employee's pre-injury weekly salary, usually one-half to two-thirds. Each state's laws set a separate ceiling for weekly benefits.)

- payment of medical expenses for doctors, hospital, rehabilitation, and therapy

- reimbursement for lost wages

- compensation for loss of limb or member of the body, based on a schedule of payments outlined in the law

- death benefits to the employee's dependents

An employee is entitled to receive other sources of compensation simultaneously, such as unemployment insurance, Social Security benefits, and health insurance payments in addition to workers' compensation.

APPLYING FOR WORKERS' COMPENSATION BENEFITS   State law requires that the employee notify the employer within a certain number of days after an injury or the onset of the first symptoms, preferably in writing and on a special form. If the employer refuses to provide benefits, the worker should consult an attorney who specializes in workers' compensation and request a hearing before the state

> *Jonathan is injured while playing baseball after work hours for the company team. Jonathan wishes to sue the league and his company in a private lawsuit for his injuries. The company desires to assist Jonathan by filing a workers' compensation claim. Jonathan retains a lawyer skilled in personal injury and workers' compensation cases. After a lengthy consultation Jonathan learns that he probably cannot file a private lawsuit because there are ample facts and evidence to demonstrate coverage under workers' compensation laws. Jonathan is advised, for example, that the fact that he wore a uniform supplied and paid for by the company, that the company transported its worker-players to the game, and the fact that food and beverage after each game was supplied and paid for by the company evidences a worker-company relationship.*

board or commission of workers' compensation. An administrative law judge usually hears the case and renders a decision. If either party is unhappy with the verdict, each state has an appeal process.

Because workers' compensation is governed by state laws, no federal agency has enforcement authority. If you have any questions regarding workers' compensation, check the phone book under State Government—Workers' Compensation Board.

Applying for Unemployment Compensation

Most employees are covered by unemployment compensation insurance and can collect benefits if they have been fired or laid off through no fault of their own. Employees who are fired for good cause or who quit without good cause can be denied benefits. Termination for good cause might include an employee's frequent absences, poor performance, or abusing drugs or alcohol on the job. Quitting for good cause could include an employer's unfair treatment of an employee, or an employee's refusal to work under hazardous working conditions.

To qualify for unemployment compensation, an applicant must show a willingness and an ability to work. If found eligible the applicant can collect benefits for 26 weeks (which may be extended depending on state and federal law). The amount is based on the highest amount the applicant earned during a particular one-year period. The quarter system (3-month period) is used to calculate benefits. For example, if you were terminated in May of 1994, the state will ignore what you earned in the previous quarter (January, February, March) and use the four quarters prior to that (all 12 months in 1993) to establish a "base period." The amount you received during the 3 months of the base period in which you received the highest salary or wages will determine the amount of benefits you'll receive for 26 weeks. Each state has a limit on benefits and usually pays no more than $400 per week. You may be able to receive benefits for an additional 13 weeks if your needs are special.

To apply for benefits, go to the state agency that handles unemployment compensation. The application process can take several hours, and if you are found eligible you may not begin receiving benefits for several weeks.

Your former employer will be notified that you have applied for benefits. If you receive opposition from your employer regarding your eligibility to collect unemployment, don't be surprised. The amount the employer has to pay into the fund on a regular basis is partly determined by the amount of unemployment compensation the state has to compensate its former employees.

You'll be required to report in person to the unemployment office every other week to confirm that you have been looking for work. You may be asked to supply the names of potential employers you've applied to and to submit copies of job applications you have made.

The benefits you receive will be offset by any additional money you earn and report.

IF YOUR APPLICATION FOR UNEMPLOYMENT BENEFITS IS CHALLENGED Once your most recent employer is notified and asked for the reasons your employment was terminated or you were laid off, the agency will decide whether to grant or deny you benefits. The losing party, you or the employer, can request a hearing within the time period specified on the initial determination notice. It's best to consult a lawyer to prepare for these hearings, and since you may be in difficult financial straits, you may qualify for free legal assistance through your state bar association.

An employer must prove claims that you were fired for good cause. If you maintain that you quit for good cause, you have the burden of proof. The decision rendered at this hearing can be appealed to a review board and, as a last resort, to the court system if you believe the agency

failed to follow the correct procedures
violated your constitutional rights
misinterpreted the laws or regulations
made its decision lacking substantial evidence

If you need help with unemployment compensation problems, contact your state department of labor, found under State Government in your phone book.

Compensation to Workers for Ideas, Designs, and Inventions
Workers frequently offer valuable suggestions, comments, ideas, designs, manufacturing processes, and inventions that often lead to money-saving and money-making devices. For example, Judith develops a manufacturing process during working hours that she thinks will save the company money. She tells her boss, and the idea is incorporated into the company's production process. Judith is not compensated for the idea. She resigns and sues to recover a percentage of the money saved by the idea's use.

Judith's case is not as strong as it appears. The reason is that ideas, plans, methods, and procedures for business operations cannot usually be copyrighted. Most ideas are presumed to be work-for-hire and the property of the employer if an employee offers them voluntarily without contracting to receive additional compensation. Judith would have a stronger case if she could prove that the idea was her own, original, unique creation not requested or developed while working on company time or on the employer's premises, and that it was furnished because of a specific promise or understanding that she would be compensated for it once it was implemented by the employer.

WHERE TO GO FOR HELP

The laws governing the workplace are enforced by a number of different federal and state agencies. Certain private organizations supply attorneys as well, depending on whether your complaint is in accord with their current goals.

DISCRIMINATION COMPLAINTS

American Civil Liberties Union
local or regional office

Equal Employment Opportunity Commission
1801 L Street, N.W.
Washington, DC 20506
800-669-EEOC
202-663-4264

National Association for the Advancement of Colored People
local chapter

SAFETY AND HEALTH PROBLEMS IN THE WORKPLACE

U.S. Department of Labor
200 Constitution Avenue, N.W.
Washington, DC 20210
202-219-6666

U.S. Department of Labor
Occupational Safety and Health Administration (OSHA)
Frances Perkins Building
200 Constitution Avenue, N.W.
Washington, DC 20210
202-219-6091

OSHA also has 10 regional offices located in Boston, New York, Philadelphia, Atlanta, Chicago, Dallas, Kansas City (Missouri), Denver, San Francisco, and Seattle.

INFORMATION ON LABOR UNIONS

AFL-CIO
Pamphlet Division
Room 208
815 Sixteenth Street, N.W.
Washington, DC 20006
202-637-5000

National Labor Relations Board
1099 Fourteenth Street, N.W.
Washington, DC 20570
202-273-1991

PENSION INFORMATION

Pension and Welfare Benefits Administration
U.S. Department of Labor
Office of Program Services
200 Constitution Avenue, N.W.
Room N5677
Washington, DC 20210
202-219-8233

9

CONSUMER RIGHTS AND OBLIGATIONS

Each day we are bombarded with advertisements on television and radio and in newspapers and magazines. An observer once called advertising "a technique which makes you believe you've longed all your life for something you've never heard of before." Fortunately, we are not as vulnerable to consumer rip-offs and unsuspecting of fraudulent claims as we were in the recent past. With the help of independent consumer groups and government regulations, the old battle cry in the marketplace of "let the buyer beware" can be more muted these days now that manufacturers and merchants must provide safer products and better warranties, more truth in advertising, and less obtrusive sales techniques. But vigilance is still required of consumers who shop for goods and services.

SALES

Buying merchandise or services by mail, telephone, or at your door provides great convenience, but all have the potential for abuse and need close monitoring. Sales abuses can still occur even when you go to a store to make a purchase; even if you have sought out the item and can see it, you can't always make an informed decision.

BUYING BY TELEPHONE AND THROUGH THE MAIL

The shopping phenomenon of the 1990s has been buying by telephone, ordering either from a catalog or a television presentation. But with the convenience these shopping methods bring come complications as well. Without the consumer having the opportunity actually to examine the merchandise, it's simple for unscrupulous sellers to misrepresent the product's quality, price, and warranties. When purchase transactions take place on the telephone, proving (in a potential dispute) what information was provided when the sale was made may become particularly difficult. The buyer is sometimes pressured with statements that "time is running out" and that this is a "one-time deal." Other problems typical of some telephone and mail purchases are late deliveries, no delivery at all, or no refund privileges.

Federal Mail-Order Protection Laws

A variety of federal legislation offers protection to consumers who order products by phone and through the mail. The degree of protection available varies with the circumstances of the purchase.

If You Pay for a Telephone Order by Mail

If you're paying for a telephone order by mail, the Federal Trade Commission (FTC) has a Mail Order Merchandise Rule to protect you. It requires a company to ship an order by the promised date. If no date was promised, the seller must ship your goods no later than 30 days after you place your order (50 days if your order was accompanied by an application for credit). If the merchant fails to meet the delivery deadlines, the merchant is required to send you an "option notice," which gives you the choice of accepting delivery on a later date or canceling the purchase and receiving a full refund within 7 business days. If you charged your order, your credit card account has to be adjusted within one billing cycle.

There are exceptions. Items not covered by the Mail Order Merchandise Rule include magazine subscriptions after the first issue has been mailed, photo finishing, COD (payment on delivery) orders, plants and seeds, and charge card orders in which you are not charged before the merchandise is shipped.

If You Charge a Purchase by Phone

The Mail Order Merchandise Rule is available to you as a remedy when you pay for a telephone order by mail. But if you charged a purchase by phone, you can turn to the Fair Credit Billing Act for additional help. This law states that the consumer can refuse to pay if there is an error regarding the transaction (e.g., failure to promptly credit for a return) or failure to deliver merchandise.

Under certain circumstances, if there is a dispute about the quality of a product or service purchased with a credit card, you may be able to withhold payment from the credit card company up to the amount of the dispute, including finance charges. To do this, you must have attempted to resolve the matter with the seller first. Second, the amount of credit involved in the transaction must have been more than $50. Third, the transaction must have occurred in the same state as your current address or within 100 miles of it. However, these distance and dollar restrictions are not applicable if the seller is also the issuer of the credit card or if a special business relationship exists

Rick purchased a jacket by telephone from a catalog company. The person taking the order told him the jacket would be shipped within 3 business days from the warehouse. Rick charged the jacket to his credit card, and the company processed the charge at the time of the sale. After processing the sale, the company realized that the jacket was not in stock and would have to be back-ordered. At that point, because the jacket would not be shipped within 3 days, the company sent Rick a postcard telling him that the jacket was back-ordered and would be shipped in 21 days and that he had a right to cancel the order. If Rick cancels his order, his credit card should reflect this cancellation within one billing cycle.

Mack called a sporting goods catalog company and ordered a new rod and reel. He paid for the rod and reel with his credit card. When the rod and reel were delivered, they were not the quality of merchandise listed in the catalog. He returned the rod and reel to the catalog company and asked it to credit his credit card account. However, the next month his credit card company included this purchase. Mack wrote the credit card company at the address it provided for billing errors and explained that he had returned this merchandise and that he should not be billed for it. When Mack paid his bill that month, he also deducted this amount from the bill and paid only the remaining balance. After investigating the matter, the credit card company found that Mack was correct and credited his account for the return of the merchandise.

between the seller and issuer. The Federal Trade Commission can provide specific information regarding the Fair Credit Billing Act.

What should you do if you have a problem with merchandise ordered by telephone and paid for by a credit card? First, if the problem is with the quality of the merchandise, contact the seller immediately and tell it of the problem. If you contact the seller by telephone, send a follow-up letter that explains the problem and relates your understanding of what you are to do (return the merchandise to them, etc.). Second, if your credit card is billed for the merchandise, contact the credit card company in writing at the address provided for billing errors. (This address should be on your credit card statement.) The credit card company must receive this notice within 60 days after you received the statement that included the error. Your letter should include both your name as it appears on the account and the correct account number, and you should explain why you believe a billing error has occurred. Be as specific as possible; include the type, date, and amount of the error. During this time you have the right to withhold payment of the contested amount, and the credit card company cannot make a finance charge on this amount. However, you must make any other payment due on the account.

The credit card company must acknowledge receipt of your letter within 30 days. If the company does not immediately agree that an error has occurred, it has two full billing cycles to investigate and notify you of the results of the investigation. If the credit card company finds the error occurred, the error will be corrected on your account. If the company concludes the error did not occur, it will notify you in writing of the reasons for finding that no error occurred and will provide documentation supporting its findings if you request it.

When You Receive Unordered Merchandise

One problem with mail-order and telephone sales involves companies sending you merchandise you never ordered. The Unordered Merchandise Statute allows you to keep products you never requested and prohibits the companies that send it from sending you bills or harassing you for payment.

You are under no legal obligation to notify the sender that you plan to keep unordered merchandise, but it's advisable that you do. Send the company a certified letter stating that you didn't order the merchandise and that you plan to keep it as a free gift. Be sure to keep a copy of the letter as well as the return receipt. This letter should prevent repeated bills and collection letters; if not, send the company another letter asking it to stop billing you, once again using certified mail.

Sometimes there's been an honest mistake in shipping, and a company believes you ordered merchandise, or it was delivered to the wrong address. Contact the sender and offer to return the merchandise if the sender is willing to cover postage and handling costs. Set a time limit for the sender either to pick up the merchandise or to make arrangements for the return shipment. Inform the sender that if you receive no response within the specified time, you have the right to keep the merchandise or do whatever you wish with it. If you have problems resolving disputes directly with the company, contact your local U.S. Postal Inspector, your local or state (often in the attorney general's office) consumer protection office, the Better Business Bureau, or the Direct Marketing Association.

Selections from Book and Record Clubs

A federal law also protects you from abuses by "negative option clubs," record and book clubs you join under the condition that you buy a certain number of selections over a certain period of time. The Negative Option Rule requires such clubs to allow their members a minimum of 10 days to reject the monthly selection before they automatically send it. The rule also requires the club to include a form that you can use to reject the automatic selection.

What follows is a hypothetical situation involving receipt of unordered products.

THE PROBLEM

Janet is a member of a book club. Each month, she receives a listing of books for sale, including that month's featured book, and a reply card, which she must return in order to avoid receiving the featured book. This form must give her at least 10 days to decide whether she wants the featured book. One month she did not receive the form until 3 days after the date on the reply card. Janet received the featured book.

WHAT TO DO

Because Janet did not receive the reply card within the prescribed time, she may return the book without obligation.

If you receive books or records and you did not have the form to refuse the selections in the time permitted by law, you can refuse to accept the goods and have the post office return them to the sender. If you receive the form after the end of the 10-day period, send the form to the company with a letter explaining that you received the form late and you do not want the selection. Make a copy of your letter for your files. If you receive the selection anyway, return it to the company.

Mail-Order Lists and Telemarketing

You may have noticed that ever since you ordered a shirt by mail or joined a book club, the volume of advertisements and catalogs in your mail has tripled. That's because many companies profit greatly by renting the lists of their customers to list brokers, who in turn rent them to other merchants. The information you provide about your family, your income, your buying preferences, and anything else you freely reveal on order forms becomes available to many merchants. It is entirely legal for companies to rent your name, but if you prefer that they not do so, write the company with your request. You can also be removed from the telephone solicitation lists of marketing companies that are members of the Direct Marketing Association by writing to:

Direct Marketing Association
Telephone Preference Service
6 East 43rd Street
New York, NY 10017

Telemarketing companies will often use your social security number to keep records of your purchases. You are under no obligation to provide your social security number to anyone other than the Internal Revenue Service.

Some states acknowledge that telephone solicitations can be intrusive and have passed legislation to regulate them. For a nominal fee, Florida allows consumers to be added to a "no-call" list. The list puts phone solicitors on notice that these consumers don't want to be called. Check with the Public Service Commission or the government agency that oversees public utilities to find out what rights you have in limiting your exposure to telephone solicitations. (In Florida call 800-342-2176 for more information.)

Under a federal law enacted in 1991, the Federal Communications Commission (FCC) enacted procedures to protect the privacy rights of residential telephone subscribers so that they will not receive telephone solicitations to which they object. Under these regulations no person may call you at home to encourage you to purchase, invest in, or rent property, goods, or services before 8:00 A.M. or after 9:00 P.M. Any telephone solicitation entity must also have instituted a system for maintaining a list of persons who do not wish to receive telephone solicitations; once you inform the solicitor that you do not want to be called, your name should be added to their list and you should not receive any more calls from that solicitor.

DOOR-TO-DOOR SALES

If you make a purchase from a door-to-door salesperson, the Federal Trade Commission provides you with a three-day cooling-off period, a chance to change your mind. When a salesperson comes to your door, be sure that person shows you some form of identification. The salesperson should also show you a sample of the product and how it works or at least provide a description of the product or services. Any contract you are asked to sign should first be fully explained. Make certain that the contract has no blank spaces and that you understand it completely after reading it and before you sign it. The salesperson must also reveal the provisions of the cooling-off period.

The Cooling-Off Period

The FTC's cooling-off rule allows a consumer three days to change his or her mind under certain circumstances:

· The purchase must have been made at home, a motel, or similar place, not by mail, phone, or in a store.
· The cost of the purchase must exceed $25.
· The rule does not protect purchasers of real estate, insurance, securities, or emergency home repairs.

If your purchase falls within the FTC provisions, the seller must:

· give you a fully completed copy of the sales contract
· attach an easily detachable written notice of cancellation to the contract
· orally inform you of your right to cancel at the time the contract is signed
· provide the name and address of the seller on the contract
· provide, in an area of the contract near where you sign, a statement of your right to cancel

If you decide to cancel your purchase, date and sign the proper cancellation forms. Send one copy by certified mail, return receipt requested, to the proper address postmarked before midnight on the third business day after the date the contract was signed. Hold on to the post office receipt as your proof that you canceled in a timely manner. Keep the second copy of the form for your records.

Under state law a cooling-off period is also provided for certain other sales, so check with the seller as well as with your state regulatory agencies for specifics.

Even if the FTC cooling-off period doesn't apply to the purchase you are making, you have the right to ask the seller to include a grace period in your contract. If the seller refuses, you should reconsider the deal.

The following hypothetical situation involves door-to-door sales.

THE PROBLEM

Margaret is at home one day when Sam comes to her door selling encyclopedias. Sam is persuasive and Margaret agrees to purchase a set of encyclopedias for $779. As required by the FTC rule, Sam tells Margaret she has three days to cancel the contract if she changes her mind, and he gives her two copies of the cancellation form as well as a copy of the fully completed contract with the name and address of the seller. After Sam leaves, Margaret reconsiders whether she wants the encyclopedias.

WHAT TO DO

If Margaret had any doubts about whether she wanted the encyclopedias, she should have decided within the three-day cooling-off period. It would have been better to cancel the contract if she had any doubts, because she could always buy the goods later if she decided she wanted them.

Remember: This right to cancel covers many purchases over $25 sold door-to-door, including cosmetics and newspaper and magazine subscriptions.

RETAIL SALES

Sales made in department, grocery, and other stores are not as closely regulated as door-to-door and telephone sales. For example, no federal or state laws require stores to allow exchanges, returns, or refunds, unless the product is defective or was misrepresented. Many shoppers believe that stores are obligated to take back a dress or shirt that turned out to be the wrong size or color. Not true. Any return policy based on customer satisfaction is purely voluntary, and some are more liberal than others. Some states require merchants to post their return policies, but it's advisable to check with a salesperson about the store's return policy before you buy anything.

Certain laws, ranging from requiring truth in labeling to rain-check compensation, do protect retail customers from fraud.

The Unavailability Rule

Prior to 1971, when consumers flocked to the stores with sale fliers and coupons in hand, it was no coincidence that they often found the advertised items either in short supply or not even on the shelves. Grocers were allowed to purposely limit the stock of such items and to use the "sale" as a come-on. To curb these abuses the FTC issued the Retail Food Store Advertising and Marketing Practices Rule in 1971 and amended it in 1989. Basically, the rule says that for a retail food store to advertise a product at a specific sale price, it has to have enough stock to meet the reasonable anticipated demand. If the product is available to the retailer on a limited basis or can be purchased only at a particular store in a chain, the advertisements have to state this clearly. If the advertising fails to mention that supplies are limited, the retailer has to offer either a rain check to purchase the same product later at the advertised sale price, a substitute of comparable value, or compensation at least equal in value to the advertised product.

If the retailer can prove to the FTC that an adequate supply of the product had been ordered in ample time prior to the sale, the retailer may not have to provide a rain check or other substitutes.

What follows is a hypothetical situation involving a store not honoring its advertisements.

THE PROBLEM

Jeremy reads in his local newspaper that a six-pack of his favorite soft drink is on sale for $.99 at his local supermarket, part of a large grocery store chain. The advertisement says there is a limit of 10 six-packs per customer, but no other limits are listed in the ad. Jeremy goes to his local supermarket and finds the soft drink priced at $2.99 per six-pack. He finds the store manager and asks where the $.99 per six-pack are located. The store manager tells him that the price is only available at the store in a nearby town.

WHAT TO DO

Because the advertisement didn't state this fact, Jeremy's supermarket is also required to honor the sale price. First, Jeremy should complain to the store manager. It would be helpful if he has a copy of the store advertisement when he makes his complaint. (As a precaution Jeremy should have taken the sales advertisement with him when he went to the shop, in case there was a problem.) If the store manager doesn't respond as Jeremy thinks she should, he should contact the district or regional manager of the chain. He should complain to the local Better Business Bureau and his state's attorney general's consumer affairs office.

GOING-OUT-OF-BUSINESS SALES

One of the biggest frauds perpetrated on consumers in retail stores is the going-out-of-business sale. Shoppers are convinced that they are buying quality merchandise at bargain prices because a business is being forced to liquidate its stock. Unfortunately, many of these businesses never plan to go out of business at all and use the "sale" as a false pretense to sell newly arrived inferior goods at jacked-up prices.

Certain states regulate going-out-of-business sales, sometimes requiring licenses or restricting the number of days or weeks the sale can run. If you are not satisfied that a store conducting such a sale is really going out of business, contact your state consumer affairs office or attorney general's office.

Kathleen often shops at Ben's Trading Post. One day, she sees a "Going Out of Business Sale" sign on the door of Ben's Trading Post. When she enters the store, she notices the prices are not any different from the regular prices. However, there is a lot of new merchandise, and it is not as nice as what she usually sees at the store. Kathleen leaves the store without buying anything. Two months later she goes back to the store; the same sign is there, but the store is still full of merchandise. Kathleen realizes from the prices and the quality of merchandise that this going-out-of-business sale is no bargain.

You should be suspicious of a "going-out-of-business" sale. Carefully check the quality of the merchandise and its prices. Notice if the store stock is being depleted or if new stock is coming in regularly. Ask if there is a date set for the store to close.

PRODUCT LIABILITY

Some consumer problems are far more serious than poor service or a product's failure to operate properly. Some products are actually defective and may cause serious injury to the people who use them. Products that are not defective may also cause injury.

In general, a product is considered defective if:

- a mistake was made in the manufacturing process (For example, you open a can of soda, take a swallow, and end up with a nail in your mouth.)

- the design or packaging of the product is defective (For example, a baby crib is designed so poorly that the vertical slats on the side are not spaced properly, allowing an infant's head to become stuck between them.)

- the manufacturer failed to provide adequate warnings or instructions on a label or packaging (For example, a pharmaceutical company fails to mention that a dangerous interaction occurs when alcohol is used with a particular medication, and the interaction can cause kidney damage.)

Prior to product liability legislation, in order to recover damages, injured parties had to sue the product's manufacturer based on the theory of negligence. In other words, a consumer had to prove that the manufacturer knew or should have known that the product was going to cause the injury it caused. Today most states have laws that allow courts to hold manufacturers "strictly liable" if the product was defective or unreasonably dangerous and caused injury or death. This latter standard is far easier to prove than is negligence, because consumers do not have to establish the state of mind of the manufacturer (an almost impossible hurdle). The condition of the product and whether it caused the injury are now the main issues.

The amount of damages or compensation you can expect to receive from a product liability case depends on the gravity of the injuries you have sustained. The extent of your medical bills, the medical prognosis for your recovery or disability, as well as your pain and suffering will all be considered in determining the amount of compensation.

In general, consumers may sue any party who caused the injury—that is, whose *actions* can be proved to have caused the injury—including the product's designer, manufacturer, wholesaler, distributor, and retailer.

Remember: Laws differ from state to state. Check the relevant laws in your area and/or consult an attorney before pursuing legal action.

Warranties

The manufacturer's confidence in a product—how long it will last or serve without problems—is often reflected in its warranties. Warranties are of different kinds, and understanding the differences is very important.

An *express warranty* is a specific promise made either in writing or verbally about a product and its quality. The manufacturer or retailer backs up that statement with a promise to repair or replace the product during the specific warranty period. A *full warranty* usu-

> *Lauren was cooking outside on her grill and started the fire on the briquettes with lighter fluid. The fire caught but not as well as she would have liked, so she gave the briquettes another squirt. The flames shot up the stream from the can, and the can exploded in her face. She was severely injured and attempted to bring a product liability lawsuit against the lighter fluid manufacturer. Lauren's case will most likely be unsuccessful, because the can's label very clearly stated that the lighter fluid should never be applied to an open flame. She misused a properly labeled product, and as a result of the labeling the company cannot be held strictly liable.*

ally covers the entire product, not just certain parts. It usually sets a specific warranty period, guaranteeing that the product will be repaired or replaced should problems arise during that period. The manufacturer is required to repair the product within a certain amount of time and at a location convenient to you. A *limited warranty* usually covers only certain parts of a product, such as a heating element in an oven, and you'll usually have to pay the cost of the labor to have the new part installed.

Although these are not supplied in writing, most products are also covered by an *implied warranty*. An *implied warranty of merchantability* means that the product is guaranteed to serve its intended purpose: A stove will cook food and a lawn mower will cut grass. An *implied warranty of fitness for a particular purpose* goes a step further and promises that a product will meet certain special needs.

Neither express nor implied warranties are provided for products that are sold "as is."

Extended Warranties and Service Contracts

An extended warranty is an "insurance policy" that a retailer tries to sell a buyer by warning that the item being purchased may need to be replaced or repaired after the original warranty runs out.

Suppose you ask a salesperson for a radio that will pick up your favorite FM station. You take it home, only to find out it picks up only AM stations. Because the salesperson promised you that the radio could do something it couldn't do, you are entitled to ask for your money back.

Extended warranties have become a high-profit center for retailers. In some instances the product may never need service after the original warranty period, or the repair costs may be so minimal that they will cost less than the purchase price of the extended warranty. For example, the cost of the coverage being offered by a service contract company may be only $20, but the salesperson adds a commission. By the time the cost of the extended warranty is quoted to the consumer, it may be doubled or tripled. Retailers will profit if you forget that you even bought the extra protection. Furthermore, you can't always assume that the retailer will still be in business when you need to use the warranty. Some businesses have been known to sell extended warranties the day before they filed for bankruptcy. You may want to check into the stability of the store or the company offering the warranty before you purchase a contract. Find out if the service can be performed at a store other than the one in which you made the purchase. Also determine if there is a fee for canceling the warranty or transferring it to the next owner of the merchandise.

Resolving Warranty and Service Contract Disputes

Make sure you know what's covered in your warranty, whether it's the original warranty that came with the product or an extended coverage contract. Not all warranties provide a refund if a product is defective; some may give the company the right to try to fix it first. The FTC regulates many aspects of warranties under the Magnuson-Moss Act and rules adopted under the Act. They require the seller or warrantor to state certain information about the warranty coverage in one, easy-to-read document, to designate the written warranty as "full" or "limited," and to ensure that warranties are available to be read before the product is purchased.

If you feel the warranty applies to your situation, explain the problem to the retailer or seller first. If the seller isn't cooperative, contact the manufacturer at the phone number and address listed on the warranty. If you're still unsuccessful, you might want to report the problem to the attorney general's office. Many states have "little FTC" acts (modeled after the FTC's prohibition of unfair and deceptive acts and practices in commerce).

If you get no satisfaction, consider the option of arbitration or another dispute resolution procedure. If the manufacturer is willing to allow the dispute to be arbitrated, check into organizations in your locale that provide these services. Your warranty may even *require* you to attempt dispute resolution procedures before filing a lawsuit.

But if filing a lawsuit is the only solution and the claim involves less than a few thousand dollars, you may be able to file a complaint in small-claims court. Each jurisdiction has different guidelines for the maximum dollar limit, so check with your local small-claims court to find out its requirements.

If the amount in dispute is too great for small-claims court, you may want to talk to a lawyer about filing a lawsuit in a state court; discuss what damages you can demand and whether you can ask the court for attorneys' fees.

Referring your problem to the FTC is also advisable. Although the agency won't become involved in or solve your individual situation, it can investigate and look for a pattern of abuses.

Warranty Disclaimers

Some warranties include a clause that disclaims the manufacturer's liability for injuries incurred as a result of a defective product.

False Advertising

The FTC reviews the commercials and advertisements that flood newspapers and magazines and radio and television airwaves, looking for "unfair" and "deceptive practices." Commercials and advertisements judged to be unfair usually involve children as their target, such as alcohol and cigarette ads that entice children to use these products. Advertisements or sales practices are also considered to be unfair if they coerce consumers to buy a product.

Aside from these examples, most ads that the FTC finds unac-

Suppose you buy a lawn mower manufactured by the Sampson Mower Company. The warranty that came with the mower states that if the mower is defective, Sampson's only obligation is to repair or replace the defective mower or defective part. While mowing the lawn the blade comes loose and is thrown out the back, lacerating your leg severely. Because the defective mower caused personal injury, the warranty disclaimer has no significance. Sampson can be held liable for your injuries, and it may become a question for a judge or jury to determine how much you are entitled to in damages.

ceptable are considered "deceptive," which means they make claims that are either misleading or just simply out-and-out lies. For example, commercials for weight-loss clinics that promise to "readjust your metabolism" have been removed from the air because of their deceptive claims. One popular trick of unscrupulous and illegal advertisers is the bait-and-switch method, in which a retailer advertises a product, perhaps a car, at a ridiculously low price or low interest rate simply to get you into the store or showroom. Once you are there, the advertiser tells you the last of the low-priced cars has been sold, but the advertiser does have a car that, you are told, is of much better and higher quality. The price, of course, is much higher too.

Given these guidelines, if you believe that an advertisement or a commercial is unfair or misleading, you can file a complaint with your state attorney general's office, the local office of consumer affairs, or the National Advertising Division (NAD) of the Council of Better Business Bureaus. If the NAD believes there might be merit to your grievance, it will contact the advertiser and request proof of their advertising claims. If the NAD finds your complaint valid, it may take it to its review board and ultimately to a governmental agency in an attempt to see that the advertising is changed or removed. Send your complaints (including the brand of the product or service as well as the manufacturer) to NAD, 845 Third Avenue, New York, NY 10022.

If you heard the commercial on the radio or television, state the date, time of day, and the station. If you saw the ad on an outdoor billboard, supply the date and location. For a newspaper or magazine ad, give the date and name of the publication and enclose a copy.

Another law in this category that protects consumers is the Fair Packaging and Labeling Act, which requires that the label on a product properly identifies its contents and net quantity.

In false advertising or labeling claims, as in most consumer problems, contact your state consumer protection office, usually found in the attorney general's office. You might also want to report the problem to the FTC. Although the FTC won't help you with your individual situation, it can investigate a company when several complaints about it are reported.

Remedies

If a company has sold you a faulty or inferior product or failed to provide satisfactory service, try to solve the problem directly with the company. Part of the trick in getting satisfaction is knowing how to lodge a complaint.

First, call the retailer or manufacturer and tell a customer service or other representative about the problem. The packaging or instructions will often include a toll-free number for the company's home office. Take notes regarding the date, time, to whom you spoke, and the information you received. Ask how soon you can expect a response to your complaint. Then follow up your call with a letter repeating what was discussed in your phone conversation. Include the information about the product or service you purchased, when you purchased it, how you paid for it (cash, check, or credit), what was wrong with it, and how you want the retailer or manufacturer to solve the problem (replacement, repair, or refunding your money). Keep a file on the product that includes the canceled check or original credit card charge slip and the actual billing for the charge. Write the product's serial number on the check or charge slip.

If the company replaces the item or a part, ask for and try to get in writing information about whether the warranty period or any portion of it starts over. Some firms will extend coverage on a repaired or replaced item past the expiration date of the original warranty.

If you receive no reply within a few weeks, send the company another letter. This time send it by certified mail, return receipt requested. Restate the problem, noting that you have already called it and notified it by mail and that you expect a resolution by a particular date. If that date comes and goes with no resolution, send another certified letter stating your intention to take the company to court, to report it to state or federal regulatory agencies such as the FTC, or to contact the Better Business Bureau. If you still receive no reply, you may want to make good on your threats of legal action against the company.

The value of the merchandise or services involved will determine where you should file the lawsuit. If it is less than $2,000, you probably will be able to handle the matter yourself in small-claims court, although the amount varies from court to court. If the product or service costs more or if the failure involves violations of state or federal laws, you should consult an attorney. Also report the matter to the office of consumer affairs in your state and the Better Business Bureau in your city as well as to those in the locale of the company against which you are lodging your complaint.

If you believe that a merchant or manufacturer has violated a federal law, contact the FTC. For problems you encounter while ordering products or services through the mail, write:

Direct Marketing Association
6 East 43 Street
New York, NY 10017
212-768-7277

For products offered door-to-door or through home parties, write:

Direct Selling Association
1776 K Street, N.W.
Suite 600
Washington, DC 20006-2387
202-293-5760

MEDICAL MALPRACTICE

A physician is guilty of negligence or medical malpractice if he or she deviates from accepted standards of medical care and injury results. An error does not constitute malpractice unless it was caused by a failure to follow standard procedures.

An unfortunate outcome—no matter how horrendous it may be for the patient—does not by itself constitute malpractice. Medical malpractice consists of unfortunate results (injuries or death) caused by avoidable medical errors.

What follows is a hypothetical situation involving medical malpractice.

THE PROBLEM

Susan (41) and Bob (46) struggled for years to have a baby. Both had endured several surgeries to enhance the potential to conceive a child. For several years the couple received state-of-the-art fertility treatments to no avail. Recently Susan's obstetrician discovered a cervical cyst and scheduled a biopsy. Dr. Smith conducted a cervical and endometrial biopsy. Dr. Smith did not do a pregnancy test before conducting these invasive procedures. At that time, although Susan and Dr. Smith did not know it, Susan was pregnant.

Later, when Susan started bleeding excessively, she suspected a miscarriage. Bob took Susan to the emergency room, where the pregnancy and miscarriage were confirmed. The emergency room doctors asserted that a biopsy could have caused the miscarriage.

WHAT TO DO

Susan and Bob should seek legal counsel to determine whether they have a case for malpractice. The facts appear to present a solid malpractice case, but the lawyer will make his or her determination based on the analysis of a medical expert. The expert will give advice about whether the doctor caused the miscarriage and whether not doing a pregnancy test before conducting a biopsy violated appropriate standards of care.

AIR TRAVEL

Your airline ticket is a contract between you and the carrier. Most airlines summarize the key terms in the Conditions of Contract that are printed on your ticket, but even this fine print doesn't tell you the full story. Your contract also "incorporates by reference" all the details appearing in a separate volume, which each airline prepares and makes available for inspection upon request. This document spells out your obligations, such as deadlines for checking in or requirements for filing a claim, and it also sets forth what rights you have (or don't have) when flights are delayed or canceled, luggage is damaged, or tickets are lost.

Flight Delays

Bad weather and mechanical problems cause most flight delays or cancellations. Airlines sometimes cancel flights that are lightly booked, but these "economic cancellations" are rare, and they'll usually tell you it's a mechanical problem; also, there's usually another flight leaving in an hour or so.

If your flight is canceled, the airline must book you on the next available flight to your destination at no extra charge, but the airline may insist that you use its next available flight, not a more convenient flight from another airline. And if you're stranded overnight, you may be able to persuade the airline to buy you dinner and put you up in a hotel, though you have to push them on this point.

Airlines differ regarding what each will provide for you if a flight is delayed. Some will pay for meals and phone calls; others will not. Some will provide these services only if the delay was caused by the airline, but don't expect the airline to pay for any financial or business losses you incurred as a result of a delayed trip. Suppose a delayed flight causes you to miss a sales meeting that could have meant $20,000 in income to you. Even if you can prove the loss, the airline is not required to make good on it.

There are no rules requiring airlines to offer any amenities when delays or cancellations occur. Decisions about whether to offer passengers a meal or a hotel room are often left to the airlines station

If you're on a tight schedule, is there something you can do to minimize the risk of delay? Yes. Airlines are required by federal regulation to publish the on-time record of each flight, which appears on the computer screen when the travel agent is making a reservation. This on-time rating is indicated for each flight by a single digit between 0 and 9, which tells you how often that flight lands on schedule (or at least within 15 minutes after scheduled arrival). A 9 indicates a 90 percent on-time arrival rate; a 5 indicates a timely arrival only 50 to 59 percent of the time, and so on. Of course, there is no guarantee that the flight you book will land on time, but this information helps you avoid the flights that are chronically late in favor of those that are more often on time.

manager (supervisor) at each airport, so if you don't get a satisfactory response from the ticket agent, ask to see the station manager. Keep in mind that there's strength in numbers, so you should try to round up as many hungry passengers as you can before speaking with that person.

What follows is a hypothetical situation involving a flight cancellation.

THE PROBLEM

Jack was sitting in the airport lounge in Chicago early one evening, waiting for his connecting flight to Denver. He was just starting out on a vacation that would last 10 days. Because he had booked a week in advance and would be gone over a Saturday night, his travel agent was able to find a cheap fare.

As he waited he chatted with Fred, a colleague from work. Fred was also on his way to Denver for an important meeting that had come up at the last minute, forcing Fred to travel at the full fare.

As they waited, there came an announcement that the flight would be delayed by an hour because of engine problems. Fred decided he couldn't wait that long and had the ticket agent switch him to a flight on another airline that was leaving in the next 20 minutes. Jack tried to do the same but was told that the other airline would not accept his low-fare ticket.

One hour stretched into two, then three, and finally Jack and the other passengers were told that the flight had been canceled and that they'd have to stay overnight and take the airline's first flight out the next morning.

WHAT TO DO

As Jack found out, passengers are often powerless when flights are delayed. Fred was able to switch to another airline because he was traveling on a full-fare ticket, and one advantage of full-fare travel is that your ticket can easily be rewritten and used on another airline. By contrast, most excursion fares—such as the one Jack was using—require you to book at least a week in advance, so you can't have your ticket rewritten at the same price once that deadline has passed.

When Jack's flight turns from a delay into an outright cancellation, he and the other passengers should ask the ticket agent if it's possible for them to switch to another airline that still has a flight departing that night. If time permits (and space is available), any remaining full-fare passengers may get out that night. Because it is now a cancellation, not just a delay, it's possible (though not assured) that the other airline can be persuaded to accept other passengers as well. (Keep in mind that if you switch airlines at the last minute, it may be too late to switch your luggage to the new flight.)

When Jack learns that he'll be spending the night, he and the other stranded passengers should ask the station manager to give them a meal and hotel room at no charge. Airlines don't necessarily volunteer such accommodations even if it's obvious you're stranded away from home, and the final decision is usually up to the station manager. Be polite, but be forceful.

Losing Your Plane Ticket

Airlines may make it difficult for you to secure a replacement or a refund when you have lost a ticket, so notify the airline as soon as you know the ticket is lost. As a precaution always write down your ticket number on a separate piece of paper (or make a photocopy of the ticket), which will let the airline trace the ticket in its computer system if the ticket is lost or stolen. Some airlines may be able to verify that you did buy the ticket and willingly issue you a replacement or refund quickly; other airlines may take several months. Either way, you will probably be charged an additional fee (often $50) for the paperwork. Some airlines require that you purchase a new ticket to replace a lost one. In these cases, a refund or credit for the lost ticket is issued at a later date. On some airlines, the restrictions that exist on the day of purchase (of the replacement ticket) rather than any offers that may have existed with the original purchase will be applied.

Getting a Refund

In most cases where airfares are low, the airlines that offer them allow no refunds after the date of purchase. Be sure you understand all the restrictions when you book a flight. Paying for a ticket with a credit card is your best protection against an airline suddenly going out of business and leaving you with an unused ticket. Notifying your credit card company should be the first step for obtaining a refund. You'll have a longer wait if you pay with cash or by check.

The following hypothetical situation involves obtaining a refund for an airline ticket.

THE PROBLEM

When Frank and Joan arrived at the airport check-in counter to start their long-awaited vacation, Joan discovered that she had left the bag containing their plane tickets in the taxi. What's more, the airline agent claimed there was no record of their having made a reservation, and that they would have to pay $1,500 to buy new tickets at the full fare.

WHAT TO DO

Fortunately, Frank had made a photocopy of their tickets, which he was careful to carry separately from the tickets themselves. These photocopies—plus a copy of his receipt from the travel agent—showed that they had purchased the tickets and had confirmed reservations on the flight, even though there had been some sort of computer error.

Because Frank and Joan had this documentation plus photo

identification, the agent canceled the old tickets and issued new ones at the same fare, plus a $50 penalty that the agent told them is required in all lost-ticket situations. The agent explained that she would have to charge Frank and Joan for the new tickets and also gave them a form to seek a refund, which she said would be applied to their credit card account once it had been processed.

If Frank and Joan experience a delay in getting the refund processed, they should follow up with the airline by letter. Because the lost tickets had been purchased by credit card, Frank and Joan also have the option of placing the cost of the tickets in dispute (by notifying the credit card company of this) if a problem should arise.

Baggage

The airlines have a 98 percent recovery rate on "misdirected" baggage. If your baggage is missing, report the missing bags to the airline office at the airport. Don't wait until you get home. You'll be asked to fill out a form describing the baggage and its contents. Hold on to a copy of the form. If you're required to turn over the baggage claim tags, be sure to note the lost baggage on the form. While the airline attempts to trace your baggage, it may advance you cash for necessities. If it refuses to do so, you have no alternative but to replace your things yourself. Save your receipts, spend frugally on the essentials, and request reimbursement later.

If your baggage is finally recovered but the contents are damaged, the airline will pay you for repairs if repair is possible. If the damage is extensive, the carrier will probably pay you the depreciated value—not the replacement value—of both the luggage and its contents. If the damaged contents are found to have been fragile or packed improperly, the airline may refuse to pay you anything. Major carriers will also deliver "found" baggage to your destination address. Be sure to ask for this service to avoid an unnecessary trip to the airport to pick up found baggage.

Under federal law airlines can limit the amount they pay each passenger for lost baggage to $1,250. This is not insurance but simply a "cap" on the airline's liability. On international trips there is a ceiling of just over $9 per pound. Although the law doesn't require it, most airlines will reimburse you for reasonable out-of-pocket expenses caused by lost baggage. If the baggage is not recovered, the airline may ask for receipts and other documents to prove how much the lost items are currently worth, regardless of how much it will cost to buy replacement items. Once you have finally agreed on a fair reimbursement, it will take 6 to 12 weeks to receive your check.

If the baggage you are taking on a flight is worth more than the airline is legally required to pay, ask the airline if you can purchase "excess valuation coverage" when you check your baggage through. This is not insurance, but it is designed to increase the $1,250 liability ceiling that would otherwise be in effect. The airline may not be willing to pay for certain items, including jewelry, cash, or fragile heirlooms. It is best not to carry items in your luggage that are valued for more than the airline will cover.

What follows is a hypothetical situation involving obtaining reimbursement for lost baggage.

THE PROBLEM

Virginia had a sinking feeling in her stomach as she watched her fellow passengers, one by one, pick up their suitcases from the carousel. By the time she was the last passenger left, she figured that her baggage had been lost.

The agent on duty assured her that the baggage would probably be on the next flight, adding that many lost bags turn up within 24 hours. Virginia filled out a form describing the two lost pieces, a suitcase plus a box containing a vase wrapped as a present for her hosts. She also asked for and received some money to purchase a toothbrush and some other toilet articles.

Two days and numerous phone calls later, Virginia was told that the pieces were still missing. When Virginia got home, she mailed in a claim form detailing the contents of her suitcase, when she bought the items, and how much she paid. She estimated their value at $1,000, and she also enclosed a receipt for the vase, which she had purchased for $300 just before the trip.

A few weeks later the airline sent Virginia a letter offering $250 to settle the claim, reflecting the airline's estimate of what the lost clothing and other items in Virginia's suitcase were worth. The letter also said that the box containing the vase had turned up but that the vase was broken; the airline added that it was refusing to pay anything for the vase because the vase had not been packed in a factory-sealed carton.

After several weeks of letters back and forth, the airline finally raised its offer to $500. By that point, Virginia was totally frustrated and not sure whether she should keep up the fight, take the money, or do something else.

WHAT TO DO

Preventive medicine is the best way to deal with the problems of baggage loss. Here are some things you should do before you leave for the airport:

1. Put your name, address, and phone number on both the outside and the inside of your luggage. That way, if the outside tag or label is lost, the airline can locate you.

2. Don't use fancy-looking luggage.

3. Lock your suitcase.

4. Pack defensively. Don't pack items you'd be lost without, such as eyeglasses, medicine you must take every four hours, etc. Carry them with you on the plane. The same advice applies to fragile or expensive items that the airline can and will refuse to pay for if they're lost.

5. If you do plan to check fragile or breakable items (skis, a guitar, a vase), call the airline and ask whether it will be liable in case of damage or loss. You should also ask if the airline has any special rules, such as the one about factory-sealed cartons, which Virginia learned about too late.

If, despite your best efforts, your suitcase(s) still disappears, you should:

1. Be aware that airlines determine your claim based on when you purchased each item and how much you paid for it, from which they calculate the present or depreciated value of each item. As a result passengers are often shocked when they receive a very low settlement offer reflecting not only this phenomenon but also some element of bargaining and negotiating on the part of the airline.

2. Be prepared to send the airline copies (never send originals) of sales slips or credit card receipts to prove the purchase price of each missing item.

3. Recognize that airlines do engage in negotiating and that some back-and-forth bargaining may be required before the airline's offer comes up to an acceptable level. Also keep in mind that airlines may drag out the claims process for weeks or months. Keep after them! Persistence pays.

When all else fails, you've got two other choices:

1. Consider small-claims court, recognizing that the most a passenger can recover is $1,250 on domestic flights. An airline might become more inclined to settle rather than litigate.
2. Talk to your insurance broker. Many homeowners policies let you recover up to $3,000.

"Bumping"

Because of the inevitable no-shows, airlines overbook to protect themselves, and sometimes they end up "bumping" passengers if more passengers than they expect actually appear for the flight. If you are not under pressure to get to your destination and the airline determines that it has more passengers than seats on a particular flight, it may offer on-the-spot cash or a free ticket if you agree to give up your seat. If the choice is yours, consider how much they are willing to pay you for the ticket and when the next available flight takes off. If you can't get another flight until the next day, will the airline pay for your meals and hotel? Airline employees usually have negotiating power when they are looking for volunteers to be bumped, so don't agree to a voluntary bumping too cheaply.

Suppose the flight you're scheduled to take is overbooked and there are no willing "bumpees." Because you were one of the last to check in at the boarding gate, you have been selected as one of those who are involuntarily bumped. You'll be given a written explanation of who may be bumped and what your rights are.

Most airlines let bumped passengers choose between a free ticket for travel within the United States (excluding Alaska and Hawaii) or cash. If you elect to be paid in cash, your compensation will depend on how soon you can get another flight and how late you will reach your destination. If the alternate flight offered to you is scheduled to arrive within one hour of your previous estimated time of arrival, the airline is not required to pay you anything. If the alternate transportation is scheduled to land one to two hours later than the original flight, you are entitled to the cost of a one-way ticket to your final destination, with a ceiling of $200. If the best the airline can do is to get you a flight scheduled to land two hours or more later than your original flight would have arrived (four hours or more on international flights), you will receive double your one-way fare, with a maximum of $400. Regardless of how much the airline wants to compensate you, you can still keep your original ticket.

These rules apply on domestic flights and outbound flights from the United States to foreign countries. They do not apply to flights on aircraft with fewer than 60 seats, to flights that are canceled, or when passengers are left at the gate because a smaller aircraft is substituted for safety or operational reasons.

Keep in mind that each airline has its own passenger deadlines for ticketing or checking in and if you're late they can refuse to pay you anything if they bump you. If they offer to give you a voucher for a future flight instead of monetary compensation, you have the right to demand the money. If you are not happy with the amount of compensation the airline is willing to give you, talk to the complaint department representatives of the airline and try to negotiate a better settlement.

What follows is a hypothetical situation involving getting "bumped" from a flight.

THE PROBLEM

It was 4:00 P.M. on the day before Thanksgiving. After waiting in line at the departure gate for half an hour, Paul finally reached the counter and was told by the ticket agent that the flight had been oversold.

WHAT TO DO

First, Paul should ask if the airline has requested volunteers who are willing to give up their seat in return for cash or a free ticket. Under federal overbooking rules, airlines must hold such an auction before they can bump anyone involuntarily. This requirement of "volunteers first" may be the most important element of these rules, because it makes it more likely that people with a pressing need to travel will actually get on an oversold flight rather than be left at the gate under a rigid last-at-the-gate-first-bumped policy. In Paul's situation, if the airline has not yet sought volunteers, it is possible that someone will step forward and that he can make the flight.

Now, suppose that Paul had arrived 10 minutes earlier, checked in without incident, then heard an announcement that the airline was looking for three volunteers to give up their seats in return for a seat on the next available flight as well as cash or a free ticket for future travel. Should he volunteer?

Before saying yes, Paul should ask the agent exactly when the airline will be able to put him on another flight. If the airline can get him on a flight that's leaving in 45 minutes, he may want to volunteer. But because he's traveling on the day before Thanksgiving (and this is true during other peak travel times of the year), the other flights that day may also be sold out, and the next available flight may not leave until the next day.

If you must get on a given flight, your best guarantee against being bumped may also be the simplest: Make sure you get to the airport in plenty of time.

Frequent Fliers

If you travel often, you should join many frequent-flier programs. Such programs provide that as you accumulate mileage on trips taken, you can trade that mileage for a free ticket to a wide variety of locations, or upgrade from coach to business or first class. (In some programs, frequent-flier mileage can be obtained through use of specified credit cards.) Some programs provide better opportunities than others, and it's in your best interest to compare them before you begin accumulating points (mileage) on a particular airline.

When you choose a frequent-flier program, read the policies, procedures, and conditions. Be sure you find out if the airline can change its point requirements for free trips or place limits on the number of seats or days of travel available after you've signed up for the program.

While most airlines claim that they can change the requirements for free trips and their availability, the issue is currently (January 1994) being examined in the courts.

In most cases, the transfer of frequent-flier awards (coupons) is limited to family members or the member's companion traveler on the same itinerary. Any other transfer is not allowed. If you sell or even attempt to sell your awards, you run the risk of losing some or all of your mileage or being evicted from the program. If you are the knowing purchaser of such an unauthorized transfer, not only will your right to board the aircraft be denied, but the ticket will also be taken from you. The airlines have the right to file a lawsuit against people who violate these conditions, but their focus is primarily on taking the agencies that trade in frequent-flier awards (coupon brokers) to court—that is, the people who join the willing seller and buyer together in a transaction.

Keep in mind that airlines limit the number of free seats that are available at any one time. On some airlines, restrictions can be bypassed by giving up additional mileage credit (over the amount required for the free ticket or upgrade). Remember, too, that most miles are earned by business travelers who want to use them for personal travel. Chances are they want to use them to visit the same places you want to go at the same time you want to travel (for example, Europe in the summer, Hawaii or Florida in the winter). Also remember that most people prefer to travel on weekends.

What this means is that you need to start planning as early as possible. Before you start building up miles in a particular airline program, set a goal for yourself. Decide which destination or destinations you'd like to visit, and start earning the number of miles you need. Before you become too heavily committed to one airline's program, call the frequent-flier desk at that airline and ask how far in advance you need to book a reservation to your preferred destination. You may need to book almost a year in advance for some of the most popular destinations, if you will be cashing in frequent-flier miles for a ticket. If possible try being flexible about departure and return dates and time when you call the airline about cashing in your mileage.

If necessary you should also ask if there would be any seats available if you took a more circuitous routing through another one of the airline's "hub" cities. For example, if you live in New England and want to visit Florida, you wouldn't normally think of going via Detroit or Chicago, but if that's the only way to get there for nothing (by cashing in frequent-flier miles), you should consider tolerating the inconvenience.

Advance booking is important for another reason. Some airlines now employ a "use or lose" approach, which requires you to use your miles by a certain date or they become worthless.

TRAVEL COMPLAINTS

If you have a complaint about a flight, including the conduct of a flight attendant, the fact that you were involuntarily bumped, or that the food was terrible, seek out the customer service representative at the airport. If your complaint is more serious or if you failed to receive satisfaction, ask the customer service representative for the address and phone number of the consumer affairs office of the airline. Write the office a letter outlining the problem as well as noting the date, time, and flight number, and attach copies of your receipts or tickets (never the originals). Clearly and specifically state what you expect the airline to do to satisfy you. Expect some response within a few weeks. If the airline fails to respond to your complaint, write or call:

U.S. Department of Transportation
Office of Community and Consumer Affairs
400 Seventh Street, S.W.
Room 10405, I-25
Washington, DC 20590
202-366-2220

The department will follow up on your complaint and try to determine why the airline never responded, but it cannot compel the airline to pay a claim or offer you any relief unless there has been some violation of a Department of Transportation rule, such as the one on overbooking.

Fewer problems arise when you travel by train, bus, or mass transit, but when they do it's important to lodge a complaint and attempt to receive satisfaction. If you are traveling on Amtrak, the country's only national, intercity passenger railroad, direct your comments or complaints to:

Director of Customer Relations
AMTRAK
60 Massachusetts Avenue, N.W.
Washington, DC 20002
202-906-2121

If your problem involves a refund and you live east of Ohio and north of Virginia, write to:

AMTRAK Refunds
30th Street Station
30th and Market Streets
Philadelphia, PA 19104

For all other refund requests, send your letter to:

AMTRAK Refunds
Chicago Union Station
210 S. Canal Street
Chicago, IL 60661

To register complaints about buses and mass transit, check the phone book White Pages for the company's local office or toll-free national number.

BANKING AND CONSUMER CREDIT

Most consumers think of banks as lenders, not borrowers. Technically speaking, however, when it comes to checking accounts, you are the lender by virtue of your depositing your money with the bank; the bank is the debtor.

Certain legal issues affect your everyday banking.

Postdated Checks

In some states, your bank will be held liable for your expenses because it cashed a postdated check. In many other states, however, you are considered responsible because you have counted on the goodwill of the merchant or the individual to whom you wrote the check not to present it for payment before the date you specified. To protect yourself, some states require you to notify your bank in advance that you have postdated a check.

A check is a contract, and by law it goes into effect when it is signed, regardless of the date, making you, not the bank, liable for the full amount.

For example, you want to buy a portable compact disc player for $400, but you are unsure about your checking account balance. Tomorrow is payday, so to be safe you "postdate" the check, writing tomorrow's date instead of today's. The merchant ignores the check's date and deposits it in your bank today. The bank honors the check and pays in cash. The withdrawal of that money leaves you with only $5 in your account, and two more checks totaling $50 come through for payment by the bank a few hours later. Your bank refuses to honor those checks because of insufficient funds and also causes you to incur $40 in check refusal fees.

Stop-Payment Orders

Stop-payment orders must be made immediately if they are to be effective. Suppose that you had a check made out to "cash" in your wallet when the wallet was stolen. You notify your bank and ask that a stop-payment order be placed on the check. If the order is made in writing, the law states that it will stand for six months and can be renewed over and over again. Bank policies vary regarding stop-payment orders made by telephone.

Altered Checks

Since the bank is supposed to examine each check it receives, it can be held responsible for paying on an altered check. Let's assume that you write a check to a merchant for $22. The merchant adds two zeros to the number and adds the word "hundred" after "twenty-two," takes it to the bank, and is given $2,200 in cash. Your bank may be held responsible, but if it is determined that you wrote out the check with spaces before and after the numbers and words, thus making alteration possible, the bank may not be held liable.

Forged Checks

Your bank becomes responsible for money lost through forgery because it has your signature card on file. Suppose that your checkbook is stolen, and that the thief writes a check, for cash, for $200, forges your name, and cashes it at your bank. The bank might possibly avoid liability if it could prove that you often sign your name differently, making it impossible for bank employees to detect a forgery.

What follows is a hypothetical situation involving a forged check.

THE PROBLEM

When Janis received her monthly bank statement, she found a canceled check for $439 that she didn't recognize. It was written to a store she had never been to, and the signature on it was clearly a forgery of her own.

WHAT TO DO

1. Janis should call the bank as soon as possible and ask to speak to a bank officer. She should explain what happened and ask how long it will take the bank to investigate the problem and get back to her. She should write a letter confirming her conversation and keep a copy.

2. If she doesn't hear that the problem has been resolved, and the amount of the forged check has not been credited to her account by the time she receives her next monthly statement, Janis should call the bank officer again. She should explain that she knows it is the bank's responsibility to verify her signature on all checks and offer to supply a copy of the forged check to show that the signature on it is obviously not hers. She should ask when she can expect the matter to be resolved and send a letter confirming this conversation. (It may not help her, but it can't hurt to mention that she's been a good customer of the bank but is prepared to take her business elsewhere.) If that doesn't resolve the problem, she should go on to step 3.

3. Janis should call the nearest Federal Reserve System office (it has Federal Reserve Banks or branches in most major cities) and ask if it has authority over her bank—or, if not, what agency does. She may also want to call her state banking department, usually located in the state capital, and ask what it can do on her behalf to resolve the problem. Janis should follow up with a letter, attaching copies of all previous correspondence, and send a carbon copy to her bank.

4. In the unlikely event that Janis's problem wasn't resolved by one of the earlier steps and if the forged check was for a large amount, she may want to consult a lawyer.

Forged or Missing Endorsements

A bank is responsible if it honors checks with forged or missing endorsements. Suppose you have lost a large refund check and it's found by someone else, who, without endorsing it, takes it to the bank where it is cashed. The bank must reimburse you, because it is required to check for endorsements as well as to ask for identification to compare signatures.

CREDIT

Credit is extended by banks, savings and loans, mortgage companies, credit unions, and trusts. There are basically three forms of

Fran, the owner of Franklin's Hardware Store, accepted a check for the purchase of a lawn mower from someone claiming to be Pam Saunders. The buyer had forged the check. When Pam discovered the fraudulent transaction after receiving her canceled check, she quickly notified her bank. Pam does not know who should make good on the forged check—the bank, Fran, Fran's bank, or Pam herself. The liability falls on the party accepting the forged check, unless Fran can prove that it was Pam's negligent handling of her checkbook that caused it to get into the hands of a thief.

consumer credit: installment credit, revolving credit, and open-end credit.

Installment Credit

Consumers who use installment credit pay off their loans in equal amounts, usually each month or within a certain period of time. For example, when you borrow money to buy a car, you are usually required to pay the same amount each month for a specified period, such as two, three, or five years.

Revolving Credit

Under revolving credit plans, used typically in department store charge accounts and with most credit cards, consumers borrow money and pay it back in monthly installments that vary in amount from a required minimum to payment in full at the option of the borrower. Interest is charged on the outstanding balance each month.

Open-End Credit

With open-end credit, the consumer is not given the option of carrying the current debt over to the next month; the full balance is to be paid when the invoice is submitted. Some credit card companies operate on the standard of open-end credit.

Applying for Credit

Federal laws protect consumers from lenders who discriminate against them; nevertheless, a potential creditor uses certain standards to determine whether you are a safe credit risk:

- Your ability to repay the loan. Lenders consider your employment situation, salary, and length of employment, as well as any other sources of income you may have in order to establish your financial stability. Then, they weigh your income against your obligations and expenses, including your mortgage, car payments, any child support and alimony you pay, credit card debts, and your basic costs of living.

- Your credit history. Have you met your past financial obligations on time? Have you ever filed for bankruptcy or had a car repossessed?

- Your assets as collateral. Do you have property, investments, or other sources of collateral to cover the amount of the loan if you become unable to repay it?

DISCRIMINATION AND CREDIT APPLICATIONS The Equal Credit Opportunity Act (ECOA) prohibits lenders from turning you down for a loan on the basis of your age, race, national origin, gender, marital status, or religion. In addition, the fact that you receive Social Security benefits or other public aid cannot be used as a reason for denying you a loan. While discrimination can involve a lender's flat refusal of a loan even though you have demonstrated that you qualify for it, it can also be something more subtle, such as discouraging you from filling out a loan application, charging you higher than standard interest, or lending you less than someone who has the same credit background.

In the past, when fewer women worked outside the home, lenders judged women as poor credit risks and often denied them credit. The ECOA has helped discourage such discrimination, for example, preventing a lender from denying a loan to a woman on the basis of her marital status. The law provides that the question of whether a woman plans to have children in the future cannot be asked and cannot become a determining factor in granting a loan. If a woman individually meets the requirements for a loan, the lender cannot demand that her husband co-sign the loan application. She also cannot be turned down for a loan simply because her husband has filed for bankruptcy.

What follows is a hypothetical situation involving discrimination in lending practices.

THE PROBLEM

Tina applied for a personal loan at her bank. Although she was able to demonstrate a more than adequate ability to repay the loan, the loan officer suggested her application would be rejected unless her husband co-signed for it.

WHAT TO DO

Tina should remind the loan officer that under current law a lender cannot require a woman to have her husband co-sign a loan application. If that doesn't work, she should ask to speak to the loan officer's supervisor and repeat this explanation of the law.

If this does not get the desired results, Tina should take her business to a more enlightened bank and report the offending bank to the FTC.

Establishing a Credit History

Lenders are hesitant to make a loan to an applicant without an established credit history. If you can't get a conventional credit card, one way to establish a credit history is to apply for a secured credit card issued by a well-established bank. You must deposit money into an interest-bearing account at that bank, which you then borrow against with your credit card. Over time, this can help establish your credit history and make you eligible for a nonsecured credit card. For a list of banks that issue secured cards, send $3 to Bankcard Holders of America, 560 Herndon Parkway, Suite 120, Herndon, VA 22070.

Another way to develop the beginning of a credit history is by co-signing on someone else's credit card account. You'll both be responsible for the debts incurred, so be sure the person you sign with is reliable and has a good credit rating. Also be sure you are a co-signer and not merely an additional cardholder who has no liability for the incurred debt.

Credit Reports

Like it or not, your creditworthiness depends in large part on what three national credit bureaus—Equifax, TransUnion, and TRW Credit Data—report that it is. When you apply for a loan or when a present creditor wants to check on your financial stability, the lender will request a report from one of these three bureaus or from one of the local bureaus they "feed." This is a rather unsettling practice for consumers, considering that informal investigations reveal a 20 percent error rate in the credit reports released by the big three. The sources of these errors range from incorrect information provided by borrowers to inaccuracies emanating from the creditors. Nevertheless, the possible effect is often the unjustified rejection for a loan, a mortgage, or a credit card.

Keep your credit report in good condition. Don't make the mistake of believing that making a late payment or two won't matter; any delay over 30 days will be reflected on your credit report and will detract from your credit rating. If someone wins a court judgment against you, be sure the court records as well as the credit bureaus are notified when you have paid it. If you have defaulted on your student loan payments, this too is a fact that may be added to your credit records. If you can't pay your loan, don't ignore it. (Deferments of up to three years are available in certain circumstances, or you may be able to negotiate a new payment plan.)

What follows is a hypothetical situation involving errors in a credit report.

THE PROBLEM

After being rejected for a charge account at a department store, Nate learned that the information that led to the decision had been supplied by a credit bureau. He called the store to find out which credit bureau was responsible. Then he requested a free credit report from that bureau, which he is entitled to because he was denied credit. When he received the credit report, Nate saw that it contained several delinquent accounts that were not his.

WHAT TO DO

1. Nate should contact the credit bureau and ask that the incorrect accounts be removed from his credit report. (If the errors involve one of his actual accounts, he should contact that creditor and ask it to correct the information that it supplied to the credit bureau.) The credit bureau is required to investigate.

2. Nate can provide a written explanation of 100 words or less regarding any information in his credit report that he believes to be in error. If the credit bureau is slow to investigate his complaint or to remove the inaccurate information, a written explanation might improve his chances of getting credit. He should call the credit bureau to find out the procedure. If that gets results, he should go on to step 3.

3. Errors in credit reports have a way of reappearing, so it's a good idea for Nate to request a copy of his report three or four months after this problem is cleared up (he'll probably have to pay for a copy this time) to make sure the error is still off his record.

To make certain that your credit report is in good order, request your credit records from each of the bureaus. The request can be made by calling or writing:

Equifax
P.O. Box 740241
Atlanta, GA 30374
404-885-8000
or a local office in your city or state

TransUnion Company
P.O. Box 390
Philadelphia, PA 19064
215-690-4955

TransUnion (Midwest)
Consumer Relations
212 South Market
Wichita, KS 67202
800-851-2674

TransUnion (South)
Consumer Relations
101 Bullit Lane, Suite G10
Louisville, KY 40222
502-425-7511

TransUnion (West)
Consumer Relations
1561 East Orangethorpe
Fullerton, CA 92633
714-738-3800

TRW Credit Data
National Consumer Relations Center
P.O. Box 2106
Allen, TX 75002
214-390-3000

If you have been denied credit, the credit bureau responsible for the information that led to your rejection is required to provide you with your report free of charge. If you are simply checking your credit, the report may cost anywhere from $2 to $20.

The credit report probably will include most or all of your creditors, how quickly you pay them, and whether there are any unsatisfied judgments against you, including liens on your property, unpaid debts, or personal bankruptcies. The report will use a system of abbreviations and numbers that are indexed on the back of the report. If you discover an error, try to clear it up immediately by writing to the creditor and explaining the mistake. Also, send a copy of your letter to the credit bureau, which is required to investigate the questionable entry within 30 days. The bureau is then required to send corrected reports to anyone who received your credit record during the preceding six months. If the creditor fails to acknowledge and correct the error, it will remain on your record, but you will be permitted to provide an explanation of 100 words or less, and it will become part of your credit report.

Certain businesses advertise themselves as "credit-repair" companies and promise to clean up bad credit records for a fee. Such companies may charge as much as $500, and there is no service they can provide for you that you can't accomplish for yourself.

Your credit report also includes the names of companies or individuals who requested to see and were provided with a copy of your credit record. The list may surprise you, for the only criterion required for this access to your private financial history is that the inquiring party have a "legitimate business need"—which includes just about anyone, from retailers wanting to sell you expensive jewelry to real estate agents wanting to sell you swampland in Florida. You can request that access to your credit records be denied to outsiders in only one area: issuers of credit cards who frequently peruse credit reports to select people who qualify for "preapproved" cards. If you prefer that such credit card issuers be prevented from using your credit records, notify one of the three bureaus; it is supposed to comply with your request and also to contact the other two bureaus.

Credit Cards

Your choices of credit cards are almost limitless. Most adults are deluged with offers for cards or even preapproved applications. It is legal for credit card companies to send you the preapproved applications, but you are not liable if someone else takes your application and sends it in on your behalf, using the card in your name.

It is against federal law for an issuer to send you a credit card if you did not request it. If you receive one, cut it in half and send it back whence it came, explaining in a covering letter that you never asked for it. Be sure to send it back! If you do not, the company *might* treat it as an open account and report the credit limit to one of the credit reporting bureaus, thus exaggerating the total amount of credit extended to you by all lending sources. This could hamper your obtaining credit you want in the future.

Consumer Credit Card Protection

Federal laws protect consumers against credit card abuse. They apply to:

- *Interest Rates.* The Truth-In-Lending Act requires credit card companies as well as other lenders to state the Annual Percentage Rate (APR) they charge.

- *Immediate Posting of Payments.* The issuer is required to credit your account on the day that payment is received. The issuer cannot delay it for a day or two, thus accumulating greater interest charges. You have the obligation to follow the proper procedures for paying your bill, including sending it to the correct address and with the correct account number. The issuer cannot be held responsible for your mistakes.

- *Refunds.* If you are owed a refund, either because you overpaid or because you returned merchandise, you have two choices. If the amount of the refund due you exceeds $1, you can request that a refund check be sent to you. It must be sent to you within seven days of the issuer's receipt of your written request. Alternatively, you may decide to keep the balance due you on your account. The issuer should attempt to refund your credit if it stays on your account longer than six months.

- *Billing Errors.* If you find a mistake on your bill, write to the issuer within 60 days after the incorrect bill was mailed to you. Within two billing cycles, the issuer must investigate your inquiry and respond to you in writing. You won't be charged for the amount in question during the period of time that the company is looking into the problem.

- *Unauthorized Use of the Card.* If your credit card is lost or stolen, you won't be responsible for any charges if you report the missing card to the company before any unauthorized charges are made; call the issuer with the card's number as soon as possible and follow your call with a confirming letter. The issuer's address and phone number are provided on the back of your monthly credit card bill.

Suppose your wallet containing six credit cards is stolen.

Suppose you bought a piece of luggage at a department store, using the store's credit card. Two days after your purchase, the bag develops a rip in a seam. You return to the store, explain that you are unhappy with the quality of the bag, and say you would like the store to credit your account. The salesperson refuses to do so but offers an identical replacement bag. You speak with the manager, explaining that you don't want another bag, but that you want your account credited. You receive no satisfaction.

If you bought the luggage with a bank card or card that was not issued by the store, you can refuse to make payment if the luggage cost more than $50, was bought in your home state or within 100 miles of your billing address, and if you attempted to resolve the dispute with the retailer. If your purchase doesn't fit these criteria, you may have to go to small-claims court for help. Or better, inform the card issuer that a mistake was made on the bill, noting that the merchant gave you an inferior product instead of the one for which you were billed.

The thief goes on a spending spree with your cards, charging about $8,000 worth of services and merchandise, and you don't report the loss to the toll-free phone number until two days later. You will be liable for a maximum of $50 per card, for a total of $300, not $8,000. This $50 maximum pertains to all credit cards, but not to lost ATM cards.

• *Disputed Purchases.* You have the right to refuse to pay the charge for damaged merchandise or another such disputed purchase as well as any finance charge resulting from it.

WHEN YOUR CREDIT CARD IS TRANSFERRED TO ANOTHER BANK Beware if your bank informs you that your credit card account has been moved to another lending institution. The new institution is legally permitted to boost the interest rate on your account (for late payments) with only 15 days' notice to you. Check the laws in your state; you may be allowed to pay off the amount due and cancel the card before the higher rate applies.

What follows is a hypothetical situation involving returning merchandise that is unsatisfactory.

THE PROBLEM

Using a credit card, Gordon bought a pair of binoculars on sale for $100 at a local camera store. The binoculars seemed to work fine in the store, but after he got them home, he discovered that they didn't focus properly. When he took them back to the store, he was told that he couldn't return them because they were on sale.

WHAT TO DO

1. Gordon should tell the store manager that he plans to exercise his rights as a credit card user and refuse to pay for unsatisfactory merchandise. He should explain that it will be less trouble for the store, as well as for himself, to return his money now. If that doesn't bring results, Gordon should follow up with a letter. (He may need written proof that he first tried to work things out with the merchant before the credit card issuer will intervene.)

2. Gordon should call the card issuer and explain the problem, asking what procedures should be followed to withhold payment for defective merchandise. He should also ask whether

the card issuer has other programs that might be helpful, such as purchase insurance. If the disputed purchase appears on Gordon's credit card bill, he should pay the balance due minus the disputed purchase and attach a note saying that he paid for a satisfactory product but received a defective one. His card issuer may accept that explanation, particularly if he's been a good customer and it wants to keep his business.

3. Gordon's credit card isn't his only weapon in these battles, though it may be the easiest one to try first. His state's consumer protection or attorney general's office may also be able to help. He should call to find out what office handles complaints like his and follow up with a letter explaining the problem and detailing his earlier attempts to resolve it with the merchant.

Merchants and Credit Cards

Since merchants must pay a fee on purchases you make with your charge card, ranging anywhere from 2.25 percent to 5 percent, they sometimes attempt to pass that cost on to you on top of the price of your purchase. This practice is legal in some states, but not in others. You can contact the Better Business Bureau in your town or city to find out if a merchant can legally charge you this fee or part of it.

Some retailers require minimum dollar purchases before allowing you to use a credit card. These restrictions violate the agreements the merchants made with the issuing banks and the credit card companies. You can report the retailer to the card-issuing institution; if you get no satisfaction, write Visa, MasterCard, American Express, or the corresponding company, and then the Better Business Bureau.

Automatic Teller Machine (ATM) Cards

Automatic teller machines enable you to do your basic banking transactions at all hours of the day or night without the need for a bank teller. But be aware that through the use of the card and the application of your own secret code, a thief can gain access to all of the money in your checking account *and* to any line of credit on the account. One-third of all users of ATMs make the mistake of writing their access code on the card itself or on a piece of paper in the same wallet. The Electronic Funds Transfer (EFT) Act protects consumers by requiring banks to state, in writing, their charge for an ATM transaction as well as other important terms. The Act also spells out a procedure for disputing a charge or mistake.

Unlike lost credit cards, where the maximum liability you have is $50, ATM cards expose you to a greater degree of liability. If your card is lost and you contact the issuer immediately before anyone else uses it, you are not responsible for any unauthorized use; however, if it is used before you report it, your liability increases the longer you wait to report it. If you call the necessary toll-free number within 2 business days after you discover the card is missing, you will be responsible for $50 of withdrawals. If you wait longer, you could be liable for up to $500. And if you don't report an unauthorized withdrawal within 60 days after receiving a statement that reflects it, you could find yourself drained of your entire balance as well as up to the credit line for overdrafts.

What follows is a hypothetical situation involving an error caused by an ATM malfunction.

THE PROBLEM

Greg tried to withdraw $100 from his savings account using an ATM, but the ATM malfunctioned and didn't give him any money. He assumed the bank would catch the error, but when he received his next account statement, he discovered that his account had been debited for the $100 he never received.

WHAT TO DO

1. Greg should call the bank and explain the error, providing any information he can about the bank branch, time of day, and specific ATM used. He should ask to have the matter investigated and the money returned to his account, and he should follow up with a letter confirming the conversation. If that doesn't resolve the matter by the time of Greg's next monthly statement, he should go on to step 2.

2. He should call the bank again and speak to an officer. Greg should explain his previous attempt to resolve the problem and, if he thinks it's likely to give him any leverage, threaten to move his accounts to another bank if the problem isn't resolved quickly.

3. If that doesn't work, he should call the nearest office of the Federal Reserve System and ask whether it has authority over his bank and, if not, what agency does. Greg should also contact his state banking department. He should file complaints with both federal and state agencies, attaching copies of his previous correspondence with the bank. The bank should also be sent copies of both complaints and previous correspondence.

WHERE TO GO WITH BANK CREDIT COMPLAINTS

Go to the source of the problem, in this case the bank. If you are unable to resolve it, contact the Federal Reserve System, which will look into the matter and attempt to respond in 15 days. The Federal Reserve has jurisdiction only over state-chartered banks, so if your complaint should be directed elsewhere, the Federal Reserve will refer you. Send your complaints concerning consumer credit law violations, or deceptive or unfair banking practices to:

Director
Division of Consumer and Community Affairs
Board of Governors of the Federal Reserve System
614 H Street, N.W., Room 108
Washington, DC 20001

District Federal Reserve Banks are also available to take your complaints and are located in Atlanta, Boston, Chicago, Cleveland, Dallas, Kansas City (Missouri), Minneapolis, New York, Philadelphia, Richmond, San Francisco, and St. Louis.

DEBTS

Owing money was once a jailable offense, but our credit economy makes that a distant custom indeed. Nevertheless, creditors use certain methods to recover their money, and consumers have legal rights to protect them from being abused in the process.

Foreclosure

If you are unable to make your monthly mortgage payments or to comply with one of the agreements you made with the institution that lent you the money for your house, the lender has the right to foreclose and to sell your home at a public auction.

The first step the lender will take is to conduct a title search to see if another creditor has a lesser lien on the property; perhaps someone holds a second mortgage, for example. If the lender's foreclosure sale nets more than the cost of the loan extended to you, proceeds may be left for the other lienholders, so the lender is required to notify these other lienholders of the foreclosure sale.

Next, the lender will file a lawsuit, which causes a copy of the complaint and summons to be served on you and anyone else who holds a lesser lien. A notice will be filed with the court, which alerts any interested party that there is a legal action pending against the property. If you have any defense to the action, you have the right to a trial. If you don't respond and therefore default, the lender will be granted a judgment decree, allowing the lender to auction off the property. You and the other defendants will be notified of the sale, and the lender will be required to announce the sale in the local newspaper.

If the auction brings less than the amount of the loan, you may be responsible for making up the deficiency, depending on the laws in your state. In some states you may have the *right of redemption*, meaning that within a certain amount of time you can redeem your house by paying the foreclosure sale price. Some states require you to pay the entire amount of the loan in order to redeem the house.

What follows is a hypothetical situation involving possible foreclosure of a mortgage.

THE PROBLEM

Because of large medical bills, Donna was unable to make her monthly mortgage payments. After she had missed several payments, the bank that issued the mortgage threatened her with foreclosure.

WHAT TO DO

1. Donna should make an appointment to speak with a bank officer and explain the reasons for her delinquent mortgage payments. She should mention that she has paid her bills reliably in the past, and she should ask if the bank can give her some time to catch up on her payments or work out an arrangement in which she pays a modest amount each month. In general, banks are more interested in getting their money back than they are in owning houses. If that doesn't work and the bank starts foreclosure proceedings, Donna should go on to step 2.

2. When she receives notice of a foreclosure proceeding, she has a right to defend herself in court. At this point she may want to consult a lawyer; if she can't afford a lawyer, her local legal aid society may be able to provide help. If she loses in court and the bank is given the authority to auction off her property, she can go on to step 3.

3. Depending on the laws in her state, Donna may have a right to buy back her house within a certain period of time. If, by that time, her financial crisis has passed, she may want to exercise that right.

Repossession

A creditor is legally permitted to take possession of your car or another possession you have financed with a loan as soon as you default, as defined in your contract; this may be as soon as you are late on one payment. Those terms can be changed if your bank or other creditor agrees to accept late payments or moves the due date to later in the month. If your creditor automatically accepts late payments every month, with no questions asked, you can submit this evidence in court to exhibit an implied agreement to allow tardy payments without default.

Suppose you are two months behind in your car payments and you've made no effort to discuss the problem with your bank, the creditor. You have officially defaulted, so the bank has the right to send someone to your home or to your place of business and repossess the car without a court order or without giving you prior notice. Your car can be repossessed at any hour, but the creditor cannot "breach the peace," destroy property, or use threats, force, or violence.

After the bank takes your car, its representatives must notify you if it plans to keep your car or whether it will be sold, either privately or through a public auction. You have the right to demand a sale instead of the bank's possession, if you believe the sale can bring in more money than you owe on the car.

If the car is to be sold to a private purchaser, the bank must tell you the date it is being put up for sale. If it is to be sold at auction, you must be informed of the date, time, and location so that you have the option of attending and bidding on it.

If you have returned to a stable financial condition and you want your car back, most states will allow you to recover the car if you pay the full amount of the loan still outstanding plus the bank's or other creditor's costs of repossession. Some states permit owners to reinstate their loan by merely making the payments they missed as well as paying the repossession costs.

Even if the bank takes your car, your obligation to the bank may still not be discharged. Some states require that you pay the difference between the amount of money brought in by the sale and the amount you owe. If you are notified of a deficiency hearing, be sure to make an appearance. If you have any valid defense showing why you should not pay the deficiency—perhaps the creditor "breached the peace" during repossession—now's your chance to be heard. If a lot of money is at stake, you might want to consult an attorney.

If a Creditor Gains Access to Your Bank Accounts and Garnishees Your Paycheck

If a creditor has gone to court and won a judgment against you and you fail to pay within a certain number of days, the creditor can legally gain access to your bank accounts and other sources of income through a court-issued "writ of execution." The creditor is not allowed to attach other entities, such as your car, the equity in your home, and your personal effects. But the creditor has the right to have 25 percent to 30 percent of your income withheld from each paycheck, and the ability to obtain the entire proceeds of your savings account. It's best to try to negotiate an installment plan with your creditor and to prevent court action.

Protecting Yourself from Abusive Creditors

Before 1973 there was no legislation in place to prevent collection agencies and other debt collectors from harassing debtors, threatening them, and generally making their lives miserable. The Fair Debt Collection Practices Act of that year greatly improved consumer protection from these abuses, prohibiting debt collectors from using certain unethical tactics. The law applies only to those who collect debts for others on a regular basis, such as collection agencies. It does not protect consumers from the creditors themselves. Nevertheless, since debt collectors are usually paid on the basis of their success, some may continue to use unethical tactics despite federal and state legislation designed to prevent it.

To exercise your rights under the Fair Debt Collection Practices Act, first, send the collector a letter stating simply that you don't want the collector to contact you again. The collector is obligated to provide you with certain information, in writing, about your debt within five days of this first contact. The collector is required to tell you how much you owe, the name of the creditor, and what you can do if you believe you don't owe the debt.

If you write within 30 days and inform the debt collector that you

Suppose you owe an appliance store $800. After several months, the store turns over the collection of your debt to a collection agency. Since the agency will receive as much as 50 percent of the amount it can collect from you, it may become quite aggressive, calling you many times a day and late at night and embarrassing you at your office. By calling you at unusual hours, calling too frequently, and basically harassing you, a collection agency is violating the Fair Debt Collection Practices Act.

don't owe the money, the collector must stop contacting you. If the collector sends you evidence of your debt, such as a bill or invoice, the collector can begin legal proceedings against you.

If you have retained an attorney, the collector may contact the attorney and no one else in regard to the payment. If you are not being represented by a lawyer, the collector may contact other individuals to find out your address and place of employment. But the collector cannot harass you, make false statements, or use unfair practices such as the following:

- publishing or advertising your name and the debt
- threatening harm or injury to you, your reputation, or your property
- using obscene language
- threatening to have you arrested
- contacting you by using a postcard (which others might read)
- overstating the amount of your debt or collecting more than you owe
- falsely claiming or implying that he or she is a lawyer or a government employee
- stating that legal action is being brought against you when it isn't

If a collector commits any of these violations or is deceptive in any other way, you have the right to file a lawsuit against the collector in either federal or state court within one year, and you may be able to recover your damages, attorney's fees, and court costs. In addition, you should contact the attorney general of your state to find out your rights under state laws and the FTC for more specific information about your rights under the Fair Debt Collection Practices Act.

What follows is a hypothetical situation involving harassment by a collection agency.

THE PROBLEM

After his small business failed, Ned found himself far behind in his debts. One of his creditors hired a collection agency to try to get its money back. The collection agent began to call Ned both at his new job and at home at night to pressure him for money. Ned still intended to pay his debts as soon as he was able, but he wanted to stop the harassment, which was interfering with his work and upsetting his family.

WHAT TO DO

1. Ned should make a note of all calls from the debt collector. If he received calls at work or at odd hours, the debt collector may have violated his rights, and he may be able to bring suit later on. If Ned didn't owe the debt, he should send a letter to that effect to the debt collector and save a copy.

2. If the calls persist, Ned may want to hire a lawyer. If the debt collector calls again, Ned should refer the collector to his lawyer. The debt collector cannot legally call anyone but Ned's lawyer regarding his case.

3. If the debt collector continues to call or violates Ned's rights in any other way, he can bring a lawsuit.

Rehabilitating Your Bad Credit

If you find yourself in deep debt, you might need counseling to assist you in rehabilitating your credit. There are 500 consumer credit counseling agencies across the country that can help develop a debt repayment plan for you and then help negotiate with your creditors. Consumer credit counseling agencies are nonprofit, so their services cost very little. For information on the office closest to you, contact:

National Foundation for Consumer Credit
8611 Second Avenue
Suite 100
Silver Spring, MD 20910-3372
800-388-2227

Bankruptcy

Debts sometimes become insurmountable, and the only way out may be to file for bankruptcy. Consumer debtors have two avenues created by the federal Bankruptcy Act: Chapter 7 and Chapter 13. Each achieves different ends, and both require the help of an attorney.

Also known as "straight bankruptcy," a Chapter 7 bankruptcy discharges or forgives some of your debts and will pay off others by liquidating certain property. Bankruptcy law provides that property can be liquidated or sold to pay off the debts that cannot be discharged, but certain property is considered exempt, or protected from creditors. This includes, up to certain dollar limits, the equity in your home, clothing, personal effects, and household items, as well as alimony, child support, and maintenance payments. Property that you may have tried to hide by transferring it to friends or family members one year before filing the bankruptcy petition will not be exempt and can be sold. "Secured debts," such as cars, where the borrower is putting up the item purchased as collateral for the loan, also cannot be discharged by bankruptcy.

What follows is a hypothetical situation involving bankruptcy.

THE PROBLEM

Hector's debts continued to mount, and he began to doubt that he'd ever be able to pay them all off. He wondered if he shouldn't file for bankruptcy protection.

WHAT TO DO

1. Hector should consult with a consumer credit counseling agency. It will try to work out a debt repayment plan for him and negotiate with his creditors. If that isn't practical, the counseling agency may suggest that Hector see a lawyer.

2. A lawyer may be able to suggest other actions Hector can take, short of filing for bankruptcy. Since bankruptcy would be a blot on Hector's credit record for years to come, he should carefully consider any alternatives at this point.

3. If filing for bankruptcy is Hector's best choice, he will need a lawyer to file a petition for bankruptcy and to guide him through the legal process. Once he has filed, his creditors can no longer try to collect from him. A trustee will be appointed to take charge of Hector's nonexempt assets, sell them, and distribute the proceeds to his creditors.

FILING CHAPTER 7 BANKRUPTCY   Once you file a petition with the federal Bankruptcy Court, you are "off-limits" to your creditors; they are not permitted to sue you or to continue efforts to collect the debt. You'll be required to file a financial statement, listing all your assets and liabilities. The Bankruptcy Court can provide you with the proper forms.

The court will notify your creditors of the bankruptcy action and the date and time of the first creditors' meeting. At the meeting your creditors will file their claims and objections to exemptions or discharges. The creditors will also select a trustee who will take title to all your nonexempt property and sell it at auction.

The court may hold hearings to consider any objections made by creditors to discharges or exemptions. In any case, the court sends all creditors a copy of its discharge order, which legally terminates any future action against you to collect the debts.

From the proceeds of the sale, certain creditors and expenses are paid according to a priority list provided in the federal Bankruptcy Act. Secured creditors are paid first. If any proceeds are left, the costs of administering the bankruptcy come next, and so on down the list until all the proceeds are exhausted.

You may decide to "reaffirm" certain debts, even though the court determines them to be exempt. For example, it might be in your best interests to pay off a debt to a business associate if you want to continue your relationship. Before the debt can be reaffirmed, however, the court will hold a hearing and examine the reasons for reaffirmation and the effects it will have.

FILING CHAPTER 13 BANKRUPTCY Only 20 percent of all personal bankruptcy filings are Chapter 13 bankruptcies. These involve an effort to pay back creditors, at least in part. In addition, if you owe more than $100,000 in unsecured debt and $350,000 in secured debt (that is, debt backed by collateral), you cannot qualify for a Chapter 13 bankruptcy. If you do, you will have to develop a proposed payment plan and have it approved by the Bankruptcy Court. Each month you'll be required to pay your creditors through a trustee. If you can't keep up with the payments, you can ask that the plan be readjusted, or you can file for a Chapter 7 bankruptcy.

WHERE TO GET HELP

Sometimes the most difficult thing about getting help with a consumer problem is knowing whom to call. The sheer number of federal, state, and local agencies and organizations, both governmental and private, is daunting. If you want to file a complaint against or make an inquiry into a business, start by contacting your state office of consumer affairs, often within the state attorney general's office, and the local Better Business Bureau.

Other times it's not enough that you handle the situation locally. It may be important that you call the problem to the attention of a federal agency, such as the FTC. The following list supplies additional information on the agencies and organizations that might help you resolve your problem.

Filing a Complaint with the Office of Consumer Affairs (OCA)
Every state has its own office of consumer affairs; check your phone book under State Government. More than half of the nation's OCAs are located within a state's attorney general's office. If you have trouble locating your local office of consumer affairs or if you want to contact a federal agency about your problem, the Office of Consumer Affairs within the U.S. Department of Commerce can refer you. Write or call:

Office of Consumer Affairs
U.S. Department of Commerce
Fourteenth Street between Constitution Avenue & E Street, N.W.
Room 5718
Washington, DC 20230
202-482-5000

Your state office of consumer affairs may be your best resource if you believe that a law has been violated. When you write the OCA office, explain the circumstances, provide dates and names, and send copies (never originals) of contracts and documentation involved in the transaction.

A counselor will screen the matter for potential infractions, but if it's found that no law has been violated, the counselor may attempt to help mediate the problem between you and the company. If the counselor finds merit in your complaint, that counselor will conduct an investigation, asking the company for an explanation, or perhaps begin an undercover investigation. If it's determined that wrongdoing has taken place, the business will be contacted and informed that if the problem is not corrected by a certain date, legal action will be taken. If the violation is ignored or not resolved, it will be turned over to the state attorney general, with a request that a suit be filed.

The Better Business Bureau

When you're in doubt about the reliability and reputation of a business, the Better Business Bureau can tell you whether complaints have been filed against that company. If you have a problem with a specific business, they can intervene and help mediate between both parties. A nonprofit organization, the Better Business Bureau can also provide educational consumer information on various topics.

The Bureau's headquarters are located at 4200 Wilson Boulevard, Arlington, VA 22209. Offices are located in every state and major city. Check your phone book for the one closest to you.

The Small Business Administration (SBA)

To file a complaint against a small business, write or call:

The Small Business Administration
409 Third Street, S.W.
Washington, DC 20416
202-205-6600

To request information, call 202-U-ASK-SBA.

The Federal Trade Commission (FTC)

The FTC is an independent regulatory body that is responsible to Congress. The FTC accepts consumer complaints about the deceptive advertising of consumer products (automobiles, appliances, electronic equipment) and service industries (employment counseling, health-care services), deceptive credit activities (mortgages, credit cards, leasing, banking), fraudulent franchises and business opportunities, deceptive sales programs (travel clubs, diet clinics, timesharing), or health and safety problems with consumer goods. Simply put, if your complaint relates to the consumer, it falls within the province of the FTC.

When the agency receives a complaint from an individual consumer, a business, or Congress or when it notices a problem on its own, it begins an investigation. If it finds that a law has been violated, FTC representatives will encourage the company to formally agree to stop the deceptive or fraudulent act. If the company fails to cooperate, the FTC can sue the company and have the case heard before an administrative law judge or in federal court. It's within the power of the court not only to order the company to cease its actions but to provide some compensation to the wronged consumer.

If you want to contact the FTC to file a complaint or request more information on their rules and programs, write or call the agency's headquarters at:

The Federal Trade Commission
Pennsylvania Avenue at Sixth Street, N.W.
Washington, DC 20580
202-326-2222

The FTC also has 10 regional offices located in Atlanta, Boston, Chicago, Cleveland, Dallas, Denver, Los Angeles, New York, San Francisco, and Seattle. The agency cannot resolve an individual problem, but if the problem indicates a pattern of violations, it will investigate.

The United States Postal Inspector and the Federal Bureau of Investigation

If your complaint has anything to do with fraudulent or deceptive sales information or advertising being sent through the mail, write:

Chief United States Postal Inspector
U.S. Postal Service
475 L'Enfant Plaza West
Washington, DC 20260

The FBI may become involved if the materials sent through the mail involve a criminal activity.

The Securities and Exchange Commission
If the complaint you have relates to the sale of stocks or other securities, write or call:

Securities and Exchange Commission
450 Fifth Street, N.W.
Washington, DC 20549
202-272-7440

Each state also has a securities commission; look in the Yellow Pages under State Government.

The Food and Drug Administration (FDA)
If your problem involves foods, cosmetics, pharmaceuticals, or medical devices, write:

Food and Drug Administration
5600 Fishers Lane
Rockville, MD 20857

Also check for the FDA's closest regional office in your local phone book.

The Federal Reserve Bank and Other Federal Banking Enforcement Agencies
The banking system is complex. If your credit grievance is with a national bank, call the Comptroller of the Currency at 202-874-5000 for information about complaint procedures. If the grievance involves a state bank that is a member of the Federal Reserve, send your complaint in writing to:

Director
Division of Consumer and Community Affairs
Board of Governors of the Federal Reserve System
Twentieth Street and Constitution Avenue, N.W.
Washington, DC 20551

If it's a federally insured state bank, call the Federal Deposit Insurance Corporation at 800-424-5488; in regard to other state banks or private financial institutions, take your complaint to the banking commissioner in your state. For problems with savings-and-loan associations, call the Office of Thrift Supervision at 800-842-6929.

10

THE LEGAL SYSTEM: HOW IT WORKS

The U.S. Constitution, enacted in 1789, could hardly contain all the rules, regulations, and ordinances our society requires. In addition to the laws outlined in the Constitution, we are subject not only to ordinances, rules, and restrictions passed by city, state, and federal agencies, but also to a large body of "common law"—another name for habit and precedent. This body of law is then interpreted by the court system.

In theory, the United States has 52 court systems—the federal system as well as a system within each of the 50 states and the District of Columbia. Each system has three layers: courts of original jurisdiction (trial courts), appellate courts (appeals), and the supreme (or highest) courts.

The cases tried in our courts fall into two categories: criminal and civil. Criminal cases involve some violation of the law; the state or federal government brings a lawsuit (as the plaintiff) against the person or entity charged with the violation (the defendant). While criminal proceedings attract more attention because of the drama they often contain, most of the cases tried in the courts are civil matters.

Unlike criminal matters, civil cases are brought by private individuals or businesses who believe they have suffered a wrong at the hands of another. When one citizen harms another person or the property of another person, the law provides a system of compensation, or a way to "right the wrong." The person bringing the action is the plaintiff; the defendant is the party being sued. The government or law enforcement agencies are neutral with no stake in such matters.

In general, a person, group, company, or agency (a party) sues another party when that party (the plaintiff) believes one of three matters has occurred:

1. The other party has breached a contract.
2. The plaintiff has been intentionally harmed.
3. The plaintiff has been hurt through negligence.

Certain behavior can result in both civil and criminal actions. For example, if someone is attacked and injured, the police will arrest the perpetrator (the attacker) and charge that person with assault and battery, a criminal offense. The injured party may personally sue the perpetrator to recover an award for the damages caused.

JURISDICTION

Jurisdiction—a court's right to "adjudicate" a case—refers to whether a particular court has the power to hear and decide certain kinds of cases. Each level of court (federal, state, and municipal) has jurisdiction in only certain kinds of cases. Some courts have jurisdiction only in civil matters, others only in criminal matters. A civil matter cannot be heard in a traffic court, for example, nor can a criminal matter be heard in a probate court. A federal tax case cannot be tried in a state court.

Jurisdiction is also determined by the "subject matter" of a lawsuit. For example, bankruptcy courts, tax courts, and juvenile courts will hear cases dealing only with those particular subjects. The right to adjudicate a case is also restricted by geography. A court can only hear cases in which the parties are residents of the jurisdiction or the events surrounding the lawsuit took place within its geographical borders; e.g., a lawsuit between two Hawaiian residents cannot be brought in a New Jersey court.

A court's power to hear a particular case can also depend on the "amount in controversy," or the dollar figure that the plaintiff can realistically demand in damages. In cases involving less than a few thousand dollars, small-claims courts have jurisdiction.

Plaintiffs who initiate lawsuits bring them in courts of *original jurisdiction*, trial courts. Parties asking a court to review a lower court's decision are required to go to a court of *appellate jurisdiction*, such as a U.S. Court of Appeals or a state supreme court.

A court is said to have *personal jurisdiction* if some kind of relationship or connection exists between the party being sued and the court—usually if the party bringing the action lives in that state, the breached contract was signed there, or the wrong in question was committed there. If the focus of the lawsuit is a thing, such as a parcel of land or a bank account, the court must have "*in rem* jurisdiction," meaning that for the court to have the power over it, the *res*, or "thing," must be situated in the state.

For example, suppose two parties are disputing the ownership of a parcel of land located in Pennsylvania. A court in that state would have *in rem* jurisdiction, the authority to hear the case because the land (the *res*) is within Pennsylvania. The court would probably have the authority to decide who owns the land, but it couldn't make other determinations, such as imposing damages, unless it also had personal jurisdiction over the parties. Residency in Pennsylvania, for example, would provide personal jurisdiction.

The Federal Courts

Your chances of going before a federal court judge are slim. Most cases are heard in state courts. In 1992 only 277,119 new federal cases were filed, compared with 94 million new cases filed in state courts.

District Courts

The United States is divided into 12 districts, or circuits, and within each are federal district courts, which are trial courts. At least one of the 94 federal district courts is in every state. They handle both civil and criminal cases, but they have jurisdiction only in certain disputes:

- when a federal law is at issue
- when the United States is a party to the lawsuit

FEDERAL COURT SYSTEM

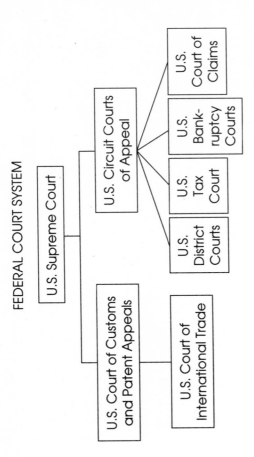

- when one state is suing another state
- when a resident of one state is suing a resident of another state and more than $50,000 is involved

Federal district court judges are appointed by the president for life, but they can be impeached by the House of Representatives and convicted by the Senate.

There are also four types of *limited jurisdiction* federal courts: the United States Bankruptcy Courts, the United States Tax Court, the United States Court of Claims (which hears suits against the federal government), and the United States Court of International Trade (which hears disputes relating to tariffs and customs).

United States Circuit Courts of Appeal

There are 12 circuit courts of appeal in the federal system, one for each circuit or district. If a district court issues a ruling against you, you can file an appeal with the appellate court in your circuit. The appellate court will not give you a new trial; it will review the trial record and briefs (written arguments) from both parties and determine if an error was made in deciding your case. If the court of appeals agrees with the decision of the district court, your last avenue of appeal is to the U.S. Supreme Court. The high court is not required

APPEALS THROUGH THE FEDERAL AND STATE COURT SYSTEMS

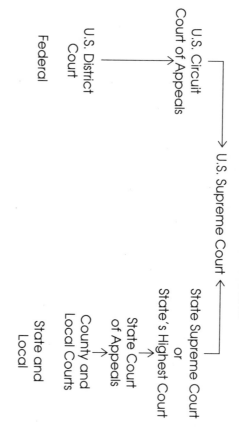

Federal

U.S. Circuit Court of Appeals → U.S. Supreme Court

U.S. District Court →

State and Local

State Supreme Court or State's Highest Court → U.S. Supreme Court

State Court of Appeals →

County and Local Courts →

to hear any case and is very selective about the cases it chooses, applying standards that are noted below.

The circuit court of appeals hears cases from the district courts, as well as the special jurisdiction courts, including the U.S. Bankruptcy Courts, the U.S. Tax Court, and the U.S. Court of Claims. The only exception is the U.S. Court of International Trade; those who appeal its decisions must do so to the U.S. Court of Customs and Patent Appeals.

The Supreme Court

The U.S. Supreme Court, the nation's highest court, has nine justices, each appointed by the president to serve for life. The Court holds session every year from the first Monday of October until late in June. It considers cases from the highest courts of each state, involving a constitutional question; the U.S. Court of Appeals; and the U.S. Court of Customs and Patent Appeals.

Only two types of cases may originate in the U.S. Supreme Court: those in which a state government is one of the parties and those involving ambassadors and foreign officials. Under certain conditions, the Supreme Court is required to hear an appeal, such as when a federal law has been declared unconstitutional by a lower court.

Most of the cases heard before the Supreme Court (112 cases were heard in the 1992–1993 term) come by way of a petition from individuals asking that the Court hear arguments for a case previously tried in a lower court. Only four "yes" votes by the justices are required to put the case on the calendar and thus to schedule oral arguments. The justices refuse to hear about 75 percent of the cases up for review.

Once the Court announces its decision to consider a case, about three months elapse before the case reaches the oral argument stage. In the meantime, the party who filed the writ has 45 days in which to submit a brief outlining its arguments; the other party, the respondent, has 30 more days to answer by brief. An interested third party with no personal stake in the case, an *amicus curiae* (friend of the court), may request permission to file a brief presenting its views. For instance, the American Civil Liberties Union (ACLU) has played a role as a friend of the court in landmark cases throughout recent U.S. legal history, including *Miranda v. Arizona* in 1966 (the advising of the right to remain silent and the right to an attorney during questioning) and *Brown v. Board of Education* in 1954 (access by blacks to equal education). Other public interest groups active in helping to make law by filing *amicus* briefs over the years include the National Association for the Advancement of Colored People (NAACP), the Anti-Defamation League, and the National Organization for Women (NOW).

After the attorneys for both parties submit their briefs and the justices have had the opportunity to review them as well as the *amicus* briefs and the record from the lower court, the attorneys representing the parties will present oral arguments. Each side is limited to 30 minutes, including the time the justices may take up in asking the attorneys questions. The arguments are taped and transcribed, and the transcript eventually takes its place in the National Archives.

The justices listen to oral arguments on the cases they have decided to hear for about two weeks; the next two weeks they spend in conference, held in strictest privacy, to consider and vote on each case. The outcome of the cases is determined by majority vote—five if the full Court is voting. One of the justices voting in the majority is assigned the task of writing the majority opinion; a minority opinion is written by one of the justices who supports that group's views. Concurring decisions may be written by any justice who has particularly strong feelings about wanting to express an opinion on the case or wishes to go on record to detail the issues that came to bear on his or her vote. Drafts are circulated and rewritten until they respectively represent the majority and minority opinion. Then the Court's decisions are read in open court.

The Supreme Court's decision is final. Only the Supreme Court can reverse itself. For example, in 1896 the Court in *Plessy v. Ferguson* ruled that school segregation—"separate but equal"—was constitutional. And 58 years later in the 1954 landmark case of *Brown v. Board of Education*, the Court held that segregation violated the Fourteenth Amendment's equal protection clause. The Court can have such diametrically opposed interpretations of the same Constitution because it has the flexibility of changing with the social and political currents of the times.

The Military Justice System

Members of the armed services who commit a violation of military laws are under the jurisdiction of the military justice system, the procedures of which are spelled out in the Uniform Code of Military Justice. For example, servicepeople who desert or otherwise disobey orders can be ordered by their commanding officers to face a court-martial, which requires them to stand trial. If the violation is also a crime under civilian law, such as murder, servicepeople will be tried in the state or federal court system as well.

State Courts

Court structures vary from state to state, but all states have general trial courts that hear divorce cases, contract disputes, personal injury cases, and criminal cases. Some courts hear only specific disputes—for example, juvenile courts, tax courts, or probate courts.

All states have a "court of last resort," usually their supreme court, to which lower court decisions can be appealed. Some states have an intermediate appellate court just below it. The U.S. Supreme Court will hear a case that comes from a state supreme court under two conditions: when a state declares a federal treaty or statute to be

STATE COURT SYSTEM

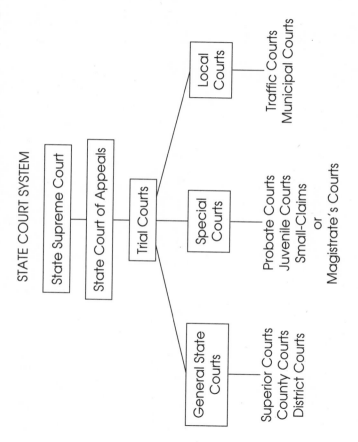

```
                State Supreme Court
                State Court of Appeals
                      Trial Courts
        ┌──────────────┼──────────────┐
  General State    Special          Local
    Courts         Courts           Courts

  Superior Courts  Probate Courts   Traffic Courts
  County Courts    Juvenile Courts  Municipal Courts
  District Courts  Small-Claims
                        or
                  Magistrate's Courts
```

unconstitutional, or when it is determined by a state supreme court that a particular state law does not contradict a federal law or the U.S. Constitution.

Municipal, town, village, small-claims, or police courts adjudicate local matters. The criminal cases handled by these courts are usually limited to traffic violations. In civil cases these courts usually hear cases involving matters that do not exceed a few thousand dollars in claims or awards.

ALTERNATIVES TO THE COURTS

Bringing a lawsuit is not cheap; filing costs, court costs, attorney's fees, court transcripts, private investigators, and even the wages lost if you miss work can mount up. Expenses can continue to grow if the litigation drags on for months or years. Moreover, open court offers little privacy, and a plaintiff's or defendant's privileged business information or personal affairs can easily become public knowledge. With growing concern over the costs and fairness of the contemporary court system, alternative means of dispute resolution are becoming more attractive. The alternatives include negotiation, arbitration, mediation, and conciliation. None of these requires retaining an attorney.

Negotiation

In this form of conflict resolution, the two disputing parties meet together and try to reach a solution that both can accept. A settlement agreement is usually drafted, releasing both parties from liability as long as they comply with the agreement.

Arbitration

The parties submit their dispute to one or more arbitrators, or neutral experts, in a private hearing or "minitrial" that can often be completed in one day. The parties agree ahead of time that the arbitrator's decision will be final and binding. This alternative dispute resolution method is used primarily in disputes involving business, insurance, or labor management.

The easiest way to provide for arbitration is to include an arbitration clause in your contracts before a conflict or dispute ever

---

Let's assume that you have entered into an agreement to pay Morris and Sons, Inc., $30,000 to gut and remodel your kitchen completely, replacing all appliances. If Morris's contract does not include one, you should insist on inserting a future-dispute arbitration clause, including language such as: "Any dispute between the parties to this agreement that involves interpretation of the terms of the agreement shall be submitted to arbitration under the rules of the American Arbitration Association, and the findings of the Arbitrator shall be binding on all parties." Should you and the contractor disagree, you will be able to avoid the high costs of litigation to resolve a contract dispute.

arises. Most business contracts are entered into with the best intentions, but somewhere down the road one of the parties may become unhappy with the contract or its performance. Anticipate this by including a clause in the contract that requires disputes to be settled through arbitration.

There are several organizations that sponsor arbitration. If you want a conflict to be arbitrated, a good starting place is the American Arbitration Association (AAA), which has its headquarters in New York City and has 35 regional offices in major cities across the country. The AAA is not for everyone, because its procedures require a minimum filing fee of $300; if your dispute involves only $500, you should probably consider another organization that conducts arbitration. Check the Yellow Pages under Arbitration for such an organization in your community.

Mediation

This form of dispute resolution is even more informal than arbitration and requires no witnesses and no opening and closing statements. The mediator is more an adviser than a judge and guides the parties through their own decision-making process, helping them to examine all sides of the conflict as well as their options. The decisions of a mediator are usually not binding.

Mediation is often used as a tool in the justice centers across the country that deal with domestic conflicts; landlord-tenant problems, and neighborhood disputes, such as barking dogs or unkempt yards. Many courts are turning to mediation as a last resort before divorce trials; the couples involved often agree to mediation as an opportunity to avoid the public proceedings, embarrassment, the high legal fees charged for a court trial, and a decision that may leave both parties unhappy.

Sometimes an attempt to resolve a dispute begins with mediation and moves into arbitration if mediation is unsuccessful. This process is called "med-arb."

Conciliation

Conciliation is the least formal alternative to a court trial. It's similar to mediation, except the mediator talks with each party separately by telephone instead of face-to-face. Conciliation is sometimes attempted as an early alternative, and if it fails, a mediation session is set up.

SMALL-CLAIMS COURT

Small-claims courts go by several other names: some locales call them magistrate's court, others, conciliation court. But all serve the same purpose: to hear cases that involve relatively small amounts of money, usually less than a few thousand dollars, and to resolve them quickly. Each state has a dollar limit on the size of the case the court will hear, based on the amount of monetary damages being demanded. For example, you may bring a case to small-claims court in California if your damages are less than $2,500. In Alaska, the limit is $5,000. You can contact your county clerk and find out the procedure for its small-claims court.

Small-claims courts handle only civil cases, never criminal matters. And the courts will award only monetary damages, never requiring a party to provide a service or perform an act.

Before you decide to bring an action in small-claims court, ask yourself a few questions:

1. How much are the damages you are requesting, and does the amount meet the statutory requirement for filing in the small-claims court instead of the state court?

2. How long ago did the violation or negligent act occur, and are you bringing the lawsuit within the statute of limitations period?

3. Was the other party at fault, or did you do something to contribute to the problem?

Suppose your swimming pool contractor walked off the job before it was completed. Your local small-claims court rules in your favor but will award only the monetary damages you have incurred: the cost of completing the pool. The judge will not demand that the contractor finish the job.

4. Are you willing to accept the decision of this court? You will not be allowed to retry the matter in a higher court once the small-claims court issues a decision.

Filing a Claim

If you have decided to make a claim in small-claims court, call the clerk to find out how to file a complaint and the amount of a filing fee, usually only about $15. The complaint you prepare doesn't have to be complex—just an explanation of what occurred, why it was the other party's fault, how you notified the person of the problem, his or her failure to correct the situation, and the amount of damages you are seeking. Be specific, noting dates and names of the individuals you contacted. When you determine how much you should be demanding, be sure to add all your expenses, including postage, telephone calls, lost wages, and transportation costs. If you had to pay for someone to serve the complaint, include that cost in your damages.

The party being served with the complaint is required to answer the complaint in one of four ways:

1. Admit the claims and attempt to settle with you, the person suing.

2. Deny the claims and go to court when scheduled.

3. Deny the claims but still attempt to settle.

The dishwasher Alex purchased from Rob's Appliance Store for $800 hasn't worked properly since the day he bought it two months ago. Rob refuses to replace it, repair it, or give Alex's money back. The amount of the reimbursement was too small to take to a state court, considering the expense Alex would have incurred in hiring a lawyer, paying court costs, and the time he would have had to take off from work. But the loss was too much simply to ignore. He took the matter to small-claims court. The judge decided in his favor and ruled that Rob must pay him $800 plus telephone and other related expenses.

4. Deny the claims and sue the other party for damages caused (counterclaim).

The summons that is served along with the complaint will tell the party being sued where to send that party's answer and will notify that party of the court date. If you and the other party decide to settle, be sure to determine who will be responsible for the court costs involved with the filing and service fee. And make certain that the lawsuit is not dismissed until all damages are paid.

If settlement is out of the question, be sure to show up for your court date. If it's difficult for you to make an appearance on the scheduled date and time, call the court and attempt to have it rescheduled. Failing to show up without notice will cause the court to dismiss the case and rule in favor of the nondefaulting party.

Preparing for the Trial

Small-claims court is informal. The litigants are not required to know and argue points of law; they merely need to argue the facts. If you need to call witnesses, ask the court to issue subpoenas when you file your claim. If a witness refuses to come willingly, the sheriff can bring that person into court. Even if the witness is your friend, a subpoena will serve as a formal excuse to show to an employer if the witness needs to miss a few hours of work. A small-claims court will sometimes accept notarized affidavits that contain the testimony of the witnesses instead of requiring them to appear in court.

Sonya filed a lawsuit in small-claims court against her landlord for failing to repair the roof in her apartment building; a heavy snow caused severe damage to her furniture. The trial date was set for January 23; however, Sonya misread it as January 28. When the landlord appeared in court, he asked the judge to dismiss the case because Sonya was not present. The judge granted the dismissal for "failure to prosecute," and Sonya automatically lost her case without being heard.

Prepare carefully for your trial. Write down the questions you plan to ask your witnesses and have all your evidence ready to present, whether documents, canceled checks that may serve as evidence of a contract, photographs, or a damaged product. Anticipate the testimony of the other party and the other witnesses, and prepare questions and rebuttal.

Most small-claims courts mail you a decision rather than "ruling from the bench." If you have been awarded a judgment, it's up to you to collect it. Make sure your opponent is aware of the award; send that person a copy of the court's decision by certified mail, return receipt requested, along with a letter demanding immediate payment. If no payment is forthcoming, contact the clerk of the small-claims court and ask the clerk what procedures are used in your county to collect judgments. This usually involves calling the other party into court with a "Petition for Notice to Show Cause," where the person is required to explain why no payment has been paid. It may be necessary to have a lien placed on your opponent's property or garnishee that person's salary or bank account.

Levying on Your Bank Accounts and Garnisheeing Your Paycheck
If a creditor has gone to court and won a judgment against you and you fail to pay within a certain number of days, the creditor can legally tap your bank accounts and your sources of income through the court issuing a "writ of execution."

There are certain things the creditor can't touch, including your automobile, the equity in your home up to a certain amount, and your personal effects. But the creditor does have the right to have a certain percentage of your income withheld from each paycheck and the ability to clean out your savings account. It is the creditor's job to find out where you have checking accounts and where you work, but the actual levying and garnisheeing is done by the clerk of the court or sheriff or marshal. Jurisdictions vary on what percentage of your assets can be taken as well as the procedure involved. Check with the clerk of the court to get the information.

WHERE TO FIND MORE INFORMATION

For more information on the federal court system, write:

Office of Legislative and Public Affairs
Public Information Center
Administrative Office of the United States Courts
1 Columbus Circle, N.E., Suite 7-110
Washington, DC 20544

For information about the U.S. Supreme Court, write:

Public Information Office
U.S. Supreme Court
1 First Street, N.E.
Washington, DC 20543

For information about your state court system, contact the office of your state's supreme court, listed under State Government in your phone book. For an overview of the state court systems throughout the country, write:

National Center for State Courts
300 Newport Avenue
Williamsburg, VA 23187

If you're interested in arbitration, or want to find out where the closest office is, call the American Arbitration Association listed in your local directory or contact its national headquarters:

American Arbitration Association
140 West 51st Street
New York, NY 10020
212-484-4000

The AAA can also provide you with information about mediation, as can your local Better Business Bureau and in some communities a neighborhood justice center. The American Bar Association also provides information about dispute resolution. Write:

American Bar Association
Standing Committee on Dispute Resolution
1800 M Street, N.W.
Washington, DC 20036

11

CHOOSING AND WORKING WITH AN ATTORNEY

Skilled, honest lawyers are professionals who can support and facilitate your negotiating the legal system. With one out of every 250 Americans being an attorney, your choices are not limited, but you need some expertise to discern under what conditions you will require the services of an attorney, how to find the appropriate one to suit your needs, and how to avoid those who are inexperienced or otherwise lack the ability to perform well on your behalf.

WHEN DO YOU NEED A LAWYER?

If you serve as your own lawyer, you are said to be acting *pro se*, or on your own behalf. Doing so can be appropriate and productive, but the pitfalls of *pro se* action are memorialized in the expression that "the lawyer who represents himself has a fool for a client." The lack of objectivity can be a drawback even if you have sufficient knowledge. On the other hand, there are many situations in which you can easily handle legal issues without professional legal assistance. Aside from conducting your own negotiations, submitting a dispute to arbitration, mediation, or small-claims court, or otherwise acting on your own behalf, you can often find appropriate guidance from nonlegal professionals. For example, if you're having a minor property dispute, a real estate broker might be able to give you some advice, or an insurance agent may assist you if you are involved in a minor accident. Certain situations, however, require a lawyer, if only for a one-time consultation. These include:

- if you are arrested and charged with a criminal action
- if you are filing for bankruptcy
- if someone is suing you
- if you are purchasing a business
- if you have sustained serious injuries in an auto accident
- if you or your spouse is filing for a separation or divorce (one that isn't uncontested)
- if you want to adopt a child
- if you want to draw up a will that involves estate planning
- if you are about to enter into a complicated contract

SELECTING AN ATTORNEY

It is extremely important to choose an attorney who is knowledgeable or expert in the matter for which you need legal assistance. The law has become so complex and specialized that it is unlikely that one attorney will have a high level of expertise in, say, estate planning, criminal law, and medical malpractice law.

Your first step is to decide what kind of specialist you need. If you have been injured on the job, for example, you want an expert in workers' compensation who has kept up with the changes in the law, knows the ins and outs of the workers' compensation board, and is familiar with the histories of the judges who will be hearing or deciding your claim. Even if your case never makes it as far as a hearing, a specialist in the field will know and be known by the insurance company attorneys who will be negotiating a settlement, and such familiarity may facilitate their work on your behalf.

Your situation will probably warrant consulting an attorney specializing in one of the following areas:

adoptions
antitrust and trade regulation
bankruptcy and debtor relief
civil rights

computer law

consumer law

corporate and banking law

creditor's rights

criminal law

divorce

employment discrimination and benefits

family law

franchise law

immigration, naturalization, customs

insurance law

intellectual property (copyrights, patents, and trademarks)

international and foreign law

labor law

legal malpractice

medical malpractice

military law

personal injury and wrongful death

probate

real property

school law

tax law

wills, trusts, estate planning

workers' compensation

Personal Characteristics

Make a list of all qualifications and traits you are looking for in your attorney. Depending on the case and your own comfort level, you might want to consider gender, age, academic training, and courtroom style. Now it's time to do some research to find the one best suited to you. Keep in mind that if your case involves your attorney making several trips to the courthouse, it might be less expensive for you if you choose an attorney located close to the court because you will often be charged for travel time.

Begin by asking your friends, family members, and co-workers for the names of lawyers they may have used and who have done a good job for them. Ask about the attorney's personality, if the person seemed to devote enough attention to their case, and if telephone calls and inquiries were responded to quickly. Did the attorney move the case along, or did constant delays or procedural errors at the attorney's office slow things down?

Another good source for referrals is other attorneys. A lawyer who handled your estate planning could probably recommend a respected colleague to handle an automobile accident case for you; however, take care to ask your own direct questions about an attorney's experience.

If friends and associates can't recommend anyone or if their referral just doesn't fit the bill, move on to your local bar association. Contact the American Bar Association, your state bar, or city or county bar associations. All provide a listing of all the attorneys licensed to practice law in your region. Many bar associations provide a referral service, which, for a small registration fee, will provide you with a list of recommended lawyers. Some bar associations provide this service free of charge.

Once you have secured the names of one or more attorneys with experience in the specialty you require, go to your library and consult *Martindale-Hubbell* for more detailed information. This is a multivolume listing of all the attorneys in the United States and their vital statistics, including their birth dates, year they were admitted to the bar, where they attended law school, and their area of expertise.

This research should tell you something about the lawyer's qualifications, but there's only one way to find out whether your personalities are compatible, and that is to talk with the attorney about your case and find out what he or she believes can be done for you. Often a phone conversation can tell you whether you want to meet with that attorney further or whether you should go on to interview someone else.

Be prepared to summarize your case or situation to save time on the phone. Develop a list of questions to ask that will help you find out more about your prospective lawyer. First, confirm that the attorney specializes in the type of case you have. Ask about fees; does the attorney have an hourly rate, a flat fee, or work on contingency or retainer basis? Is there a charge for the initial consultation?

Call several lawyers so you can make a comparison and have a choice. Set up appointments with those you like well enough to go to the next step: a consultation at their office.

When you come to the lawyer's office, be prepared. Bring all the information you have relating to the legal matter or case you wish to bring. If you have been in a car accident and are meeting with a personal injury attorney, bring the police report, the damage estimates you have obtained, any photographs you may have taken, doctor bills, the names and telephone numbers of any witnesses, and any information you may have obtained about the other driver. Answer any questions the attorney may have about you and your situation, and be ready with your own questions, which can include:

- What percentage of the attorney's practice involves this kind of law?
- How large is the firm?
- Will the attorney be handling your case personally or will a great deal of the work be handled by a younger and less experienced attorney or paralegal?
- Is the attorney willing to provide client references?
- What is the attorney's initial reaction to your case or legal situation?
- Does the attorney believe that you have legal grounds for your action?
- What is the attorney's opinion of your chance of success?
- Is the attorney experienced in litigation, or do other members of the firm go to court when this is necessary?
- Review once again the attorney's fee structure and arrangements. Is there a flat fee, or does the attorney work on contingency (percentage of settlement or award)?
- Is the attorney willing to specify the fee agreement in writing?
- Assuming that your case becomes more complex than anticipated as the proceedings unfold, how great a fee might you be facing? Get specifics, if possible, which will also indicate the attorney's experience.

In addition, ask any other questions that pertain specifically to your case.

After your meeting be sure to call one or two of the references you obtained. Find out whether the parties were pleased with the handling of their case. Was the attorney responsive to their questions and phone calls?

Once you have decided which attorney you think will do best with your case, call the state bar association and make sure the attorney is in good standing and has received no reprimands or suspensions.

THE EMPLOYMENT AGREEMENT

When you are ready to commit your case to an attorney and all the details have been worked out, the agreement between you should be put in writing. Your lawyer will probably have a standard printed contract that reflects much of the agreement you have made verbally. Be sure it specifies the type of fee structure you have agreed upon and that it spells out the details you have discussed. Most such employment agreements should include details about the following.

COSTS   One of the biggest complaints clients have about their attorneys is that they have not been properly informed about the attorney's fee. If an attorney tells you that your uncontested divorce will cost you only $400, find out what the fee includes. Does it cover court costs, photocopying, and anticipated long-distance calls? What other fees does the attorney anticipate? Be sure they are part of the agreement. Can some of the work be done by a junior person in the firm? If so, it should not be billed at the same hourly rate as your attorney receives. Both rates should be specified in the agreement.

EXPENSES   No matter what kind of fee arrangement you make, whether flat, hourly, or contingency, you'll also have to pay for the expenses the attorney incurs in handling the case. Normal expenses include:

- court costs—fees for filing a lawsuit
- court reporter and copies of transcripts—for depositions

(recorded testimony taken out of court) and trial transcripts (if the case is being appealed)

· expert witness fees—doctors and other professionals charge either an hourly or daily fee for their testimony by deposition or in court

· private investigator—if your attorney requires the services of an investigator to locate the defendant or gather evidence

· postage and courier costs

· photocopying

· long-distance telephone calls

· computerized legal research

· out-of-town air or car transportation

· hotel and meal expenses—if overnight stays are required to conduct discovery and/or depositions

Although your attorney has no way of giving you an exact prediction of the expenses your case will entail, the attorney should be able to give you a realistic estimate of what to expect. The attorney will probably use a retainer collected from you to cover immediate expenses. Ask that an accounting of expenses incurred on your case be submitted to you each month, and be sure that this monthly obligation is spelled out in the fee agreement.

Travel can be a costly item, so remember to develop guidelines for it in writing. If you are going to be billed for an attorney's travel time, specify how much per hour. If the attorney is required to fly rather than drive, is the trip by coach or first class?

You might want to handle certain matters on your own to save on expenses. Rather than paying a courier company to deliver documents across town or a member of your attorney's staff to check and copy documents at the courthouse, tell the attorney that you are available to do it. The savings add up. Certain research and "legwork" can also be handled by clients; discuss whether this is possible in your case.

HOURLY FEES Many lawyers charge by the hour, with the hourly fee determined by the amount of experience and expertise the lawyer has. Lawyers fresh out of law school with little expertise in any area of the law may charge as little as $80 per hour, while specialists in complex areas of the law may command more than $500 an hour.

Historically, charging an hourly fee has been the lawyers' bread and butter. But as both the number of lawyers and their hourly rates continue to creep higher and higher, the job of getting and keeping clients is becoming more difficult and competitive. Some clients, particularly corporate clients, are demanding alternative billing methods, including fixed fees, capped fees, more contingency cases, and competitive bidding.

The attorney's location may also help determine the fee. Practitioners in the suburbs and rural areas tend to charge less than those in big cities. And large prestigious law firms demand much heftier hourly fees than sole practitioners.

Be sure to find out how the attorney bills for a fraction of an hour, and discuss how telephone time is charged. Some lawyers will break an hour down into 1-minute or 5-minute intervals, while others won't bill for less than 15 minutes, no matter how short a telephone call or other service lasts. If your lawyer bills at $100 an hour, a 3-minute phone call can cost you less than $5 if you are billed in increments of one minute. If the smallest billable fraction is one-quarter of an hour, a 3-minute phone call can cost you $25. Billing in 6-minute intervals, which amounts to one-tenth of an hour, is standard. Be sure the smallest interval of a billable hour is spelled out in the fee agreement you make. If your lawyer wants to charge you based on a quarter of an hour, you might want to start looking for someone else to represent you.

FLAT FEES   Some lawyers run advertisements and commercials that offer an uncontested divorce for a flat fee of $75, or a first-time-defense driving-under-the-influence for $100. Such types of legal matters are usually uncomplicated, and an attorney can complete them relatively quickly; the service is often a way of making "quick money" for an attorney and serves as a way of signing on new clients for more complex cases later on. Prospective clients of such proposals must be careful to find out what other expenses they will have to pay, such as filing and court costs that may not be included in the quoted flat fee, as well as any expenses.

CONTINGENCY FEES   When a lawyer takes a case on a contingency basis, the lawyer is making a calculated gamble. The attorney will be investing time and energy in your case, possibly all the way through to a complete trial, and if the case is won, the lawyer may earn a healthy fee—usually 25 percent to 50 percent of the final settlement or judgment in the case. If the case is lost, the lawyer gets nothing. Contingency arrangements are almost always used in personal injury cases, but are prohibited for divorce and criminal cases in many states.

Regardless of whether the attorney wins or loses your case, you will have to pay the costs of court fees, filing fees, and other expenses that your case may require (see chapter 12).

Before you agree on a contingency arrangement with your attorney, be sure to ask if the expenses that you are required to pay are to be deducted before or after your attorney takes a percentage of an award or settlement. For example, suppose an attorney won a $75,000 medical malpractice settlement for her client, Randolph. Over the course of the case, the expenses climbed to $4,200 for doctor's depositions, private investigators, court costs, and other fees.

Randolph's share has been calculated two ways below. The first and standard method reflects his share when expenses are subtracted before the attorney takes a one-third share. The second way subtracts attorney's fees first, and only then deducts expenses.

A.

$75,000	recovery in case
− 4,200	expenses
$70,800	balance
− 23,600	attorney's ⅓ share
$47,200	plaintiff's share

B.

$75,000	recovery in case
− 25,000	attorney's ⅓ share
$50,000	
− 4,200	expenses
$45,800	plaintiff's share

Remember: *Laws differ from state to state. Check the relevant laws in your area and/or consult an attorney before pursuing legal action.*

Connie filed for divorce against Martin, and the case required that each of them seek legal representation. Martin was not wealthy, but he had too many assets to qualify for assistance from the local Legal Aid Society. He called a divorce attorney and asked if the attorney could take the case on a contingency basis rather than an hourly rate. The attorney refused; lawyers are prohibited from taking on divorce cases on contingency because, unlike personal injury or medical malpractice cases, none of the parties is seeking damages. The services provided in a divorce case often involve child custody and child support issues, awards from which attorneys' fees cannot be legally deducted.

Notice how Randolph's share will be $1,400 less if his attorney insists upon taking out one-third before expenses.

Insist that you want the case's expenses taken out of the recovery before the attorney's share is calculated. As with any fee arrangement, be sure you specify the method to be used in writing. If your attorney refuses, decide whether you want to look for another attorney or whether this one is worth the extra fee.

Retainers

There are actually three different kinds of retainers. Be certain that the type of retainer is spelled out very clearly ahead of time and written into the fee agreement.

When an attorney agrees to represent you in a particular case or matter, the attorney may ask for a retainer. Suppose the attorney will be incorporating your company for a *flat fee* of $500. You will probably be asked to pay the attorney a retainer to cover court costs as well as expenses, such as photocopying and mailing. Be sure the amount of the retainer is written into the fee agreement and that it specifies whether the retainer will be applied to the attorney's hourly fee or to expenses.

The two other forms of retainers are used by companies or individuals who need legal services frequently. They pay a *monthly* or *annual retainer* to their attorney or law firm to ensure that when they need advice or consultation, the attorney will be available. In "pure" retainer situations, the client has to pay for the legal services provided, in addition to the retainer. In other referral arrangements, the retainer covers basic legal services, such as reviewing contracts, simple litigation, and advice given on the telephone. The attorney will charge for legal services over and above the retainer only if the problem requires more than general advice, such as negotiating a complex contract or preparing for a lengthy trial.

Billing

Be sure that your fee agreement with the attorney stipulates monthly statements. And if you and the attorney have worked out an easy payment plan allowing you to stretch your payments over time, make this perfectly clear in the written agreement.

The agreement should also spell out what information is to appear on your bill. For each service provided, the bill should state

Dean belonged to a prepaid legal service plan at work and paid an annual "retainer" of a few hundred dollars. After being a member of the plan for two years and never having needed its services, he was sued personally by a former business partner for breach of contract. The legal services he required involved extended litigation, and Dean expected his legal plan to cover it. Unfortunately, he didn't understand that such prepaid plans generally pay only for basic services such as wills or advice given by telephone or letter. The litigation Dean requires may be provided at a discount through the plan, but he should make certain that the lawyer who handles the matter has the expertise to do so. The services provided by retainer arrangements should be understood in detail before any agreement for them is signed.

the date of service, the service performed, the individual who did the work, and the length of time it took. The bill should also reflect all expenses, the amount, and the purpose.

Requiring a monthly bill accomplishes several things. Obviously, it lets you know how much you owe your attorney, but it also gives you a report of what the attorney has done on your case during this period. Whenever you meet with the attorney or speak together on the phone, keep track of how much time the attorney spent with you, and compare your notes against the bill you receive. Some attorneys "pad" their bills, and the practice can be difficult to determine, especially in activities that don't require your involvement, such as research or reviewing documents. But a detailed billing makes an attorney more accountable to the client, and makes it less likely that unearned billable hours will be added.

After your attorney has had a chance to discuss your case with you, ask for a general idea of how the attorney thinks the case will progress. Does it have a good chance of being settled? If it goes to trial, how long might this take, and how long a trial is envisioned? The practice of law and the workings of the courts are hardly an exact science, but the attorney should be able to give you a sense of what lies ahead. Such an estimate should be included in the employment agreement and referred to as the case progresses.

OTHER OBLIGATIONS AND RESPONSIBILITIES YOU AND THE ATTORNEY HAVE TO EACH OTHER

The attorney-client relationship is a two-way street; each of you has certain obligations to the other. The employment agreement should spell those out very clearly.

The attorney's obligations to you should include:

- submitting a monthly, itemized billing that lists fees and expenses
- providing you with copies of any documents relating to your case (be prepared to pay for the photocopying)

- following as closely as possible to the schedule estimated in the employment agreement as well as staying within the guidelines for the anticipated fees and expenses
- providing you with periodic telephone or written updates
- responding to your telephone inquiries promptly
- advising you and consulting with you about any settlement offers, regardless of the attorney's opinion about whether you should accept them
- getting your permission if it is necessary to turn over some portion of your case to an associate or another attorney
- ensuring total confidentiality—this responsibility extends to the attorney's staff, including paralegals, investigators, and any employee of the firm

You, the client, have the following obligations:

- being available to your attorney to answer questions or provide information
- being entirely honest with the attorney, even if your answers are not what you think the attorney wants to hear

Edwina called her divorce attorney, David, and told him to discontinue the property settlement negotiations temporarily, because in a few days there would be less property to quibble over. She told him she had hired an arsonist to "relieve" her husband of the family residence as well as the Porsche in the garage. She revealed all this to David under the misconception that the attorney-client privilege would prohibit him from sharing the information with the police. Edwina was wrong because David is required by law to report the intent to commit a crime that can be prevented. In contrast, had Edwina admitted to burning down a house in the past, the attorney-client privilege would have protected her.

- clearly spelling out, in advance, whether you wish to become involved in doing some of the legwork on your own case
- looking over the attorney's bill as soon as you receive it and, if everything seems to be in order, paying it promptly
- calling your attorney immediately with any new occurrences or information that will affect your case
- being prepared when consulting with the attorney (Shuffling through paperwork only wastes time, and if you are being billed by the hour, you will be charged for this wasted time at the same rate as if it were productive.)

Anticipating Disputes

The best of relationships sometimes run into problems, and attorney-client relationships are no exception. Expect these problems and plan for them.

In your employment contract the parties should agree that if a dispute arises, both will work toward an amicable resolution. If this is impossible, specify that arbitration, mediation, or another alternate dispute resolution method will be used to settle your differences rather than the courtroom. Be sure to specify that your attorney should not bill you for any time spent in resolving the problem.

If You Have a Problem with Your Attorney

Routine problems with attorneys can run the gamut from a simple billing error to a costly mistake, such as missing a filing deadline.

The first step in resolving any conflict is to confront it. Call the attorney and explain the problem. Sometimes it involves only a misunderstanding that a simple conversation can clear up; sometimes it involves much more.

Firing Your Attorney

Perhaps the problem you are experiencing with your attorney is not resolvable. If you believe this is so, it may be time to end your attorney-client relationship and cut your losses. If your legal matter does not involve litigation or if your case is still in its early stages, call the attorney on the phone and explain why you are unhappy with the services being supplied and that you intend to retain another attorney. Document the conversation with a letter. Ask that the attorney send you your file, which includes all the work done on the case so far.

What follows is a hypothetical situation involving firing an attorney.

THE PROBLEM

Sanford, a well-known personality in the social circles of a small New York suburb, confided in his divorce attorney, Bill, that he was an alcoholic and that this was one of the major problems in his marriage. Two weeks later, Bill told his golfing buddies about his client's drinking problem. Sanford found out about Bill's indiscretion and wants to act immediately. Sanford paid Bill a large retainer up front as an advance against fees and expenses.

WHAT TO DO

1. Before he fires Bill, Sanford has to be sure that another attorney can step in and do as good a job. He has to be sure that selecting a new lawyer won't jeopardize his divorce case. Once he makes that determination, he can go on to step 2.

2. Sanford determines that any good divorce attorney can handle his case, so he writes Bill a letter firing him. He includes an explanation for his dismissal and informs him that since Bill has violated the canon of professional ethics by disclosing confidential information, he will be reporting him to the state bar association.

3. Sanford should write a letter to the state bar association explaining how Bill violated the code of ethics. The bar association will usually allow the attorney to respond, and it may take some action, including a reprimand, suspension, or disbarment, depending upon the severity of the infraction.

4. Sanford wants a refund on the retainer paid up front. He is willing to allow Bill to keep the money he spent on expenses, but he is not willing to pay his hourly fee. Violating the attorney-client privilege is one of the "good cause" grounds for dismissing an attorney, and in many states this is sufficient reason for refusing to pay attorneys' fees. If he is not successful in getting his retainer back, either partially or in full, he should go on to step 5.

5. Sanford should check with the state or local bar association for an arbitration program that helps resolve fee disputes. If Bill refuses to participate or it does not solve Sanford's problem, he should go on to step 6.

6. Sanford may have to go to court if all else fails. If the amount in dispute is low enough, he can probably do it himself in small-claims court. If it exceeds the dollar limit in the small-claims court in his jurisdiction, he may have to hire an attorney and sue Bill in a higher court.

If your case has already gone to trial, you should think long and hard about whether you want to change attorneys at this point. But if the lawyer is doing a poor job for you and you don't want the attorney to proceed any further with your case, you may have to ask the court's permission to dismiss that attorney and hope that you are allowed enough of a postponement in which to responsibly retain another attorney.

If your attorney has been working on a contingency basis and has not orchestrated a settlement for you, you owe the attorney nothing. If your agreement is based on an hourly fee, you must pay for the work that the attorney has put in on the case. If the attorney has been working on a flat fee, you may be required to pay a portion of this, depending on how much work the attorney had done when you terminated the attorney's services.

STANDARDS OF PROFESSIONAL BEHAVIOR FOR ATTORNEYS

Every state has its own Code of Professional Responsibility, which details the rules that govern a lawyer's conduct. They are uniform from state to state because they are based on a code developed by the American Bar Association. Depending on the severity of the attorney's violation, they specify the conditions under which attorneys can be reprimanded either publicly or privately, suspended, or disbarred from the practice of law.

Reprimands

The most frequently administered punishment the Code provides is a private reprimand; a minor or unintentional infraction of the code of ethics could cause an attorney to receive a private admonition without its being revealed to others. For more serious infractions, reprimands are made public in the state's legal publication. Infractions that may result in a public reprimand include:

- an attorney's abrupt withdrawing from a case without sufficient notice to the client
- failing or refusing to return a fee that has been paid in advance but was never earned after withdrawing from a case
- threatening to bring criminal charges against an individual in order to gain an advantage in a civil action the attorney is handling—for example, threatening to file criminal adultery charges against a client's wife if she fails to sign a divorce agreement
- behaving in an undignified or disruptive manner in court
- investing in a company that is opposing the attorney's client in litigation
- helping a nonlawyer practice law

Reprimands are embarrassing, but they do not interfere with an attorney's ability to practice law in the state.

Suspensions, Disbarments, and Voluntary Surrender of License

When a violation is found to be more serious, an attorney's license may be revoked, either for a set period of time (suspension) or indefinitely (disbarment).

Violations that may result in disbarment include:

- being convicted of a felony or misdemeanor involving moral turpitude (which, more than being simply illegal, involves malicious behavior or dishonesty)
- withholding evidence that the attorney is obligated to reveal
- advising a witness to go into hiding to avoid giving testimony
- accepting a case that the attorney knows he or she is not competent to handle without associating with another attorney
- allowing personal funds to be commingled with those of a client

A disbarred attorney may ask to be reinstated three to five years after being disbarred; a panel investigates and acts on the request, either granting or denying the reinstatement.

388 · CHOOSING AND WORKING WITH AN ATTORNEY

How to File a Complaint

In 1992 over 102,000 complaints were filed against lawyers in the United States, but fewer than 3 percent were determined to have any merit. What clients believe is irresponsible representation does not always violate the state's Code of Professional Responsibility for attorneys. Before you file a complaint with your state grievance agency, be aware of what standards the code provides. A law library, either at a county courthouse or at a law school, will have a copy of your state's "Code of Professional Responsibility." If no such libraries are close to you, call the state bar office and ask them to send you a copy of the code. If you believe that your attorney has violated the code, contact the state or local bar association for the forms and the information necessary to file a complaint.

Fill out the forms thoroughly, giving a detailed explanation of the events and occurrences that have prompted your complaint. Make copies of all letters, invoices, receipts, or paperwork that support your contentions and submit them with the complaint.

The bar association's grievance staff will review your complaint, and if it alleges that the lawyer's code of ethics has been violated, your complaint will be investigated. This means that the accused attorney will be contacted and asked to make a response to the charge. The agency will sometimes investigate further, and if it decides that the complaint has merit, it will conduct a hearing.

If a hearing is held, you will be asked to testify before a panel of three people, which will include at least two attorneys. Prepare as if you were a witness in a trial: Develop and present your complaint so that it is clear and concise. Using documentation, explain why you retained the attorney, what the attorney's obligations were, the specific grievance you are filing, and what ethical code you believe is being violated.

How the hearing is conducted varies from state to state. Some allow the testimony of witnesses, others do not. Some permit complaints to question the lawyer they are accusing, others do not. Be sure you understand how the hearing will be conducted and what your rights are when you prepare for it.

Once the hearing has been completed, the panel will make a

determination about whether your attorney violated the state code. If the panel finds that a violation has taken place, it will decide whether the attorney should be reprimanded, suspended, or disbarred. Be aware that if the state bar association takes action against the attorney, all that has been done is to prevent someone else from suffering the same incompetency or illegality. The bar association's action does not compensate you for your damages, though you have other avenues for relief through the courts.

Settling Fee Disputes

Since money matters are often the cause of attorney-client problems, a majority of the states have developed fee arbitration programs to settle conflicts quickly and cheaply. These programs provide a method of resolving a fee dispute by an impartial panel of arbitrators, with the parties deciding before the hearing whether they want the decision to be binding or merely to serve as a guide through future negotiations.

If you have a fee dispute with your attorney, contact the state bar association to find out how fee arbitration works and how to initiate it.

If Your Attorney Steals from You: The Client Security Trust Fund

Lawyers are officers of the court and, of course, are not allowed to steal money from clients. But the phenomenon does occur, and to help remedy such serious injury, lawyers in many states contribute to a special fund that compensates clients who have been swindled by other members of their profession. These client security trust funds exist in most states.

If you believe that your lawyer has stolen from you, perhaps by pocketing an advance you gave the attorney that will not be refunded, contact your state's client security trust fund office, and ask for the necessary forms and information needed to file a complaint.

Even if the panel of lawyers that oversees the fund determines that you have been victimized by your attorney, you will most likely not receive the full amount stolen. To recover the rest, you may have to sue your lawyer.

Suing for Legal Malpractice

If your attorney has been incompetent or careless enough to cause you some kind of loss, either personal or financial, you may have grounds for taking the attorney to court for malpractice.

Sometimes, lawyers are sued because they have intentionally caused their harm, for example, by leaving town with a client's settlement check. But malpractice cases usually arise because an attorney either breached the attorney-client contract or because of negligence in handling a client's legal matters.

When an attorney is retained by a client, the attorney is expected to meet a certain standard of performance, that of a "reasonable lawyer," as well as meeting certain standards of competency, knowledge, and skill.

Suppose the attorney is required to write a brief supporting the pivotal premise of your case. The attorney assigns a first-year law student to the research, and the student is so inexperienced that a major case that conclusively supports your claim is not cited. You can sue your attorney for malpractice because the attorney was negligent. It is the attorney's duty to prepare for your case diligently, and this means either entrusting the research to a competent professional or doing it personally. Failing to meet filing deadlines or not showing up for court appearances or hearings also constitutes negligence and is a clear breach of the attorney-client relationship.

In order to be successful in bringing a lawsuit against your lawyer, you will be required to prove four elements:

1. that a client-attorney relationship existed (Fee contracts or paperwork performed by the attorney is generally valid evidence of the relationship.)

2. that the attorney violated a duty to you as your attorney

3. that you suffered injuries because of the attorney's violation of duty

4. that your injuries caused you monetary loss

If you can prove all four points, you may be entitled to compensation. This can include remedying any monetary losses you suffered, such as legal expenses for another attorney, or the judgment you may have been awarded had your lawyer not missed a filing deadline or had represented you more competently. "Foreseeable damages," may also be awarded, including, for example, an increase in car insurance you have suffered because your attorney did a poor job for you in a vehicle-related lawsuit. If your attorney is found to have committed intentional violations, you may be entitled to damages three times the amount you actually suffered. And if the lawyer disappeared with your money, you may be able to collect "extraordinary damages."

IF YOU CAN'T AFFORD AN ATTORNEY

If you have decided that you need the services of a lawyer but cannot afford to pay one, a number of alternatives are available.

If your income and assets do not exceed a certain amount and if you need legal representation for a divorce, an eviction, or another civil matter, your local legal aid society may be willing to represent you without fee. And many law firms, including top-notch ones, volunteer their services to the community, doing *pro bono* (for the public good) work. Call your local bar association to find out what free or reduced legal services are available in your community.

Even if the attorney's behavior is clearly negligent, remember that a trial can be a long, expensive process and a drain on your time and emotions. If there is a chance that you can get adequate compensation through negotiation, mediation, or arbitration, pursue these alternatives. If not, and if you are committed to seeing the matter through, find a lawyer who specializes in suing other lawyers. Several years ago it was very difficult to find an attorney who would consent to challenge colleagues in a lawsuit, but attitudes are changing. Attorneys who specialize in legal malpractice suits are no longer considered pariahs in their profession.

If you believe that your constitutional rights have been violated, contact a local chapter of the American Civil Liberties Union (ACLU), the National Association for the Advancement of Colored People (NAACP), or the National Organization for Women (NOW).

If you are facing criminal charges, you may qualify for a court-appointed lawyer, a public defender. Find out the requirements in your state; if you qualify, the court will appoint one at your request during your first appearance before the judge.

Community legal clinics in many locales sometimes provide basic legal services well below the standard rate. But compare prices first, and be sure to know what you are getting for your money. Is the quality of representation equal to that of a higher-priced advocate? Will you be getting the services of an actual attorney, or will your matter be turned over to a paralegal? Find out precisely what representation you will be getting.

Some unions provide free or low-cost legal advice for their members.

12

THE TRIAL

In 1992 over 94 million new lawsuits were filed in the nation's state and federal courts. This figure does not include the millions of court cases previously filed and still pending.

Even if you are not a party to one of these cases, you might be among the number of witnesses who are called to testify through deposition or in court. And if you are registered to vote or own a car or property, your name is probably on a list of potential jurors.

THE PREAMBLE TO A TRIAL

The following hypothetical scenario is intended to provide a background for what occurs before a trial.

Joe, a promising 35-year-old sales executive for a Fortune 500 company, is out jogging one evening just before dusk. As he begins to cross the street, a car swings around the corner, hitting him with great force and sending him through the air.

The car slows down, but when the driver sees Joe's body lying motionless, he panics and speeds off. Several neighbors see the accident and jot down a description of the car and its license number. One of the neighbors who sees the accident runs into her home to call 911 and request an ambulance and a police car. Joe is taken to the hospital.

Joe stays in the hospital for seven days, being treated for a concussion, a broken leg, and a sprained back. Three weeks after the accident, he goes back to work part time, but he has not recovered enough to work a regular schedule. Joe is under the care of several doctors, and it's uncertain when he will be able to walk normally.

Vincent, the driver, can be tried in criminal court for his reckless driving as well as for leaving the scene of the accident. But Joe also has the right to sue Vincent personally in a civil action in order to be compensated for the injuries he received as a result of Vincent's negligent driving.

As soon as he is able, Joe should find a lawyer who specializes in personal injury cases. To his first appointment with the attorney, Joe should bring all his medical records, the accident report, a list of witnesses, any correspondence that has taken place between him and the driver or the driver's insurance company, or anything else relating to the accident.

Joe's lawyer will examine all the facts and the documentation of his injuries, and determine whether the driver's actions constituted negligence. But before spending more time on Joe's case, the lawyer must first consider certain important questions.

The Statute of Limitations

First, the attorney will determine whether the action is barred by the statute of limitations. Is there still time to file a lawsuit, or has too much time elapsed since the injury occurred? In personal injury cases, the statute of limitations clock starts ticking as soon as any substantial injury has occurred. Joe, a resident of California, has two years from the date of the accident to file a lawsuit. The statute of limitations varies from state to state: Some may block a personal injury lawsuit if more than two years has elapsed since the injury; others are more lenient and allow a limit of six years.

The law makes some allowances for children. Minor children are

Remember: *Laws differ from state to state. Check the relevant laws in your area and/or consult an attorney before pursuing legal action.*

not required to file personal injury actions within these limits; the statute does not start to run until the injured child is no longer a minor. Most states consider an 18-year-old to be an adult.

In certain cases the statute of limitations begins to run only when the injury is discovered. For example, if a doctor leaves a sponge inside a patient during surgery and it goes undetected for months, the statute of limitations starts to run only when the mistake is discovered. If the lawsuit is being brought for wrongful death, the time starts running when the individual dies. In contract cases the statute of limitations (often six years) is measured from the time the breach of contract occurs.

If the statute of limitations has elapsed in Joe's case, he may not bring suit no matter how severe his injuries may be or how excellent a case he may have. If the attorney was at fault for having missed a deadline and thus failed to file the case before the statute of limitations expired, Joe might have grounds to sue the attorney for legal malpractice.

Is There a Legitimate Cause of Action?

In Joe's case, there is still ample time to bring an action. It is important that Joe and his attorney evaluate the case thoroughly before filing a lawsuit. If the case is groundless, Joe will have wasted his time and money in court costs. Moreover, the defendant could sue both Joe and his attorney for malicious prosecution. Joe's attorney will have to show that Vincent, the driver, failed to meet his obligation to use proper care in operating his car because he was driving too fast. The attorney must also prove that Vincent's negligence caused the injuries. Since Joe's attorney believes that he has a good case and can show clear-cut negligence on the part of Vincent, client and attorney decide to proceed with the lawsuit and enter into a fee agreement (see chapter 11).

Jurisdiction and Venue

It's clear that Joe's negligence case falls within the jurisdiction of a state court, which is therefore where it will be filed. Next, the venue (the proper county) will have to be determined. In a personal injury action, the proper venue will probably be either in the county where the defendant resides or where the accident occurred; the venue is spelled out in each state's laws.

If Vincent, the driver of the car, were a well-known and popular individual in town and Joe believed that getting a fair trial with unbiased jurors would be difficult, or if the location of the trial was inconvenient to the parties and several witnesses, Joe's attorney could ask the court for a change in venue. If the reasons were legitimate, the court would probably grant the request.

Jury Trial or "Bench" Trial?

Joe will have to choose whether he wants a judge or a jury to decide the guilt or innocence of the driver and how much compensation will be awarded.

The following factors should be considered in making this choice:

- Is expense an important consideration? Jury trials cost more and last longer than "bench" trials. Even if the attorney's fee is based on how much is awarded to you if you win (a contingency fee), you will still be required to pay the costs of a trial.

- Are you in a hurry to resolve your case? Jury trials take longer than bench trials to reach a court calendar; so if expediency is important to you, you might want your case decided in a bench trial, where the judge not only presides over the proceedings but also takes the role of the jury.

In a personal injury case like Joe's, a panel of jurors would probably be more sympathetic than a judge. The jurors would tend to empathize and identify more than a judge might with Joe's discomfort and the disruption to his life. Joe's lawyer would also have the advantage of choosing the jurors through the *voir dire* (pronounced *vwor der*) process (a preliminary examination to determine the competency of a juror or witness), asking them questions about their experiences and biases and exercising certain options to reject those the attorney believes will be prejudiced against Joe or his claim.

The pros and cons in each case should be discussed carefully before deciding to proceed. Plaintiffs are offered a certain period of time (usually 10 days) after filing the last pleading in which to demand a jury trial.

What Damages Can You Ask For and Expect?

Awarding damages is the legal system's way of compensating an injured party for any harm suffered as the result of another's actions. The awarding of damages is an attempt at least to restore the injured party as close as possible to the position and condition he or she was in before the injury took place.

Joe can demand that the other driver (actually the driver's insurance company) pay for his medical expenses (including doctor and hospital bills, prescriptions, and therapy), anticipated medical expenses, lost wages, and loss of future earning capacity. The fact that Joe was a potentially successful executive at the time of the accident will be figured into the equation. In some circumstances the court will award attorneys' fees as well as court costs.

The physical and emotional pain and suffering Joe has experienced is also compensable. There is no set magic formula for juries to use to determine the value of a plaintiff's pain and suffering, disfigurement, or the loss of a limb. The courts have to use their own judgment, evaluating each case. For example, a jury would most likely award a larger verdict to a surgeon or a piano player who has lost a finger than to a stockbroker.

Suppose the court awards Joe $40,000. The defendant in Joe's case carried sufficient liability insurance to cover this amount, so Joe should have little trouble in collecting his judgment. If Vincent has no insurance but does have personal assets, Joe can institute legal action that will freeze Vincent's checking accounts, wages, and property to satisfy the judgment. If Vincent has no assets that can be garnisheed or levied upon (perhaps he has hidden them), he is considered to be "judgment proof," and Joe will very likely never receive much of the court's award.

How a Lawsuit Begins: Filing the Complaint

Joe's lawsuit begins when his attorney files a "complaint" with the proper court. It will name Vincent as the defendant, state the facts of the case, the charges of negligence, the injuries Joe incurred, and the damages to which he believes he is entitled.

The court will issue a summons along with a copy of the complaint and have it personally served on Vincent, usually by a sheriff or an officer of the court.

Responding to the Complaint: The Answer

The defendant usually has 20 to 30 days to respond to the lawsuit with an "answer." Although Vincent is the defendant in this case, attorneys for his car insurance company will be defending the action. It is the insurance company that will ultimately be paying any judgment or settlement that Joe's attorney can secure.

The defendant has three options in responding to the complaint: He may deny the allegations, admit them but plead that there is some excusable reason for the accident (for example, that his brakes failed), or admit some allegations and deny others. He will most likely deny Joe's charges and claim that he was not traveling too fast but was unable to stop because Joe ran directly into his path.

Vincent could also file a counterclaim in his answer, in which he sues Joe and charges, for example, that he, Vincent, suffered neck injuries because Joe negligently ran into the path of his car.

Regardless of how Vincent responds, if he fails to file an answer within the specified time (usually a grace period is allowed), he automatically defaults (loses) without a chance to defend himself in court.

Motions

Vincent also has the right to respond by presenting motions, which are requests that the lawsuit be dismissed or altered in some way. When the complaint and answer have been filed, Joe may file a motion for "judgment on the pleadings" (immediate judgment) if the defendant's answer neither denies the allegations nor provides any positive defense that would refute Joe's complaint.

Pretrial Discovery

The time between filing the complaint and actually going to trial is spent gathering evidence. Joe's attorney will probably visit the location where the accident occurred and have him demonstrate how it took place. The attorney will take pictures of the intersection from the angle of the car and a photograph of where Joe landed after the car threw him; the attorney will also measure how far Joe was from the curb when he was hit and how far the car propelled him.

The attorney will try to interview anyone who was a witness to the accident as well as anyone who can testify about how the accident changed Joe's life.

Joe and his attorney will also attempt to gather information about Vincent. First, Joe's attorney will send Vincent's counsel a set of written "interrogatories," basic questions about Vincent, the type of insurance he carries, and what kind of driving record he has.

Vincent's lawyers will send "interrogatories" to Joe, through his lawyer, asking him similar questions and requesting information about his medical history, how the "alleged" incident occurred, and whether he has filed other lawsuits before. Both parties will have a specified amount of time to answer the questions and return the answers by mail.

DEPOSITIONS   Depositions are another form of "discovery." Vincent's attorney will request that Joe appear on a specified date and time, usually at his attorney's office, to be questioned about the accident and his injuries. The questioning will be done under oath, with a court reporter recording the testimony on a stenograph machine using a form of shorthand. Joe's attorney will be permitted to cross-examine Joe. Vincent's lawyers may also want to depose the doctors who have treated Joe both before and after the accident if Vincent is attempting to prove that the injuries were not all accident-related. Joe's attorney has the same right to "depose" the defendant under the same set of circumstances.

Depositions are used to collect information and facts about the case, to impeach (discredit) the testimony of a witness, and to let both sides know how solid (or weak) a case the other has. Depositions also save time, because the testimony given during the deposition can be introduced later during the trial without the witness having to reappear. (It is easier to take a doctor's deposition at a convenient time and place, often in the doctor's office, than to subpoena the doctor to the court during the trial.) And since "expert" witnesses usually charge by the hour, it is usually less expensive for the parties to pay a doctor for a deposition that will take an hour or two instead of possibly having to pay the doctor for a full day—or more—in court.

Examining the Witness

Of the two kinds of witnesses, *expert witnesses* are those who are experienced and knowledgeable in a particular technical area, and they are paid well to come into court or testify during a deposition to explain the area of their expertise, to supply supporting background information, or to refute evidence to the jury. Most expert witnesses are retained not only for their knowledge but also for their ability to communicate to a judge or jury.

Lay witnesses are those who are called to testify in court or during a deposition if they have witnessed an incident, have personal knowledge of certain facts, or were involved in a transaction that became the subject of a lawsuit.

Being a lay witness requires no special skills or technical knowhow, but it does require preparation and knowledge of how the courtroom operates.

Not everyone is eligible to serve as a witness. The court may deem certain people incompetent to provide credible information. For example, if a six-year-old boy witnessed the accident, some states would prohibit his testimony because of his age. Witnesses may also be disqualified because they have low mental acuity, failing eyesight, or poor hearing.

Let's assume that you are one of Joe's neighbors and saw the accident from start to finish. You told the police at the scene that Vincent was clearly at fault, driving recklessly on a residential street and negligently running down Joe, whom you described as a cautious jogger. Your name will be noted on the accident report.

Joe's lawyer will contact you to get more details of the accident. The lawyer will also evaluate how credible you will be in the eyes of a judge or jury. Although the lawyer could force you to testify at the trial as a "hostile witness" by issuing you a subpoena, the attorney would probably prefer to convince you to testify freely, thus having you appear as a "friendly witness" for the plaintiff.

If it is possible that you will not be available to testify at the trial, Joe's attorney may want to take your *deposition*—your recorded testimony taken out of court. Because your testimony will be critical to the strength of Joe's case, Vincent's attorney will most likely request your deposition in order to determine how good a witness you will be and what steps the attorney must take to refute your testimony and/or to destroy your credibility. Vincent's attorney may also send you *interrogatories* (questions in written form), but you are not required to respond. Only the parties to a case must answer interrogatories.

Let's assume that Vincent's attorney subpoenaed you for a deposition, requesting your presence at the office of Joe's attorney on a particular date and time. If you cannot be present on the date the attorneys have selected, be sure to call them and suggest a date and time that is convenient for everyone. If you ignore the notice to appear for a deposition, Vincent's attorney can file a motion with the court compelling you to comply. If you ignore a court order for your appearance, you can be held in contempt of court and face a jail sentence until you comply.

Other Information

In addition to interrogatories and depositions, the parties may also request that the other party provide them with documents, photographs, maps, or other information for inspection related to the case.

Motion for Summary Judgment

After discovery is completed, either party may bring a motion for summary judgment, asking that the judge decide in their favor before a trial is conducted. Such a motion is granted when the depositions, interrogatories, and all of the other evidence fail to show that some facts are in dispute. If, for example, Vincent's attorney has been unable to provide any evidence illustrating that Vincent was not negligent, the judge might grant Joe's motion for summary judgment and rule in his favor.

Remember: When you testify at a deposition, you will be under oath, and the penalties for perjury (lying) are just as severe during a deposition as they would be during the trial.

Keep in mind that you may very well be called to appear in court to testify at a later time, and Vincent's attorney will refer to your deposition transcript to point out any discrepancies between a statement you make during the deposition and your later testimony during the trial.

For example, Trent, a witness to an auto accident, received a subpoena to testify at a deposition. He decided to ignore it. Trent can be found in contempt of court, which could result in a fine and/or a jail sentence. The testimony provided in depositions can be read in court just as if the witness were on the stand testifying. Failing to appear or to tell the truth during a deposition is equivalent to doing the same in court before a judge.

The Pretrial Conference

Before the trial, the judge may request a conference with the attorneys for both parties in order to consider ways to consolidate the issues and move the actual trial along more quickly. The judge will encourage the parties to reach a settlement at this conference and to forgo an expensive and time-consuming trial. Settlement can take place at any time. The defendant's insurance company in a personal injury case will have to decide whether it would be cheaper for them in the long run to settle the matter in advance or to pay their attorneys to defend it in court.

Certain unwritten guidelines are often followed in arriving at reasonable settlement agreements, depending on the type of case involved. For example, in personal injury claims that don't involve catastrophic injuries, lawyers often attempt to settle a case by demanding three times the amount of the *special damages* the plaintiff incurred. Special damages include medical expenses and lost wages. So, if Joe's medical expenses amounted to only $2,000, and he lost about $600 in wages because of work he missed, $7,800 would be a reasonable starting place to negotiate a settlement. However, Joe's case is more complicated and involves future earnings as well.

THE PROCEDURE OF A TRIAL

Judges, either elected or appointed, have complete control over their courtrooms, and any disrespect shown to them by any parties, including attorneys, can elicit a contempt citation, which can mean that the party cited pays a fine and/or serves a jail sentence. The judge's job is to rule on points of law and procedure before, during, and after the trial. During a bench trial, the judge also acts as the jury and renders a final verdict.

The *bailiff*, or court officer, is responsible for the jury, taking its members back and forth from the jury room to the courtroom and carrying communications between them and the judge. It's also the bailiff's job to call each witness to the stand and swear them in.

The *court clerk* handles much of the trial's paperwork before, during, and after the proceedings. The clerk also accepts physical evidence when it is formally submitted, tags it, and is responsible for its safe handling.

The entire proceedings of the trial are recorded by a *court reporter* and later transcribed into transcript form if the attorneys or judge requests it.

The Jury

There are two kinds of juries, petit and grand. *Grand juries* are used only in criminal trials and have no power to decide guilt or innocence. The grand jury's only job is to decide if the government's attorney has presented sufficient evidence to indict an individual and bring him or her to trial. *Petit juries* are called to hear and decide the outcome of both civil and criminal cases. The jury referred to in the hypothetical *Joe v. Vincent* case would be a petit jury.

The required number of members on a jury varies from jurisdiction to jurisdiction. In the past the standard jury was composed of 12 members, but today many courts allow 6-member juries. Often, some extra jurors are selected to serve as alternates in case a regular juror becomes ill or otherwise cannot serve.

The jury is selected from a pool of eligible citizens whose names are selected randomly from voter or vehicle registration, tax assessments, or other comprehensive lists within a county or district. Being called for jury duty does not necessarily mean that a person will be asked to serve on a jury.

When a judge is ready to preside over a trial, prospective jurors are usually brought into the courtroom in groups, or panels, of 12 to go through the process of *voir dire* (literally, "to speak the truth"). During this process the attorneys for both the plaintiff and the defendant have the opportunity to ask the prospective jurors personal questions. It is hoped that the answers will reveal any biases or preferences on the part of the juror that would prevent that juror from rendering a verdict favorable to the respective attorney's client. Prospective jurors are often asked about their educational background, their profession, their family, and their experiences.

If one of the attorneys believes that an error was made in the manner in which the jury pool was selected, the attorney can ask that none of those on the panel be permitted to serve as jurors, a request that is called "challenge to the array."

A prospective juror may be "challenged for cause"—that is, for a reason. For example, if the juror is related to one of the lawyers in the case, is mentally disabled, or appears to have any kind of bias that might affect the trial's outcome, either attorney can ask the judge to "strike" the potential juror. A judge is entitled to grant attorneys as many challenges for cause as the judge deems appropriate.

Attorneys may also move to eliminate prospective jurors whom they believe would not be sympathetic to the party they represent. These "peremptory challenges" are limited, however, and each side is allowed only a certain number of strikes. An attorney need not offer any reason for peremptory challenges. Once the jury has been selected, its members are sworn in and the trial is ready to begin. Suppose you have been called for jury duty. Because democratic government perceives jury service as a privilege and an obligation, it's your civic duty to serve. Most states make it difficult to avoid. Before you respond to a jury summons, ask yourself if you meet the following requirements. If not, you may not qualify to be a juror in most states.

1. Are you an American citizen?
2. Are you age 18 or older? (This varies from state to state.)
3. Have you been a resident of the United States for at least one year? (This may also vary.)
4. Can you read and speak English?
5. Are you mentally and physically capable of serving as a juror?
6. Is your record clear of any criminal conviction?

If you cannot answer yes to all of the above, call the phone number provided on your summons and inform the clerk's office of the situation.

Suppose you meet all the qualifications, but you have a newborn baby or a business that cannot survive without you. Courts differ regarding what might be required to be excused from jury duty. Some will excuse you for a funeral, for example, while others will not. But if jury service would create a major hardship for you, call or write (as specified on the summons) the clerk of the court and explain your situation. Perhaps your service can be postponed for a few months. In any case, you must answer a jury summons; do not make the mistake of not appearing on the given date without having reached an agreement in advance about your appearance.

The courts are moving toward a "one day, one trial" system, which means that when you report for jury duty, you will often be needed for only one day or one trial (which usually lasts for only a few days). This reform eliminates the antiquated system of prospective jurors waiting for an entire week to be called, or serving as a jury member for several short trials.

Getting a notice doesn't necessarily mean you will be required to report to the courthouse. Some jurisdictions ask that you call the court the night before the date on the summons and find out from a recording whether or not you will be needed. If you are required to report, be sure you know to which court you are being summoned, whether state or federal, and where it is located. Your summons will provide this information. Be sure to report on time, and then be prepared to wait, possibly for hours.

JURY PAY   The most you can expect to earn from a day of jury duty in state court is about $40. Some states don't pay for the first three days of service, but compensate you $50 per day thereafter. Some courts will pay you at the end of the day and others will mail you a check. Some jurisdictions will pay for your round-trip travel expenses to the courthouse.

Most states require your employer to pay you your normal salary while you are on jury duty. In these cases, it is often customary that the check for jury service be turned in to the juror's employer. If your employer refuses to pay you or will not allow you to take the time off after you have shown him/her your summons, report the employer to the court. Federal law, the Judiciary and Judicial Proceedings Act, as well as some state laws prohibit an employer from preventing an employee from serving on jury duty or terminating anyone because he or she was called and served on jury duty. If you have been fired for serving, consult a lawyer.

JURY SELECTION   Attorneys have preconceived ideas about what kind of juror they need on a particular kind of case. For example, a plaintiff's lawyer in an automobile personal injury case will most likely want to select jurors who have been injured themselves in auto accidents. If lawyers have the time or the resources to do so, they research the backgrounds of those on the prospective jury list before the day of the selection. They want to know the prospective juror's occupation, marital status, number of children, economic situation, political leanings, and religious beliefs.

Some courts will send prospective jurors a questionnaire to fill out and bring to court, asking whether they have ever been a party to or a victim in a civil or criminal case, or whether they or anyone in their family is associated with a police department. The attorneys will use this information in the *voir dire*.

In an automobile personal injury case such as Joe's, his attorney will probably begin by asking the prospective jurors if they know the defendant, Vincent, or his attorneys. Joe's attorney will also want to know whether they or any family member had ever been a plaintiff or defendant in a lawsuit involving an automobile accident.

During his/her turn in the *voir dire* process, Vincent's attorney might ask if any of the jurors are joggers or might try to establish whether any of them have a special bias in favor of the plaintiff. The attorney may also ask if anyone on the panel has ever been treated by the plaintiff's doctor.

Panel members who survive the *voir dire* process without being stricken by either attorney become members of the jury. Alternate jurors are then selected and sit through the entire trial in the event that one of the regular jurors becomes ill or otherwise cannot finish out his or her jury service.

Once the jurors are sworn, the judge prohibits them from discussing the case with anyone, including parties, witnesses, attorneys, and the news media. They are also cautioned to avoid newspaper, television, or radio reports on the case or the trial.

If, at any time, a juror sees a fellow juror violating the judge's instructions—for example, speaking with the defendant or his attorney or reading a prohibited newspaper article—it's that juror's obligation to inform the judge of the indiscretion. The errant juror will most likely be removed, found in contempt of court, and be given a fine and/or a jail term.

As Max was riding the bus to the courthouse where he was serving as a juror on a high-profile divorce case, he noticed the headlines of the local newspaper of another passenger, which referred to the lawsuit. The judge had warned Max and his fellow jurors that they were to avoid any news accounts of the trial in the newspapers, radio, or television. Regardless of whether Max believes that the newspaper headline will influence his decision as a juror, he is obligated to report it to the court and let the judge decide whether he is still capable of being an impartial juror.

Opening Arguments

Since the plaintiff, Joe, has the burden of proving his case against the defendant, Vincent, Joe's lawyer presents an opening statement first. The attorney will state the basic facts of the case and what the evidence and testimony should prove. In this case, Joe's attorney will most likely explain to the jury how the accident occurred, what injuries his client sustained, and how these injuries will affect his future. The attorney will also mention the witnesses he expects to testify and how they, along with any physical evidence, will prove that it was Vincent's negligence that caused Joe's extensive injuries. In the opening statement, Joe's attorney is not permitted to claim that he will prove something if, in fact, he doesn't plan to do so. Opening statements can vary in length depending on the complexity of the case.

The defendant's attorney may either present the opening statement after the presentation of the plaintiff's, or may wait until the attorney for the plaintiff has called all of his or her witnesses and rested. Then the defendant's attorney, like the plaintiff's, will explain what the testimony and evidence he or she will present should prove.

The Plaintiff's Case

In this case, it is the responsibility of Joe's attorney, through the use of witnesses and physical evidence, to prove "beyond a preponderance of the evidence" that Vincent was negligent. "Preponderance of the evidence" is the standard of proof used in civil cases, which is easier to prove than the standard of "beyond a reasonable doubt" used in criminal cases. Joe's evidence has to convince the judge or jury that Vincent's negligence more likely than not—but *not* necessarily "beyond a reasonable doubt"—caused Joe's injuries.

The plaintiff's attorney will question each witness called on "direct examination." A competent attorney knows how to elicit the necessary information from the witnesses to prove the case, while still following the strict rules of evidence required by the court. "Leading questions"—questions loaded with the information that the attorney wants the witness to bring out in testimony—are not permitted. A leading question in this case might be "Is it not true, Doctor

Jones, that had it not been for Vincent's reckless driving, Joe would be able to run today?" Nor is testimony admissible if it is irrelevant or immaterial, and there is a fine distinction between the two. *Irrelevant* evidence doesn't prove the point at issue; *immaterial* evidence proves something that is not even at issue and is unimportant to the case.

Hearsay is another type of evidence that is inadmissible. With some exceptions, a witness's testimony about what someone else said outside of the courtroom is not admissible.

When a question or testimony is improper, the opposing attorney has the right to object. The judge may either "deny" the objection and allow the witness to answer or "sustain" it, requiring the examining attorney to rephrase it or move on to another question. Witnesses should not answer a question that is objected to until the judge rules on the objection. If the witness has already answered before the judge sustains an objection, the judge can rule that the response be stricken from the record, meaning that the court reporter will eliminate it from the transcript. The jury will also be asked to disregard the improper question and the answer.

Cross-Examination

After the plaintiff's attorney has completed the direct examination, the defendant's attorney may cross-examine the witness in an effort to discredit that person's testimony or to present the information in a different light. Leading questions *are* permitted on cross-examination.

Witnesses called to testify on Joe's behalf would probably include those who saw the accident take place, the police officer who arrived on the scene, medical experts, and Joe's employer and family members. Joe will most likely take the stand himself.

Testifying in Court

If you are summoned to court as a witness, it probably will be through a subpoena. Never ignore a subpoena. If for some reason you cannot be present on the date specified, notify the court. Ignoring a subpoena can result in a fine, an imprisonment, or both. If one of the attorneys considers your testimony crucial to the case, the attorney may ask the judge for a continuance, or postponement, if you cannot appear.

Sometimes, the court will issue an order (*subpoena duces tecum*) requesting that you bring documents to court as evidence on the day you are asked to appear.

You may be called as a friendly witness by the party whom you believe was in the right; or you could be summoned against your will as an "unfriendly" witness and be required to testify on behalf of the opposition. Either way, you must tell the truth. Penalties for perjury are severe: 1 to 14 years in prison.

REHEARSING AND PREPARING FOR COURT TESTIMONY It's best to plan and prepare your testimony before you take the witness stand in order to ensure that your testimony will be clear, concise, and easy to understand. The "friendly" lawyer will want to know ahead of time how you will respond to certain questions and may guide you in your manner of presentation without changing your meaning or veracity.

If you have previously been "deposed," you should reread the deposition to refresh your memory, because the opposing attorney may try to confuse you or make you contradict your earlier testimony.

Unlike an expert witness, you have not been retained by one side to clarify or teach the jury the technical substance of a certain topic. Nor are you being paid to convince the jury of a certain fact or to provide your opinion. Your only responsibility is to tell the facts as effectively as you can so that a judge or jury can make an informed decision about a case.

COMPENSATION You will probably be compensated only for your transportation to the court and for your lunch. States vary about how much compensation they pay, but no more than $15 per day and a gas allowance is a general maximum.

A WITNESS'S CREDIBILITY One of the most important traits of a good witness is credibility. Its ingredients include a witness's sincerity, clarity, intelligence, empathy, appearance, and objectivity when testifying.

Depending on the nature of the case, the witnesses may be

sequestered, which means that they are not permitted to sit in the courtroom while others testify but will be called in individually to testify so that another's testimony does not influence theirs.

ANSWERING THE QUESTIONS   In general, if you are a witness you must answer all the questions put to you by the attorneys and judge. You cannot arbitrarily decide that you would prefer not to answer a question. But under certain circumstances you are protected from having to respond.

Conversations between you and your doctor, psychotherapist, lawyer, clergyman, and spouse are considered *privileged.* In other words, what is said in the sanctity of these professional or personal relationships is legally private, and if an attorney tries to elicit information from you that you gained through a conversation with these individuals, you may refuse to respond. You probably will not need to decline such questions yourself, because a competent lawyer will probably object before you have a chance to reply.

Another reason you may legitimately refuse to answer is if a truthful response will implicate you in a criminal act. For example, let us assume that when you witnessed the accident, you were burglarizing someone's home. Because such an illegal activity is hardly one you wish to divulge in court when an attorney asks what you were doing when you witnessed the accident, you may plead the Fifth Amendment, stating that your response would tend to incriminate or implicate you.

When you can answer, answer as honestly as you know how. If you don't know the answer to the question, simply say so. Remember that you are under oath and that any fabrication is a lie, punishable by a fine, imprisonment, or both.

If you cannot remember whether something is true, say so. Most judges will not allow you to have notes in front of you when you testify; they want your testimony to be fresh and spontaneous. If you don't understand the question, ask the attorney to repeat it or to reword it so that you do. If the question has several parts, ask to have it broken down for you, one part at a time.

If the plaintiff has called you as a witness, the plaintiff's attorney will ask you questions on direct examination. Since you probably have already spoken at length with the attorney about your testimony, you need not expect any surprises.

Opposing counsel will question you on cross-examination. The opposing counsel's job is to challenge either your credibility or your testimony.

After counsel completes the cross-examination, the attorney who asked you to testify can question you on "redirect" about any new issues that may have come out on cross-examination. The other attorney then has an opportunity to recross-examine you.

If you have been well prepared and have been confident in relating what happened as clearly and honestly as possible, you have done your job as a witness. If you realize after leaving the witness stand that you have made a mistake in your testimony, don't ignore it. Tell the attorney who asked or subpoenaed you to testify to report it to the judge. You may be called back to the witness stand.

Exhibits

In addition to eliciting testimony from witnesses, the plaintiff may enter documents or other physical matter as evidence that the jury or judge can consider in reaching a verdict. In our hypothetical case, these may include a diagram and photographs taken of the accident scene, photographs of Joe's injuries, his medical records, and an affidavit detailing the hours he has not been able to work since the accident. These will be identified and labeled as Exhibit A, Exhibit B, etc., for the record.

At the plaintiff's request, the jury may also be allowed to visit the scene of the accident as a group. But individual jury members are prohibited from going there on their own or as a group without the court's express direction.

Motion for Dismissal

After the plaintiff's attorney has presented his or her case, the plaintiff "rests," or concludes, this part of the trial. Depending on how strong a case the attorney has made, the defendant's attorney may "move," or make a motion, that the case be dismissed at this point because the plaintiff's attorney failed to carry the burden of proof.

The judge then considers the motion; it may be granted, dismissed, or denied. If it is denied, the trial continues with the defendant mounting the defense. If the defendant's attorney has already made his/her opening statement after the plaintiff's, then the defendant's evidence and witnesses open to cross-examination will now be presented.

Rebuttal and Closing Arguments

When the defendant's attorney has completed the presentation of the defense's case, the plaintiff's attorney then has the right to present rebuttal witnesses. After both parties have rested, it is time for the presentation of closing arguments. The plaintiff's attorney goes first, addressing the issues in the case, reviewing the evidence, and pointing to what conclusions the jury "should" draw from them. The defendant's attorney will follow with his/her closing statement.

Deciding the Verdict

The jury should listen carefully when the judge reads the charges. If they don't understand them, they will have a chance to ask the judge about them after deliberations begin.

Often the real drama in a trial takes place in the jury room, where 6 to 12 individuals will have to come to some consensus. The foreman is sometimes selected by the court, with the first juror selected in *voir dire* often becoming the foreman. In other courts, the jurors themselves vote for a foreman. He or she is basically the chairperson or leader, conducting discussions and calling for votes. If any communication between the jury and court/bailiff is necessary, it will be conducted through the foreman.

There is no set agenda for how a jury is supposed to deliberate. Some judges discourage taking a vote immediately, feeling that the jurors should be open to new opinions and observations. Jury deliberations are a team sport. All members should be willing to express their views, examine the evidence, apply the law, and reach a conclusion. But they must also be willing to change their minds if someone else's reasoning makes more sense. It's a give-and-take situation with justice as the end result.

Charging the Jury

Before the jury can begin its deliberations, the judge must instruct them on the law that applies to the case before them, thus "charging the jury." Charges are statements of law that attorneys generally research in "charge books" that provide instructions applying to cases by category.

Both attorneys will submit their suggested charges to the judge prior to the trial, but it is up to the judge to decide how the jury should be charged. For example, one of the charges that the defendant might request the judge to use is "I charge you that if you believe that the injury to plaintiff was caused by pure accident and the plaintiff and defendant were both free of fault, the plaintiff cannot recover." The plaintiff, however, might hope that the following charge is used: "I charge you that in order for a party to be held liable for negligence, it is not necessary that he should have been able to anticipate the particular consequences that ensued. It is sufficient if in ordinary prudence he might have foreseen some injury which would result from his act or omission and that consequences of a generally injurious nature might result." It is possible that the judge may select both these charges, in addition to several others. Both attorneys have the right to object to portions of the charge.

There are times when a jury does not understand the judge's charges, and on these occasions they have the right and the duty to send a note to the judge during the deliberations to ask for clarification.

Deliberation

After the charges are read, the jurors retire to the jury room where they begin the deliberations. If a judge believes that publicity or other outside influences may have some effect on the jury's verdict, the judge may require the members to be sequestered (secluded in hotel rooms each night after deliberations in the jury room) until the trial is concluded. Newspapers and magazines as well as television and radio news broadcasts are off-limits to the jurors. If the trial becomes lengthy, family members are sometimes permitted to visit sequestered jurors with the stipulation that they not discuss the case or the trial.

Throughout its deliberations, the jury will take votes to determine where each member stands on a verdict. Some jurisdictions require unanimous decisions; others, only a majority vote.

The Verdict

When a decision is reached, the foreman will inform the bailiff that the jury has completed its job. The judge is then notified, and the attorneys and the parties to the action return to the courtroom for the announcement. The jury is called in and the judge asks: "Ladies and gentlemen of the jury, have you arrived at a verdict?" The foreman speaks on behalf of the entire jury and responds: "Yes, Your Honor, we have." "How do you find?" asks the judge. If the jury has decided in favor of Joe, believing that he deserves an award, the foreman will respond: "We find for the plaintiff in the amount of $_____." If the jury has found that the plaintiff has failed to prove his case, they will decide in favor of the defendant.

A losing party will sometimes request that the jury be polled, which means that each juror will be asked individually if he or she did, in fact, vote as the verdict reflects. If any discrepancies arise, the verdict is stricken and the jury must continue its deliberations.

A judge occasionally disregards a jury's verdict because it is contrary to the facts of the case or the law and enters the judge's own decision instead, which is called a "judgment notwithstanding the verdict." However, most jury verdicts are not challenged by judges, and the judgments become final, or *res judicata*, after the time of appeal has lapsed. Litigants who are dissatisfied with the outcome of the trial have the right to challenge it through several avenues.

If the required number of jurors cannot agree on a verdict, the trial ends in a mistrial with a hung jury. The plaintiff may ask that the case be tried again with a new jury or may decide that a second trial wouldn't be any more successful and choose to abandon the case.

After the verdict has been read, the judge will thank the jury members for their service and dismiss them. If this has been a high-profile case, the news media may want to get the jurors' comments. The "gag order" is now lifted, so they may comment if they wish but not to the extent of revealing any information about the other jurors, including their names, their views, or how they voted. The attorneys, too, might want to talk with the jurors to find out why they decided the way they did in order to find out what they did right and what they did wrong. Jurors are permitted to speak with them, too, if they wish to do so.

AFTER THE TRIAL

New Trials and Appeals

Parties to a completed court trial have a time limit in which they may ask for a new trial. A new trial may be granted if

- new evidence is discovered
- the verdict is inconsistent with the weight of the evidence
- the damages granted in the verdict are considered by either party to be too great or inadequate
- errors of law were made during the trial

Unsatisfied litigants can also appeal a final judgment from the court. The process by which this is accomplished does not require beginning again, as a new trial does. Instead, the court reporter will be asked to prepare the transcript of the trial, which will be sent to the appellate court.

The party bringing the appeal is the *appellant*; the other party is the *appellee*. The appellant will submit a brief along with its petition for appeal, outlining why that party believes that the lower court erred and citing statutes and case law. The appellee will have an opportunity to respond, arguing why the lower court decision should stand.

Individuals or groups who are not parties to the case but who have some interest in its outcome may file a brief as a "friend of the court."

Proving that a significant mistake was made during a trial and that the error prejudiced the outcome of the case is difficult. Be aware that the success rate of appeals is very low—only about 6 percent.

While the court system and trial by jury does effectively settle disputes, it is a lengthy and expensive process. Knowledge of the law is your best way to guard against problems that might occur through carelessness or ignorance. If a problem does occur, the information in this book should help you deal with the situation quickly and effectively.

See the Appendixes for additional information and guidance.

Useful Addresses and Phone Numbers

1 THE FAMILY

Adoption

National Adoption Information
    Clearinghouse
11426 Rockville Pike
Suite 410
Rockville, MD 20852
301-231-6512

The Child Welfare League of
    America, Inc.
440 First Street, N.W.
Suite 310
Washington, DC 20001
202-638-2952

The National Committee for
    Adoption
1930 Seventeenth Street, N.W.
Washington, DC 20009
202-328-1200

2 PLANNING YOUR ESTATE

Funerals

Continental Association of Funeral
    and Memorial Societies
6900 Lost Lake Road
Egg Harbor, WI 54209
414-868-3136

Living Wills

Choice in Dying
200 Varick Street
New York, NY 10014
212-366-5540

Organ Donations

The Living Bank
P.O. Box 6725
Houston, TX 77265
713-528-2971

5 CARS AND DRIVING

*Information on the Consumer
Leasing Act (CLA)*

The Federal Trade Commission (FTC)
Bureau of Consumer Protection
Credit Practices Division
Room 4037
601 Pennsylvania Avenue, N.W.
Washington, DC 20580
202-326-3222

Car Complaints

American Automobile Association
    (AAA, AUTOSOLVE)
Check your phone book for a local
    office.

Automotive Consumer Action
    Program (AUTOCAP)
8400 Westpark Drive
McLean, VA 22102
703-821-7144

The Better Business Bureau (BBB
    Auto Line)
Check your phone book for a local
    office.

Center for Auto Safety
2001 S Street, N.W.
Washington, DC 20009
202-328-7700

Federal Trade Commission (FTC)
Bureau of Consumer Protection
601 Pennsylvania Avenue, N.W.
Washington, DC 20580

Car Safety

National Highway Traffic Safety
Administration
400 Seventh Street, S.W.
Washington, DC 20590
Safety hotline: 800-424-9393

Auto Insurance

Insurance commissioner's office
Check your phone book for a state
office.

Insurance Information Institute
110 William Street
New York, NY 10038
212-669-9200

*Questions on Licensing,
Registration, or Titles*

Department of Motor Vehicles
Check your phone book under State
Government for local offices.

**6 CIVIL RIGHTS AND PERSONAL
FREEDOMS**

Civil Rights Violations

American Civil Liberties Union
132 West 43 Street
New York, NY 10036
212-944-9800

U.S. Commission on Civil Rights
624 Ninth Street, N.W.
Washington, DC 20425
202-376-8177
800-552-6843

National Association for the
Advancement of Colored People
(NAACP)
4805 Mt. Hope Drive
Baltimore, MD 21215
410-358-8900
Call your state or local chapter.

National Organization for Women
(NOW)
1000 Sixteenth Street, N.W.
Suite 700
Washington, DC 20036
202-331-0066

*Discrimination Against Older
Americans*

American Association of Homes for
the Aging
901 E Street, N.W.
Suite 500
Washington, DC 20004
202-783-2242

American Association of Retired
Persons (AARP)
601 E Street, N.W.
Washington, DC 20049
202-434-2277

National Council on the Aging
409 Third Street, S.W.
Suite 200
Washington, DC 20024
202-479-1200

Social Security Administration
800-772-1213

State Office of Aging
Check the State Government listing
in the phone book.

Discrimination in Education

U.S. Department of Education
Office of Civil Rights
400 Maryland Avenue, S.W.

Washington, DC 20202
202-205-5413

Housing Discrimination

Office of Fair Housing and Equal Opportunity
U.S. Department of Housing and Urban Development (HUD)
451 Seventh Street, S.W.
Room 5100
Washington, DC 20410
202-708-4252
800-669-9777

Employment

Equal Employment Opportunity Commission (EEOC)
1801 L Street, N.W.
Washington, DC 20507
202-663-4900
800-669-4000

Pension and Welfare Benefits Administration
U.S. Department of Labor
1730 K Street, N.W.
Washington, DC 20006
202-254-7013

Immigration

Immigration and Naturalization Services (INS)
U.S. Department of Justice
425 I Street, N.W.
Washington, DC 20536
202-514-4316

7 BUYING OR RENTING A HOME

Housing Discrimination

U.S. Department of Housing and Urban Development (HUD)
451 Seventh Street, S.W.
Room 5100
Washington, DC 20410

202-708-4252
800-669-9777

Homeowner's Insurance

Insurance Information Institute
110 William Street
New York, NY 10038
212-669-9200

Information on Timeshares

Federal Trade Commission (FTC)
Division of Marketing Practices
Pennsylvania Avenue at Sixth Street, N.W.
Washington, DC 20580
202-326-2222

Real Estate Commission
Check your phone book for a local office.

8 THE WORKPLACE

Employment Discrimination

American Civil Liberties Union (ACLU)
132 West 43 Street
New York, NY 10036
212-944-9800

Check your phone book for a local or regional office.

Equal Employment Opportunity Commission (EEOC)
1801 L Street, N.W.
Washington, DC 20507
800-669-4000
202-663-4264

U.S. Department of Labor
200 Constitution Avenue, N.W.
Washington, DC 20210
202-219-6666

National Association for the Advancement of Colored People
4805 Mt. Hope Drive
Baltimore, MD 21215
410-358-8900

Safety and Health Problems

U.S. Department of Labor
Occupational Safety and Health
Administration (OSHA)
Frances Perkins Building
200 Constitution Avenue, N.W.
Washington, DC 20210
202-219-6091

OSHA has regional offices located in
Atlanta, Boston, Chicago, Dallas,
Denver, Kansas City, Philadelphia,
New York, San Francisco, and
Seattle.

Information on Labor Unions

AFL-CIO
Pamphlet Division
815 Sixteenth Street, N.W.
Room 208
Washington, DC 20006
202-637-5000

National Labor Relations Board
(NLRB)
1099 Fourteenth Street, N.W.
Washington, DC 20570
202-273-1991

Pension Information

Pension and Welfare Benefits
Administration
U.S. Department of Labor
Office of Program Services
200 Constitution Avenue, N.W.
Washington, DC 20210
202-219-8233

Travel Agent Scams

The American Society of Travel
Agents (ASTA)
1101 King Street

Alexandria, VA 22314
703-739-2782

Health Scams

Medicare
800-368-5779

or write:

HHSOIG Hotline
P.O. Box 17303
Baltimore, MD 21203-7303

Mail-Order Lists

Direct Marketing Association
Telephone Preference Service
6 East 43 Street
New York, NY 10017
212-768-7277

False Advertising

National Advertising Division (NAD)
845 Third Avenue
New York, NY 10022
212-754-1320

*Remedies for Defective
Manufacturing*

Direct Marketing Association
6 East 43 Street
New York, NY 10017
212-768-7277

Direct Selling Association
1776 K Street, N.W.
Suite 600
Washington, DC 20006
202-293-5760

Travel Complaints

U.S. Department of Transportation
(DOT)
Office of Community and Consumer
Affairs
400 Seventh Street, S.W., I-25
Washington, DC 20590
202-366-2220

9 CONSUMER RIGHTS AND
OBLIGATIONS

AMTRAK

Director of Customer Relations
AMTRAK
60 Massachusetts Avenue, N.E.
Washington, DC 20002
202-906-2121

AMTRAK Refunds (east of Ohio and
north of Virginia)
30th Street Station
30th and Market Streets
Philadelphia, PA 19104
215-824-1600

AMTRAK Refunds (all other
locations)
Chicago Union Station
210 S. Canal Street
Chicago, IL 60603
312-558-1075

Credit History

Bankcard Holders of America
560 Herndon Parkway
Suite 120
Herndon, VA 22070
703-481-1110

Credit Reports

Equifax
P.O. Box 740241
Atlanta, GA 30374
404-885-8000

National Consumer Feedback
5641 Yale Boulevard
Dallas, TX 75206
214-890-9913

TransUnion—Consumer Relations
P.O. Box 7000
N. Olmsted, OH 44070
216-779-7200

TRW Credit Data
P.O. Box 2106

Allen, TX 75002-2106
214-390-3000

Bank Credit Complaints

Director
Division of Consumer and
Community Affairs
Board of Governors of the Federal
Reserve System
614 H Street, N.W.
Room 108
Washington, DC 20001
202-727-7000

District Federal Reserve Banks
Located in Atlanta, Boston, Chicago,
Cleveland, Dallas, Kansas City,
Minneapolis, New York,
Philadelphia, Richmond, San
Francisco, and St. Louis

Rehabilitating Bad Credit

National Foundation for Consumer
Credit
8611 Second Avenue
Suite 100
Silver Spring, MD 20910
301-589-5600
800-388-2227

Filing a Complaint

Better Business Bureau
(headquarters)
4200 Wilson Boulevard
Arlington, VA 22209
703-524-6581
Check your phone book for the local
office nearest you.

Office of Consumer Affairs
U.S. Department of Commerce
Fourteenth Street and Constitution
Avenue, N.W.
Room 5718
Washington, DC 20230
202-482-5000

Food and Drug Administration (FDA)
5600 Fishers Lane
Rockville, MD 20857
301-443-3170
Check your phone book for the closest regional office.

Chief United States Postal Inspector
U.S. Postal Service
475 L'Enfant Plaza West
Washington, DC 20260
202-268-2000

Securities and Exchange Commission
450 Fifth Street, N.W.
Washington, DC 20549
202-272-7440
Look under the State Government phone listing for your state's securities commission.

Small Business Administration (SBA)
409 Third Street, S.W.
Washington, DC 20416
202-205-6600
To request information: 800-827-5722

The Federal Trade Commission (FTC)
Pennsylvania Avenue at Sixth Street, N.W.
Washington, DC 20580
202-326-2222
FTC also has regional offices located in Atlanta, Boston, Chicago, Cleveland, Dallas, Denver, Los Angeles, New York, San Francisco, and Seattle.

Complaints with National Banks
Comptroller of the Currency
Compliance Management
Mail Stop 7-5
Washington, DC 20219-0001
202-874-4820

Complaints with State Banks (members of Federal Reserve)
Director
Division of Consumer and Community Affairs
Board of Governors of the Federal Reserve System
Twentieth Street and Constitution Avenue, N.W.
Washington, DC 20551
202-452-3000

Complaints with State Banks (federally insured state banks)
Federal Deposit Insurance Corporation (FDIC)
550 Seventeenth Street, N.W.
Washington, DC 20429
800-424-5488
800-934-3342

Complaints with Other State Banks or Private Financial Institutions
Banking Commissioner
Check your local phone book.

Complaints with Savings and Loan Associations
Office of Thrift Supervision
800-842-6929

Information on the Federal Court System
Office of Legislative and Public Affairs
Public Information Center
Administrative Office of the United States Courts

10   THE LEGAL SYSTEM: HOW IT WORKS

1 Columbus Circle, N.E.
Suite 7-110
Washington, DC 20544
202-273-1120

Information on U.S. Supreme Court

Public Information Office
U.S. Supreme Court
1 First Street, N.E.
Washington, DC 20543
202-479-3000

Information on State Supreme Courts

National Center for State Courts
300 Newport Avenue
Williamsburg, VA 23187
804-253-2000

Also check your phone book under State Government for your state's supreme court.

Information on Arbitration

American Arbitration Association
140 West 51st Street
New York, NY 10020
212-484-4000

Also check your phone book for a local office.

Information on Dispute Resolution

American Bar Association (ABA)
Standing Committee on Dispute Resolution
1800 M Street, N.W.
Washington, DC 20036
202-331-2200

Offices of State Attorneys General

ALABAMA

Attorney General
State House
Montgomery, AL 36130
205-242-7300

ALASKA

Attorney General's Office
Department of Law
Capitol Building
P.O. Box 110300
Juneau, AK 99801
907-465-3600

ARIZONA

Attorney General
1275 West Washington
Phoenix, AZ 85007
602-542-5025

ARKANSAS

Attorney General
Office of the Attorney General
200 Tower Building
323 Center
Little Rock, AK 72201
501-682-2007

CALIFORNIA

Attorney General
Office of the Attorney General
Department of Justice
1515 K Street
Suite 511
Sacramento, CA 94244
916-445-9555

COLORADO

Attorney General
1525 Sherman Street
Fifth Floor
Denver, CO 80202
303-866-3617

CONNECTICUT

Attorney General
55 Elm Street
Hartford, CT 06106
203-566-2026

DELAWARE

Attorney General
Carvel State Office Building
820 North French Street
Wilmington, DE 19801
302-577-3047

FLORIDA

Attorney General
Department of Legal Affairs
The Capitol
Tallahassee, FL 32399
904-488-2526

GEORGIA

Attorney General
40 Capitol Square, S.W.
Atlanta, GA 30334
404-656-3300

HAWAII

Attorney General
425 Queen Street
Honolulu, HI 96813
808-586-1500

IDAHO

Attorney General
Office of the Attorney General
210 Statehouse
Boise, ID 83720
208-334-2400

ILLINOIS

Attorney General
500 South Second Street
Springfield, IL 62706
217-782-1090

INDIANA

Attorney General
217 State House
Indianapolis, IN 46204
317-232-6201

IOWA

Attorney General
Hoover Building
Second Floor
Des Moines, IA 50319
515-242-6235

KANSAS

Attorney General
Kansas Judicial Center
Second Floor
Topeka, KS 66612
913-296-2215

KENTUCKY

Attorney General
State Capitol
Frankfort, KY 40601
502-564-2200

LOUISIANA

Attorney General
Department of Justice
P.O. Box 94005
Baton Rouge, LA 70804
504-342-7013

MAINE

Attorney General
State House Station 6
Augusta, ME 04333
207-626-8800

MARYLAND

Attorney General
200 Saint Paul Place
Baltimore, MD 21202
410-576-6300

MASSACHUSETTS

Attorney General
One Ashburton Place
Room 2010
Boston, MA 02108
617-727-2200

MICHIGAN

Attorney General
Law Building
P.O. Box 30212
Lansing, MI 48909
517-373-1110

MINNESOTA
Attorney General
102 State Capitol
St. Paul, MN 55155
612-296-6196

MISSISSIPPI
Attorney General
P.O. Box 220
Jackson, MS 39205
601-359-3680

MISSOURI
Attorney General
Supreme Court Building
P.O. Box 899
Jefferson City, MO 65102
314-751-3321

MONTANA
Attorney General
Department of Justice
215 North Sanders
Helena, MT 59620
406-444-2026

NEBRASKA
Attorney General
2115 State Capitol
P.O. Box 98920
Lincoln, NE 68509
402-471-2682

NEVADA
Attorney General's Office
Capitol Complex
Carson City, NV 89710
702-687-3510

NEW HAMPSHIRE
Attorney General
208 State House Annex
Concord, NH 03301
603-271-3671

NEW JERSEY
Attorney General's Office
Department of Law and Public Safety
Justice Complex, CN 081
Trenton, NJ 08625
609-984-1548

NEW MEXICO
Attorney General
P.O. Drawer 1508
Santa Fe, NM 87504
505-827-6000

NEW YORK
Attorney General
Department of Law
State Capitol
Albany, NY 12224
518-474-7330

NORTH CAROLINA
Attorney General
Department of Justice
P.O. Box 629
Raleigh, NC 27602
919-733-3377

NORTH DAKOTA
Attorney General
State Capitol
First Floor
600 East Boulevard Avenue
Bismarck, ND 58505
701-224-2210

OHIO
Attorney General
30 East Broad Street
Seventeenth Floor

Columbus, OH 43266
614-466-3376

OKLAHOMA

Attorney General
112 State Capitol
Oklahoma City, OK 73105
405-521-3911

OREGON

Attorney General
Department of Justice
100 Justice Building
Salem, OR 97310
503-378-6002

PENNSYLVANIA

Attorney General
Strawberry Square
Sixteenth Floor
Harrisburg, PA 17120
717-787-3391

RHODE ISLAND

Attorney General
72 Pine Street
Providence, RI 02903
401-274-4400

SOUTH CAROLINA

Attorney General
P.O. Box 11549
Columbia, SC 29211
803-734-3970

SOUTH DAKOTA

Attorney General
State Capitol
500 East Capitol Avenue
Pierre, SD 57501
605-773-3215

TENNESSEE

Attorney General
500 Charlotte Avenue
Nashville, TN 37243
615-741-3491

TEXAS

Attorney General
Price Daniel, Sr. Building
P.O. Box 12548
Austin, TX 78711
512-463-2100

UTAH

Attorney General
236 State Capitol
Salt Lake City, UT 84114
801-538-1015

VERMONT

Attorney General
109 State Street
Montpelier, VT 05609
802-828-3171

VIRGINIA

Attorney General
101 North Eighth Street
Richmond, VA 23219
804-786-2071

WASHINGTON

Attorney General
905 Plum Street
Building #3
P.O. Box 40100
Olympia, WA 98504
206-753-6200

WEST VIRGINIA

Attorney General
State Capitol

East Wing, Room 26
Charleston, WV 25305
304-348-2021

WISCONSIN
Attorney General
Department of Justice
P.O. Box 7857
Madison, WI 53707
608-266-1221

WYOMING
Attorney General
123 State Capitol
Cheyenne, WY 82002
307-777-7841

DISTRICT OF COLUMBIA
Corporation Council
441 Fourth Street, N.W.
Suite 1060N
Washington, DC 20001

AMERICAN SAMOA
Attorney General
P.O. Box 7

Pago Pago, AS 96799
684-633-4163

GUAM
Attorney General
Law Department
2-200E Guam Judiciary Center
120 West O'Brien Drive
Agana, Guam 96910
671-472-3324

PUERTO RICO
Secretary
Department of Justice
P.O. Box 192
San Juan, PR 00902
809-721-7700

U.S. VIRGIN ISLANDS
Attorney General
Department of Justice
Kronprindsens Gade, GERS Complex
Second Floor
Charlotte Amalie
St. Thomas, VI 00802
809-774-5666

ATLANTA—Alabama, Florida, Georgia, Mississippi, North Carolina, South Carolina, Tennessee, Virginia
1718 Peachtree Street, N.W.
Room 1000
Atlanta, GA 30367
404-347-4837

BOSTON—Connecticut, Maine, Massachusetts, New Hampshire, Rhode Island, Vermont
10 Causeway Street
Room 1184
Boston, MA 02222
617-565-7240

CHICAGO—Illinois, Indiana, Iowa, Kentucky, Minnesota, Missouri, Wisconsin
55 East Monroe Street
Suite 1437
Chicago, IL 60603
312-353-8516

CLEVELAND—Delaware, District of Columbia, Maryland, Michigan, Ohio, Pennsylvania, West Virginia
668 Euclid Avenue
Suite 520-A
Cleveland, OH 44114
216-522-4210

DALLAS—Arkansas, Louisiana, New Mexico, Oklahoma, Texas
100 North Central Expressway
Suite 500
Dallas, TX 75201
214-767-5503

DENVER—Colorado, Kansas, Montana, Nebraska, North Dakota, South Dakota, Utah, Wyoming
1405 Curtis Street
Suite 2900

Denver, CO 80202
303-844-2271

LOS ANGELES—Arizona, southern California
11000 Wilshire Boulevard
Suite 13209
Los Angeles, CA 90024
310-575-7890

NEW YORK—New Jersey, New York
150 William Street
Suite 1300
New York, NY 10038
212-264-1207

SAN FRANCISCO—Northern California, Hawaii, Nevada
901 Market Street
Suite 570
San Francisco, CA 94103
415-744-7920

SEATTLE—Alaska, Idaho, Oregon, Washington
915 Second Avenue
2806 Federal Building
Seattle, WA 98174
206-553-4656

APPENDIX D
Sample Letters

The following sample letters are intended to help consumers communicate their complaints or requests to the proper authorities. In all cases, be sure to make a copy of all correspondence. Send letters via certified mail, return receipt requested. Unless otherwise requested, send copies (keep originals) of invoices, receipts, letters, and so forth.

In some states consumers have a three-day period in which to change their minds and cancel an agreement. The Cooling-Off Rule requires sellers to inform you of your rights to cancel and to provide a cancellation form along with the sale contract. If the seller has failed to provide one, you can use this FTC model form.

NOTICE OF CANCELLATION

Date of Transaction: _____

You may cancel this transaction, without any penalty or obligation, within three business days from the above date.

If you cancel, any property traded in, any payments made by you under the contract or sale, and any negotiable instrument executed by you will be returned within 10 business days following receipt by the seller of your cancellation notice, and any security interest arising out of the transaction will be canceled.

If you cancel, you must make available to the seller at your residence, in substantially as good condition as when received, any goods delivered to you under this contract or sale; or you may, if you wish, comply with the instructions of the seller regarding the return shipment of the goods at the seller's expense and risk.

If you do make the goods available to the seller and the seller does not pick them up within 20 days of the date of your notice of cancellation, you may retain or dispose of the goods without any further obligation. If you fail to make the goods available to the seller or if you agree to return the goods to the seller and fail to do so, then you remain liable for performance of all obligations under the contract.

433

To cancel this transaction, mail or deliver a signed and dated copy of this cancellation notice, or send a telegram, to (name of seller) at (address of seller's place of business) not later than midnight of (date), saying,

I hereby cancel this transaction.

_____   _____
Your Signature   Date

Letter When Cooling-Off Rule Has Been Violated

Your street address
City, State, Zip Code
Date

Name of state, county, local consumer protection office or state attorney general's office
Street Address
City, State, Zip Code

Dear _____:

On (date), I purchased a (name of product, model, and serial number) for $_____ at my home from (name of company). Exercising my option to cancel the sale within three business days from the date of purchase, I sent the company a notice of cancellation on (date), certified mail, return receipt requested.

After waiting (number of days or weeks), I received no response from the company. Despite a follow-up letter on (date), the company still has not responded.

Enclosed please find copies of the sales agreement, signed cancellation notice and certified mail receipt, my canceled check, and two letters I sent the company.

I feel this company is violating the Cooling-Off Rule and I would greatly appreciate it if you would contact the company and investigate this matter. The company address is _____. I can be reached at the address at the top of this letter or by telephone at _____ during the day, and _____ in the evening.

Thank you for your assistance.

Sincerely,
(your name)
Enclosures

Letter to Company Regarding a Sales Problem

Your street address
City, State, Zip Code
Date

Customer Service Department
Name of company
Street Address
City, State, Zip Code

Dear _____:

On (date), I purchased a (name of product, model, and serial number) at (store and location). However, I have been dissatisfied with this purchase because (reason for dissatisfaction in detail).

I have attempted to resolve this matter by (explanation of attempts to resolve), but was given no satisfaction.

I am asking your company to give me a full refund in the amount of $_____ (or whatever other action you would like them to take). I have enclosed copies of the sales receipt and my canceled check (if applicable, include copies of warranties, guarantees, contracts, and any other records involving the transaction).

I am sending a copy of this letter to (local, county, or state consumer affairs office, state attorney general's office, Better Business Bureau, trade organization). I would like a resolution to this problem by (date). If there is no resolution by that time, I will call on these agencies to investigate my complaint.

I can be reached at the address at the top of this letter or by telephone at _____ during the day and _____ in the evening.

Sincerely,
(your name)

Enclosures
cc: agencies that are receiving copies

Letter to a Better Business Bureau Office

Your street address
City, State, Zip Code
Date

Better Business Bureau
Street Address
City, State, Zip Code

Dear _____:

Enclosed please find a letter I sent on (date) to (name of company) regarding a product I felt was inferior. As you will note, my letter asked the company to remedy the situation. They have refused to answer my letter; therefore, I am asking for your assistance in investigating this matter. I would also like to know if other complaints have been filed against this company and if they were of a similar nature. I can be reached at the address at the top of this letter or by telephone at _____ during the day and _____ in the evening. Thank you for your help.

Sincerely,
(your name)

Enclosures

Letter to the Direct Selling Association for Assistance When the Company You Are Complaining About Is a Member

Your street address
City, State, Zip Code
Date

The Direct Selling Association
1730 M Street, N.W.
Washington, DC 20036

Dear _____:

Enclosed please find a letter I have sent to (name of company) regarding a defective product I purchased from them. The company is a member of the Direct Selling Association. As my letter indicates, I feel my rights as a consumer have been violated because (reason stated briefly).

Since (name of company) is a member of your organization, I would appreciate it if you would look into this matter and encourage its resolution. I can be reached at the address at the top of this letter or by telephone at _____ during the day and _____ in the evening. Thank you for your kind assistance.

Sincerely,
(your name)

Enclosures

Letter of Complaint to the Mail Order Action Line Regarding a Mail-Order Problem

Your street address
City, State, Zip Code
Date

Mail Order Action Line
6 East 43rd Street
New York, NY 10017

Dear _____:

On (date), I ordered three items from (name of company), paying with a check in the amount of $_____. After waiting two months for my order to arrive, I contacted the company and asked them about the delay. (Name of person) in the Customer Service Department informed me that they had temporarily run out of all three items and would send them as soon as possible.

I waited one more month and when there was no response from the company, I called them again and told them to refund my money and cancel the order. I sent those instructions in a letter on (date). I still have not received my money back, but I know that my check was cashed by the company.

Since (name of company) is a member of your organization, I would appreciate your intervention in this matter. I have included copies of the order, the canceled check, and all my correspondence with (name of company). I can be reached at the address at the top of this letter or by telephone at _____ during the day and _____ in the evening. Thank you for your help.

Sincerely,
(your name)

Enclosures

Letter to the Federal Trade Commission

Your street address
City, State, Zip Code
Date

The Federal Trade Commission
Sixth and Pennsylvania Avenue, N.W.
Washington, DC 20580

Dear _____:

Enclosed please find a letter I have sent to (name of company) regarding very poor service provided by them. As my letter indicates, I feel my rights as a consumer have been violated because (reason stated briefly).

I understand that the Federal Trade Commission does not resolve individual problems, but I wanted to file this complaint with the FTC in the event that other complaints are made against this company and possibly prompt an investigation. I have sent a copy of the letter to (names of consumer agencies).

I can be reached at the address at the top of this letter or by telephone at _____ during the day and _____ in the evening. Thank you for your kind assistance.

Sincerely,
(your name)

Enclosures

Letter to the Insurer of a Credit Card Disputing a Credit Charge

Your street address
City, State, Zip Code
Date

Name of Bank or Retailer
Street Address
City, State, Zip Code

Re: Name of Account; Type of Account (VISA, MasterCard, American Express, department store, etc.); Account number; Expiration date

Dear _____:

Enclosed please find a copy of your billing notice of (date) reflecting a charge made on the above referenced account on (date) at (name of restaurant, store, gas station, etc.). This is a billing error because (explain why). Please look into this situation and eliminate this charge from my bill. Thank you for your cooperation.

Sincerely,
(your name)

Enclosures

Letter Requesting Your Credit Report

Your street address
City, State, Zip Code
Date

Equifax, TRW Credit Data, TransUnion
Consumer Relations
Street Address
City, State, Zip Code

Dear _____:

Please send a copy of my credit record to the address at the top of this letter. My Social Security number is _____. My former address (if applicable) was _____. My spouse's name (if applicable) is _____. I have enclosed a check for $_____. Thank you.

Sincerely,
(your name)

Enclosures

Letter Requesting Your Credit Report After Being Denied Credit

Your street address
City, State, Zip Code
Date

Equifax, TRW Credit Data, TransUnion
Consumer Relations
Street Address
City, State, Zip Code

Dear _____:

On (date), I was denied credit by (name of company or individual) based on a credit report provided by your company. My Social Security number is _____. My former address (if applicable) was _____. My spouse's name (if applicable) is _____.

Please send a copy of this credit report as soon as possible to the address at the top of this letter. Thank you.

Sincerely,
(your name)

Enclosures

Letter to File Complaint in a Case of Discrimination During a Job Interview

Your street address
City, State, Zip Code
Date

Name of official
Title
Name of Agency
Address

Dear _____:

This letter is a formal protest against certain hiring practices of (name of employer) that I believe are illegal.

On (date), I was interviewed by (name and title of employee) for the position of (job title). The interview took place at (location). During the interview, (name of employee) asked the following questions that I believe are illegal under federal and state law: (specify).

I explained to the interviewer that such questions were improper and refused to answer them. The interviewer told me such questions were routinely asked of all job candidates and that the interview would be terminated immediately if I chose not to answer them. The interviewer then told me I had an "attitude problem" and that the position was no longer available.

Based on this, I believe I have been the victim of discrimination, because I am highly qualified for the job and was never given the opportunity to display my qualifications and be considered. I authorize you to investigate this matter to determine if these charges have merit. You may also institute legal proceedings if appropriate.

I am available to meet with you at your office at a mutually convenient date and can furnish you with additional facts upon your request. Thank you for your cooperation and attention in this matter.

Sincerely,
(your name)

Enclosures

Letter Protesting Sexual Harassment

Your street address
City, State, Zip Code
Date

Name and title of supervisor
Name of Company
Address

Re: *Complaint of sexual harassment*

Dear (Name of Supervisor):

I have recently been subjected to a number of offensive, harmful, and disruptive acts that I believe constitute sexual harassment in violation of my rights.

The acts I am specifically complaining about occurred on (date, time, and place) and were as follows: (describe the acts committed, by whom, if witnesses were present, etc.).

After being subjected to such acts, I requested of (specify the individual) that they cease and stated that they were unwelcome. However, on (date) they continued (specify new acts, place, what occurred, etc.).

Such acts are intimidating and repugnant and have had severe emotional and physical impact on my working efforts (specify other harm resulting, if appropriate).

Unless such conduct ceases immediately, be advised that I will take all necessary steps to protect my rights, including contacting a representative from the State Human Rights Commission or the federal Equal Employment Opportunity Commission.

I hope such actions will not be necessary, and I thank you for your attention and cooperation in this matter.

Sincerely,
(your name)

Enclosures

Letter to Mail Preference Service Requesting that Your Name Be Removed from a Direct Mail List

Your street address
City, State, Zip Code
Date

Mail Preference Service
P.O. Box 3861
Grand Central Station
New York, NY 10163

Dear _____:

I would be grateful if you would remove my name from all direct mail lists. I can be reached by telephone at _____ during the day and _____ in the evening. Thank you for your assistance.

Sincerely,
(your name)

Enclosures

Letter to Telephone Preference Service Asking that Your Name Be Removed from Telephone Solicitation Lists

Your street address
City, State, Zip Code
Date

Telephone Preference Service
6 East 43rd Street
New York, NY 10017

Dear _____:

I would be grateful if you would remove my name from all telephone solicitation lists. I can be reached by telephone at _____ during the day and _____ in the evening. Thank you for your assistance.

Sincerely,
(your name)

Enclosures

The Constitution of the United States

We the People of the United States, in Order to form a more perfect Union, establish Justice, insure domestic Tranquility, provide for the common defence, promote the general Welfare, and secure the Blessings of Liberty to ourselves and our Posterity, do ordain and establish this Constitution for the United States of America.

ARTICLE I

Section 1. All legislative Powers herein granted shall be vested in a Congress of the United States, which shall consist of a Senate and House of Representatives.

Section 2. (1) The House of Representatives shall be composed of Members chosen every second Year by the People of the several States, and the Electors in each State shall have the Qualifications requisite for Electors of the most numerous Branch of the State Legislature.

(2) No Person shall be a Representative who shall not have attained to the Age of twenty five Years, and been seven Years a Citizen of the United States, and who shall not, when elected, be an Inhabitant of that State in which he shall be chosen.

(3) Representatives and direct Taxes shall be apportioned among the several States which may be included within this Union, according to their respective Numbers, which shall be determined by adding to the whole Number of free Persons, including those bound to Service for a Term of Years, and excluding Indians not taxed, three fifths of all other Persons. The actual Enumeration shall be made within three Years after the first Meeting of the Congress of the United States, and within every subsequent Term of ten Years, in such Manner as they shall by Law direct. The Number of Representatives shall not exceed one for every thirty Thousand, but each State shall have at Least one Representative; and until such enumeration shall be made, the State of New Hampshire shall be entitled to chuse three, Massachusetts eight, Rhode-Island and Providence Plantations one, Connecticut five, New-York six, New Jersey four, Pennsylvania eight, Delaware one, Maryland six, Virginia ten, North Carolina five, South Carolina five, and Georgia three.

443

(4) When vacancies happen in the Representation from any State, the Executive Authority thereof shall issue Writs of Election to fill such Vacancies.

(5) The House of Representatives shall chuse their Speaker and other Officers; and shall have the sole Power of Impeachment.

Section 3. (1) The Senate of the United States shall be composed of two Senators from each State, chosen by the Legislature thereof, for six Years; and each Senator shall have one Vote.

(2) Immediately after they shall be assembled in Consequence of the first Election, they shall be divided as equally as may be into three Classes. The Seats of the Senators of the first Class shall be vacated at the Expiration of the Second Year, of the second Class at the Expiration of the fourth Year, and of the third Class at the Expiration of the sixth Year, so that one third may be chosen every second Year; and if Vacancies happen by Resignation, or otherwise, during the Recess of Legislature of any State, the Executive thereof may make temporary Appointments until the next Meeting of the Legislature, which shall then fill such Vacancies.

(3) No Person shall be a Senator who shall not have attained to the Age of thirty Years, and been nine Years a Citizen of the United States, and who shall not, when elected, be an Inhabitant of that State for which he shall be chosen.

(4) The Vice President of the United States shall be President of the Senate, but shall have no Vote, unless they be equally divided.

(5) The Senate shall chuse their other Officers, and also a President pro tempore, in the absence of the Vice President, or when he shall exercise the Office of President of the United States.

(6) The Senate shall have the sole Power to try all Impeachments. When sitting for that Purpose, they shall be on Oath or Affirmation. When the President of the United States is tried, the Chief Justice shall preside: And no Person shall be convicted without the Concurrence of two thirds of the Members present.

(7) Judgment in Cases of Impeachment shall not extend further than to removal from Office, and disqualification to hold and enjoy any Office of honor, Trust, or Profit under the United States: but the Party convicted shall nevertheless be liable and subject to Indictment, Trial, Judgment, and Punishment, according to Law.

Section 4. The Times, Places and Manner of holding Elections for Senators and Representatives, shall be prescribed in each State by the Legislature thereof; but the Congress may at any time by law make or alter such Regulations, except as to the Place of Chusing Senators.

(2) The Congress shall assemble at least once in every Year, and such Meeting shall be on the first Monday in December, unless they shall by Law appoint a different Day.

Section 5. (1) Each House shall be the Judge of the Elections, Returns, and Qualifications of its own Members, and a Majority of each shall constitute a Quorum to do Business; but a smaller Number may adjourn from day to day, and may be authorized to compel the Attendance of absent Members, in such Manner, and under such Penalties as each House may provide

(2) Each House may determine the Rules of its Proceedings, punish its Members for disorderly Behavior, and, with the Concurrence of two thirds, expel a Member.

(3) Each House shall keep a Journal of its Proceedings, and from time to time publish the same, excepting such Parts as may in their Judgment require Secrecy; and the Yeas and Nays of the Members of either House on any question shall, at the Desire of one fifth of those Present, be entered on the Journal.

(4) Neither House, during the Session of Congress, shall, without the Consent of the other, adjourn for more than three days, nor to any other Place than that in which the two Houses shall be sitting.

Section 6. (1) The Senators and Representatives shall receive a Compensation for their Services, to be ascertained by Law, and paid out of the Treasury of the United States. They shall in all Cases, except Treason, Felony and Breach of the Peace, be privileged from Arrest during their Attendance at the Session of their respective Houses, and in going to and returning from the same; and for any Speech or Debate in either House, they shall not be questioned in any other Place.

(2) No Senator or Representative shall, during the Time for which he was elected, be appointed to any civil Office under the Authority of the United States, which shall have been created, or the Emoluments whereof shall have been encreased during such time; and no Person holding any Office under the United States, shall be a Member of either House during his Continuance in Office.

Section 7. (1) All Bills for raising Revenue shall originate in the House of Representatives; but the Senate may propose or concur with Amendments as on other Bills.

(2) Every Bill which shall have passed the House of Representatives and the Senate, shall, before it become a Law, be presented to the President of the United States; If he approve he shall sign it, but if not he shall return it, with his Objections to the House in which it shall have originated, who shall enter the Objections at large on their Journal, and proceed to reconsider it. If after such Reconsideration two thirds of that House shall agree to pass the Bill, it shall be sent, together with the Objections, to the other House, by which it shall likewise be reconsidered, and if approved by two thirds of that House, it shall become a Law. But in all such Cases the Votes of both Houses shall be determined by Yeas and Nays, and the Names of the Persons voting for and against the Bill shall be entered on the Journal of each House respectively. If any Bill shall not be returned by the President within ten days (Sundays excepted) after it shall have been presented to him, the Same shall be a Law, in like Manner as if he had signed it, unless the Congress by their Adjournment prevent its Return, in which Case it shall not be a Law.

(3) Every Order, Resolution, or Vote, to Which the Concurrence of the Senate and House of Representatives may be necessary (except on a question of Adjournment) shall be presented to the President of the United States; and before the Same shall take Effect, shall be approved by him, or being disap-

proved by him, shall be repassed by two thirds of the Senate and House of Representatives, according to the Rules and Limitations prescribed in the Case of a Bill.

Section 8. (1) The Congress shall have Power To lay and collect Taxes, Duties, Imposts and Excises, to pay the Debts and provide for the common Defence and general Welfare of the United States; but all Duties, Imposts and Excises shall be uniform throughout the United States;

(2) To borrow money on the credit of the United States;

(3) To regulate Commerce with foreign Nations, and among the several States, and with the Indian Tribes;

(4) To establish an uniform Rule of Naturalization, and uniform Laws on the subject of Bankruptcies throughout the United States;

(5) To coin Money, regulate the Value thereof, and of foreign Coin, and fix the Standard of Weights and Measures;

(6) To provide for the Punishment of counterfeiting the Securities and current Coin of the United States;

(7) To Establish Post Offices and Post Roads;

(8) To promote the Progress of Science and useful Arts, by securing for limited Times to Authors and Inventors the exclusive Right to their respective Writings and Discoveries;

(9) To constitute Tribunals inferior to the supreme Court;

(10) To define and punish Piracies and Felonies commited on the high Seas, and Offenses against the Law of Nations;

(11) To declare War, grant Letters of Marque and Reprisal, and make Rules concerning Captures on Land and Water;

(12) To raise and support Armies, but no Appropriation of Money to that Use shall be for a longer Term than two Years;

(13) To provide and maintain a Navy;

(14) To make Rules for the Government and Regulation of the land and naval Forces;

(15) To provide for calling forth the Militia to execute the Laws of the Union, suppress Insurrections and repel Invasions;

(16) To provide for organizing, arming, and disciplining the Militia, and for governing such Part of them as may be employed in the Service of the United States, reserving to the States respectively, the Appointment of the Officers, and the Authority of training the Militia according to the discipline prescribed by Congress;

(17) To exercise exclusive Legislation in all Cases whatsoever, over such District (not exceeding ten Miles square) as may, by Cession of particular States, and the Acceptance of Congress, become the Seat of the Government of the United States, and to the exercise like Authority over all Places purchased by the Consent of the Legislature of the State in which the Same shall be, for the Erection of Forts, Magazines, Arsenals, dock-Yards, and other needful Buildings; —And

(18) To make all Laws which shall be necessary and proper for carrying into Execution the foregoing Powers, and all other Powers vested by this Constitu-

tion in the Government of the United States, or in any Department or Officer thereof.

Section 9. (1) The Migration or Importation of Such Persons as any of the States now existing shall think proper to admit, shall not be prohibited by the Congress prior to the Year one thousand eight hundred and eight, but a tax or duty may be imposed on such Importation, not exceeding ten dollars for each Person.

(2) The privilege of the Writ of Habeas Corpus shall not be suspended, unless when in Cases of Rebellion or Invasion the public Safety may require it.

(3) No Bill of Attainder or ex post facto Law shall be passed.

(4) No capitation, or other direct, Tax shall be laid, unless in Proportion to the Census or Enumeration herein before directed to be taken.

(5) No Tax or Duty shall be laid on Articles exported from any State.

(6) No Preference shall be given by any Regulation of Commerce or Revenue to the Ports of one State over those of another: nor shall Vessels bound to, or from, one State be obliged to enter, clear, or pay Duties in another.

(7) No money shall be drawn from the Treasury, but in Consequence of Appropriations made by Law; and a regular Statement and Account of the Receipts and Expenditures of all public Money shall be published from time to time.

(8) No Title of Nobility shall be granted by the United States: And no Person holding any Office of Profit or Trust under them, shall, without the Consent of the Congress, accept of any present, Emolument, Office, or Title, of any kind whatever, from any King, Prince, or foreign State.

Section 10. (1) No State shall enter into any Treaty, Alliance, or Confederation; grant Letters of Marque and Reprisal; coin Money; emit Bills of Credit; make any Thing but gold and silver Coin a Tender in Payment of Debts; pass any Bill of Attainder, ex post facto Law, or Law impairing the Obligation of Contracts, or grant any Title of Nobility.

(2) No State shall, without the Consent of the Congress, lay any Imposts or Duties on Imports or Exports, except what may be absolutely necessary for executing it's inspection Laws: and the net Produce of all Duties and Imposts, laid by any State on Imports or Exports, shall be for the Use of the Treasury of the United States; and all such Laws shall be subject to the Revision and Controul of the Congress.

(3) No State shall, without the Consent of Congress, lay any duty of Tonnage, keep Troops, or Ships of War in time of Peace, enter into any Agreement or Compact with another State, or with a foreign Power, or engage in War, unless actually invaded, or in such imminent Danger as will not admit of delay.

ARTICLE II

Section 1. (1) The executive Power shall be vested in a President of the United States of America. He shall hold his Office during the Term of four Years, and, together with the Vice President, chosen for the same Term, be elected, as follows:

(2) Each State shall appoint, in such Manner as the Legislature thereof may direct, a Number of Electors, equal to the whole Number of Senators and Representatives to which the State may be entitled in the Congress; but no Senator or Representative, or Person holding an Office of Trust or Profit under the United States, shall be appointed an Elector.

(3) The Electors shall meet in their respective States, and vote by Ballot for two Persons, of whom one at least shall not be an Inhabitant of the same State with themselves. And they shall make a List of all the Persons voted for, and of the Number of Votes for each; which List they shall sign and certify, and transmit sealed to the Seat of the Government of the United States, directed to the President of the Senate. The President of the Senate shall, in the Presence of the Senate and House of Representatives, open all the Certificates, and the Votes shall then be counted. The Person having the greatest Number of Votes shall be the President, if such Number be a Majority of the whole Number of Electors appointed; and if there be more than one who have such Majority, and have an equal Number of Votes, then the House of Representatives shall immediately chuse by Ballot one of them for President; and if no Person have a Majority, then from the five highest on the List the said House shall in like Manner chuse the President. But in chusing the President, the Votes shall be taken by States, the Representation from each State having one Vote; A quorum for this Purpose shall consist of a Member or Members from two thirds of the States, and a Majority of all the States shall be necessary to a Choice. In every Case, after the Choice of the President, the Person having the greatest Number of Votes of the Electors shall be the Vice President. But if there should remain two or more who have equal Votes, the Senate shall chuse from them by Ballot the Vice President.

(4) The Congress may determine the Time of chusing the Electors, and the Day on which they shall give their Votes; which Day shall be the same throughout the United States.

(5) No person except a natural born Citizen, or a Citizen of the United States, at the time of the Adoption of this Constitution, shall be eligible to the Office of President; neither shall any Person be eligible to that Office who shall not have attained to the Age of thirty five Years, and been fourteen Years a Resident within the United States.

(6) In case of the removal of the President from Office, or of his Death, Resignation, or Inability to discharge the Powers and Duties of the said Office, the same shall devolve on the Vice President, and the Congress may by Law provide for the Case of Removal, Death, Resignation or Inability, both of the President and Vice President, declaring what Officer shall then act as President, and such Officer shall act accordingly, until the Disability by removed, or a President shall be elected.

(7) The President shall, at stated Times, receive for his Services, a Compensation, which shall neither be encreased nor diminished during the Period for which he shall have been elected, and he shall not receive within that Period any other Emolument from the United States, or any of them.

(8) Before he enter on the Execution of his Office, he shall take the following

Oath or Affirmation: "I do solemnly swear (or affirm) that I will faithfully execute the Office of President of the United States, and will to the best of my Ability, preserve, protect and defend the Constitution of the United States."

Section 2. (1) The President shall be Commander in Chief of the Army and Navy of the United States, and of the militia of the several States, when called into the actual Service of the United States; he may require the Opinion, in writing, of the principal Officer in each of the executive Departments, upon any subject relating to the Duties of their respective Offices, and he shall have Power to Grant Reprieves and Pardons for Offenses against the United States, except in Cases of Impeachment.

(2) He shall have Power, by and with the Advice and Consent of the Senate, to make Treaties, provided two thirds of the Senators present concur; and he shall nominate, and by and with the Advice and Consent of the Senate, shall appoint Ambassadors, other public Ministers and Consuls, Judges of the supreme Court, and all other Officers of the United States, whose Appointments are not herein otherwise provided for, and which shall be established by Law: but the Congress may by Law vest the Appointment of such inferior Officers, as they think proper, in the President alone, in the Courts of Law, or in the Heads of Departments.

(3) The President shall have Power to fill up all Vacancies that may happen during the Recess of the Senate, by granting Commissions which shall expire at the End of their next Session.

Section 3. He shall from time to time give to the Congress Information of the State of the Union, and recommend to their Consideration such Measures as he shall judge necessary and expedient; he may, on extraordinary Occasions, convene both Houses, or either of them, and in Case of Disagreement between them, with Respect to the Time of Adjournment, he may adjourn them to such Time as he shall think proper; he shall receive Ambassadors and other public Ministers; he shall take Care that the Laws be faithfully executed, and shall Commission all the Officers of the United States.

Section 4. The President, Vice President and all civil Officers of the United States, shall be removed from Office on Impeachment for, and Conviction of, Treason, Bribery, or other high Crimes and Misdemeanors.

ARTICLE III

Section 1. The judicial Power of the United States, shall be vested in one supreme Court, and in such inferior Courts as the Congress may from time to time ordain and establish. The Judges, both of the supreme and inferior Courts, shall hold their Offices during good Behaviour, and shall, at stated Times, receive for their Services a Compensation which shall not be diminished during their Continuance in Office.

Section 2. (1) The judicial Power shall extend to all Cases, in Law and Equity, arising under this Constitution, the Laws of the United States, and Treaties made, or which shall be made, under their Authority;—to all Cases affecting Ambassadors, other public Ministers and Consuls;—to all Cases of admiralty and maritime Jurisdiction;—to Controversies to which the United States shall be a Party;—to Controversies between two or more States;—between a State and Citizens of another State;—between Citizens of different States;—between Citizens of the same State claiming Lands under the Grants of different States, and between a State, or the Citizens thereof, and foreign States, Citizens or Subjects.

(2) In all Cases affecting Ambassadors, other public Ministers and Consuls, and those in which a State shall be Party, the supreme Court shall have original Jurisdiction. In all the other Cases before mentioned, the supreme Court shall have appellate Jurisdiction, both as to Law and Fact, with such Exceptions, and under such Regulations as the Congress shall make.

(3) The trial of all Crimes, except in Cases of Impeachment, shall be by Jury; and such Trial shall be held in the State where the said Crimes shall have been committed; but when not committed within any State, the Trial shall be at such Place or Places as the Congress may by Law have directed.

Section 3. (1) Treason against the United States, shall consist only in levying War against them, or in adhering to their Enemies, giving them Aid and Comfort. No Person shall be convicted of Treason unless on the Testimony of two Witnesses to the same overt Act, or on Confession in open Court.

(2) The Congress shall have Power to declare the Punishment of Treason, but no Attainder of Treason shall work Corruption of Blood, or Forfeiture except during the Life of the Person attainted.

ARTICLE IV

Section 1. Full Faith and Credit shall be given in each State to the public Acts, Records, and judicial Proceedings of every other State. And the Congress may by general Laws prescribe the Manner in which such Acts, Records and Proceedings shall be proved, and the Effect thereof.

Section 2. (1) The Citizens of each State shall be entitled to all Privileges and Immunities of Citizens in the several States.

(2) A Person charged in any State with Treason, Felony, or other Crime, who shall flee from Justice, and be found in another State, shall on demand of the executive Authority of the State from which he fled, be delivered up, to be removed to the State having Jurisdiction of the Crime.

(3) No Person held to Service or Labour in one State, under the Laws thereof, escaping into another, shall, in Consequence of any Law or Regulation therein, be discharged from such Service or Labour, but shall be delivered up on Claim of the Party to whom such Service or Labour may be due.

Section 3. (1) New States may be admitted by the Congress into this Union; but no new State shall be formed or erected within the Jurisdiction of any other State; nor any State be formed by the Junction of two or more States, or Parts of States, without the Consent of the Legislatures of the States concerned as well as of the Congress.

(2) The Congress shall have Power to dispose of and make all needful Rules and Regulations respecting the Territory or other Property belonging to the United States; and nothing in this Constitution shall be so construed as to Prejudice any Claims of the United States, or of any particular State.

Section 4. The United States shall guarantee to every State in this Union a Republican Form of Government, and shall protect each of them against Invasion; and on Application of the Legislature, or of the Executive (when the Legislature cannot be convened) against domestic Violence.

ARTICLE V

The Congress, whenever two thirds of both Houses shall deem it necessary, shall propose Amendments to this Constitution, or, on the Application of the Legislatures of two thirds of the several States, shall call a Convention for proposing Amendments, which, in either Case, shall be valid to all Intents and Purposes, as part of this Constitution, when ratified by the Legislatures of three fourths of the several States, or by Conventions in three fourths thereof, as the one or the other Mode of Ratification may be proposed by the Congress; Provided that no Amendment which may be made prior to the Year One thousand eight hundred and eight shall in any Manner affect the first and fourth Clauses in the Ninth Section of the first Article; and that no State, without its Consent, shall be deprived of its equal Suffrage in the Senate.

ARTICLE VI

(1) All Debts contracted and Engagements entered into, before the Adoption of this Constitution shall be as valid against the United States under this Constitution, as under the Confederation.

(2) This Constitution, and the Laws of the United States which shall be made in Pursuance thereof; and all Treaties made, or which shall be made, under the Authority of the United States, shall be the supreme Law of the Land; and the Judges in every State shall be bound thereby, any Thing in the Constitution or Laws of any State to the Contrary notwithstanding.

(3) The Senators and Representatives before mentioned, and the Members of the several State Legislatures, and all executive and judicial Officers, both of the United States and of the several States, shall be bound by Oath or Affirmation, to support this Constitution; but no religious Test shall ever be required as a Qualification to any Office or public Trust under the United States.

ARTICLE VII

The Ratification of the Conventions of nine States shall be sufficient for the Establishment of this Constitution between the States so ratifying the Same.

Articles in addition to, and amendment of, the Constitution of the United States of America, proposed by Congress, and ratified by the legislatures of the several states pursuant to the Fifth Article of the original Constitution.

AMENDMENT I (1791)

Congress shall make no law respecting an establishment of religion, or prohibiting the free exercise thereof; or abridging the freedom of speech, or of the press; or the right of the people peaceably to assemble, and to petition the Government for a redress of grievances.

AMENDMENT II (1791)

A well regulated Militia, being necessary to the security of a free State, the right of the people to keep and bear Arms, shall not be infringed.

AMENDMENT III (1791)

No Soldier shall, in time of peace be quartered in any house, without the consent of the Owner, nor in time of war, but in a manner to be prescribed by law.

AMENDMENT IV (1791)

The right of the people to be secure in their persons, houses, papers, and effects, against unreasonable searches and seizures, shall not be violated, and no Warrants shall issue, but upon probable cause, supported by Oath or affirmation, and particularly describing the place to be searched, and the persons or things to be seized.

AMENDMENT V (1791)

No person shall be held to answer for a capital, or otherwise infamous crime, unless on a presentment or indictment of a Grand Jury, except in cases arising in the land or naval forces, or in the Militia, when in actual service in time of War or public danger; nor shall any person be subject for the same offence to be twice put in jeopardy of life or limb; nor shall be compelled in any criminal case to be a witness against himself, nor be deprived of life, liberty, or property, without due process of law; nor shall private property be taken for public use, without just compensation.

AMENDMENT VI (1791)

In all criminal prosecutions, the accused shall enjoy the right to a speedy and public trial, by an impartial jury of the State and district wherein the crime shall have been committed, which district shall have been previously ascertained by law, and to be informed of the nature and cause of the accusation; to be confronted with the witnesses against him; to have compulsory process for obtaining witnesses in his favor, and to have the Assistance of Counsel for his defence.

AMENDMENT VII (1791)

In Suits at common law, where the value in controversy shall exceed twenty dollars, the right of trial by jury shall be preserved, and no fact tried by jury, shall be otherwise re-examined in any Court of the United States, than according to the rules of the common law.

AMENDMENT VIII (1791)

Excessive bail shall not be required, nor excessive fines imposed, nor cruel and unusual punishment inflicted.

AMENDMENT IX (1791)

The enumeration in the Constitution, of certain rights, shall not be construed to deny or disparage others retained by the people.

AMENDMENT X (1791)

The powers not delegated to the United States by the Constitution, nor prohibited by it to the States, are reserved to the States respectively, or to the people.

AMENDMENT XI (1798)

The Judicial power of the United States shall not be construed to extend to any suit in law or equity, commenced or prosecuted against one of the United States by Citizens of another State, or by Citizens or subjects of any foreign State.

AMENDMENT XII (1804)

The Electors shall meet in their respective states and vote by ballot for President and Vice-President, one of whom, at least, shall not be an inhabitant of the same state with themselves; they shall name in their ballots the person voted for as President, and in distinct ballots the person voted for as Vice-President, and they shall make distinct lists of all persons voted for as President, and of all persons voted for as Vice-President, and of the number of votes for each, which lists they shall sign and certify, and transmit sealed to the seat of the government of the United States, directed to the President of the Senate;—The President of the Senate shall, in the presence of the Senate and House of Representatives, open all the certificates and the votes then be counted;—The person having the greatest number of votes for President, shall be the President, if such number be a majority of the whole number of Electors appointed; and if no person have such majority, then from the persons having the highest numbers not exceeding three on the list of those voted for as President, the House of Representatives shall choose immediately, by ballot, the President. But in choosing the President, the votes shall be taken by states, the representation from each state having one vote; a quorum for this purpose shall consist of a member or members from two-thirds of the states, and a majority of all the states shall be necessary to a choice. And if the House of Representatives shall not choose a President whenever the right of choice shall devolve upon them before the fourth day of March next following, then the Vice-President shall act as President, as in the case of the death or other constitutional disability of the

President.—The person having the greatest number of votes as Vice-President, shall be the Vice-President if such number be a majority of the whole number of Electors appointed, and if no person have a majority, then from the two highest numbers of the list, the Senate shall choose the Vice-President; a quorum for the purpose shall consist of two-thirds of the whole number of Senators, and a majority of the whole number shall be necessary to a choice. But no person constitutionally ineligible to the office of President shall be eligible to that of Vice-President of the United States.

AMENDMENT XIII (1865)

Section 1. Neither slavery nor involuntary servitude, except as a punishment for crime whereof the party shall have been duly convicted, shall exist within the United States, or any place subject to their jurisdiction.

Section 2. Congress shall have power to enforce this article by appropriate legislation.

AMENDMENT XIV (1868)

Section 1. All persons born or naturalized in the United States, and subject to the jurisdiction thereof, are citizens of the United States and of the State wherein they reside. No State shall make or enforce any law which shall abridge the privileges or immunities of citizens of the United States; nor shall any State deprive any person of life, liberty, or property, without due process of law; nor deny to any person within its jurisdiction the equal protection of the laws.

Section 2. Representatives shall be apportioned among the several States according to their respective numbers, counting the whole number of persons in each State, excluding Indians not taxed. But when the right to vote at any election for the choice of electors for President and Vice-President of the United States, Representatives in Congress, the Executive and Judicial officers of a State, or the members of the Legislature thereof, is denied to any of the male inhabitants of such State, being twenty-one years of age, and citizens of the United States, or in any way abridged, except for participation in rebellion, or other crime, the basis of representation therein shall be reduced in the proportion which the number of such male citizens shall bear to the whole number of male citizens twenty-one years of age in such State.

Section 3. No person shall be a Senator or Representative in Congress, or elector of President and Vice-President, or hold any office, civil or military, under the United States, or under any State, who, having previously taken an oath, as a member of Congress, or as an officer of the United States, or as a member of any State legislature, or as an executive or judicial officer of any State, to support the Constitution of the United States, shall have engaged in insurrection or rebellion against the same, or given aid or comfort to the enemies thereof. But Congress may by a vote of two-thirds of each House, remove such disability.

Section 4. The validity of the public debt of the United States, authorized by law, including debts incurred for payment of pensions and bounties for services in suppressing insurrection or rebellion, shall not be questioned. But neither the United States nor any State shall assume or pay any debt or obligation incurred in aid of insurrection or rebellion against the United States, or any claim for the loss or emancipation of any slave; but all such debts, obligations and claims shall be held illegal and void.

Section 5. The Congress shall have power to enforce, by appropriate legislation, the provisions of this article.

AMENDMENT XV (1870)

Section 1. The right of citizens of the United States to vote shall not be denied or abridged by the United States or by any State on account of race, color, or previous condition of servitude.

Section 2. The Congress shall have power to enforce this article by appropriate legislation.

AMENDMENT XVI (1913)

The Congress shall have power to lay and collect taxes on incomes, from whatever source derived, without apportionment among the several States, and without regard to any census or enumeration.

AMENDMENT XVII (1913)

(1) The Senate of the United States shall be composed of two Senators from each State, elected by the people thereof, for six years; and each Senator shall have one vote. The electors in each State shall have the qualifications requisite for electors of the most numerous branch of the State legislatures.

(2) When vacancies happen in the representation of any State in the Senate, the executive authority of such State shall issue writs of election to fill such vacancies: *Provided,* That the legislature of any State may empower the executive thereof to make temporary appointments until the people fill the vacancies by election as the legislature may direct.

(3) This amendment shall not be so construed as to affect the election or term of any Senator chosen before it becomes valid as part of the Constitution.

AMENDMENT XVIII (1919)

Section 1. After one year from the ratification of this article the manufacture, sale, or transportation of intoxicating liquors therein, the importation thereof into, or the exportation thereof from the United States and all territory subject to the jurisdiction thereof for beverage purposes is hereby prohibited.

Section 2. The Congress and the several States shall have concurrent power to enforce this article by appropriate legislation.

Section 3. This article shall be inoperative unless it shall have been ratified as an amendment to the Constitution by the legislatures of the several States, as provided in the Constitution, within seven years from the date of the submission hereof to the States by the Congress.

AMENDMENT XIX (1920)

(1) The right of citizens of the United States to vote shall not be denied or abridged by the United States or by any State on account of sex.

(2) Congress shall have power to enforce this article by appropriate legislation.

AMENDMENT XX (1933)

Section 1. The terms of the President and Vice President shall end at noon on the 20th day of January, and the terms of Senators and Representatives at noon the 3d day of January, of the years in which such terms would have ended if this article had not been ratified; and the terms of their successors shall then begin.

Section 2. The Congress shall assemble at least once in every year, and such meeting shall begin at noon on the 3d day of January, unless they shall by law appoint a different day.

Section 3. If, at the time fixed for the beginning of the term of the President, the President elect shall have died, the Vice President elect shall become President. If a President shall not have been chosen before the time fixed for the beginning of his term, or if the President elect shall have failed to qualify, then the Vice President elect shall act as President until a President shall have qualified; and the Congress may by law provide for the case wherein neither a President elect nor a Vice President elect shall have qualified, declaring who shall then act as President, or the manner in which one who is to act shall be selected, and such person shall act accordingly until a president or Vice President shall have qualified.

Section 4. The Congress may by law provide for the case of the death of any of the persons from whom the House of Representatives may choose a President whenever the right of choice shall have devolved upon them, and for the case of the death of any of the persons from whom the Senate may choose a Vice President whenever the right of choice shall have devolved upon them.

Section 5. Sections 1 and 2 shall take effect on the 15th day of October following the ratification of this article.

Section 6. This article shall be inoperative unless it shall have been ratified as an amendment to the Constitution by the legislatures of three-fourths of the several States within seven years from the date of its submission.

AMENDMENT XXI (1933)

Section 1. The eighteenth article of amendment to the Constitution of the United States is hereby repealed.

Section 2. The transportation or importation into any State, Territory, or possession of the United States for delivery of use therein of intoxicating liquors, in violation of the laws thereof, is hereby prohibited.

Section 3. This article shall be inoperative unless it shall have been ratified as an amendment to the Constitution by conventions in the several States, as provided in the Constitution, within seven years from the date of the submission hereof to the States by the Congress.

AMENDMENT XXII (1951)

Section 1. No person shall be elected to the office of the President more than twice, and no person who has held the office of President, or acted as President, for more than two years of a term to which some other person was elected President shall be elected to the office of President more than once. But this Article shall not apply to any person holding the office of President when this Article was proposed by the Congress, and shall not prevent any person who may be holding the office of President, or acting as President, during the term within which this Article becomes operative from holding the office of President or acting as President during the remainder of such term.

Section 2. This article shall be inoperative unless it shall have been ratified as an amendment to the Constitution by the legislatures of three-fourths of the several States within seven years from the date of its submission to the States by the Congress.

AMENDMENT XXIII (1961)

Section 1. The District constituting the seat of Government of the United States shall appoint in such manner as the Congress may direct:

A number of electors of President and Vice President equal to the whole number of Senators and Representatives in Congress to which the District would be entitled if it were a State, but in no event more than the least populous state; they shall be in addition to those appointed by the States, but they shall be considered, for the purposes of the election of President and Vice President, to be electors appointed by a State; and they shall meet in the District and perform such duties as provided by the twelfth article of amendment.

Section 2. The Congress shall have power to enforce this article by appropriate legislation.

AMENDMENT XXIV (1964)

Section 1. The right of citizens of the United States to vote in any primary or other election for President or Vice President, for electors for President or Vice President, or for Senator or Representative in Congress, shall not be denied or abridged by the United States, or any State by reason of failure to pay any poll tax or other tax.

Section 2. The Congress shall have power to enforce this article by appropriate legislation.

AMENDMENT XXV (1967)

Section 1. In case of the removal of the President from office or of his death or resignation, the Vice President shall become President.

Section 2. Whenever there is a vacancy in the office of the Vice President, the President shall nominate a Vice President who shall take office upon confirmation by a majority vote of both Houses of Congress.

Section 3. Whenever the President transmits to the President pro tempore of the Senate and the Speaker of the House of Representatives his written declaration that he is unable to discharge the powers and duties of his office, and until he transmits to them a written declaration to the contrary, such powers and duties shall be discharged by the Vice President as Acting President.

Section 4. Whenever the Vice President and a majority of either the principal officers of the executive departments or of such other body as Congress may by law provide, transmit to the President pro tempore of the Senate and the Speaker of the House of Representatives their written declaration that the President is unable to discharge the powers and duties of his office, the Vice President shall immediately assume the powers and duties of the office as Acting President.

Thereafter, when the President transmits to the President pro tempore of the Senate and the Speaker of the House of Representatives his written declaration that no inability exists, he shall resume the powers and duties of his office unless the Vice President and a majority of either the principal officers of the executive department or of such other body as Congress may by law provide, transmit within four days to the President pro tempore of the Senate and the Speaker of the House of Representatives their written declaration that the President is unable to discharge the powers and duties of his office. Thereupon Congress shall decide the issue, assembling within forty-eight hours for that purpose if not in session. If the Congress, within twenty-one days after receipt of the latter written declaration, or, if Congress is not in session, within twenty-one days after Congress is required to assemble, determines by two-thirds vote of both Houses that the President is unable to discharge the powers and duties of his office, the Vice President shall continue to discharge the same as Acting President; otherwise, the President shall resume the powers and duties of his office.

AMENDMENT XXVI (1971)

Section 1. The right of citizens of the United States, who are eighteen years of age or older, to vote shall not be denied or abridged by the United States or by any State on account of age.

Section 2. The Congress shall have power to enforce this article by appropriate legislation.

AMENDMENT XXVII (1992)

No law, varying the compensation for the services of the Senators and Representatives, shall take effect, until an election of Representatives shall have intervened.

Glossary

ADJUDICATION: a final decision handed down by the court

AFFIDAVIT: a written statement made under oath and witnessed by a notary public or another authorized person

AGENT: an individual designated to act on behalf of another, particularly in business transactions

ALIMONY: also called "marital support" or "maintenance," money the court orders an individual to pay an estranged or former spouse

AMICUS CURIAE: Latin term meaning "friend of the court"; a person or group who provides information to the court but is not party to the lawsuit

ANNULMENT: a court order that declares a marriage void from its beginning

ANSWER: the defendant's response to a complaint filed by the plaintiff

APPELLANT: the individual who appeals a court decision

ASSAULT AND BATTERY: the intentional and unlawful touching of another; assault is the attempt to do bodily harm, and battery is the actual touching

BAILMENT: delivery of property to another for safekeeping, repair, or for another specific purpose

BEQUEST: a gift made through a will involving personal property or money, but not real property

BREACH: a violation of a contract or promise

BRIEF: a written document drafted by a lawyer outlining the reasons and citing cases to justify her/his legal arguments

CASE LAW: a body of law dictated by the courts' holdings in all prior cases

CAVEAT EMPTOR: Latin term meaning "let the buyer beware"; before statutes protecting consumers were introduced, consumers often felt dependent upon the integrity of merchants and the quality of their products

CIVIL ACTION: lawsuit brought among individuals or companies seeking damages when a contract has been breached or a party has been injured; opposite of a criminal action involving the government bringing the action

CLOSING: the final step in the process of buying or selling a home, with money and deeds changing hands

CODICIL: an amendment to a will

COLLATERAL: security for repayment of a debt in the form of money or property

COMMON LAW: body of law based on court decisions rather than statutes and legislation

COMMON-LAW MARRIAGES: recognized in some states, they are created without a ceremony, requiring only the present intent to be married, the representation to the public that they are married, and cohabitation

COMMUNITY PROPERTY: property attained during marriage, with each partner owning one half

COMPLAINT: the formal written accusation filed by the plaintiff in a lawsuit against the defendant

CONDEMNATION: taking of private property by the government for public use

CONSIDERATION: something of value exchanged in the performance of a contract

CONTESTED DIVORCE: divorce in which parties cannot agree on property settlement, alimony, or child issues, or in which one of the parties wants to remain married

CONTINGENT FEES: attorney fee based on a percentage of the amount recovered

CONTINUANCE: a postponement in a court proceeding

CONTRACT: binding agreement or promises to do or provide something; requires an offer, an acceptance, and consideration

CONVERSION: wrongful taking or use of another's property

COOLING-OFF PERIOD: the time given in sales, usually three days, to reconsider the purchase and return the product

COUNTERCLAIM: claim brought by the defendant against the plaintiff in the same lawsuit

COVENANT: a promise or contract

CROSS-EXAMINATION: one party's attorney questioning the opposing party and/or witnesses

DAMAGES: money awarded by the court to compensate for injuries suffered

DEED: written document passing title of land

DEFAMATION: damaging the reputation or good name of another; if published, it is libel; if spoken, slander

DEFENDANT: party who is being sued

DEPOSITION: part of the pretrial discovery process in which parties and witnesses are questioned under oath

DEVISE: a gift of real property made through a will

DISCOVERY: pretrial procedure of gathering information and evidence, including depositions, interrogatories, and production of documents

DISMISSAL: ending of a lawsuit prematurely or a trial before a verdict is rendered

DOCKET: court calendar listing cases to be heard

DUE PROCESS: constitutional guarantee that certain requirements must be fulfilled before the deprivation of life, liberty, or property

EASEMENT: an agreement to allow another to use land or property for a specific purpose

ESTATE: all personal and real property a person owns

EVICT: removal of a tenant by a landlord

EXECUTE: to sign a document or fulfill the terms of an agreement

EXECUTOR/EXECUTRIX: individual appointed to carry out terms of a will

FORECLOSURE: termination of one's ownership of property

GUARDIAN: an adult entrusted with the care and control of a minor or incompetent and/or her/his estate

HOLOGRAPHIC WILL: a handwritten will

HUNG JURY: a jury unable to reach a verdict because the required number of jurors could not agree

INTESTATE: dying without leaving a valid will

JOINT TENANCY WITH RIGHT OF SURVIVORSHIP: ownership of real property by two or more persons, with ownership rights reverting to the survivor when the first dies

JUDGMENT: a final decision by the court

JURISDICTION: the authority of a court to hear and rule on a particular type of case

LIEN: a claim or hold on another's property as security for debt

LIVING WILL: a document directing a physician to refrain from providing extraordinary life-supporting measures in the event of a terminal illness or vegetative state

MAGISTRATE: judge of a local court, such as municipal or police court

MALICIOUS PROSECUTION: bringing an action with malice and lacking probable cause

MISDEMEANOR: type of lesser crime that is usually punishable by a fine or short sentence

MOTION: an oral or written application to the court asking for a ruling in favor of the applicant

NEGLIGENCE: failing to meet the standards of a reasonable person

NO-FAULT DIVORCE: fault of a spouse is not needed to obtain a divorce, only that the parties cannot reconcile their differences

NOLO CONTENDERE: Latin term meaning "I do not wish to contest"; a plea made to the court that is neither an admission nor a denial, often used in first-time DWI cases to receive a lighter punishment

NUNCUPATIVE WILL: oral will, valid in some states

PALIMONY: a form of alimony for a couple living together but not legally married

PLAINTIFF: party bringing the lawsuit

POWER OF ATTORNEY: the authority to act on behalf of another in a personal or business context

PRENUPTIAL AGREEMENT: also known as antenuptial agreement, a contract made in contemplation of marriage that establishes property rights of each partner

PROBATE: court procedure that establishes the validity of a will

PRO SE: Latin term meaning "in one's own behalf"; representing oneself in a legal action without the assistance of legal counsel

QUITCLAIM DEED: a document that conveys only that title, which the seller has, with no guarantees that she/he holds property free and clear of any liens or encumbrances

RESIDUARY CLAUSE: provision in a will that conveys property left over after all the specific devises have been made

STATUTE OF FRAUDS: law requiring certain contracts to be in writing in order to be valid, including those conveying real property

STATUTE OF LIMITATIONS: period of time in which a legal action must be brought

STRICT LIABILITY: liability without having to show negligence or fault, usually occurring when dangerous activities are involved

TESTATOR: individual drafting a will

TITLE: ownership with right to possess and convey

TORT: a civil wrong or injury

TRESPASS: unlawful entry or injury to another's property

TRUST: legal arrangement where one party is appointed to hold property for the benefit of another

VENUE: geographical location where the court can exercise its power or jurisdiction

VOIR DIRE: French term meaning "to speak the truth"; the questioning of jurors conducted prior to trial in order to select a jury

WARRANTY: guarantee or assurance that defects do not exist

WRONGFUL DEATH: individual causes the death of another through an intentional act or negligence

List of Contributors

The following individuals contributed the hypothetical situations as well as their expertise (area of expertise indicated in parentheses).

RANDOLPH AMENGUAL has been practicing law for 19 years and is the Senior Real Estate Partner at Esanu Katsky Korins & Siger. He is also an adjunct lecturer in real estate at the New York University School of Continuing Education and a member of the Real Property Law Committee of the Association of the Bar of the City of New York. (Real estate.)

DAVALENE COOPER, a graduate of the University of Kentucky College of Law, is currently an Instructor in the Legal Practice Skills Program at Suffolk University Law School in Boston, Massachusetts. From 1988–1990, she was a staff attorney with Appalachian Research and Defense Fund of Kentucky. During the summer of 1993, Ms. Cooper was an Attorney Fellow at the National Consumer Law Center. She gratefully acknowledges the assistance of Robert Hobbs, Deputy Director, National Consumer Law Center, in the work done for this book. (Contracts, sales, and advertising.)

GREG DAUGHERTY is the economics editor of *Consumer Reports* and the author of *Consumer Reports Mutual Funds Book*. Before joining *Consumer Reports* in 1989, he was the executive editor of *Sylvia Porter's Personal Finance* magazine. (Credit, banking, insurance, and consumer rights.)

MARIAN F. DOBBS practices matrimonial and family law in her own law firm in New York City. She has held numerous positions of distinction in her specialty, including fellowship in the American Academy of Matrimonial Lawyers, and chairman or member of various committees in the Family Law Section of the American Bar Association as well as New York State and local bar associations. (Family law.)

LAWRENCE GOLDHIRSCH, a member of the New York Bar, has been a trial lawyer for over 20 years. He holds a B.S. in Physics from City College of New York and J.D. from Brooklyn Law School. The author of numerous articles, he is also the author of *The Warsaw Convention Annotated,* a guide for lawyers representing persons injured on international flights. (Wrongful injury.)

463

MICHAEL S. GOLDSTEIN is an attorney specializing in adoption law. He is an adoptive father of three as well as a New York State certified social worker. Goldstein has been practicing law for 12 years. His principal office is located in Rye Brook, New York. (Adoption.)

CORNISH HITCHCOCK is a lawyer with Public Citizen Litigation Group in Washington, D.C., where he specializes in aviation issues. He was formerly the Director and longtime Legal Director of the Aviation Consumer Action Project (ACAP), which was founded by Ralph Nader in 1971 to be an advocate for airline passengers on a variety of issues involving airline service and safety. (Travel.)

DAVID A. HOFFMAN is a member of the Boston law firm of Hill & Barlow, where his practice is concentrated in the areas of litigation and alternative dispute resolution. Mr. Hoffman is on the governing council of the American Bar Association's Section of Individual Rights and Responsibilities, and is a former staff attorney for the Civil Liberties Union of Massachusetts. (Civil rights and personal freedom.)

LINDA LIPSEN is Legislative Director for the Washington, D.C., Office of Consumers Union. Lipsen represents the consumer interest on a range of issues, including civil justice and liability, product safety, insurance reform, health care, and antitrust issues. Ms. Lipsen is frequently interviewed by the national media and has lectured on a variety of public policy issues before numerous organizations and academic institutions throughout the country. She is a member of the Washington, D.C., bar. (Product liability, health service.)

CHARLES K. PLOTNICK is an attorney in Jenkintown, Pennsylvania, whose practice is limited to estate planning and estate administration. He is co-author together with Stephan R. Leimberg of *How to Settle an Estate* (Consumer Reports Books) and five other books on estate planning and estate administration. He is the author of numerous magazine articles on estate planning. (Estate planning.)

STEVEN MITCHELL SACK has maintained a private law practice in New York City devoted primarily to labor matters. Mr. Sack is the author of eight books on legal subjects including *Don't Get Taken: How to Avoid Common Consumer Rip-Offs* (Consumer Reports Books). He is a graduate of Boston College Law School and serves as a commercial arbitrator for the American Arbitration Association. (The law in the workplace.)

Index